MW00837417

TECHNOLOGY COMMERCIALIZATION

TECHNOLOGY COMMERCIALIZATION:

DEA AND RELATED ANALYTICAL METHODS FOR EVALUATING THE USE AND IMPLEMENTATION OF TECHNICAL INNOVATION

Edited by Sten A. Thore,

Gregory A. Kozmetsky Centennial Fellow Emeritus, IC^2 Institute,
The University of Texas, Austin
Former Chair in Commercialization of Science and Technology,
Instituto Superior Técnico, Lisbon

Kluwer Academic Publishers
Boston/Dordrecht/London

Distributors for North, Central and South America:
Kluwer Academic Publishers
101 Philip Drive
Assinippi Park
Norwell, Massachusetts 02061 USA
Telephone (781) 871-6600
Fax (781) 871-9045
E-Mail: kluwer@wkap.com

Distributors for all other countries:
Kluwer Academic Publishers Group
Post Office Box 322
3300 AH Dordrecht, THE NETHERLANDS
Telephone 31 786 576 000
Fax 31 786 546 474
E-mail: services@wkap.nl

Electronic Services <http://www.wkap.nl>

Library of Congress Cataloging-in-Publication Data

Thore, Sten A.O.
Technology commercialization : DEA and related analytical methods for evaluating the use and implementation of technical innovation / Sten A. Thore.
p. cm.
Includes bibligraphical references and index.
ISBN 1-4020-7017-9 (alk.paper)
1. Technological innovations—Evaluation. 2. Technological innovations—Management. 3. Data envelopment analysis. I. Title.

HC79.T4+

2002022123

Printed on acid-free paper.

Printed in the United States of America.

Contents

Contributors

Cristina Abad is a Ph. D. student at the Department of Accounting and Finance, University of Seville. E-mail: cristina.abad@uca.es

Adisa Azapagic is a Reader in the Department of Chemical and Process Engineering at the University of Surrey, UK. E-mail: A.Azapagic@surrey.ac.uk

Carlos A. Bana e Costa is a Professor in Operations Research at the Department of Operational Research, London School of Economics, and at the Department of Engineering and Management, Instituto Superior Técnico, Lisbon. E-mail carlosbana@netcabo.pt or c.bana@lse.ac.uk

Roland Clift is a Professor at the University of Surrey, UK, and Director for the Centre for Environmental Strategy. E-mail: r.clift@surrey.ac.uk

Paulo Ferrão is an Assistant Professor at the Instituto Superior Técnico, Lisbon where he is responsible for the graduate program in Energy and Environment. E-mail: ferrao@dem.ist.utl.pt

Fausto M. Freire is a teaching and research assistant at the Faculty of Sciences and Technology, the University of Coimbra, and a Ph.D. student at the Instituto Superior Técnico, Lisbon. E-mail: fausto.freire@dem.uc.pt

Boaz Golany is a Professor in the Faculty of Industrial Engineering and Management, the Technion, Haifa, Israel. E-mail: golany@ie.technion.ac.il

Tom L.C.M. Groot is a Professor at the Vrije University, Amsterdam, The Netherlands. E-mail: tgroot@feweb.vu.nl

J.-N- Huang obtained his M.S. degree from the Institute of Management of Technology, National Chiao Tung University, Taiwan.

Luis Lapão is a graduate student at the Instituto Superior Técnico, Lisbon. E-mail: llapao@mail.telepac.pt

Warren Mellor is a research fellow in the Centre for Environmental Strategy, the Polymer Research Centre and the Department of Chemical and Process Engineering at the University of Surrey, UK. E-mail: w.mellor@surrey.ac.uk

Fernando Pimentel is a graduate of the Instituto Superior Técnico, Lisbon, currently employed at the central bank of Portugal, Banco de Portugal, Lisbon. E-mail: Fernando.Lobo.Pimentel@bportugal.pt

Gary Rich is the Director of Marketing at Baker Hughes Inc., Houston. He holds a M.Sc. of Commercialization of Science and Technology, a new graduate program offered by the IC^2 Institute, The University of Texas at Austin. E-mail: gary.rich@hugheschris.com

Gary Stevens is Director for the Polymer Research Centre at the University of Surrey, UK. E-mail: g.stevens@surrey.ac.uk

Sten A. Thore is the Gregory A. Kozmetsky Centennial Fellow Emeritus at the IC^2 Institute, The University of Texas at Austin. He held a personal chair in the Commercialization of Science and Technology, the Instituto Superior Técnico, Lisbon, Portugal, 1997-1999. Website: www.stenthore.com, E-mail: thore@mail.telepac.pt

Teresa Garcia Valderrama is Professor at the Department of Business Economics, University of Cadiz, Spain. E-mail: teresa.garcia@uca.es

Elizabeth Williams is a research fellow in the Centre for Environmental Strategy, the Polymer Research Centre and the Department of Chemical and Process Engineering at the University of Surrey, UK. E-mail: Elizabeth.Wright@surrey.ac.uk

Benjamin Yuan is Associate dean and a Professor at the Institute of Management of Technology, the National Chiao Tung University, Taiwan, E-mail: benjamin@cc.nctu.edu.tw

Foreword

TECHNOLOGY CHOICES AND THE NEW DISCIPLINE OF TECHNOLOGY COMMERCIALIZATION

by Robert Ronstadt, The IC² Institute,
The University of Texas at Austin, www.ic2.org

You won't read about it in the Sunday Times, but I'm predicting that the application of Data Envelopment Analysis (DEA) will be seen in the years ahead as a major achievement in the history of technology commercialization.

If you're reading this book, you probably know that DEA means something other than the Drug Enforcement Agency. But just in case... DEA is a statistical methodology that permits the setting of commercial priorities while taking into account a wide array of factors where outcomes are calculated against a "frontier or best practice," as oppose to some statistical average. For those of you who never resonated to statistical regression, DEA is much more palatable. Think of it as "progressing to an optimum, versus regressing to a mean." Who wants to be "average," anyway?

Certainly, the authors don't. Led by Senior IC^2 Fellow, Sten Thore, they have produced a book that shows how to apply theory to difficult real world problems. In the process, they've enriched a stream of seminal research started by IC^2 Fellows, Bill Cooper and Abe Charnes over 20 years ago. IC^2 Institute has regularly supported the early theoretical work and the subsequent applications work of DEA over the last two decades. We've done so because we believed this work has the potential to improve the efficacy of: 1) national and corporate research laboratories; 2) university research investments; 3) venture incubator portfolios; 4) venture capital portfolios; and, in fact, any portfolio where choices must be made about capital allocations.

In fact, this array of applications is telltale. They reveal that this extremely readable book is more than one more step in the arduous journey to quantify research and development (R&D) projects. Despite the limitation of the book's subtitle, Technology Commercialization is much more. From my perspective, this book is part of a larger movement whose outline is now barely visible on the horizon, a movement whose goal is more than the demonstration of a new quantitative technique, but part of an effort to create an entirely new discipline around a critical wealth producing process known as technology commercialization.

What is technology commercialization? Technology commercialization can be defined simply as "the movement of ideas from the research laboratory to the market place." The value of this simple definition is its ease of understanding. People can be perplexed about "technology commercialization," but they generally comprehend that the "lab to market" description implies a conversion of ideas into products and services. Also, it's easy to expand this definition to be more precise about the starting and ending points of the technology commercialization process. For instance, a more realistic starting point sees technology commercialization commencing at the very moment of ideation versus some laboratory workbench... and ending at that point when a venture actually creates real wealth.

These latter stipulations aren't just semantics. The recent dot.com bubble illustrates how new businesses can reach the market place, even go public, without creating real wealth. And breakthrough ideas are just as likely (perhaps more likely) to hit us after a good night's sleep, or in the shower, versus at some research laboratory.

Why are applications of DEA important? History shows us the discovery of new scientific tools often opens the floodgates of scientific breakthroughs and eventually commercial application. For instance, many scientific theories and new technologies would never have seen the light of day without Galileo's telescope, the electron microscope, or the computer instruments enabling the Gnome.

Less appreciated, but equally true, history shows us that analytic methodologies can have the same impact on science and technology commercialization. Examples range from the scientific method itself, to mathematical advances in geometry, calculus, classical statistics, Bayesian statistics, to linear programming and other operations research techniques.

But whether the innovation is a tool or a method of analysis, it must be demonstrated before it is deemed worthwhile. Even Galileo's telescope was viewed with great skepticism until a large number of scientists confirmed his celestial sightings. That's why the demonstration of DEA by Thore and company is so important. Their application of DEA breathes life into the theory, incenting others to use it, while showing how the methodology will improve productivity.

How will DEA impact technology commercialization? Sometimes scientific advances lead to commercial innovations that improve the human condition. In most instances, they do not, *even when the intent behind the original research work is to produce a commercial outcome*.

For instance, billions are spent each year on science and technology research at universities, national labs, and corporate laboratories located around the world. A huge chunk of this investment leads to journal articles, patents, more journal articles, and even scientific fame without ever having any commercial impact. In other instances, commercialization occurs but the net impact on society is negative, especially when environmental and other social objectives are ignored. All the best evidence indicates that only a minute share of our investments in science and technology result in knowledge that creates real wealth.

To be fair, I'd be the last to imply that the nexus of science and commercialization does not present daunting challenges for scientists, entrepreneurs, and everyone else in between. For instance, calculating the value of a specific research project is fraught with difficulties given the nature of discovery and the usual uncertainties associated with computing financial returns. This difficulty is compounded when one attempts to assess the cost/benefits of pursuing one set of technology pathways versus another set. Ascertaining an accurate time period covering the calculation can also be a hazardous task... especially when a scientific discovery with seemingly zero commercial potential today may have great impact in the market place once future discoveries are made decades down the road. Factoring into the equation those variables that represent environmental and other social concerns presents still more dilemmas.

The authors make no claims that DEA will solve all the challenges presented by mankind's attempt to improve the human condition via science and technology commercialization. But they have made a step forward, especially when it comes to assessing environmental issues… and history suggests it may be a giant step, one that gives us a critical building tool to create a discipline around technology commercialization.

This thought, I must admit, gives me some pause. The creation of a new discipline is something akin to a breach birth. It's a painful, drawn-out, often tortuous process that leaves career fatalities and setbacks in its wake. The good news is that all the trauma is worth the effort.

Personal experience is speaking now. I've been fortunate to play a small role in the creation of two disciplines. The first was a very minor role in the 1960's and 1970's when huge research and teaching efforts on multinational enterprise at Harvard Business School (and eventually elsewhere) led to the legitimization of international business as a core business discipline, one that became part and parcel of every business curriculum. The second occurred at Babson College in the 1970's and early 1980's where my efforts as Department Chair, Planning Director, and the first Director of the Entrepreneurship Program contributed to the eventual acceptance of entrepreneurship as an accepted discipline…first at Babson and then elsewhere.

I should note that it took about 15 years for entrepreneurship to be fully accepted as a valid discipline, one with a concrete body of knowledge that had hard value for practitioners. Acceptance was rarely easy, especially in the early years, and resistance came not only from academicians, but also from corporate boardrooms and government offices. Even successful entrepreneurs rejected the notion that their success was explained as something more than a biological trait.

Yet the evidence shows that entrepreneurship is a learnable process where the odds of success are improved through knowledge discovery. Now new concepts, tools, organizational entities, and methods must be innovated for technology commercialization. Sten Thore and others at IC^2 have opened the doors for us. We only need the courage to pass through to a new knowledge arena. Let your journey begin with this fine book.

Austin, February 2001

Acknowledgements

This book is the product of a vision, long nourished, and an opportunity. I shall have more to say about the vision in the Prologue (below).

Here is the place to record the opportunity. It occurred in the spring of 1997 when I found myself installed at the Instituto Superior Técnico (IST) in Lisbon, appointed to a freshly minted Chair in The Commercialization of Science and Technology. It had all happened because of the inspired intervention of my friend and then IST deputy president Manuel Heitor, and the financial backing of the Luso-American Foundation guided by the enlightened policies of Charles Buchanan. I owe them my deepest gratitude.

Surrounded by a bunch of smart and well-trained Ph.D. students, I realized that here was my dream research team, bristling with enthusiasm. They form the inner core, as it were, of the roster of researchers coauthoring this book (see the List of Contributors). Eventually, the team expanded as I invited (and as my students invited) others to join in. The end result is a true mix of nationalities, backgrounds, and academic careers - - for some authors, this is their very first published piece; others again are veterans of great recognized scholarly standing. What joined us was our common quest, exploring a new and promising research field. To all my contributors, I would like to express my sincere thanks for their cheerful cooperation and their willingness to submit to picky criticism and to my endless requests for new drafts of their papers.

My editor, Mr. Gary Folven of Kluwer Academic Publishers, has shepherded this volume to publication right from its first inception. His wise advice and gentle nudging has been much appreciated.

The Algarve, Portugal

S.Th.

Prologue

Sten A. Thore
IC² Institute, The University of Texas at Austin

Abstract: The editor explains the origin of the present volume, the general motivation of the research effort, and provides a brief introduction to each chapter.

Key words: IC² Institute, Instituto Superior Técnico, knowledge economy, investment in human capital, technology breakthroughs, startup companies, technology incubators, strategic alliances, technopolis, venture capitalists

1. BACKGROUND

The theme of this volume is the development of analytical tools to rate and prioritize a given set of R&D projects, paying regard to, if need be, to the environmental consequences of those projects. For present purposes, a "project" may be the development and commercialization of a product, a manufacturing process, or a complex of products and processes packaged and marketed as a single unit (such as a new satellite technology). In general, the ranking will be part of an attempt to gauge the commercialization of a project, that is, the potential of a project to move from the laboratory to the market ("technology commercialization").

Such ranking of projects and selection of the ones to be pursued was once the province of a few advanced R&D laboratories in large corporations. Nowadays, however, these kinds of considerations have to be made, explicitly or implicitly, by any corporate entity participating in the race of launching ever superior high tech products meeting the demands of ever more sophisticated consumers. Collectively, these decisions determine the path of future technology. This is so not only because the R&D&C (research, development and commercialization) decisions determine the technological evolution of a single company, but also because there occurs in society a "locking in" (Arthur, 1989) of technology so that future technology choices will be conditioned by past ones. In short, the R&D&C decisions in society jointly determine the path of evolution of technology and of our material civilization.

My interest in these matters was formed during those 20 years (1977 – 1997) when I was associated with the IC^2 Institute at the University of Texas, a unique research institution dedicated to the furthering of our understanding of the process of commercialization of high technology, initially through research, but later through teaching and also actually operating a high technology business incubator. These activities all reflected the vision of the founder and first director of the Institute, George Kozmetsky.

When I and my colleagues started researching these matters in the late 1970s, we moved into unchartered territory that up to then had been left outside the field of scientific inquiry and had been left to be exercised by the entrepreneurs of the practical world. Indeed, it was felt by many those days that successful commercialization was an art that could never be boxed into the format of an analytical framework. Much of the work of the Institute during those early years consisted of organizing conferences on the commercial potential of various spectacular developments of high technology, such as the commercial potential of the supercomputer (Kirkland and Poore, 1987), of the superconducting superaccelerator, of "Star Wars" (Nozette and Kuhn, 1987), and of biotechnology (Mabry, 1987).

A few far-sighted researchers had ventured to develop the first tentative analytical structures for how such commercialization decisions are made; among them was a study by Charnes and Stedry (1966) on the allocation of R&D funds to various departments inside a large university. During all these years, I always kept a reprint of that paper lying on my desk. It showed that it was indeed possible to construct a sophisticated operations research format (employing chance constrained programming) to model such issues, even providing funding contingencies for the occurrence of unexpected scientific breakthroughs.

George Kozmetsky had unique insights into both the practical commercial world and the scholarly world, being the co-founder and co-director of Teledyne, growing into one of the largest high tech companies in the country, and the dean of the business school at the University of Texas at Austin. In his capacity as a scholar, George had formed life-long ties of friendship with two of the giants in operations research, Abe Charnes (1917 – 1992) and W.W. (Bill) Cooper, who eventually both joined him accepting chairs at the business school. Since 1978, Abe and Bill were engaged in a feverish development of a new and sensational mathematical technique called data envelopment analysis (DEA). It is designed to rank the performance of entities (called "decision making units") when an entire vector of characteristics rather than a single figure of merit measure the fruits of their labors. Supporting the work by Abe and Bill through conferences and publications, the IC^2 Institute quickly became a leading institution in the pursuit of the new opportunities that DEA offers.

In 1991 the research director of the IC^2 Institute Fred Phillips and I were invited by the 3M Corporation which had recently established its research headquarters in Austin, to participate in the design of formalized procedures for the prioritization of R&D telecommunications projects. We learned with some stupefaction that this division of 3M employed a conventional but elaborate system of calculating net present values to prioritize and monitor every single R&D project. (For the 3M technical audits, see Krogh, Prager, Sorenssen and Tomlinson, 1988.) Management had realized for some time that these procedures were highly unsatisfactory, but where was the alternative? With data provided by 3M, I ran the first DEA programs and presented the resulting rankings to local managers.

A couple of years later, in 1994, I was contracted by a consulting firm in Washington D.C. to look into the possibility of using DEA to rank the performance of NASA aeronautics investments. Here was an application that went beyond purely commercial considerations, because NASA explicitly emphasized societal returns, such as local employment provided. The unique power of DEA of incorporating a range of performance criteria (rather than a single criterion like net profit) was thus brought to the fore. The NASA material came too good use when I developed a case study for my students at the Department of Aerospace Engineering at the University of Texas, where I developed and taught a Ph.D. course in the Commercialization of Space Technology.

In the spring of 1996, the IC^2 Institute launched its new Master program in the Commercialization of Science and Technology. Finally, after 18 years of intellectual preparation, George Kozmetsky's dream of creating a new academic discipline was coming to fruition, as my colleagues and I started sharing with students the insights and knowledge that we had accumulated over the years.

One of the students in the Austin class (a second and parallel class was taught in Washington D.C.) was Gary Rich, who at the time was manager of product development at Baker-Hughes Inc., Houston, a Texas company developing high technology systems for oil drilling. Gary had already earlier been involved in an effort to rate the R&D projects he was responsible for at Baker-Hughes, and had extensive data available, both on completed and on-going projects. Our report of the DEA calculations is presented as Chapter 2 in the present volume (see also the introductory comments below).

As I retired from my position at the IC^2 Institute in 1997, a fortuitous chain of events enabled me to establish a new academic home at the Instituto Superior Técnico, Lisbon. Under the dynamic leadership of its deputy president, Manuel V. Heitor, the IST had concluded an agreement of cooperation with the University of Texas. Lisbon was to become the European bridgehead of the new Texas master program of Commercialization of Science and Technology. Thus it came to be that I in 1998 found myself helping teaching in Portugal the very program that my colleagues and I had developed in Texas two years earlier, and which now became a spearhead effort in the new medium of distance learning. We had certainly come a long way. What 20 years earlier had been thought to be an art resisting any attempt at analytical study was now being disseminated and taught in a multi-continental multi-media classroom.

Manuel Heitor opened my eyes to the importance of technology policy. Being a major graduate school of technology in a small country like Portugal, the IST in its research activities directly and indirectly influences the allocation of high tech R&D efforts in the entire nation. The moral responsibility is indeed a daunting one, and again the question presents itself: is it possible to develop a framework for the ranking and prioritization of these activities?

Technology policy does not only deal with choices between alternative paths of economic well-being. It very much is concerned with the avoidance of economic “bads”: of negative externalities of production and consumption afflicting the environment. On the European academic scene I discovered an intense interest in the subject matter of environmental economics and in technology policy for a sustainable economy. As the research reported in this book evolved, I realized that the prioritization of R&D projects should incorporate an assessment of their environmental impact as well. In this respect, as in many others, this book probes beyond the standard procedures of DEA.

2. R&D AND ECONOMIC GROWTH

To explain the role of R&D in the modern economy, it is useful to consider the distinction between real capital such as machinery and industrial plants, and "human capital" or knowledge and know-how. These are economic stocks; the corresponding economic flows (additions to the stock over time) are

- investment in real capital;
- investment in human capital = R&D.

The economies of the Western world grew during the 19th century and the first half of the 20th century as a result of a rapid accumulation of real capital. The driver of economic growth was high investments in real capital. When growth abated, as it did during the downturn of the business cycle, the culprit was flagging real investments.

Toward the end of the 20th century, the nature of the advanced economies changed, and an explosion in communication and information technology, biotech and pharmaceutical sciences occurred. Ours became a "knowledge economy." In this economy there is a rapid accumulation of human capital in the form of new technology and new knowledge. The driver of the new economy is R&D, mainly as it is carried out by private corporations but also by institutions such as universities, foundations, and investment banks. Also, new economic agents have sprung up, serving as intermediates in the R&D process: venture capitalists, business incubators, R&D stock funds and government research institutions.

In order to explain the evaluation, ranking and determination of investment in real capital, economists traditionally employ a diagram as in Fig. 1 below, showing how the marginal rate of return gradually would

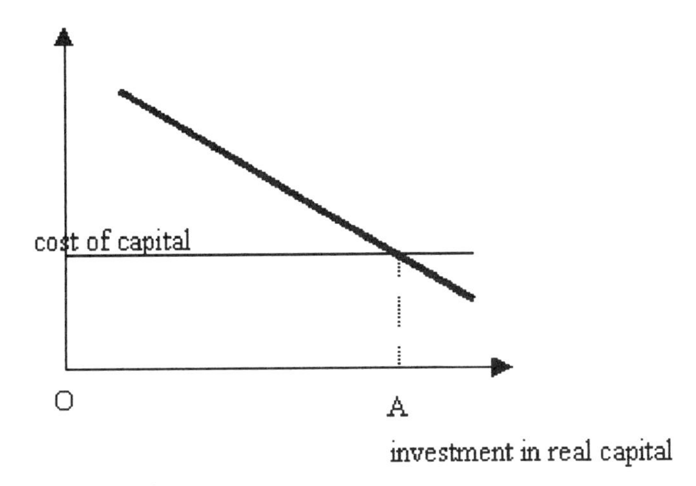

Figure 1. Schedule of returns to investment in real capital

decline as investments are extended from the most profitable opportunities at hand to those with slightly less promising prospects. The "equilibrium" rate of investment, for a single corporation, or for an entire industry, is indicated by the intersection of the downward-sloping curve with the horizontal line marking the cost of capital. This is investment *OA* in Figure 1.

Turning now to the evaluation, ranking and determination of R&D, which is the subject of the present volume, one may adapt the same diagram as shown in Figure 2. The schedule M - M exhibits falling returns as the R&D is gradually extended from the most promising projects to less promising ones. (In the tradition of the sweeping simplifications of textbook economics, I have drawn a continuous downward sloping curve. The reality, of course, is a discrete number of points on that curve, each point displaying the expected return of a single R&D project. The projects are evaluated, ranked, and reordered in the order of monotonically falling return rates.)

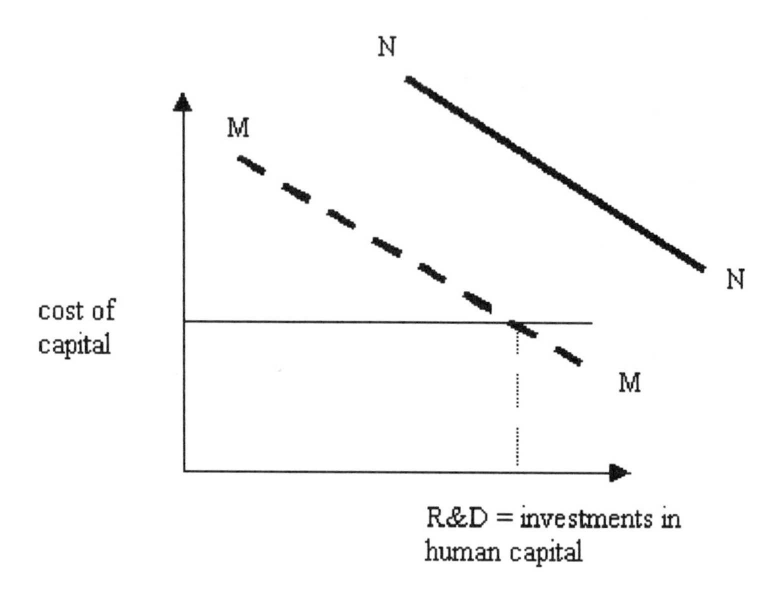

Figure 2. Schedules of return to R&D. Legend:
M-M: marginal rate of return, original schedule
N-N: marginal rate of return after technology breakthrough

Presently, however, a new and significant factor comes into play, changing the entire picture. In Figure 1, investments are carried out in known and existing technologies. In Figure 2, the investment is carried out in new and unknown technologies so that the rates of return are not only shrouded in uncertainty, but they are subject to dynamic evolution. As a result of some successful projects, new technology vistas will be opened up -- new products, new uses, new possibilities will emerge that were earlier entirely unforeseen. There will be technological breakthroughs. A new range of promising possibilities will present itself, as illustrated by the new schedule N - N. Capitalizing on the breakthroughs, these projects will yield superior returns so that schedule N - N is located above, and to the right of, schedule M - M.

There is no need here to describe further, or to exemplify, this process of the stepwise unfolding of new technologies and new knowledge. Suffice it to point out that the process is

- *hierarchical*, so that new technology links almost always have technology precursors, now combined and arranged in new ways (see also Thore, 1998);
- *self-enforcing*, in that many new technologies carry the seeds of their own prospective future growth (Arthur 1994, Thore, 2001).

As a result of repeated breakthroughs, the actual path *ex post* of a corporation or of an industry can therefore exhibit marginally increasing returns to scale, see the stippled curve in Figure 3 below.

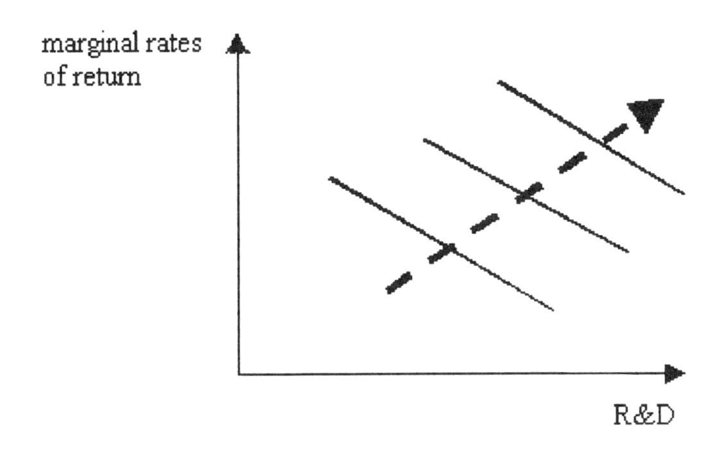

Figure 3. Dynamic path of corporation/ industry with increasing marginal returns over time

The mechanisms illustrated in Figure 3 lie behind the modern view of the creative potential of high technology capitalism. During the last 10-15 years, the view has become common among economists and policy-makers alike that unfettered stock markets, a vigorous presence of venture capitalists and a steady flow of startup companies and other characteristic features of high technology capitalism can be a ticket to rapid economic growth. The rising curve traced in Figure 3 cannot be climbed without a multiplicity of actors pursuing a multiplicity of technological leads - - some actors eventually trapped in commercial dead-ends and going bankrupt, other actors seeing opportunities that no one else saw and profiting handsomely. Through a chaotic shakeout, an evolutionary path of the technologies gradually emerges. All these features are offered by capitalism. (For a discussion of high tech capitalism, see Thore 1995 and 1999.)

As the 1990's wore on, and as the new technologies at an accelerating pace were transforming the economic climate of the Western world, many observers have come to revise their former, often hostile views about capitalism, and to see it as an engine of high technology growth. This changing attitude was all the more remarkable because it occurred in the absence of any generally embraced new theoretical understanding - - or even a single towering figure in the academic world. As so many times before, economic events overtook academic economic thinking.

We do not yet know how future economists will describe the high tech revolution that swept the Western world during the last decades of the 20th century. Researchers at the IC^2 Institute have pointed at the following driving factors:

The role of startup companies and technology incubators. A business incubator houses and aids startup companies, providing manufacturing and office space and other amenities; it may also offer secretarial support, computer services and management consulting services. Hopefully, after a few years, the tenants at the incubator will "graduate," moving out from the incubator and making it on their own. Business incubators can be operated by local government, spun off from academic institutions, or be run by private business The Austin Technology Incubator, operated by the IC^2 Institute, has been a major success story in the nation. It serves as a major outlet for the commercialization of technology developed at the University of Texas at Austin.

Much of the same mix that once produced Silicon Valley is currently driving the growth along the San Antonio-Austin corridor: a major national university, an industry park operated by the university, and strong synergy with a rapidly expanding business community.

The role of strategic alliances. In their book Winning Combinations, J. Botkin and J. Matthews (1992) described a coming wave of entrepreneurial partnerships between small and large companies. Small companies can benefit in many ways from collaboration with larger ones. Large companies often have particular strengths in marketing, distributing and selling as well as sources capital. . Technologies and products that are still in the R&D pipeline, awaiting commercialization, are often the subjects of collaborative efforts. Corporations conduct flexible policies of entering into coalitions of cooperation with some partners, while perhaps letting other coalitions break up. US corporations have entered into thousands of research coalitions with other partners, both domestic and foreign. The management of the portfolio of strategic alliances of a high tech corporation requires consummate skill and diplomatic tact.

The role of high tech synergies and the "technopolis." The first technopolis (=technology city) was Silicon Valley. Others are Route 128 (drawing on the expertise of the Massachusetts Institute of Technology), the Research Triangle in North Carolina, Sophia Antipolis at the French Riviera, Tsukuba City in Japan and the Shenzhen Special Enterprise Zone in China. A number of other similar aggregations are now emerging in the US and in other parts of the world. There are powerful so-called positive externalities present in the technopolis: the growth of one corporation builds infrastructure and stimulates the emergence and growth of other corporations. The technopolis feeds on the development of new technology -- a continuous flow of new products and new designs that leave the laboratories and enter the marketplace. Some of these new products and new designs are brought to the market by the developers of the products themselves. Others are transferred to spinout companies or even to competitors.

The role of venture capitalists. The venture capital industry specializes in high-risk equity investments and is generally oriented toward investing in new companies introducing new technologies and helping their managements with advice and help as required. Many venture capitalists (or venture capital companies, as the case may be) center their attention on emerging high technology corporations whose expansion is restricted by a lack of equity capital. With few assets and without a proved cash flow, such corporations are often unable to raise capital from conventional sources. Venture capitalists build enduring relationships with fledgling client corporations, providing successive rounds of financing as the corporation grows, and eventually assisting with an initial public offering (IPO) in the stock market.

Cooperation between private corporations, academia, and local and central government. The high tech economy needs to spawn a continuous stream of new technologies and this has generated a need for new institutional arrangements to help develop new methods of collaboration between industry, academia and local and national government. Increasingly, much new high tech will come from universities and federal laboratories. A key function in the future economy will be the transfer of technology from the not-for-profit sector to private industry. To smooth the transfer of technology, society needs new institutions and a new social framework. The precise nature and function of these institutions is not yet clear. The IC^2 Institute - - where IC^2 = ICC = Innovation, Creativity, and Capital - - at the University of Texas is a novel type of academic institution, pioneering new ways of commercializing university science and technology. The institute has a unique mission to explore new organizational and management structures that can facilitate the commercialization of university-developed technology.

3. THE VISION

Most of the readers of this book will probably agree that the commercialization of science and technology is a powerful driving agent during the process of economic growth. Many will agree that we need a scholarly analysis of this mechanism. Some may even agree that we need to create a new academic discipline of technology commercialization.

But, most people will no doubt say, why then all this mathematics of data envelopment analysis? Do we really need a new esoteric mathematical technique to study something as mundane and obvious as the considerations of an entrepreneur in bringing a new product or service to the market?

To answer this question, it may be helpful to draw a comparison with the development of the science of finance in the early 1960s. In those days, college textbooks in finance essentially contained descriptive material about the functioning of various financial institutions, and the calculation of present values of future income streams. Then, in 1956, Harry Markowitz published a paper demonstrating how a quadratic mathematical programming problem could be employed to solve an abstract problem of portfolio selection. The solution establishes an optimal balance between return and risk. A few pioneers followed his lead, developing that ubiquitous capital asset pricing model that eventually would sail in a triumphal procession through a new generation of textbooks in finance.

Scholarly analysis needs a logical and mathematical backbone. As it so happened, quadratic programming provided that rigor of analysis that made it possible to create the modern theory of finance.

Technology commercialization is still a discipline in search of itself. The idea and the vision that motivates the present work is that perhaps - - just perhaps - - a simple mathematical programming model called DEA can be harnessed to provide the mathematical rigor that will enable the discipline of technology commercialization to get off the ground.

To begin with, it was just a stray idea. The application of DEA to the immediate problem of ranking R&D projects in a commercial corporation (see Chapter 2 below) was straightforward. Encouraged by these first results, my students and I were tempted to try the DEA model on other similar situations of evaluation of research, development and commercialization, in a variety of institutional settings. As more authors were brought into the joint effort, our ambition increased. We came to see the DEA model as a general mathematical principle for the ranking and selection of uncertain projects. We were able to model the selection of research projects by government development banks, by venture capitalists, and even by academic research institutions. We have accounted for the pricing of initial public offerings (IPOs) on the stock market. We spent considerable efforts on the evaluation and ranking of projects with possible harmful ecological side effects.

Yet, what follows is just the beginning. There were more papers on the drawing board that never made it to this volume. Hopefully, we shall all have an opportunity to revisit some of these themes in the future, in other publications. If other researchers will be inspired to follow in our footsteps, our efforts have not been in vain.

4. OVERVIEW OF CHAPTERS

This volume contains two tutorials, nine editorial introductions, and ten original research papers. The tutorials and the introductions provide brief accounts of material that is relevant to the evaluation and prioritization of R&D projects. Their purpose is to make this book accessible to readers outside the narrow realm of research. They are written for a broad readership, including R&D professionals. Much of this material is standard textbook material.

The chapters have been grouped into two parts: Commercial Priorities (chapters 1-8), and Environmental Concerns (chapters 9-11) There is no need for the reader to study each single chapter. Once the basic approach has been understood, the reader may turn to the subject matter or the field of application that may be of interest.

Chapter 1 (Tutorial). The Many Dimensions of an R&D Project: Multi-criteria Analysis. A casual observer will immediately be struck by the complexity of the R&D problem. It involves questions of engineering, financing and marketing of a product that is still just on the drawing board. Multi-criteria analysis is a method of surveying and handling such complex situations of decision-making. Often data on key issues are missing entirely. Opinions and judgments often have to substitute for data. Yet, these decisions have to be made. The tutorial briefly describes some well-known procedures to help organize and evaluate such complex information and to help arriving at decisions. The procedures include methods of rating and ranking, scorecards, evaluation sheets, and the construction of utility indices.

The aim of the volume is to discuss and provide examples of the ranking of the attractiveness of a series of R&D projects. If there were a single criterion of the attractiveness of each project, such as the expected profit, the ranking would be easy and immediate. But when many criteria are included, as the potential for follow-up developments of each project, the expected approval of the marketing department and of consumers, sales in the domestic market and overseas, the ranking becomes problematic. Data Envelopment Analysis (DEA) is a mathematical technique that was developed precisely for ranking items characterized by several criteria rather than a single one. The chapter ends up comparing Multi-criteria analysis and DEA.

Chapter 2. Using Frontier Analysis to Rate the R&D Projects of a Commercial Corporation. This chapter introduces the basic and simplest DEA calculations underlying most work in the present volume. The *editorial introduction* offers some comments on the concept of Pareto-efficiency and economic "equilibrium." The winners of the DEA rankings are located on the efficiency frontier. Economic textbooks would recognize them as being statically "adjusted." But those projects that fall behind the frontier are launched on a path of dynamic or even possibly chaotic adjustment.

The *research paper* ("Prioritizing a Corporation's R&D Activities, Employing 'Data Envelopment Analysis') reports on two practical applications of DEA for the prioritization of R&D projects:

- in a Texas company manufacturing high tech oil drilling equipment, and
- for the rating of NASA aeronautics investments.

DEA accords each R&D project an efficiency rating or "score". The projects are split into two groups: the "efficient" ones lying on the performance frontier or "envelope", and those that fall behind the frontier, called sub-efficient projects. Efficient projects are all assigned an efficiency rating of 1.0 and no distinction is made between them. The sub-efficient projects are assigned an efficiency rating less than 1.0 and are ranked in order of decreasing scores.

The example brought from NASA aeronautical investments is particularly instructive. One of the indicators of the performance of each investment was taken to be the social priority of the project, as measured by the prospective number of jobs created. As it turned out, these considerations became crucial for the DEA ratings. Some projects that would otherwise have been ranked as inefficient were then thrust to the efficiency frontier with ratings of 1.0.

Chapter 3. The Life Cycles of Sales and Profits: Dealing with the Uncertainties of the Commercialization Process. This chapter extends the time perspective of the DEA calculations to cover the entire life cycle of a new product or a new technology. Since the life cycle may cover several years, it then also becomes necessary to deal with the issue of uncertainty - - technological uncertainty and market uncertainty.

The *editorial introduction* surveys some elementary techniques of rating income streams and profit streams including rate-of-return analysis and present value. The so-called logistics curve of modeling life cycles is described. To account for the presence of uncertainty, some simple procedures of "scenario analysis" are reviewed. Scenario analysis is a shortcut way of dealing with uncertainty where a number of possible outcomes or states of the world have been identified but no explicit probability measures are attached to these states

The *research paper* ("Prioritizing Commercial R&D Projects in the Face of Uncertainty: Combining Scenario Analysis and DEA") describes the rating of a portfolio of R&D projects in a large international telecommunications company, here called "X-TEL.". The uncertainty facing high tech companies in the digital age is daunting, involving question marks about the direction and feasibility of new technology such as optical electronics. The market prospects of companies selling on the European scene might seem equally bewildering, depending on matters like the future of the new European currency (the EURO), the possible expansion of the European union etc.

To measure these matters and to handle the uncertainty that is inherent in any study of the commercialization potential of R&D, this chapter proposes a combination of DEA and scenario analysis. In the present application, five different scenarios for the long-run macroeconomic development are spelled out, each associated with a different pattern of the life cycle of sales. The authors account explicitly for a five-year time frame of analysis, assuming that each R&D project would pass through a typical life cycle of market introduction, upswing and maturation. The DEA calculations then yield 25 efficiency ratings for each project: five ratings for each year under each of the five scenarios. The results are plotted in five time diagrams, one for each scenario. A simple rank ordering procedure is used to establish the final ranking of the projects, and the validity of the priorities established is tested using a non-parametric test.

Chapter 4. Investment Policies by Venture Capital Firms and Government Development Foundations. The *editorial comments* introduce an important group of intermediaries in the R&D process: private or government organizations that specialize in the funding of R&D projects. These intermediaries will conduct their own independent evaluation and ranking of projects under consideration for possible funding.

The text surveys some common practices by venture capital firms to screen, evaluate, and structure their investment deals.

The *research paper* {"Applying Data envelopment Analysis to Evaluate the Efficiency of R&D Projects - - A Case Study of R&D Projects in Energy Technology) describes the ranking and analysis of a series of energy project proposals in Taiwan. Non-profit organizations, research institutes, university researchers or private corporations file the proposals. A government research-funding program administered by the Taiwan Ministry of Economic Affairs is responsible for the prioritization, funding and on-going monitoring of the projects. The paper describes the administrative processing and evaluation of the proposals, and the ranking of them using DEA. The Ministry currently use the procedures outlined for its internal review of projects (but not yet as a regular screening/ranking device).

Chapter 5. Ranking Academic Research. The *editorial introduction* traces the R&D process back to the development and evolution of basic knowledge inside university institutions. The relation between basic research and applied industrial developments is often tenuous, but it is important for our understanding of long economic waves. There seem to be "echo effects" between basic inventions and commercial innovations (Mensch, 1979).

Once, the academic world was left on its own to pursue truth and knowledge wherever it found it. Modern university administrators, however, often attempt to manage the research efforts of their institutions, directly and indirectly. Is it possible, or even wise, to lay down guidelines for such efforts?

The merits and weaknesses of "bibliometric" information to quantify the results of academic research are discussed.

The *research paper* ("Controlling the Efficiency of University Research in the Netherlands") makes use of some unique data being collected by the Dutch university authorities, rating academic research in the country by peer review. Each research program is rated with respect to four characteristics: scientific quality, scientific productivity obtained, relevance, and long-term viability. The authors use these scores as inputs into DEA, calculating the efficiency of 90 research programs in economics and econometrics.

Chapter 6. Investing in IPOs of Technology Stocks. The *editorial introduction* takes a look at those large R&D ventures that are launched on the stock market as initial public offerings (IPOs). For such projects, there are available not only the standard technical and engineering evaluations and market assessments - - there is also a wealth of financial information in the form of profit and loss statements and balance sheets. And, of course, there is also that ultimate evaluator of the future prospects of a stock: its market price. How can all this *embarrassement de richesse* of information be coordinated to yield a clear-cut evaluation of an IPO?

The text surveys some standard textbook material on portfolios of common stock. The concept of an efficient portfolio is explained, balancing the return on the portfolio against its risk. The geometric locus of efficient portfolios is calculated using the well-known Markowitz theory. The introduction ends up demonstrating that the same locus of efficient portfolios can alternatively be calculated by quadratic DEA.

The *research paper* ("Pricing IPOs, using Two-stage DEA to Track Their Financial Fundamentals") starts out explaining how the recent so-called Fundamental Analysis of stocks can be implemented using the mathematical model of two-stage DEA. The first of the two stages ties current financial data of a stock to its future earnings. The second stage ties future earnings to firm value (and the stock price). For each of the two stages, a piecewise linear frontier is estimated. The procedure is illustrated by a numerical example, analyzing all manufacturing firms quoted on the Madrid stock exchange during the years 1991-96.

The frontier calculations now indicated can be used to estimate the frontier earnings and the frontier stock price not only of all existing stocks, but also of an IPO. Such calculations would seem to be of considerable interest. The consortium launching the new stock on the market certainly wants to fetch as high an introductory price as possible. On the other hand, no party would benefit by having the IPO priced above its market potential. To illustrate, the frontier opening prices are calculated for five manufacturing IPOs.

Chapter 7. Monitoring the Dynamic Performance of Portfolio of R&D Projects over Time. The brief *editorial introduction* discusses the task of monitoring and assessing the performance of a portfolio of ventures over time, as the projects step by step advance from the laboratory to the market.

A few comments are offered on so-called "window analysis," which is one way of organizing the DEA calculations to provide a picture of how the efficiency standings of a group of projects develop over time.

The *research paper* ("Evaluating a Portfolio of Proposed Projects, Ranking them Relative to a List of Existing Projects") distinguishes two categories of projects: "old" and "new" ones. The old projects are those that have already been implemented or commercialized. The new projects are those still under development, in the laboratory. The task of the prioritization at any point in time is to identify the next candidate(s) to be moved from the "new" category to the "old" one. Ranking the new projects, there will then exist two different reference sets: ranking each proposed new project relative to the other proposed projects, and ranking it relative to the already adopted old ones. In DEA terminology, there will exist two efficiency frontiers or envelopes: the frontier of the new projects, and the frontier of all projects, both new and old ones. Furthermore, these two frontiers will typically shift over time, as individual projects are moved from the one category to the other.

An application is described, relating to the planning and constructing of student housing in Lisbon. The example should be representative of a wide range of other similar instances where the performance of new proposed projects can be compared with that of the already completed ones. The comparison is not only in terms of costs and financial returns but in terms of a list of attitudinal variables as well, reflecting the views of "experts" or consumers (in the present case, a sample of students).

Chapter 8. R&D Budgeting: Assessing the Efficiency of R&D Projects in the Presence of Resource Constraints. The *editorial introduction* turns to the situation that arises when the management of a company wants to use the DEA rankings to allocate resources (such as labor and funding) to projects still under development in its laboratory. Is it reasonable to open up the purse strings for the efficient projects, while starving the inefficient ones for both labor and funding? This is a difficult question, because it converts the DEA rankings into a tool for selection, budgeting, and investments.

By way of background, a brief review of capital budgeting is provided.

The *research paper* ("On the Ranking of R&D Projects in a Hierarchical Organization Structure subject to Global Resources Constraints") deals with a large organizational structure, where some overarching body controls the resources, and R&D decisions are delegated via research departments to individual managers. In such situations, routines for hierarchical evaluation and control need to be developed, and then delegated from the center to the research departments. While the aims of R&D management are the enhancement of project performance at the bottom level of the R&D organizational structure, the means of policy are laid down through resource allocations at earlier levels.

The paper suggests several mathematical formats for ranking projects in a hierarchical organization with resource constraints. One format embeds the conventional DEA rankings inside a global resource-constrained program with binary (accept/do not accept) variables. Another format is goal programming, which can handle situations when management contemplates curtailing the use of inputs of resources to individual projects. The various programming formats are illustrated by numerical examples

Chapter 9 (Tutorial). The Environmental Impact of New Products. The second and final part of the volume, on Environmental Concerns, moves our inquiry to the rapidly expanding field of sustainable economics. A few years ago, considerations of ecology might concern at most the packaging and marketing departments of a manufacturing company. Today, they are at the heart of serious R&D efforts, prompting the search for new technologies that are neutral to the environment, or even restoring the environment. No prioritizing of the R&D projects can any longer be undertaken without paying regard to the ecological impact of new technologies and new products developed and marketed.

The tutorial provides a survey of the subject of the environmental consequences of new industrial processes and new products. This includes the study of recycling, life-cycle analysis of products, adverse ecological effects of new products and the sustainability of industrial production.

Chapter 10. A New Mathematical Programming Format for Activity Analysis and the Life Cycle of Products. The *editorial introduction* probes the theoretical foundations of Data Envelopment Analysis, re-examining the subject of economic efficiency of production in the presence of environmental impacts. These include air acidification, aquatic eco-toxicity, eutrophication, the greenhouse effect, and the depletion of the ozone layer.

The text recaptures some standard textbook on material on classical activity analysis, originated by T. Koopmans. To prepare the way for the subsequent empirical work, mathematical programming formulations are used throughout.

The *first research paper* ("Activity Analysis with Environmental Variables and Recycling: An Example from the Portuguese Bottled Water Industry") demonstrates how the concept of linear activities can be generalized to include environmental goods (or, rather, environmental "bads" such as pollution of other negative externalities). The environmental impacts of the industrial activities along the production and distribution chain are calculated explicitly, including the environmental impacts of the use of the final product itself, and of its disposal. Furthermore, allowance is made for the possible presence of loops or feedback in this chain, representing recovery of the used product and its subsequent re-use or recycling. The developments are illustrated by an example brought from the Portuguese glass industry, featuring the recycling of both glass and plastics.

The *second research paper* ("Life Cycle Activity Analysis: A Case Study of Plastic Panels") further explores the potential of activity analysis with environmental variables. The paper extends the programming format further, accounting for environmental effects along the entire life cycle of the product. The life cycle spans the production chain all the way from its upstream sources (extraction of natural resources and use of energy) to its downstream effluxes (disposal of the used product). The mathematical developments are illustrated by an application examining the end-of-life options for plastic panels used in electrical and electronic products. There are two ways used panels can be recovered and re-inserted in the production process: Degraded plastic panels can be refurbished, repainted and used again. Or, the panel material itself can be recycled, breaking it down mechanically to yield recovered granulate.

Chapter 11. Ranking Commercial Products with Harmful Environmental Effects. The *editorial comments* return to the main theme of the book: the prioritization of R&D projects, using data envelopment analysis. The obvious question is this: How can we modify the DEA rankings so that proper allowance is made for possible harmful effects on the environment of new products and processes currently under development?

In many cases, environmental impacts cannot be avoided. The task of environmental policy is not to reduce the environmental harms to zero, but to keep them within manageable bounds. Suppose that policy-makers in local and central government have laid down a list of environmental goals. Only environmental impacts that exceed these goals should be penalized in the DEA calculations.

The technique of goal programming is explained, invented by A. Charnes and W.W. Cooper in 1958.

The *research paper* ("Using DEA to Rank the Performance of Producers in the Presence of Environmental Goals") proposes a new model type within the family of DEA models, recognizing three kinds of variables: inputs, outputs and environmental variables. For each environmental variable, a goal in the sense of goal programming is formulated. That is, the goal is not a "hard" upper limit but rather a "soft" goal that may be violated, but at a cost (or exceeded with a possible associated benefit). A piece-wise linear efficiency frontier is defined, at which the producers would make optimal use of their inputs, producing and distributing the final product to the consumers, while adhering to the environmental goals as closely as possible. The producers are ranked relative to their affinity to the frontier.

How is it possible to see to it that individual producers adhere to the goals, which may not necessarily reflect their own inclinations but rather the concerns of society at large? One way of implementing the goals is for government to levy an environmental fee or tax (an excise tax) on any use of a harmful environmental variable that exceeds the goal.

To illustrate, this paper returns to the data from the Portuguese bottled water industry, ranking individual bottlers.

Mathematical Appendix. The present volume illustrates the range and potential of the powerful ranking technique of data envelopment analysis (DEA). Also readers who are not familiar with DEA should be able to read this book. The basic application of DEA to the ranking of R&D projects is described in Chapter 1. In addition, there is a more formal *Appendix* on "The Mathematics of Data Envelopment Analysis", which can be used as a reference as the need arises. The appendix also lists a standard DEA computer code written in GAMS (= *g*eneral *a*lgebraic *m*odeling *s*ystem).

REFERENCES

Arthur, W.B. (1989). "Competing Technologies, Increasing Returns, and Lock-In by Historical Events," *The Economic Journal,* Vol. 99, March, pp. 116-131.

Arthur, W.B. (1994). *Increasing Returns and Path Dependency in the Economy,* University of Michigan Press, Ann Arbor, Mich.

Botkin, J.W. and Matthews, J.B. (1992). *Winning Combinations: The Coming Wave of Entrepreneurial Partnerships between Large and Small Companies*, Wiley, New York, N.Y.

Brockett, P.L. and Golany, B. (1996). "Using Rank Statistics for Determining Programmatic Efficiency Differences in Data Envelopment Analysis," *Management Science*, Vol. 42:3, pp. 466 – 472.

Charnes, A. and Stedry, A.C. (1996). "A Chance-Constrained Model for Real-Time Control in Research and Development Management," *Management Science*, Vol. 12:8, pp. B353-B362.

Kirkland, J.R. and Poore, J.H., editors (1987). *Supercomputers,* Praeger, Westport, Conn.

Koopmans, T. (1957). *Three Essays on the State of Economic Science*, McGraw Hill, New York, N.Y.

Krogh, L.C., Prager, J.H., Sorensen, D.P. and J.D. Tomlinson, J.D. (1988). "How 3M Evaluates its R&D Programs," *Research and Tehchnology Management*, Vol. 31:6, pp. 10-14.

Mabry, T.J., editor (1987). *Plant Biotechnology: Research Bottlenecks for Comnmercialization and Beyond,* IC^2 Institute, The University of Texas at Austin, Texas.

Mensch, G. (1979). *Stalemate in Technology: Innovations Overcome the Depression,* Ballinger Publishing, Cambridge, Mass. (German original *Das Technologische Patt,* Umschau Verlag, Frankfurt, 1975).

Nozette, S. and Kuhn, R.L., editors (1987). *Commercializing SDI Technologies*, Praeger, Westport, Conn.

Thore, S. (1995). *The Diversity, Complexity, and Evolution of High Tech Capitalism,* Kluwer Academic Publishers, Boston 1995. Pp. 203. Published on the Internet, see http://www.ic2.org/pubs/sten.pdf (see also the website www.stenthore.com).

Thore, S. (1998). "Innovation in an Industry Network: Budding, Cross-Fertilization, and Creative Destruction," in *Operations Research: Methods, Models and Applications*, edited by Aronson, J.E. and Zionts, S., honoring Gerald L. Thompson on the occasion of his 70th birthday, Quorum Books, Westport, Conn. 1998, pp. 179-200.

Thore, S. (1999). "Enterprise in the Information Age," in *Twenty-First Century Economics,* ed. By W.E. Halal and K.B. Taylor, St. Martin's Press, New York, N.Y.

Thore, S. (2001). "Economies of Scale in the Digital Industry," in *Knowledge for Inclusive Development,* edited by Conceição, P., Gibson, D., Heitor, M., Sirilli, G., and Veloso, F., Quorum Books, Westport, Conn. 2001.

PART I

COMMERCIAL PRIORITIES

Chapter 1

The Many Dimensions of an R&D Project: Multi-Criteria Analysis

A Tutorial

C. Bana e Costa and S. Thore
Instituto Superior Técnico, Lisbon

Abstract: The need to evaluate a series of R&D projects may arise in many instances: in a commercial corporation upgrading new technology or developing new one, in a business incubator, in a venture capitalist firm, or in the management of government research programs. For each of these applications, some elementary concepts and procedures of Multi-Criteria Analysis are explained and discussed.

Key words: Problematique, fundamental points of view, descriptors, evaluation criteria, multi-criteria analysis (MCA), cognitive map, causal network, value functions, bisection technique, scales, scorecards, evaluation sheets, weights

1. THE MANAGEMENT OF CORPORATE R&D

As we enter the 21st century, industrial R&D has become a major growth engine of national economies and of the global economy. The management of R&D is becoming a major preoccupation of corporations of all sizes. It is no longer just the very large corporations that find it profitable to maintain state-of-the art laboratories and research facilities. Small companies in computer software and hardware, and in biotechnology, are demonstrating again and again that a successful bet on developing and commercializing the right product at the right time can lead to market breakthroughs and spectacular growth. A surprising number of corporations listed on Wall Street actually do nothing but R&D. An ever-increasing share of GNP is devoted to R&D, with the US leading the pack of nations devoting 2.7 % of its GNP to industrial R&D. [1]

The matter of the management of corporate R&D is not a well-developed academic discipline. There are no standard handbooks on the subject. There are no generally accepted procedures. R&D is always a venture into an uncertain future. How do you manage the future itself?

The purpose of corporate R&D is to identify and to develop new industrial processes, new products, or product designs, or new means of marketing them. Corporate R&D typically takes place in a laboratory setting, the manufacturing of prototypes, or test marketing. R&D of digital products such as software, or audio or visual products take the form of programming and, perhaps, animation.

From the point of view of the CFO of the company, R&D is an investment - - a costly investment that needs to be balanced against its prospective return. But conventional investment models are of little help to gauge the financial rewards of several competing R&D projects. How do you measure the prospective returns to the corporation of a single R&D project, which may not even be technically feasible, let alone have a sustainable market potential?

A host of different considerations must enter the mind of the entrepreneur or manager who develops and launches a new product or process in the marketplace. There are the technological aspects of course, the engineering and the manufacturing questions, the technical feasibility of the new idea. There are questions of marketing and the responses of the would-be consumers. There is the matter of how the competitors will react. How will the community at large react - - organized labor, local politicians, environmental groups? There are many stakeholders in a modern corporation and in a new venture. They all want their say, and they all can make or break a new product.

As one ponders these matters, the first problem that confronts the analyst is to understand "what is the problem?" from the decision-maker's perspective (called the *decision-making problematique*, see Bana e Costa 1996). This is essential to get a wise answer to the question "how shall the study approach the problem?" (the *decision-aiding problematique*). For the managers of a corporation the problem typically is to choose between a list of several proposed alternative R&D projects, and the priority, funding and personnel to be assigned to each of them. Furthermore, once a project has been initiated, it needs to be monitored and its progress needs to be assessed at regular intervals. There may be unexpected breakthroughs calling for

[1] An interesting discussion of these matters as seen from the Portuguese perspective can be found in P. Conceição, D. Durão, M. Heitor and F. Santos (1998), Chapter 1.

additional resources allocated to the project, or there may be setbacks. During the R&D phase, the priority of a project may be upgraded or downgraded. Unsuccessful projects will be terminated.

Denoting the set of current and proposed R&D projects by $A = \{A1, A2, A3, \ldots\}$ a vector of actions relating to each element of the set may then be defined, including such actions as "initiate project and provide initial funding", "upgrade priority of project and provide additional funding", or "reject project proposal." Note that actions taken on different projects are not necessarily independent of each other because development work carried out on one project may benefit other current or potential projects. For instance, project *A1* may benefit from the successful completion of project *A2* and *A3*. Project *A4* may be just a follow-up investment on an earlier project that was completed some time ago. And so on. Our way of dealing with such dependencies will be a procedure of "successive choice" (see Bana e Costa 1996), formulating the problem in terms of a sequence of choices of the best action. A project selected at a choice stage is taken out of the set for the next stage, and before going ahead the problem is re-framed to incorporate the repercussions of the previous choice over the performances of the remaining projects.

Fundamental points of view and their descriptors. Having defined the technical *problematique* of a study and the type of set of potential actions, the next decision-aiding activity is to identify the "fundamental points of view" (see Bana e Costa, 1992) in terms of which the R&D projects should be compared. A fundamental point of view (FPV) focuses on one or several aspects of a project in the context of the operations of the company such as product development, production or marketing (see the five headings in Table 1 below). For each fundamental point of view, several individual impact *descriptors* or criteria are identified:

- Product Development and Design
    - Difficulty or practicality of converting idea into marketable product
    - In-house resources available for R&D work
    - R&D time and cost
- Production
    - Availability of facilities, work-force and know-how
    - Need for investments in plant or machinery
    - Availability of raw materials, parts, and supplies
    - Worker health, risks for accidents
- Marketing
    - Complementarity with existing product line

Potential market size
Competition
Availability of sales force and distribution networks
- Financial
  Profit margin, time to break-even
  Product lifetime and rate of return over life cycle
  Equity capital and borrowing needed
- Community and Environmental
  Location and traffic
  Environmental discharges

Table 1. List of fundamental points of view and descriptors of R&D projects

A descriptor or evaluation criterion may be defined as "a tool allowing comparison of alternatives according to a particular point of view" (Bouyssou 1990). In a few instances, a single piece of numerical information will provide what is required. In most cases, there are long stories to be told. However, a listing like Table 1 can at least be used as a starting-point trying to understand the logical structure of the problem of managing corporate R&D. In the table, the various criteria are grouped into groups and subgroups. As one pursues the various issues even further, one may decide to introduce a third or a fourth tier of criteria. See e.g. Islei *et al.*, 1991.

Even such a simple breakup of the criteria into a hierarchical structure is not without its problems and difficulties, however. Criteria on the same tier, or even on different tiers, may not be independent of each other, so that they cannot really be evaluated and assessed independently of each other. For instance, most of the factors listed in Table 1 will impact on the financial results of the proposed project. Or, environmental factors may influence the product design (choosing a recyclable design or packaging material, for instance).

The formal analysis of hierarchical structures of criteria is called *multi-criteria analysis* (MCA). Decision-making based on such analysis is called *multi-criteria decision analysis* (MCDA).

2. THE MANAGEMENT OF INCUBATORS AND VENTURE CAPITAL PORTFOLIOS

The problem of managing a portfolio of R&D projects is encountered in a slightly different form in industrial incubators nurturing start-up firms. A business incubator houses and aids start-ups, providing manufacturing and office space and other amenities; it may also offer secretarial support, computer services and management consulting services. Hopefully, after a few years, the tenants at the incubator will "graduate", moving out from the incubator and making it on their own.

The problem of managing the incubator is first, to select companies to be admitted to the incubator, and second, to monitor their progress, to assist management, and, if necessary, to terminate the contracts of unsuccessful tenants. Since each start-up company typically will manufacture or sell only a single product, each company may again be identified as a "project." The logical structure of the management problem at hand is then very similar to running an industrial R&D laboratory.

There may be a difference, however: The very purpose of the incubator may be to stimulate local businesses, local employment, or the development of one or several particular industrial sectors. States and communities in the U.S. seized on incubators as a job-creation vehicle in the early 1980s. Most incubators are nonprofit and receive financing from state or local agencies or from a university. One of the most successful incubators is the Austin Technology Incubator, serving as a major outlet for the commercialization of technology developed at the University of Texas.

Other incubators have failed to live up to their expectations because they have played it safe by taking on as tenants only those businesses that were likely to succeed anyway. The intents of the incubator may also be lost when the graduates relocate far away, providing no stimulus to the local economy.

The start-up and the running of a corporation typically involve high risk. It is a "venture." The venture capital industry specializes in high-risk equity investments, holding a portfolio of equity stakes in new ventures. The problem of managing a venture capital portfolio is to select projects among applicants, to tailor a package of financing for each project, and to monitor the progress of each project.

Just as the incubator wants its tenants eventually to "graduate," the venture capitalist wants to shepherd its clients to eventual disengagement and to free up its funds. It wants throughput. As the client-corporation expands, the moment eventually will arrive when the venture capitalist helps the client to draft a prospectus and to offer new equity on the stock market. If the initial public offering (IPO) is successful, the venture capitalist will cash out.

3. THE MANAGEMENT OF GOVERNMENT RESEARCH FUNDING PROGRAMS

The problem of managing a portfolio of R&D projects is encountered in yet another form in the operation of huge government-financed research funds that many governments have set up to stimulate applied academic research. For instance, the German Federal Ministry of Education, Science, Research and Technology operates a research funding program that provides approximately 200 million deutsche mark annually in the area of chemical research. The goals of the program are to promote R&D of new and possibly next generation technologies, to strengthen the educational basis in chemistry towards research and application of new technologies, and to create new jobs. (See Baselt, Tiebes, Wagemann and Zickler, 1998.) The Korean government established in 1993 its Institute of Information Technology Assessment, evaluating the huge national R&D program in the areas of information technology. The program is divided into a subsidies program and a loans program. (See Yi, Kang and Yoon, 1998).

In situations like these, a government agency is charged with the task of evaluating and ranking R&D proposals, and of allocating funds to the accepted ones. The agency may also monitor the progress of the projects, possibly allocating follow-up funding in the case of research breakthroughs.

Table 2 lists some fundamental points of view (FPsV) and their descriptors that government administrators may apply in judging the priority of funding proposals.

- Meeting stated R&D objectives:
  - Following the working plan and meeting the time schedule
- Impact on the scientific community:
  - Number of patents and scientific publications.
- Availability of facilities, work-force and know-how:
  - Need for investments in plant or machinery
  - Availability of raw materials, parts, and supplies
  - Worker health, risks for accidents.
- Transfer to industrial R&D:
  - Complementarity with existing product line
  - Potential market size
  - Competition
  - Availability of sales force and distribution network.
- Financial indicators:
  - Product lifetime and rate of return over life cycle
  - Equity capital and borrowing needed
- Community and Environmental:
  - Location and traffic
  - Environmental discharges

Table 2. List of fundamental points of view and descriptors of R&D funding proposals

4. THE MANAGEMENT OF ACADEMIC R&D

The traditional role of universities and academic institutions is to engage in basic or fundamental research that more or less by definition is supposed to have no immediate commercial application. Academic institutions promote the search for truth, not for financial gain.

A number of developments during the last decades have challenged this age-old distinction. For one thing, much "basic" research, notably in the areas of computer science and biotechnology, has turned out to have immediate commercial potential with huge attendant profit possibilities. Many both private and state universities in the U.S. are nowadays looking at some of their academic laboratories as veritable cash cows. Sometimes a university sets up a formal Office of Intellectual Property, reporting directly to the chancellor of the university, charged with managing activities like patenting and licensing university-developed technology. The office may be staffed with patent lawyers and top-notch managers.

As competition between academic institutions has intensified and as the number of enrolled students have grown, academic administrators have become more cost-conscious and are looking ever more desperately for additional means of funding. In this climate, administrators tend to be more selective and they tend to prioritize departments and research activities that are demonstrably "useful" to contemporary society and to the school itself. One may regret this development, but it seems to be part of an ongoing process of shaping society in a more secularized and utilitarian manner.

Modern society is rapidly being transformed by high technology and much of this new technology is born, directly or indirectly, within the academic sphere. It lies near at hand to conclude that universities not only have an opportunity but actually a moral responsibility to assist in shepherding the new technologies to commercial fruition. The old view used to be that a university has absolved its obligations once the research results had been published, gathering dust in some library. The new view is that the university also needs to assist its researchers in developing the full commercial potential of their research.

This argument gains strength when one looks at the role of academic institutions in small countries, with limited research resources. The research that obtains funding certainly must not be left to wither on the rocky ground. Universities and academic institutions in small countries can be powerful agents of technological and economic change. They face the responsibility of moving new technology from the study chamber and the laboratory to the national marketplace.

The conclusion seems to be, to paraphrase an often-used expression, that academic research is too important to be managed by academic researchers alone. Professional managers should manage it. European observers rarely appreciate the degree to which professional managers are involved in the management of U.S. academic research, directly and indirectly. Managers set the directives and researchers strive to accomplish what is expected from them. This happens when the director of a research institution is recruited from outside, often from an entirely different discipline, based on his or her academic management record of accomplishment. It happens when a department chairman initiates new department research projects, or closes down existing lines of research. It happens when research funded by the National Science Foundation has to adhere to strict guidelines and milestones.

As a result, the academic sector in the US has been and is quite responsive to market opportunities. Rosenberg, 1998, traces the growth of university departments and academic programs in the US during 150 years as a response to demands for increased knowledge and increased skills in society at large.

Is it possible to develop management criteria for the monitoring of academic R&D? A series of chapters in the present volume are devoted to answering this question. No one should be under the illusion that there exist easy answers. The transition from an academic R&D laboratory may take many, many years. The passage will not only take a longer time, it will also be much more uncertain, with greater risks of failure. The ultimate commercial benefits may be only indirectly or in a roundabout fashion linked to the original academic research. There is a problem of attribution here, of tying basic research to the eventual commercial application. Can we even today, in retrospect, determine the return on university research on lasers, carried out in the 1950s? What will be the return of research in optical computing carried out today, assuming even a most optimistic future scenario?

5. STEPS IN MULTI-CRITERIA ANALYSIS: THE STRUCTURING PHASE

To help systematize our inquiry into the motivations of R&D managers, one may draw on various procedures of multi-criteria analysis to help set up empirical investigations and to understand the information collected. Some of these procedures will precede and help identifying the list of fundamental points of view (FPsV) and their descriptors such as those exemplified in Tables 1-2. This will be referred to as the *structuring phase* of the problem. The purpose of structuring is to build a more or less formal manageable representation that integrates the objective components of the decision context. These include the various characteristics of the R&D projects, with objective with possible subjective concerns that make relevant values of interest more explicit.

The process of structuring involves three steps: cognitive mapping, identification of FPsV, and identification of descriptors.

5.1 Cognitive mapping

The cognitive map highlights the logical structure of the various points of view. Each node represents a fundamental point of view (FPV) or even an individual point of view (PV). An FPV can usually be seen as a cluster of several interrelated elementary PsV. Nodes are linked by arrows, relating the PsV to one another. They indicate how one PV influences, leads to, or has implications for another PV. In this fashion, the map illustrates the logical structure of a set of PsV and FPsV.

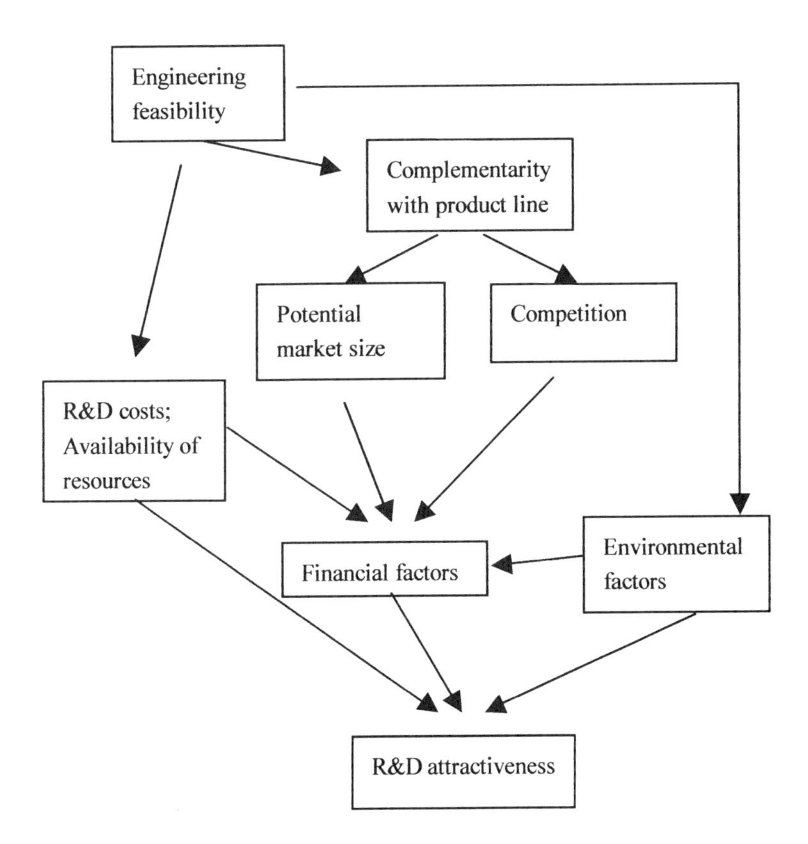

Figure 1. Causal network of R&D attractiveness

The points of view should possess suitable properties of independence, non-redundancy, inclusiveness and exhaustiveness. Arguments that are partly overlapping are to be avoided. They should cover all relevant aspects of the R&D decisions. Factors of importance must not be omitted. If data are collected in interviews, it is helpful if the investigator has given some thought to such matters already when designing the interview questionnaire.

A simple example may convey the flavor of some of these procedures. Suppose that for a study of commercial R&D decisions, a network of causal factors determining the attractiveness of a project has been developed as exhibited in Figure 1. Factors that motivate or prompt the R&D decisions are treated as "causes." Factors that describe the nature of the R&D decisions made are "effects." The joint causal structure takes the form of a causal network. There are causal interdependencies between variables. Most variables are effects of one or several upstream variables while at the same time they are causes to one or several downstream variables.

Causal networks are well known in statistical analysis and standard multivariate procedures are available to trace and test the presence and strength of the individual causal relationships in a given set of observations, including factor analysis, analysis of variance, etc. In the present instance, we use the cognitive map and the causal network as a preparatory tool to construct the simple hierarchies listed in Tables 1 and 2.

5.2 Building a tree of fundamental points of view (FPsV)

The process of building a tree of FPsV from the underlying cognitive map is an "art" left to the individual analyst (see the discussion in Bana e Costa *et al.*, 1999). There exist several computer-based techniques for generating the cognitive map, but no computer-based system to compress it into a tree of FPsV. Instead, a cyclic process of structuring involving repeated evaluations of the various points of view and the reasons why they are considered to be relevant will help selecting the final construction of the tree.

5.3 Identification of descriptors of impact

A descriptor is associated with each FPV to make an operational description (quantitative or qualitative) of the degrees to which the values stated by the FPV can be satisfied. The descriptor is an ordered set of plausible impact levels, serving to describe the impacts of alternatives. This is similar to the classical notion of an "attribute" and it fits with the use of the term "criterion."

6. STEPS IN MULTI-CRITERIA ANALYSIS: EVALUATION MODEL

In the present context, our interest goes beyond the causal understanding of the R&D decisions carried out by companies in some statistical universe. We want to arrive at guidelines for management. Once a blueprint for the causal structure has been established, we want to design numerical techniques for the rating and prioritizing R&D projects. This step requires the formal design of an *evaluation model.*

Building value functions. In order to measure the (partial) attractiveness of the R&D projects in the dimension of each FPV, cardinal value functions are constructed using the respective descriptors as function arguments.

To characterize the commercialization potential of a given R&D project, a long array of numerical information may need to be recorded. Some of the data may be cardinal, such as the expected sales of the product, the estimated financing needs and so on. But much information will typically be qualitative rather than quantitative, and to provide an account of this information a long list of categorical variables may be specified. (A categorical variable ranges over a set of discrete categories.) The information may be collected as responses from a formal or informal interview with a manager of the R&D department of the corporation, or other knowledgeable persons

For a simple example of a constructed discrete value function, consider the case of constructed attribute measuring the "market appeal of a new product", as follows

++ = the product has a good market image, it fills a real need and is seen by the consumers as superior to competing existing brands;

\+ = the product has a good market image, it fills a real need but is seen by the consumers as comparable to existing brands;

0 = the product has a good market image, it does not fill a real need but is seen by the consumers as superior to competing existing brands;

\- = the product has a good market image, it does not fill a real need and it is seen by the consumers as comparable to existing brands;

\- - = the product has not a good market image.

The constructed variable is a single-attribute value function with five discrete possible outcomes. One forms it by amalgamating three separate criteria, each with two possible discrete outcomes.

Continuous value functions can be constructed by *bisection techniques.* The techniques involve identifying "a most preferred stimulus and a least preferred stimulus...subsequently a midpoint stimulus is found that is equidistant from both extremes" (von Winterfeldt and Edwards, 1986). For instance, a team of marketing specialists is asked to rate the market appeal of a number of new products currently under development. Using the bisection technique, they might assign a point rating system ranging from the minimum of 10 points (poor appeal) to 500 points (maximum appeal). Denoting the value function to be determined by $F(x)$ where x is the number of points scored by a particular new product, one then puts $F(10) = 0$ and $F(500) = 100$. Next, one asks the experts to determine the half-way intermediate score x_1 which has the property that the increase from the score from 10 points to x_1 points is as attractive as the increase from x_1 points to 500 points. Define $F(x_1) = 50$. Next, subdivide the two intervals $(10, x_1)$ and $(x_1, 500)$ into four equally attractive intervals, etc.

MACBETH is a software package for building value functions. The questioning procedure consists in asking the evaluator to verbally judge the difference of attractiveness between two stimuli.

Constructing scales and defining weights. To facilitate the numerical analysis, it will often be advantageous to convert several qualitative or quantitative variables into a single criterion measured according to an ordinal or cardinal scale. We now discuss various approaches to constructing scales. The scaled variable may be referred to as a *single-attribute value function.*

Weights are normalized to add to 1. One or several "experts" who have experience from analyzing and comparing R&D projects may set the weights. Each expert may determine the weights directly or some software package like MACBETH may be used during an interactive session with the expert. If several experts are asked, or if some kind Delphi analysis is employed asking each expert to revise his or her earlier estimates in the light of the ratings of their co-evaluators, some mechanism of averaging the weights is necessary.

7. A SIMPLE EVALUATION TOOL: SCORECARDS OR EVALUATION SHEETS

Many companies make use of a simple rating system for assessing the prospects of R&D projects, called scorecards or evaluation sheets. One card or sheet is completed for each project. The sheet is circulated among various experts inside or outside the company, each expert being asked to evaluate those aspects of the proposed project that falls under his or her expertise. Returning to the case of Table 1, the engineer in charge of the R&D work is asked to evaluate the section on Product Development and Design. The line production manager is given the section on Production, the corporate financial officer the section on Financials and so on. Each expert is asked to evaluate each criterion, rating it on a scale of "excellent", "good", "fair", "poor", and "bad."

There are ways of formalizing this procedure, converting it into a single numerical score for each R&D project. First, the evaluation of each criterion $i = 1,...m$ is translated into a numerical value V_i such as excellent = 100, good = 75, fair = 50, poor = 25 and bad = 0. Second, each criterion is given an a priori weight w_i, like 20 percent or 30 percent, with the weights summing to one, $\Sigma_i w_i = 1$.

How should those weights be determined? They should reflect the overall assessment of top management, in balancing the various fields of specialized knowledge represented by the experts.

The total weighted score

$$\Sigma_i w_i V_i \tag{1}$$

is really a kind of subjective *utility function* for management, reflecting its balanced evaluation of the R&D project.

It is easy to criticize this approach. Laying down those weights, are we not really sneaking in the solution to the entire evaluation problem through the back door? Fortunately, the main emphasis of the mathematical techniques to follow in the present volume, called *data envelopment analysis*, is to determine the weights endogenously, as part and parcel of the problem at hand, rather than postulating them a priori.

Judging faculty research papers at Villanova University. The following example is brought from Liberatore, Nydick and Sanchez, 1992 (see also the introductory text Clauss, 1996, pp. 430 ff.). The Business College at Villanova University developed a weighted ranking procedure for judging research papers submitted by its faculty. The papers were judged according to the criteria listed in Table 3 below.

	Relative weight
Clarity of objective of the research	0.167
Justification of research	0.100
Design of research	0.239

Execution and implementation	0.193
Recommendations and implications	0.301

Table 3. Criteria used to judge faculty research papers

The weights listed in Table 3 were established after extensive deliberations in the faculty, and they reflect the consensus of its members. That is, a "panel of experts" was asked to determine the weights. The sum of the weights is one. Next, each paper was rated on each criterion according to a five-point scale, with the following numerical values:

- "outstanding" = 0.53,
- "good" = 0.24,
- "average" = 0.13,
- "fair" = 0.06,
- "poor" = 0.04.

(Various ways of translating qualitative scores into cardinal ones were discussed in Section 6 above.) Finally, the total weighted score of each research paper was determined, using the weights listed in Table 3.

To see how this works, consider three research papers, A, B and C. Listing the scores in the order of the criteria in Table 3, *Paper A* received the scores 0.53, 0.13, 0.13, 0.24, 0.04. The total weighted score is then $0.167 \times 0.53 + 0.100 \times 0.13 + 0.239 \times 0.13 + 0.193 \times 0.24 + 0.301 \times 0.04 = 0.1909$.

Paper B received the scores 0.13, 0.24, 0.24, 0.53, 0.24 and its total weighted score is $0.167 \times 0.13 + 0.100 \times 0.24 + 0.239 \times 0.24 + 0.193 \times 0.53 + 0.301 \times 0.24 = 0.2776$.

Paper C received the scores 0.24, 0.04, 0.53, 0.06, 0.06. Its total weighted score is $0.167 \times 0.24 + 0.100 \times 0.04 + 0.239 \times 0.53 + 0.193 \times 0.06 + 0.301 \times 0.06 = 0.1909$.

Conclusion: Paper B is ranked the winner, followed by paper C. Paper A is the loser, receiving the lowest score.

Valuation of biotechnology stocks. The head of the health care group of the investment banking division, Paine Webber Inc, has described an interesting application of the scoring approach; see Papadopoulos, 1998. For many reasons, investment analysts find it difficult to assess the intrinsic value of biotechnology stocks. Biotechnology is risky, with huge potentials for sales and financial gain if a new drug turns out to be viable and if it is approved by the FDA, but also with great risks of failure. Many biotech companies should be seen as specialized R&D companies, preferring to leave large-scale manufacturing and marketing to others. Once a drug or a new biotech process has been developed, the company often licenses it to a large drug manufacturer.

The basic premise of the Paine Webber method is that the future success of a young biotech company is based on how effectively it has invested in R&D in the past. First, the analyst assesses the performance of the company in three areas: science, business and strategy. The quality of the scientists is examined, the approaches they use in their work, their historical performance compared to that of competing groups, and the extent of collaboration with quality university scientists. The depth and breadth of experience of management is examined, its success in negotiating contracts with corporate partners, and its expertise in regulatory and legal affairs. The overall strategic plan of the company is examined in the context of market realities, and the interaction between the technical and business staff of the company. For each individual category, a score is assigned which reflects the performance of the company over the past several years.

Second, the analyst calculates the cumulative R&D expenditures of the company over several years. Research funded internally is postulated to be more valuable than research in a corporate alliance and earlier R&D spending is considered more valuable than recent spending. In this way, a weighted R&D index is obtained, modulated by the efficiency of managing that effort.

Pain Webber uses the resulting rankings as a screening tool for isolating potentially overvalued or undervalued stocks. Papadopoulus sums up:

> "What Wall Street needs now is a new metric that would be able to evaluate and combine, with an appropriate weighting system, the multiple factors driving biotechnology values. These factors would include management, science, market opportunity, proprietary position, competition, regulatory issues, commercial agreements, cash and interest rates into a single value parameter."(*ibid.*, p.56)

8. DETERMINING THE WEIGHTS

A number of different procedures have been suggested for determining the relative weights w_i to be assigned to different criteria in forming the weighted average (1). It should be noted that weights have specific meanings, linked to the impacts on the criteria involved. For instance, in Table 3 the criterion "recommendations and implications" was assigned a weight (0.301) almost exactly three times the weight given to "justification of research" (0.100). This means that upgrading the score of "recommendations and implications" from "fair" to "average", say, would be 3 times more attractive than increasing the score of "justification of research" in the same fashion.

The procedures for determining the weights include:

- The trade-off procedure (Keeney and Raiffa, 1976). The key idea here is to compare two alternative evaluations of a pair of criteria. The first evaluation features the best impact on the first criterion and the worst impact on the second one. The other has the worst on the first criterion and the best on the second. Choosing the preferred alternative of the two, the decision-maker is able to decide on the more important criterion. Next, the impact level is adjusted to yield indifference between the two alternatives. This is accomplished in the following manner: worsen the best impact under the chosen alternative, or improve the worst impact under the non-chosen alternative.
- The swing weighting procedure (von Winterfeldt and Edwards, 1986). Consider first the hypothetical possibility of the worst impacts in all the listed criteria. Next, one investigates the change from worst impact to the best one in one single criterion at a time. The respondent is asked to identify which swing from worst to best impact would result in the largest improvement of global attractiveness. The criterion with the most preferred swing is assigned 100 points. The magnitudes of all other swings are expressed as percentages of the largest swing.
- The ratio procedure (Edwards and Newman, 1982).
- MACBETH (Bana e Costa and Vansnick, 1997-98).

9. MULTI-CRITERIA ANALYSIS AND DATA ENVELOPMENT ANALYSIS

The purpose of the scorecards and weights is to convert an essentially multi-dimensional problem - - that of rating and prioritizing R&D projects with many characteristics and attributes - - into a single dimension, that of the utility function (1). But is it really necessary to compress the given data into a single dimension?

The answer is that recently a new and exciting technique has become available that allows the analyst to perform the ranking of R&D projects in *all* the dimensions of the list of project attributes at the same time. The ranking is carried out without assigning a priori weights to the various attributes; instead, the weights are treated as unknowns and are obtained as part and parcel of the mathematical ranking technique.

The new technique is called Data Envelopment Analysis (DEA). It is due to A. Charnes, W.W. Cooper and their numerous collaborators and Ph.D. students at the University of Texas and Carnegie Mellon University. The original paper is Charnes, Cooper and Rhodes, 1978. A main purpose of the present volume is to show how this technique can be applied to provide a rating and prioritization of both commercial and academic R&D projects. The text of the volume is self-contained and no prior knowledge of DEA is necessary. The basic concepts will be introduced by means of some simple empirical applications reported in Chapter 2 below. In subsequent chapters, a range of various applications will be demonstrated, including the rating of venture capital projects, and government research projects. Thus, the reader will gradually be introduced to these matters, with the emphasis placed on application rather than mathematics (dealt with in a separate Appendix to this book).

It is helpful to regard multi-criteria analysis and DEA as complementary approaches, each having its characteristic strengths and weaknesses (see also Belton and Stewart, 1999). The decided strength of multi-criteria analysis is the identification of objectives and assessment criteria, the mapping of the logical and causal relationships between them, and the construction of categorical or cardinal variables to measure criteria. A ranking carried out by multi-criteria analysis establishes a winning R&D project (#1), a runner-up (#2), and so on. Each project is compared with the winner. The difficulty with this kind of information is that it gives no obvious *diagnostic* clue as to how the performance of a particular project could be improved.

DEA simply assumes a given list of inputs and outputs (performance criteria). No clue is provided how these variables should be identified, selected and measured. In many ways, one may therefore say that DEA starts where the multi-criteria analysis ends

Characterizing DEA in terms of the procedures of multi-criteria analysis, DEA is a technique of determining the weights to be assigned to the various criteria. Rather than postulating fixed weights that are the same for all projects, however, *DEA proceeds by determining individual weights for each project*.

The great innovative idea of DEA that is entirely absent from multi-criteria analysis is the concept of a *frontier* or *best practice*. Those projects that are located on the frontier are all ranked as winners. The projects that fall behind the frontier are compared with best practice and it is suggested that the management of the project could be improved by replacing it by best practice. In other words, DEA provides management with consulting advice, pinpointing how the performance of a given project could be improved. In the chapters to follow, the reader will meet a number of examples, brought from both the commercial and the academic world. In every instance, DEA serves not only as a ranking device but also as a monitoring and diagnostic tool.

Differences of emphasis. Naturally, the main occupation of multi-criteria is the analysis of the criteria themselves, their logical structure and how they can be measured. DEA, on the other hand, was developed as a tool of ranking and is mainly concerned with comparing the performance of the various units examined. Therefore, current practice often reflects some differences of emphasis.

DEA has often been used for *ex post* evaluation for the purpose of monitoring and control. Multi-criteria analysis is typically presented as a tool of *ex ante* evaluation to support planning and choice. However, there is no inherent reason why the two techniques should be limited in this fashion. Indeed, one of the purposes of the papers in the present volume is to extend the use of DEA to situations of evaluating prospective and uncertain R&D projects - - that is, to applications of *ex ante* rankings.

Another difference of emphasis in the existing literature might also be pointed out. DEA typically makes use of available cardinal statistical measures, that is, of "objective data," whereas multi-criteria analysis puts considerable effort into the collection, interpretation and processing of value judgements and other "subjective data." Again, this distinction only reflects actual practice and is not inherent in the two techniques. In the papers to follow, we shall meet the joint use of both

- objective data such as statistics of current and sunk costs of the various R&D projects to be ranked, and
- subjective data such as the success evaluation of projects as seen by one or more "experts."

A very real difference between the two approaches, however, has to do with the number of observations or units to be ranked. Whereas many of the techniques of multi-criteria analysis work well also in situations where there may be only half a dozen units present for the rankings, DEA typically requires a considerable number of observations. The mathematics of DEA otherwise becomes over-determined so that there are no degrees of freedom left and most or all of the observed units end up lying on the calculated "frontier. "

Banker et al., 1989, actually recommend that the number of observations in DEA should be greater than 3 times the number of inputs plus outputs. In many applications, this rule dramatically forces the DEA analyst to limit the list of inputs and outputs. In such situations, recourse to the various techniques of multi-criteria analysis is not only called for but may be the only way to provide a more realistic picture of the causal structure.

9.1 Joint use of multi-criteria analysis and DEA

After these preliminary comments, we now outline a format for the joint use of multi-criteria analysis and DEA. To fix the ideas, consider an application involving the ranking and comparison of a number of university research projects (see Section 4 above). Suppose that a detailed questionnaire has been developed probing the nature and promises of each project. In-depth interviews are conducted and a large number of performance characteristics of each project are recorded. Let the projects be indexed $j = 1,2,...,n$. The total number of projects n may be several dozen projects, but typically not more than one hundred. (Long interviews are costly and difficult to administer.)

The first step of analysis is a cognitive mapping of all factors of relevance, both on the input side and on the output side of each project. Next, the tree of fundamental points of view is constructed. Assume that the FPsV can be divided into two classes:

- FPsV that relate to the use of inputs or resources spent on each project, say X_{ij}, $i=1,2,...,m$
- FPsV that relate to the use expected outputs or results stemming from each project, say Y_{rj}, $r = 1,2,...,s$.

Next, assume that the descriptors of the FPsV on both the input and the output side have been quantified and given cardinal measures. Denote the descriptors of the input X_{ij} by X_{igj}, $g = 1,2,...,t$ and the descriptors of the outputs Y_{rj} by Y_{rhj}, $h = 1,2,...,u$.

Presumably, a fair number of descriptors will be used to characterize each FPV. In some instances perhaps three or four descriptors will suffice; for other FPsV as many as 10 or 12 descriptors will be required. We mention this because the dimensions of the problem are important. All in all, counting the descriptors on both the input and the output side, as many as forty or fifty descriptors will be defined.

To the reader who is familiar with multi-criteria analysis, the dimensions now indicated will present no problems. But the DEA analyst will immediately recognize a difficulty: there may be too few observations (research projects) compared to the number of variables (descriptors) and the DEA calculations can easily become meaningless. Without going into the details of the calculations, it will suffice here to mention that DEA is a method of fitting a piece-wise linear "frontier" to the given observations. But if the number of observations is too small relative to the number of dimensions, every single observation will lie on the frontier. To illustrate, consider this numerical example:

Number of FPsV on the input side: 1. Number of descriptors: 6.

Number of FPsV on the output side: 8. Number of descriptors of each: 5.

Number of observations: 40.

The total number of dimensions, counting both descriptors on the input side and the output side is here $1 \times 6 + 8 \times 5 = 46$, which is greater than the number of observations 40. Geometrically, one is confronted with 40 points in a 46-dimensional space. It is possible to draw a 46-dimensional plane that joins all the 40 points. In other words, every single observation is located on the calculated frontier and the DEA calculations become meaningless.

Even if the number of observations were to be slightly larger than the number of descriptors, there may still be too few degrees of freedom left for the DEA observations and the calculated DEA ratings may not be robust.

To overcome the problems now mentioned, *we propose first to use the procedures of multi-criteria analysis to determine weights of the descriptors relating to each FPV. The sum of weights inside each FPV should equal 1. In this manner, a weighted measure of each PFV on the input side and each FPV on the output side is determined. Second, we propose using DEA to rate the observations in the dimensions of the FPsV only.*

Let the weights of the input descriptors be $w_{igj.}$, $g = 1,2,...,t$ and form the weighted average of each input FPV

$$X^\wedge_{ij} = \sum_{g=1}^{g=t} w_{igj} \times X_{igj} \tag{2}$$

In the common manner, $X^\wedge_{ij}$ may be interpreted as a utility function indicating the use of inputs of category $i = 1,2,...,m$. Similarly, let the weights of the output descriptors be $w_{rhj.}$, $h = 1,2,...,u$ and form the weighted average of each output FPV

$$Y^\wedge_{rj} = \sum_{h=1}^{h=t} w_{rhj} \times Y_{rhj} \tag{3}$$

The weighted value $Y^\wedge_{rj}$ is a utility function indicating the amount of output of category $r = 1,2,...,s$ obtained. Our proposal amounts to using these input utility functions and output utility functions as the inputs and outputs for the DEA calculations.

This approach represents a compromise between DEA using the full output data, and a conventional utility function. It involves defining a list of aggregate performance statistics, each aggregate being formed as a weighted average of its constitute detailed indicators. Standard DEA will then be employed ranking the projects, using the aggregate performance indicators as outputs.

REFERENCES

Baselt, J.P., Tiebes, D., Wagemann, K., and Zickler, A. (1998). "Assessment of Publicly Sponsored R&D Projects in Chemistry and Chemical Engineering Related to Ecological and Economic Sustainability," presented at the 2nd International Conference on Technology Policy and Innovation, Lisbon.

Bana e Costa, C.A. "Structuration, Construction et Exploitation d'un Modele Multicritere d'Aide á la Decision," Ph.D. thesis, Instituto Superior Técnico, Lisbon.

Bana e Costa, C.A. (1996). "Les Problematiques de l'Aide á la Decision: vers l'Enrichissement de la Trilogie Choix-tri-Rangement," *Recherche Operationelle /Operations Research*, Vol. 30:2, pp. 191-216

Bana e Costa, C.A., Ensslin, L., Correa, E.C., and Vansnick, J.-C. (1999). "Decision Support System in Action: Integrated Application in a Multicriteria Decision Aid Process, " *European Journal of Operational Research*, Vol. 11:3, pp. 315-335.

Banker, R., Charnes, A., Cooper, W.W., Swarts, J., and Thomas, D.A. (1989). "An Introduction to Data Envelopment Analysis with some of its Models and their Uses", *Research in Governmental and Nonprofit Accounting*, Vol. 5, pp. 125-163.

Belton, V. and Stewart, T.J. (1999). "DEA and MCDA: Competing or Complementary Approaches?" in *Advances in Decision Analysis*, ed. der Reus, N. and Roubeus, M., Kluwer Academic Publishers, Boston, 1999, pp. 87-104.

Bouyssou, D. (1990). "Building criteria: A Prerequisite for MCDA," in Bana e Costa, C.A., editor, *Readings in Multiple Criteria Decision Aid*, Springer Verlag, Berlin, 1990, pp. 58-80.

Charnes, A., Cooper, W.W., and Rhodes, E. (1978). "Measuring the Efficiency of Decision Making Units," *European Journal of Operational Research*, Vol. 2, pp. 429-444.

Clauss, F.J. (1996). *Applied Management Science and Spreadsheet Modeling*, Duxbury Press, Wadsworth Publishing company, Belmont, Calif.

Conceição, P., Durão, D., Heitor, M. and Santos, F. (1998), editors. *Novas Ideias Para a Universidade*, IST Press, Lisboa.

Isley, G., Lockett, G., Cox, B., Gisbourne, S. and Stratford, M. (1992). "Modeling Strategic Decision Making and Performance Measurements at ICI Pharmaceuticals," *Interfaces*, Vol.21: 6, pp. 140-149.

Goodwin, P. and Wright, G. (1991). *Decision Analysis for Management Judgment*, Wiley, New York, N.Y.

Keeney, R.L. (1992). *Value-Focused Thinking: A Path to Create Decision-making*, Harvard University Press, Cambridge, Mass.

Keeney, R.L. and Raiffa, H. (1976). *Decisions with Multiple Objectives: Preferences and Value Tradeoffs*, Wiley, New York, N.Y.

Liberatore, M.J., Nydick, R.L., and Sanchez, P.M. (1992). "The Evaluation of Papers (or How to Get an Academic Committee to Agree on Something)," *Interfaces*, Vol.22, pp. 91-100.
Papadopoulos, S. (1998). "Quantifying the Dream: Valuation Approaches in Biotechnology," *Nature Biotechnology*, Vol. 16, supplement, May, pp. 55-56.
Rosenberg, N. (2000). "Knowledge and Innovation for Economic Development: Should Universities be Economic Institutions?" in *Knowledge for Inclusive Development*, ed. by Conceição, P., Gibson, D.V., Heitor, M.V., Sirilli, G. and Veloso, F., Quorum Books, Greenwood Publishing Group, Westport, Conn.
von Winterfeldt, D. and Edwards, W. (1986). *Decision Analysis and Behavioral Research*, Cambridge University Press, Cambridge, Mass.
Yi, C.-G., Kang, K.-B., and Yoon, S.H. (1998). "Meta-evaluation on the Information and Communications R&D Program in Korea," presented at the 2nd International Conference on Technology Policy and Innovation, Lisbon.

Chapter 2

Using Frontier Analysis to Rate the R&D Projects of a Commercial Corporation

Editorial Introduction

Abstract: Frontier analysis classifies a number of R&D projects into two categories: efficient and sub-efficient ones. Efficient units are said to be in equilibrium; sub-efficient ones are in disequilibrium. There is always the potential for a future technological breakthrough, also for projects that currently rank far below the efficiency frontier.

Key words: Non-economic man, suboptimality, data envelopment analysis, efficiency frontier, envelope, disequilibrium, chaos theory,

1. ECONOMIC MAN - - AND NON-ECONOMIC MAN

The ranking methods discussed in the present volume build on a classical concept in theoretical economics: the concept of efficiency (sometimes called Pareto efficiency, after the Italian economist V. Pareto, 1848-1923). Students of economic textbooks encounter efficiency as a tool of equilibrium economics, expostulating the presumed rational behavior of "economic man" - - a hypothetical person choosing optimal production methods and making optimal consumption decisions. As seen from the ivory tower of economic theory, the key to the understanding of the real world lies in an examination of such rational economic behavior.

The technique of data envelopment analysis (DEA for short), invented in the late 1970's represents an important step forward in the study of economic efficiency. It is a method for analyzing observations of real-life producers and consumers and other economic agents to see if indeed they do behave according to the premises of "economic man." In other words, DEA moves the analysis of economic man from theory to empirical testing. Among a collection of economic agents operating in a market, DEA will identify *some* units as being optimal or "efficient." These units do indeed behave according to the premises of economic man. The majority of units, however, will of course not be found living up to these exacting standards. We shall call such behavior "sub-optimal" or "sub-efficient." Furthermore, for those sub-performing units, DEA delivers a numerical estimate of their shortcomings, so that DEA can be used as a tool for ranking the units in terms of their performance.

In the case of a number of R&D projects conducted by a commercial corporation or by an academic research facility, DEA will similarly identify *some* projects as optimal or "efficient." The others are falling behind this optimal ideal. Their performance is sub-optimal or sub-efficient. DEA will provide the desired ranking of the projects.

In this fashion, DEA has led to a revolutionary insight in economics: the discovery of sub-optimal or even irrational behavior. Rather than dismissing sub-optimality as a kind of noise in the economic system, distracting the observer from the postulated equilibrium optimizing behavior, sub-optimality is now being recognized as an often-true characteristic of the real world.

Rather than sweeping the failings of human decision-making under the carpet, economists now possess a numerical procedure for identifying the presence of "non-economic man", and for measuring numerically the extent of these failings. In terms of the analysis of R&D projects, we shall similarly identify the presence of sub-optimal projects and we shall measure the shortcomings of these numerically.

We offer some introductory comments on the merits and possible shortcomings of economic man under two headings: efficiency frontiers, and chaotic processes.

The research paper immediately following this editorial introduction ("Prioritizing a Portfolio of R&D Activities, Employing Data Envelopment Analysis") is a good starting point for the reader who is not familiar with the techniques of DEA. That paper is the oldest one in the present volume. It was completed already in 1996 and can be viewed as the seed from which much of the work in the volume eventually developed.

2. EFFICIENCY FRONTIERS - - AND LOOKING BEHIND THOSE FRONTIERS

Frontier analysis is a recent development in economics that explicitly recognizes that some decision-makers use sub-optimal solutions. The purpose of frontier analysis is to distinguish the optimal (efficient) decision making units, which are said to be located at the frontier, from the sub-optimal (inefficient) ones that are located away from the frontier. Since there may be several optimal decision-making units located on the frontier, the multiple answers provided by frontier analysis indicate that an optimizing decision-making unit may exist in several forms. These correspond to different ways of organizing and managing the unit. However, units that are not on the frontier do not make as efficient use of their inputs as some linear combination of other ones, indicating that their performance might be improved by changing some of their production or management procedures.

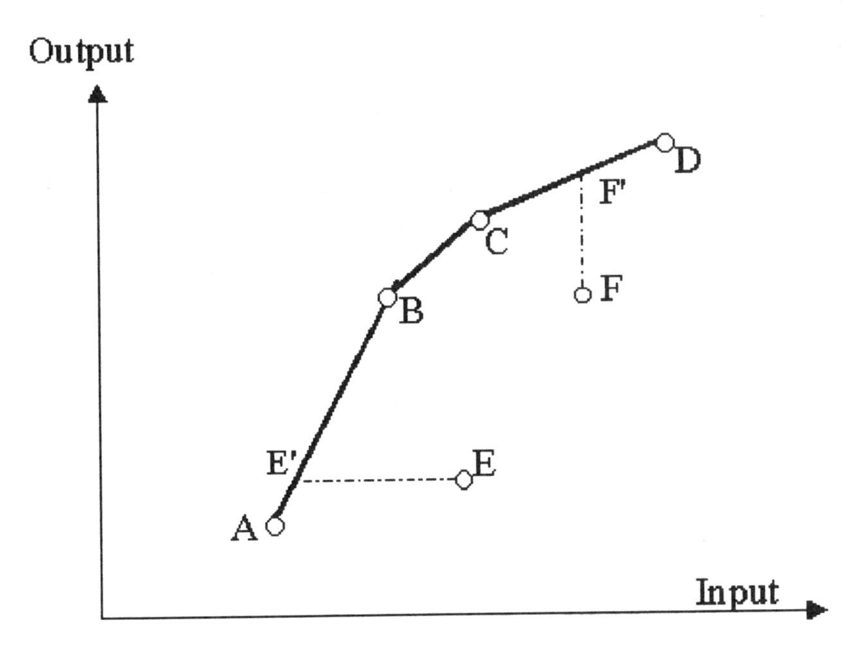

Figure 1. Illustration of input-output frontier

A simplified illustration of a technology frontier is provided in Figure 1. Six different technologies convert a single input into a single output. The observed input-output pairs have been marked by the six points A,B,C,D,E and F. The resulting efficiency frontier A-B-C-D is piece-wise linear. It consists of three linear facets: AB, BC, and CD.

The frontier is said to be "spanned" by the four technologies A,B,C,and D. These four technologies are located on the frontier. They are efficient. The two remaining technologies E and F are located behind the frontier. They are inefficient.

Quite generally, in a multidimensional space with many inputs and outputs, the efficiency frontier can be drawn as a multifaceted multidimensional surface, a so-called linear polyhedron. The polyhedron can be obtained by constructing the convex *envelope* to the observed points.

There are two ways of characterizing the inefficiency of points like E and F. One way is to take an *input-oriented* look at things, noting that the use of inputs are excessive. Given the output produced, it should be possible to reduce the use of inputs. For instance, projecting point E horizontally to the left onto the frontier, one finds point E'. Note that E' is not an observed point; rather, it is a hypothetical point using the same output but less inputs. Another way of examining an inefficient point is *output-oriented*, noting that the outputs obtained fall short of what should be possible. Given the input actually used, it should be possible to increase the output. Projecting point F vertically upwards toward the frontier, one finds point F'. It is a hypothetical point using the same inputs as F but generating more output.

Data Envelopment Analysis is a method of constructing empirically and numerically the frontier, given a set of observations like A,B,C,D,E and F. For inefficient observations, the observed performance is compared with a hypothetical optimal or "best" performance at the frontier. Thus, DEA is not only *diagnostic* in that it identifies those technologies that perform optimally, but it is also *normative* or *prescriptive* in that it delivers information how the actual performance of a sub-optimal technology might be improved.

When assessing and ranking a collection of R&D projects, we shall be able to

- identify the optimal projects, and separate them from the sub-optimal ones;
- pinpoint the shortcomings of lagging projects and provide advice for corrective action.

3. CHAOTIC PROCESSES

Just as in economics, natural science was traditionally dominated by concepts of optimum and equilibrium. During the last thirty years, however, a large body of knowledge has been brought together concerning the evolution of dynamic systems in general. Such systems typically are in disequilibrium. The breakthrough occurred in thermodynamics, in physics, and in meteorology. At its core, this theory is mathematical, dealing with the behavior of nonlinear systems. This is the modern theory of *chaos*.

The basic premise of chaos theory is the universal tendency toward disorder, dissolution, and decay. Be it a piece of machinery, a living organism, or a corporation: for a brief moment, life is a triumph over death. But the triumph is forever evanescent. Life has to be re-established every second.

To fight the cosmic compulsion for disorder, agents are constantly organizing and reorganizing themselves into larger structures through the clash of mutual accommodation and mutual rivalry. Molecules form cells, neurons form brains, species form ecosystems, and corporations form industries. At each level, entirely new properties appear. At each stage, entirely new laws, concepts, and generalizations are necessary. Each system has many niches. The very act of filling one niche opens more niches. The system is always unfolding, always in transition. New technologies and startup companies representing new ways of doing things are forever nibbling away at the edges of *status quo*, and even the most entrenched old production methods eventually have to give way.

The winds of change are sweeping new industries and old industries alike. To prosper, a company needs to bring a continuous flow of new product designs successfully to the market. The new industrial climate requires rapid decision-making, a lean and horizontal organizational structure, and a willingness to take risks. The optimal innovation policy is to pursue an entire portfolio of technological development projects. Many of these will fail the test of commercialization, but a few will survive. Those that do survive will have only a limited life span, and will soon need to be replaced by superior products

A surprising result of modern nonlinear mathematics is that the tendencies to order and chaos - - to build and to destroy, to invent the new and to discard the old - - somehow can keep each other in balance. The system never locks into a fixed pattern, nor does it dissolve into uncontrolled turbulence. The balance is called "the edge of chaos." At the edge, the system has enough stability to sustain itself and enough creativity to evolve.

Chaos theory looks at systems that are located *far away* from equilibrium, and that may stay away from equilibrium *all the time*. We shall invoke frontier analysis to demonstrate empirically the presence of such disequilibrium processes.

Under this perspective, one may not even be sure that frontier performance like A-B-C-D in Figure 1 is desirable. The very presence of disequilibrium may act as a creative driver of the system. Some of technologies that are presently listed as under-performing may actually hold the promise of major future breakthroughs.

Examples abound. Chester Carlson (1900-1968) succeeded in making the first xerographic copy in 1938. He used an electrostatic method rather than the cumbersome photographic and chemical copying processes of his day. His first patent was dated 1940. For the next four years, he tried unsuccessfully to interest someone in developing and marketing his invention; more than twenty companies turned him down. Finally, in 1947, the Haloid Company, Rochester N.Y. (later the Xerox Corporation) acquired the commercial rights and in 1958, Xerox introduced its first office copier.

Edwin Armstrong (1890 - 1954) invented FM broadcasting back in 1933. FM (= frequency modulation) modulates the frequency (number of waves per second) rather than the amplitude or power of radio waves. It was an entirely new way of scrambling the sound waves in the transmitter and unscrambling them again in the receiver. It eliminates static. The era of high-fidelity broadcasting had been ushered in. But Armstrong had to fight an uphill battle to get his invention commercialized. The large radio corporations wanted to protect their own systems (short wave and medium wave). They fought him all the way. Exhausted by interminable patent suits and despairing, he finally, in 1951, took his own life. Today FM is the preferred system in radio and the required sound system in television.

To use a term of chaos theory, these are examples of new ways of doing things that cause a *phase transition* of the underlying technology system. The transient state is characterized by order and chaos intertwined in a dance of evanescent technologies, product designs and corporate structures. Eventually, from the shakeout, a new state of technology arises.

Modern technology is in a perennial state of disequilibrium: a gap between on the one hand the perceived technological potential of the future and on the other existing practices that are fast becoming obsolete. It is a never-ending quest toward technological targets and market potentials that are forever evolving.

So, how can we gauge the potential for future growth (and system change) of sub-efficient technologies like E and F, falling behind the frontier A-B-C-D?

4. GAUGING THE POTENTIAL FOR A TECHNOLOGICAL BREAKTHROUGH

It would be pretentious, of course, to claim that the kind of miscalculations that I have now illustrated couldn't occur again. They occur all the time.

On the other hand, modern U.S. venture capitalism provides many opportunities that were absent on the R&D scene during the first half of the past century. It is helpful to think of these opportunities in terms of a multiplicity of technology and market niches, and a multiplicity of actors.

There still are the lone one-of-a-kind inventions, but they are less common. The typical invention of today has a multiplicity of technological and marketing attributes that can be packaged in many different combinations. The digital camera, or the hand-held cell phone, provides literally an entire "menu" of services. Each manufacturer carefully blends these services to hit its marketing targets. Each manufacturer conducts an R&D program to develop further the technological characteristics of each attribute. Some of these developments are fairly mundane (such as providing greater speed, connectivity, and so forth), others are more experimental and may contain the seeds of future breakthroughs.

In other words, there are close alternatives - - technological and marketing variations in many dimensions. The task of the management of the R&D department is not just to accept or to reject, but rather to choose between many competing models still under development. Those alternatives all need to be *ranked* and *prioritized.*

There are also more actors and new kinds of actors involved in gauging the future potential of technology. Some of these actors are listed below:

- The very business of *venture capitalists* is to spot new technological and market opportunities, and to find and steer clients toward those opportunities.
- *Competitors* looking for partners for new strategic alliances may suggest joint research efforts (and funding to go with them).
- *Buy-out capitalists* may ponder the possibility of an outright acquisition.
- *Stock market analysts* continuously examine the path of technological progress in their field of specialization, and assess the market opportunities of corporations quoted on Wall Street.

Financial actors and analysts like these have a personal stake in their evaluations. Seasoned by past mistakes, they learn. The most successful ones thrive. Their judgments are not to be taken lightly.

In addition, the management of corporate R&D may seek the advice of both in-house and outside *experts*. Some corporations establish a panel of experts monitoring the progress and prospects of all ongoing research projects. Such a panel should include both production and marketing people, gauging both the technical feasibility of each project and its potential market.

From a mathematical point of view, this multiplicity of technologies and actors takes the form of *vectors* of performance attributes. Technologies do not just have a single "input" and "output", as in Figure 1, but rather long lists of inputs and outputs. Furthermore, many outputs are *subjective* evaluations.

In the mathematical space of all these dimensions, there will still exist an efficiency frontier - - a multidimensional polyhedron enveloping and spanning a few efficient observations. And there will still be inefficient observations, falling behind the frontier. The precise inefficiency score, calculated by DEA, depends upon the expected performance of a given R&D project along all measured dimensions. A shortfall of a single performance variable can easily be compensated for by a superior performance in terms of other variables. The project may then still be given a green light. Or, a shortfall in one variable may be reinforced by a predicted poor showing all around. Such projects are candidates for termination.

REFERENCES

The reader who would like to learn more about chaos theory may consult some of the works mentioned below.

Gleick, J. (1987). *Chaos: Making a New Science*, Viking Penguin, New York, N.Y.
Lewin, R. (1993). *Complexity: Life at the Edge of Chaos*, Macmillan, New York, N.Y.
Waldrop, M.M. (1993). *Complexity: The Emerging Science at the Edge of Order and Chaos*, Simon and Schuster, New York, N.Y.

Prioritizing a Portfolio of R&D Activities, Employing Data Envelopment Analysis

A Research Paper

S. Thore[1] and G. Rich[2]

[1] *IC² Institute, The University of Texas*

[2] *Baker Hughes Corporation*

Abstract: A system of monitoring, ranking and prioritizing the R&D projects of a commercial enterprise or of an academic institution is presented. To characterize the progress and commercial potential of an R&D project, an entire range of criteria need to be considered. The choice of these may vary from one application to another, but will certainly include characteristics of the new product and its market, the strategic opportunities that the new product will offer, and some suitable indicator(s) of expected financial return. Environmental and societal considerations may also enter the picture. A new mathematical technique called data envelopment analysis (DEA) permits the ranking of projects in the presence of such multiple performance criteria. The basic DEA calculations are explained. Two practical applications illustrate the choice of criteria and the nature of the calculations, first for a Texas corporation engaged in the development of new drilling equipment for the oil industry, and, next, for the ranking of NASA aeronautics investments.

Key words: New product screening, data envelopment analysis, performance criteria, efficiency frontier, efficiency score, best practice, social indicators, monitoring and control

1. INTRODUCTION: THE PROBLEM OF RANKING R&D PROJECTS

In order to meet the pressing demands of the market place, the high-tech corporation needs to be engaged in continuous product development, upgrading its present product line and preparing for the timely launching of new successor technology. Even medium-sized corporations often run extensive R&D departments. To monitor such operations, corporations need a mechanism for evaluating and ranking both proposed new projects and projects currently under development. Furthermore, and perhaps most importantly, corporations need to put in place a management *process* that translates such rankings into daily routines for the management of their R&D departments.

Unfortunately, the existing literature on the management of R&D projects and capital budgeting provides little guidance to the manager or the scholar who wants to understand the scientific principles for selecting and maintaining a portfolio of R&D projects. The present paper is offered in an attempt to fill this lacuna in present knowledge.

In various ways, corporations try to grapple with the problem. Some companies, heavily dependent of their R&D activities, have developed systematic procedures of assessing their R&D projects. They range from the intuitive to the formal. The telecommunications division of 3M Corporation ranks projects by calculating their conventional net present values. For each project, expected annual sales and expected operating costs are estimated for the first four years, and the net present value (NPV) is calculated using a predetermined discounting factor. That is, only the direct impact on cash flow is considered.

NPV calculations make sense when it comes to comparing long-term investments, such as the purchase of machinery or real property. But they are unsatisfactory for monitoring a portfolio of revolving short-term projects such as R&D in the electronic, computer, or biotech industries. In such portfolios, the sequencing of projects over time is important, and the technology grows hierarchically with one project laying the technological foundations for the feasibility of the next (see Thore, 1996). Purely financial considerations need to be complemented with strategic ones. Ideally, the strategic attractiveness of a project should include its potential for unfolding critical new technology, that is, for opening up new technology perspectives and possibilities that were not visible before. One generation of technology breeds the next generation and, in an important sense, the R&D operations of a corporation sets the stage for its future operations.

Each business entity faces a different set of influential factors that might be incorporated into the ranking of R&D projects and the decision-making process. In what follows, we shall say that these factors indicate the "attractiveness" of a project. There is no such thing as a standard list of factors of attractiveness. Instead, the list of factors should be developed for a particular corporation at a particular time to reflect its strategic position and its goals. In this manner, a list of factors of attractiveness can make the evaluation of projects sufficiently flexible to fit various circumstances. Note that even social criteria such as the creation of local jobs or the enhancement of local industry may enter the decision-making picture in the form of factors of attractiveness. Such criteria may figure importantly in the considerations of government research as conducted by the departments of defense and energy, in government laboratories, and by NASA.

In order to evaluate its R&D programs, 3M Company conducts "technical audits" which provide internal peer reviews of its laboratory activities. The audit is a tool to help the operating unit plan and implement programs and allocate resources. Programs are rated according to both technical and business factors (Krogh *et. al.*, 1988). In order to shelter embryonic efforts, small programs and ideas in early stages are exempted from the audit.

The need to rank R&D projects is encountered in a slightly different institutional setting in the management of a business incubator. The IC^2 Institute at the University of Texas operates the Austin Technology Incubator (ATI), one of the nation's most successful business incubators and recipient of several national awards. The tenants of the incubator are permitted to stay in the sheltered environment for three years and must then move out to free up office and manufacturing space to new startup firms. Thus, a third of the tenants are renewed each year; the success of the incubator obviously is crucially dependent upon the selection of new entrants.

This paper presents and discusses a new mathematical method called "data envelopment analysis" (or DEA for short) which quite generally makes it possible to rank units (such as corporations) or projects (such as investment projects or R&D projects) when there is more than one ranking criterion. Ranking the performance of R&D projects, it thus permits the assessment of financial factors such as cash flow *and* strategic factors at the same time. Furthermore, there is no need to affix a predetermined weight to the score of each individual factor; instead, the mathematical method itself will determine all the unknowns.

DEA evaluates the expected performance of each R&D project in relation to the "cutting edge" or "frontier" as defined by the best-performing projects of the company. Carried out quarterly or yearly, it will provide a current check-up on the performance of each project as it advances through the R&D process. In particular, it may assist in identifying promising projects that should be considered for enhanced funding, and in identifying project laggards that are candidates for termination.

Section 2 briefly surveys some conventional procedures of R&D screening. Section 3 provides some introductory comments on the mathematical method of DEA. Section 4 presents an application ranking the R&D projects of a private Texas corporation engaged in developing systems for oil drilling. Section 5 discusses a second application ranking NASA aeronautics investments. Section 6 offers some concluding comments on the use of DEA for monitoring and control of the R&D budget.

2. SOME COMMON SCREENING METHODS: A BRIEF REVIEW

In his 1988 book *Managing New Products* Thomas Kuczmarski discusses the selection of R&D screening criteria, which will in any case typically be different for different companies with different strategic aims. Qualitative criteria may include market indices, indicators of the strategic role of that management wants to accord the new product, the various engineering and financial internal strengths of the company, and the competition. Examples of quantitative criteria mentioned by Kuczmarski are the expected minimum revenue, minimum gross margin, the expected payback period, the expected return on invested capital and (for new-to-company products) the expected return on assets.

Discussing a computer paper manufacturer and marketer looking for improved margins, Kuczmarski suggested the following qualitative criteria:

- the product must be sold to an existing target customer base,
- the product should not require post-sale maintenance or service by the company,
- the product should be distributed via current channels,
- product performance should be as good or better than competition,
- limited exposure to product liability,
- product based on low technology,
- product should require little advertising support.

Turning to quantitative criteria, Kuczmarski divided the potential R&D projects into three strategy classes: new-to-company products, product line extensions, and product line "flankers". For each such strategy class, quantitative criteria were laid down as follows:

- second year revenues, in millions of dollars,
- cumulative revenue by 3rd year, in millions of dollars,
- gross profit margin, per cent,
- pre-tax margin, per cent,
- time to breakeven, in years,
- payback period on invested capital, in years.

Once the prioritization has been carried out, Kuczmarski recommends dividing the projects into four categories:

- the top ten new products approved for development,

- backburner projects that have passed the screening (but which are considered to be of a lower priority),
- refrigerator projects that may possibly warrant consideration in the future,
- "freezer projects" that clearly do not pass muster but which may be reviewed at a later date.

In their 1993 book *New Product Screening: A Step-Wise Approach*, William C. Lesch and David E. Rupert discuss a slightly more formalized approach, assigning weights to the various factors considered. They describe a model and a software package called PIES-II, based on early work carried out at the University of Oregon and the University of Wisconsin. The model evaluates each proposed R&D project according to a list of criteria, including expected demand, market acceptance, business risk, the competition and societal factors. For instance, the demand factors include

- market potential,
- trend of demand,
- stability of demand,
- length of product life cycle,
- potential of product line (opportunities for related applications, different markets etc.).

The market acceptance factors include

- compatibility with existing products,
- learning,
- need,
- visibility,
- promotion,
- distribution,
- service.

Each factor is assessed using a seven-point scale, generating a vector of numbers for each proposed R&D project. To rank the vectors, several fancy mathematical methods are proposed. The "linear compensatory" approach sums all scores for each project. The 'conjunctive approach" drops projects that fail to meet some specified minimum value for each factor. The "disjunctive" approach drops projects that fail to satisfy minimum requirements for a set of "critical factors".

Finally, we briefly mention the 1993 book *A Knowledge-Based Approach for Screening Product Innovations*, written by Sundaresan Ram and Sudha Ram. These authors take the numerical approach discussed a moment ago a step further, introducing the concept of "weights" to be attached to each criterion considered. Experts assign the weights. Each weight reflects both the importance of a criterion and its certainty. Each criterion is assessed on a

5-point scale. The resulting score is multiplied by its weight. To assess a proposed R&D project, the (weighted) sum of all its criteria is added up.

The general idea of ranking a series of R&D projects by an *expert-weighted performance index* is fairly obvious, and is no doubt being applied in practice in many connections. We have ourselves had an opportunity to watch the use of this approach at Baker Hughes, a Texas company developing high technology systems for oil drilling. To implement the prioritization of proposed R&D projects, the company employs a scoring process that allows for a multitude of market and engineering considerations. Operations personnel from the company's various international divisions rank projects by the following list of criteria of attractiveness, using a ten-point scale:

- strategic compatibility of a project with existing products,
- market demand,
- competitive intensity,
- probability of technical success,
- the proprietary position of the company,
- manufacturing and maintenance complexity.

Each criterion is assigned a fixed weight, determined in advance by "experts" (a team of managers). An average score for each criterion for each project is calculated based on the scoring from the participants. A composite score for each project is then calculated by multiplying the weights of each criterion, as determined by the experts, with its average score. The composite score thus obtained is taken to represent the over-all attractiveness of each project.

3. WHAT IS DATA ENVELOPMENT ANALYSIS?

DEA was invented in 1978 by the research team of A. Charnes and W.W. Cooper, known for a series of pioneering contributions in applied mathematics and operations research. (The original reference to data envelopment analysis is Charnes, Cooper and Rhodes, 1978; for surveys, see Seiford and Thrall, 1990 and Charnes, Cooper, Lewin and Seiford, 1994.) The purpose of DEA is to determine the *efficiency frontier* that envelops all observations as tightly as possible. In general, several projects will lie on the frontier. The envelope projects are all assigned the efficiency rating of 100 percent. Projects falling behind the envelope are assigned ratings less than 100 percent. In other words, the new metric splits all projects into two classes: frontier projects and sub-frontier projects. Sub-frontier projects are ranked by their proximity to the frontier.

For an explanation of elementary concepts, turn to Figure 2 which illustrates the ranking of six projects, projects P, Q, R, S, T, U. Only two ranking criteria can be shown in a two-dimensional figure like this; the two dimensions chosen for this illustration are: annual net income from commercialization, in millions of dollars (being here the sole indicator of the performance of the project), and the cost of the project, also in millions of dollars. Each project is indicated as a point in the diagram. Together, the six points form a scatter or swarm of points. Data envelopment analysis proceeds by constructing the envelope to this scatter of points, the line PQRS. The envelope shows, for any given level of cost, the highest attainable net income. Also, for any given level of net income, it shows the lowest required cost. In other words, directions in the diagram toward the northwest - - upward and to the left - - are favorable and the envelope shows the frontier of the attainable positions.

In Figure 2, projects P, Q, R, S lie on the envelope. These projects are said to span the envelope. Their rating is put equal to 100 percent. But T and U lie below the envelope. These projects are sub-frontier, with ratings less than 100 percent. Take a look at project T! Projecting it horizontally to the left, one hits the envelope at point (t). At this frontier point, the performance of the project is the same (same annual net income) but the cost is lower. The rating assigned to project T is set equal to the percentage possible reduction of the cost. It is less than 100 percent.

Envelopment analysis has been employed to rank corporations engaged in manufacturing or in distribution or marketing, and also to rank not-for-profit bodies such as electric utilities, public schools (see Charnes, Cooper and Rhodes, 1981) and hospitals. The purpose of the calculations is in every such instance to trace the technology frontier and to rate each individual unit relative to the frontier. Some notable applications reported in the literature involve U.S. army recruiting districts, U.S. Air Force wings, and even Chinese cities!

The calculations were brought to the attention of the public in the early 1980s with the successful site selection of the super-conducting super-collider to Waxahachie, Texas, south of Dallas. The Texas legislature had funded a four-university study to identify feasible sites for the location of a high-energy physics lab in Texas. Six feasible sites were identified and a comparative site analysis was made, incorporating project cost, user time delay, and environmental impact data. The Waxahachie site was preferred under a wide range of conditions (Thompson, Singleton, Thrall and Smith, 1986).

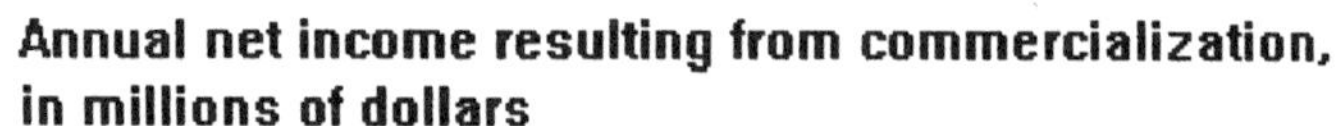

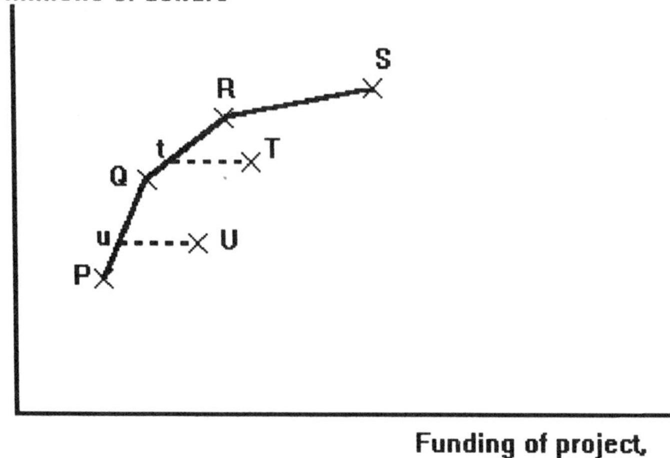

Figure 2. Illustration of Data Envelopment Analysis

3.1 The mathematics of DEA [1]

Suppose that there are $j = 1,2,...,n$ R&D projects to be ranked. Each project is characterized by $r = 1,2,...,s$ criteria; the performance of each project j in terms of these criteria is measured by the vector $Y_r = [Y_{rj}]$. The scalar X_j gives the required cost of each project j.

Consider one particular project, indicated as project $j=0$. The performance and the cost of this project are $Y_0 = [Y_{r0}]$ and X_0, respectively. The task at hand is to rank project $j=0$ relative to the "frontier", to be defined. Let the λ_j , $j=1,...,n$ be weights attached to each project. The weights are unknown, to be determined. They are nonnegative:

$$\lambda_j \geq 0, \; j=1,...,n \tag{1}$$

Further, in the so-called BCC model (Banker, Charnes and Cooper, 1984), the sum of weights is required to equal unity. Form the convex combinations $\Sigma_j \lambda_j Y_j$ and $\Sigma_j \lambda_j X_j$. The weights are to be determined so

[1] Only a brief introduction is provided here, dealing only with the case of a single input. For a complete review, see the Mathematical Appendix to the present volume.

that these sums reflect "frontier performance" and "frontier cost", respectively.

Ranking project $j = 0$, if it so happens that the weight of this project is one and the weights of all other projects are zero, then the project will be said to lie on the frontier. A few projects will always be located on the frontier, and the frontier is defined by or "spanned" by these frontier projects.

In order to find out whether a given project $j=0$ is located on the frontier, or behind it, the following procedure is introduced. One attempts to reduce or shrink the required cost, from the actual cost level X_0 to a reduced level θX_0, where θ is a reduction or contraction factor to be determined. That is, one wants to determine the frontier cost so that, if possible, it is only some fraction of the actual cost requirements (or less):

$$\theta X_0 - \Sigma_j \lambda_j X_j \geq 0 \tag{2}$$

At the same time, frontier performance must not fall short of actual performance:

$$\Sigma_j \lambda_j Y_j \geq Y_0 \tag{3}$$

For an intuitive explanation, refer again to Figure 2. Let project T be the project currently evaluated, that is, $T = (X_0, Y_0)$. The rating of the project proceeds by forming the projection on the frontier, point $t = (\Sigma_j \lambda_j X_0, \Sigma_j \lambda_j Y_0)$. The frontier costs are only some fraction θ of actual costs (or less), as spelled out by relation (2). The frontier point is sometimes referred to as "best performance."

The mathematical problem at hand is now to minimize θ while satisfying the constraints (1), (2), and (3), that is

$$\text{Min } \theta \tag{4}$$

subject to

$$\Sigma_j \lambda_j Y_j \geq Y_0$$

$$\theta X_0 - \Sigma_j \lambda_j X_j \geq 0.$$

$$\Sigma_j \lambda_j = 1, \text{ and } \lambda_j \geq 0, \; j=1,\ldots,n.$$

It is easy to see that it is always possible to drive down the contraction factor θ to the value $\theta=1$. The constraints in program (4) are then all satisfied, if one also puts the weight of project $j=0$ equal to unity and the weights of all other projects equal to zero. If it so happens that $\theta = 1$ is also the lowest possible value that program (4) permits, then the project currently rated is a frontier point. But if it is possible to drive $\theta < 1$, then the project lies behind the frontier. The optimal contraction ratio θ is termed the *efficiency rating* of the project.

The significance of these mathematical developments will become clearer to the reader when we now turn to a couple of illustrations.

4. FIRST ILLUSTRATION: RANKING R&D PROJECTS IN A PRIVATE CORPORATION

Baker Hughes is a Texas corporation developing high technology systems for oil drilling (see their website www.bakerhughes.com). The information provided below gives a stylized indication of the nature of the operations (to protect the company, the actual data have been replaced by a numerical example). At one point in time, the company was involved in pursuing 14 projects involving so-called "directional drilling," say projects *P1 - P14*. The company had identified some of these as derivative projects, such as short radius systems, re-entry motors, thrusters and work-over motors. Others were identified as (oil drilling) platform projects, such as a new reservoir navigation tool, an expandable stabilizer, and a new motor design. Others, again, were identified as "breakthrough" projects, such as coiled tubing drilling, a 200 degrees Celsius air motor, active thrusting, and closed loop drilling. There is no need to describe the details of these projects here; the shorthand labels now mentioned should suffice to evoke the general nature of the engineering involved.

The projects are listed in Table 1, column (i). There is a single input into each project - - the expected cost to complete it, in millions of dollars. It is written X and it is listed in column (ii).

Turning next to the performance of each project, data for the following $r=1,2,3,4$ criteria are exhibited in Table 1, columns (iii) – (vi):

Y_1 estimated market size, in millions of dollars

Y_2 strategic compatibility with existing products

Y_3 projected market demand, in millions of dollars

Y_4 competitive intensity

We explained in Section 2 how the company employs "experts" to assess and calculate the average score for each criterion for each project. This time, however, we shall no longer attach any fixed weights to the various criteria.

Table 1. Costs and performance data for 14 oil-drilling R &D projects

Project	X_j	Y_{1j}	Y_{2j}	Y_{3j}	Y_{4j}
P1	1.07	32	8.2	7.5	8.0
P2	1.06	50	7.6	7.2	6.4
P3	0.325	40	7.6	7.1	5.3
P4	1.60	30	7.1	7.2	5.5
P5	0.55	25	7.0	7.0	5.1
P6	0.20	8	6.0	6.1	6.9
P7	0.35	2	5.9	6.2	6.6
P8	0.53	12	5.8	5.8	5.4
P9	0.21	10	5.8	5.8	4.7
P10	0.16	0.8	5.4	5.6	6.1
P11	0.07	3	5.3	5.4	6.5
P12	1.95	300	6.8	6.1	6.4
P13	5.59	60	6.2	6.9	6.8
P14	3.10	240	6.5	6.6	7.1

No attempt will be made to form a single weighted average score of each project (thus reducing the dimensionality of the problem at hand). Instead, we shall confront directly and up front the task of ranking projects that are characterized by an entire vector of attributes.

We are now prepared to perform the envelopment analysis. Program (4) reads

$$\text{Min } \theta \tag{5}$$

subject to

$$\Sigma_j \lambda_j Y_{1j} \geq Y_{10}$$

$$\Sigma_j \lambda_j Y_{2j} \geq Y_{20}$$

$$\Sigma_j \lambda_j Y_{3j} \geq Y_{30}$$

$$\Sigma_j \lambda_j Y_{4j} \geq Y_{40}$$

$$\theta X_0 - \Sigma_j \lambda_j X_j \geq 0$$

$$\Sigma_j \lambda_j = 1, \text{ and } \lambda_j \geq 0, j=1,\ldots,n.$$

In simple words, program (5) determines the frontier point ("best performance") by searching for the greatest possible proportionate contraction of the observed cost input. The contraction should be carried out while seeing to it that the frontier performance does not fall short of the observed performance, and that frontier cost does not exceed the contracted cost

The linear program (5) consists of five inequalities and one equality. The number of unknowns is $n+1$, that is, the factor θ is unknown and there is one unknown weight λ_j for each project. In order to rank all projects, program (5) has to be solved repeatedly, once for each project.

4.1 Results of the envelopment analysis

For the numerical solution of the data envelopment, several commercial software packages are now widely available. Essentially, the numerical problem at hand is one of solving a sequence of linear programming (LP) problems - - in the present small example there are 14 successive LP problems to be solved. For instance, this numerical task can be carried out using the standard mathematical programming package GAMS (general algebraic modeling system); see Thompson and Thore, 1992.

Solving program (4) repeatedly, one then finds the efficiency scores displayed in Table 2. It turns out that six projects are efficient, getting a perfect score of $\theta = 1$: projects *P1, P3, P6, P11, P12* and *P14*. These are the elite projects, they rank ahead of the other projects and they are all equally "good." They are all located at the efficiency frontier; indeed, the frontier is spanned by these six projects.

Table 2. Ranking 14 oil-drilling R&D projects: the efficiency scores

Project	Efficiency score
P1	1
P2	0.654
P3	1
P4	0.320
P5	0.564
P6	1
P7	0.596
P8	0.249
P9	0.619
P10	0.625
P11	1
P12	1
P13	0.136
P14	1

Looking at a single sub-efficient project, say project *P2* with the efficiency score 0.654, this score has the following interpretation: Management should be able to obtain the same output performance (in terms of the output variables listed in Table 2) or better, while incurring only 65.4 % of its estimated costs.

The efficiency rating is the percentage reduction in total "input" needs (here: costs) that would be possible at the frontier while still delivering the same performance data (or more).

For projects with efficiency ratings equal to 1.00, that is, for projects located at the frontier, actual performance coincides with frontier performance. But for sub-frontier projects, the hypothetical frontier performance is better than (or equal to) actual performance. And the frontier inputs are less than (or equal to) actual inputs.

Are the efficiency scores now calculated just a play with numbers, or do they reveal something about the true comparative opportunities of the various projects? What, if anything, would one mean by the "true" ranking of the projects? One way to answer this question is to look at the predictive value of the scores, that is, to compare them with the outcomes of the projects *ex post.* Table 3 below lists the outcomes of the projects, as they had become apparent to Baker Hughes a couple of years later, in December of 1996.

There are three or four clear success stories which all go back to projects that were originally rated as located on the efficiency frontier (efficiency score = 1.0). Projects 1 and 6, also located on the frontier, were never started. Perhaps they should have been - - one will never know. Today the company rates as "moderate" or "marginal" successes five projects only. These projects were all sub-efficient, with efficiency scores less than one.

Table 3. Eventual outcomes of 14 oil-drilling projects

Project	**DEA efficiency score**	**Eventual outcome**
P1	1	Project never started
P3	1	Major project success
P6	1	Project never started
P11	1	Failed to meet technical objective
P12	1	Major project success
P14	1	Commercial in 1998 – expecting big success
P2	0.654	Commercial in 1997
P10	0.625	Moderate success
P9	0.619	Moderate success
P7	0.596	Marginal success
P5	0.564	Outsourced product – marginal success
P4	0.320	Commercial in 1997
P8	0.249	Marginal success
P13	0.136	Project never started

The other eight projects all obtain efficiency scores less than 1. They are all sub-efficient. Ranking them in the order of their efficiency scores, from the highest score to the lowest, one finds the order *P2, P10, P9, P7, P5, P4, P8* and *P13*.

Numerical examples like these are suggestive, but obviously provide circumstantial evidence only. They do not constitute a strict statistical test of the usefulness of the efficiency ratings. For that, much more in-depth studies are required.

As this illustration shows, DEA can provide indication of the commercialization potential of R&D projects still under development. If such calculations are carried out regularly, for instance each quarter, they may serve as a monitoring device. As such, they will provide guidance for managers about the progress of the various projects. In addition, DEA can be used for diagnostic purposes, to spot the shortcomings of a particular project and indicate how its performance can be improved. DEA does this by comparing the actual performance of a project with "best practice," i.e. its projection on the frontier. To see how this is done, we now turn to another numerical example.

5. SECOND ILLUSTRATION: RANKING NASA AERONAUTICS INVESTMENTS

NASA research in aeronautics in the early 1990s could be broadly categorized as follows:

- Research in *subsonic aircraft*, with aims such as reducing drag, improving lift, designing quieter and more efficient engine concepts, reducing aircraft weight through increased use of composite materials. Much of this research has a potential for commercialization, and conventional private-sector investment criteria may then be employed, together with indicators of technological and social priority.
- Research in *high-speed transportation*, providing for the world's transoceanic air routes in the next century. The commercialization potential of this research is sometimes moot, particularly when it comes to NASA research in environmental issues. Indicators of technological and social priority provide the main motivation for this research.
- Research in *high-performance military aircraft*, both fixed- and rotary-wing aircraft. This research has immediate commercial application, suggesting the use of conventional private-sector investment criteria.
- Research in *hypersonic/ trans-atmospheric vehicles* (the X-30 space plane and future hypersonic vehicles). No

commercialization potential at this time, and the motivation is provided almost exclusively by technological priorities.

- Research in *critical disciplines*, including the development of innovative concepts and theoretical, experimental and computational tools. This is fundamental research, in many instances not very different from what the National Science Foundation would fund. It has virtually no direct commercialization potential, and most common social indicators (such as the creation of jobs) are absent. Furthermore, even the technological priorities are uncertain.

Assume that the task at hand is to rank 18 NASA investment projects, identified as follows:

A1,A2,A3,A4,A5,A6,
B1,B2,B3,B4,
C1,C2,C3,
D1,
E1,E2,E3,E4.

For instance, in a ranking of NASA long-term aeronautics projects, the *A* projects could be projects in the area of materials and structures. The *B* projects refer to subsonic aircraft, the *C* projects to high-performance military aircraft. Projects *D* and *E* are projects in critical disciplines.

It is not obvious that one would want to rank all NASA aeronautics projects in one common pool. Alternatively, one may prefer to do the ranking just for hypersonic/trans-atmospheric vehicles alone, say. There is actually a major policy issue hidden here: should aeronautics projects compete with each other *across* divisions, such as projects in subsonic aircraft competing with the maintenance of NASA national facilities? Some observers would no doubt think that it is unfair to expose the maintenance of the facilities to such rigid tests. The alternative approach is to apportion the total NASA cost budget between major divisions, and only determine the ranking of individual projects inside each division.

The expected required COSTS of the projects are listed in Table 4, column (ii). These costs are calculated as the sum of cumulated past costs (sunk costs) and projected additional funding. The figures are in millions of dollars. The investment projects *A* are all of moderate size. Project categories *B* and *E* comprise new projects that have not been funded before. Project *D* is a quite small project. Projects *B4* and *C1* are very large. Other characteristics of the projects will be described in a moment.

The projects are to be ranked by three performance criteria, listed in Table 4, columns (iii)-(v):

- A conventional private-sector return criterion called INCOME, being the estimated annual net operating income generated by a project after commercialization. It is computed as expected annual sales revenues minus costs of goods sold, multiplying by a risk factor measuring the estimated probability of successful commercialization.
- A measure of the technological PRIORITY of the project, measured along a scale from 1 to 10. PRIORITY is supposed to indicate the relative importance of the project in terms of raising the technology horizon and unfolding new secondary technologies. Attempts should be made to ensure that the scale is cardinal, i.e. so that a PRIORITY of 8, say, is twice as important as a PRIORITY of 4.
- A social criterion, here chosen to be the number of JOBS created, multiplied by the estimated probability that successful commercialization can be accomplished.

Table 4. Costs and performance data for 18 NASA aeronautics projects

Project	**COST**	**INCOME**	**PRIORITY**	**JOBS**
A1	15.5	1.80	7	18.0
A2	23.0	2.70	7	45.0
A3	39.5	2.70	7	7.2
A4	80.0	9.00	7	108.0
A5	14.5	1.35	7	6.3
A6	13.5	2.25	7	40.5
B1	30.0	9.60	8	240.0
B2	220.0	16.00	10	160.0
B3	180.0	6.80	10	64.0
B4	980.0	25.20	9	560.0
C1	1050.0	20.70	6	1170.0
C2	15.0	4.50	6	18.0
C3	40.0	19.80	6	544.5
D1	5.5	0.75	10	1.0
E1	110.0	0	8	0
E2	350.0	0	8	0
E3	350.0	0	8	0
E4	110.0	0	8	0

The project categories can now be further characterized as follows. The projects in the categories *A, B,* and *C* have all a fair chance of successful commercialization (80% or more). But project *D1* has only a 50-50 chance of commercialization, and projects *E* have no commercialization potential at all - - they involve pure fundamental research. Projects *B2, B3* and *D1* have the highest technological priority; the *C* projects have the lowest technological priority.

5.1 DEA results

For the purpose of DEA, we now define the input of each of the projects as $X_j = COST_j$, $j=1,2,...,18$ and the outputs of each project as $Y_j = (INCOME_j, PRIORITY_j, JOBS_j)$, $j=1,2,...,18$. Reading the data into the DEA software and executing, the results displayed in Table 5 are obtained.

The entries in column (ii) are the efficiency ratings of the projects. Five projects are located at the performance frontier: projects *B2, B4, C1, C3* and *D1*. These are the elite projects. They span the envelope.

Table 5. Results of DEA analysis of 18 NASA aeronautics projects

Project	**Efficiency rating**	**Frontier cost**
A1	0.478	7.4
A2	0.393	9
A3	0.229	9
A4	0.256	20.4
A5	0.454	6.6
A6	0.609	8.2
B1	0.718	21.5
B2	1	220
B3	0.503	90.6
B4	1	980
C1	1	1050
C2	0.819	12.3
C3	1	40
D1	1	5.5
E1	0.05	5.5
E2	0.016	5.5
E3	0.016	5.5
E4	0.05	5.5

The remaining projects are all sub-frontier. Ranking them in relation to their distance from the frontier, with those closest to the frontier first, one obtains *C2, B1, A6, B3, A1, A5, A2, A4, A3*, in this order. The *E* projects come last; they are all very poor, falling way below the frontier. Remember that the *E* projects were all pure research projects, with no commercialization potential. Yet they were all assigned a technological priority index of 8, that is, a quite high technological priority. Apparently, that did not help.

The two very large projects (*B4* and *C1*) are at the frontier. But so is *D1*, which in terms of the required cost is the smallest of them all. *B2* is a large project; *C3* is small.

Additional insight is provided by the result figures listed in Table 5, column (iii). These figures exhibit the *optimal* sufficient cost requirements of each investment project, that is, the cost that would have been sufficient, *had this project been located at the frontier.* To illustrate, comparing the data in Table 4 with column (iii) in Table 5, the actual cost of project *A1* was $ million 15.5. However, project *A1* is located behind the frontier; its efficiency rating is 0.478. This means that it should have been possible to *shrink* the cost by the factor 0.478, to $0.478 \times 15.5 = 7.4$ million dollars.

Frontier performance (often termed “best practice”) can always be represented as a weighted average of the performance of one or several frontier projects, with the sum of weights equal to unity. Returning for a moment to Figure 1, we note that a frontier project like *(u)* can be represented as a weighted sum of the two corner projects *P* and *Q*.

In order to examine these same matters in our current numerical example, turn to Table 6. Starting with project *A1*, one sees that the hypothetical frontier performance for this project is a weighted average of projects *C3* and *D1*. The weight of project *C3* is only 0.055; the weight of project *D1* is 0.945.

Geometrically, the frontier projection of project A1 is located on the (linear) facet spanned by projects C3 and D1. The projections of *A2, A3, A4, A5, A6, B1* and *C2* are also located on this facet. The projection of *B3* is located on the facet spanned by *B2* and *D1*. As it so happens, project *D1* is a "role model" for every single inefficient project.

Table 6. DEA results, continued. Each row shows the frontier performance of each project as a weighted average of the five elite projects listed in the heading.

Project	***B2***	***B4***	***C1***	***C3***	***D1***
A1				0.055	0.945
A2				0.102	0.898
A3				0102	0.898
A4				0.433	0.567
A5				0.031	0.969
A6				0.079	0.921
B1				0.465	0.535
B2	1				
B3	0.397				0.603
B4		1			
C1			1		
C2				0.197	0.903
C3				1	
D1					1
E1					1
E2					1
E3					1
E4					1

Finally, note the importance of the social indicator, *JOBS*. Three projects, *C1, B4* and *C3* (in this order) were the greatest job-creators. They were all catapulted to the frontier. (Separate calculations show that without the boosts obtained from the social scores, these projects would all have ended up being inefficient.) Social advantage was no *sine qua non*, however. Frontier performance could be established even in the almost complete absence of social indication. Project D1 achieved its extraordinary performance while scoring a social criterion of only 1.0 (see Table 4).

6. PRIORITIZATION BY DEA AS A MANAGEMENT PROCESS

DEA can, as shown in the examples above, provide a ranking of R&D projects. It is attractive when an entire vector of attributes characterizes each project (rather than a single attribute, such as the net present value). The full potential of the envelopment analysis, however, would only be realized if a corporation puts in place a management process that translates the DEA rankings into daily routines for the management of its R&D department.

There are many stakeholders in the outcome of an organizational prioritization process, such as the engineering department, the marketing department, financing etc. Successful implementation will be predicated on the confidence each of these stakeholders has in the process. Based on our experience, many of these stakeholder groups should be directly involved in laying the groundwork for the rankings, such as defining the range of attributes to be recorded for each project. The evaluation of each project must involve those individuals within the organization that are best qualified for the task at hand. In some organizations, this will likely involve many people with diverse background providing their assessments, as was the case in the Baker Hughes example. Having the assessments completed by such diverse individuals seems to help the organization/ the stakeholders agree that the process becomes valid.

Accountability of the R&D budget: Monitoring and control. In the mathematical account of DEA above, and in the numerical examples, a single ranking of all R&D projects was carried out, at some given point in time. The full potential of the envelopment analysis, however, would only be realized within the setting of an organizational framework that included an ongoing data collection and analysis at regular time intervals such as every half-year. In other words: an organizational setup employing DEA for regular monitoring and control.

Top management sometimes complains that not enough information is received from the company's R&D department, and that they lack crucial information about the progress of individual projects. In the light of such comments, it is worth pointing out that the envelopment analysis described in the present report is not just a mathematical tool. It is a blueprint for complete R&D accountability.

Such accountability requires that it be possible to follow each single investment project from inception to successful commercialization (or termination), recording its entire life history (longitudinal studies). It requires that, at any given point in time, the future time paths of the totality of all investment projects have been charted and accounted for. This includes an assessment of their cost requirements and their potentials, to the corporation, and perhaps even to society at large (cross-section studies).

In order to proceed according to plan, an R&D project needs to pass various engineering, financial and marketing milestones. As long as these milestones are passed according to schedule, the original calculations remain valid. But any one of several intervening scenarios can disturb to this standard picture. For one thing, there is the looming possibility of notorious *cost overruns*. Such cost overruns are particularly difficult to foresee when the administration of an investment project has to answer to both private and public constituencies, as is often the case with NASA projects (including some of the leading space efforts). Cost overruns may cause the efficiency rating of a project to drop precipitously.

Even worse, *technological miscalculations* may become known, delaying the projected completion of the investment project. Such miscalculations do not necessarily have to have their roots in human errors. They may simply be due to the unfolding nature of technological research. Events beyond the current technological horizon are always shrouded in uncertainty. They may portend setbacks and even ultimate failure.

On the other side of the coin, *unexpected breakthroughs* are also a possibility. In any research organization, is it crucial to maintain sufficient slack in the allocation of research resources and in capital budgeting, so that such breakthroughs can be quickly followed up, moving resources from less promising projects to breakthrough projects. Here again, the envelopment calculations and the resulting efficiency ratings will provide the needed guidance, suggesting to management how to reallocate resources from low-efficiency to high-efficiency projects.

The most common form of breakthrough is the sudden and discontinuous appearance of a sought-after solution to an R&D problem, thus rapidly moving a particular NASA investment project to potential commercialization. But even greater potential advance may be involved if the breakthrough is in the nature of *unfolding technological horizons*, opening up new vistas and new potentials that were not within sight before. This may lead to an upgrading of the technological priority *and* the efficiency rating of the project, since new future successor projects are now becoming visible.

In summary, the development of an operational monitoring and control tool for the R&D department of a corporation based on envelopment analysis would conceivably include the following steps:

- A dialogue with top management to determine a suitable array of performance indicators and cost statistics of each project. A dozen criteria or more would easily be accommodated. (The few factors identified in the numerical examples above can only serve as a first simplified approximation of what is involved.)
- The development of office routines for data collection. These routines would have to be established at the project office, monitoring the performance of each single R&D contract from inception to termination. Essentially, this step involves modifying existing computer routines for the accounting and financial control of existing and new R&D projects. This step is crucial. The envelopment calculations will deliver results that are just as good, or as poor, as the data that go into the calculations.
- Adapting a suitable software package for envelopment analysis that is already available, to include data acquisition and suitable report generators. The software package GAMS for mathematical programming has rapidly emerged as the industry standard for large integrated mathematical programming systems. (See further the Mathematical Appendix to the present volume.) This package has the additional advantage that small subsets of it are available for students and for the classroom; the central layout of the software can be learned in a couple of hours.
- The successful implementation of a system of the nature now outlined, requires yearly updates, not only to evaluate new investment proposals as they arrive but also, and most importantly, to follow the progress of ongoing projects. It will then be possible to spot both unexpected breakthroughs leading to the upgrading of the priority of a project, and cost overruns requiring renewed evaluation.

ACKNOWLEDGEMENTS

The authors would like to thank A. Ferguson of 3M Company for sharing his experience of the R&D prioritization process. Portions of the present paper draw on a 1994 consulting report on the ranking of NASA aeronautics investments, written by the senior author and acquisitioned through Nysmith Associates, Washington D.C.

REFERENCES

Banker, R.D., Charnes, A., and Cooper, W.W. (1984). "Some Models for Estimating Technical and Scale Inefficiencies in Data Envelopment Analysis," *Management Science*, Vol.30, pp. 1078-1092.

Charnes, A. , Cooper, W.W., and E. Rhodes, E. (1978). "Measuring Efficiency of Decision Making Units," *European Journal of Operational Research*, Vol.2, pp. 429-444.

Charnes, A., Cooper, W.W., and Rhodes, E. (1981). "Data Envelopment Analysis as an Approach for Evaluating Program and Managerial Efficiency - with an Illustrative Application to the Program Follow Experiment in U.S. Public School Education," *Management Science*, Vol. 27, pp. 668 - 697.

Charnes, A., Cooper, W.W., Lewin, A.Y., and Seiford, L.M. (1994). *Data Envelopment Analysis: Theory, Methodology and Applications*, Kluwer Academic Publishers, Boston .

Krogh, L.C., Prager, J.H., Sorensen, D.P., and Tomlinson, J.D. (1988). "How 3M Evaluates its R&D Programs," *Research Technology Management*, Vol.31:6, pp. 10-14.

Kuczmarski, T.D. (1988). *Managing New Products*, Prentice Hall, New Jersey.

Lesch, W.C. and Rupert, D.E. (1993). *New Product Screening: A Step-Wise Approach*, Haworth Press, New York, N.Y.

Ram, Sundaresan and Ram, Sucha (1993). *A Knowledge-Based Approach for Screening Product Innovations*, Marketing Science Institute, Cambridge, Mass.

Seiford, L. and Thrall, L.M. (1990). "Recent Developments in DEA: The Mathematical Programming Approach to Frontier Analysis," *Journal of Econometrics*, Vol.46, pp. 7-38.

Thompson, R.G., Singleton, F.D., Thrall, R.M. and Smith, B.A. (1986). "Comparative Site Evaluations for Locating a High-Energy Physics Lab in Texas," *Interfaces*, Vol.16, pp. 35-49.

Thompson, G.L. and Thore, S. (1992). *Computational Economics: Economic Modeling with Optimization Software*, Scientific Press, South San Francisco.

Thore, S., Phillips, F.Y., Ruefli, T.W., and Yue, P. (1995). "DEA and the Management of the Product Cycle: The U.S. Computer Industry," *Computers and Operations Research*, Vol. 23:4, pp. 341-356.

Thore, S. (1998). "Innovation in an Industry Network: Budding, Cross-Fertilization, and Creative Destruction," in *Operations Research: Methods, Models, and Applications*, ed. by Aaronson, J.E. and Zionts, S., Quorum Books, Westport, Conn., pp. 179-200.

Chapter 3

The Life Cycles of Sales and Profits: Dealing with the Uncertainties of the Commercialization Process

Editorial Introduction

Abstract: The text briefly revisits some basic techniques of planning under uncertainty, including the calculation of net present value (NPV), the internal rate of return of a project, and scenario analysis.

Key words: Planning under uncertainty, net present value, internal rate of return, life cycles of sales and profits, diffusion processes, logistics curve, scenario analysis

1. LOOKING BACK AT A FEW SIMPLE TOOLS OF PLANNING UNDER UNCERTAINTY...

We now bring into our analysis an explicit account of an element that has been conspicuously missing so far: the time element. The revenues from commercial R&D and the associated costs are all flows over time, and their time profiles are important determinants of the net returns of projects. Furthermore, future revenues and future costs are typically highly uncertain (perhaps the revenues even more so than the costs). To deal with the time dimension, we therefore need recourse to general procedures of planning under uncertainty.

To the present-day DEA specialist, it may be surprising to learn that DEA is not the first technique invented to evaluate and rank investment and R&D projects. (Obviously, R&D projects are special cases of capital investments.) Such rankings were commonplace in the business world already back in the late 1940s, drawing on the writings of Joel Dean whose books on capital budgeting (notably Dean, 1951a and 1951b) provided the theoretical rationale for such procedures. Through his consulting company

Joel Dean Associates, Dean exerted a powerful influence on business practices of his day.

In an influential paper, Lorie and Savage described the ranking procedure with the following words:

> "The ... solution to the problem of allocating a fixed sum of money - - without reference to cost of capital - - among competing proposals is to order the proposals according to their rate of return and to proceed down the ladder thus created until the available funds are exhausted." (Lorie and Savage, 1955, reprinted in Solomon, ed., 1959, pp. 64-65.)

The "rate of return" mentioned here is referred to in the financial literature of today as the "internal rate of return." Calculations of net present value and of the internal rate of return are the hallmarks of Joel Dean. For a brief review, see below.

Through the device of a single return rate, the entire time profile of revenues and costs is compressed into a single number. The rates of return for an entire group of projects can then be ordered into a "ladder".

The extension to the multi-dimensional case is immediate. Assume that a series of investment or R&D projects have been evaluated; the indicators include the time profiles of expected revenues and costs. Standard DEA is then available to effect the desired rankings.

The treatment of uncertainty is much more difficult. Again, one can try to convert an essentially multi-dimensional problem into a single dimension. In the case of uncertainty, the time-honored way of doing this is to look at the mathematical expectations of all uncertain variables. In a way, that is of course what we have been doing up to now.

Problems of planning under uncertainty involve joint probability distributions. Those are nasty creatures featuring the co-variance matrix spelling out the co-variability between any pair of unknowns. Probability distribution theory is bad enough. Its practical application is fraught with difficulties as the analyst attempts to estimate those co-variances statistically. Is there no other way of dealing with uncertainty? In many applied business problems, a simplistic alternative approach is that of "scenario analysis," singling out a few possible "states of the world" (= drawings from the joint probability distribution of all unknowns) and looking at them in depth.

The research paper featured in Chapter 3 considers the task of ranking five R&D projects involving some very uncertain and risky high technology. Three scenarios are distinguished: one quite optimistic reading of the future, one involving status quo, and one "painting the devil on the wall" - - a scenario where everything goes wrong. Ranking the projects across the probabilistic drawings, there are then 5 × 3 = 15 possible "events" (an event being a particular project under a particular probabilistic outcome) to be ranked. Finally converting the DEA ratings into *ordinal* rankings, the authors are able to establish an ordinal ranking of the R&D projects themselves.

2. NET PRESENT VALUE (NPV) AND THE INTERNAL RATE OF RETURN

Given the future sales S_t that are expected to derive from a current R&D project, we calculate the *net present value* of these sales as

$$NPV = P \times \sum_{t=0}^{t=H} p_t S_t / (1+r)^t \quad (1)$$

where the following notation has been used:

$t = 0,1,2,...,H$ an index of the time periods of the expected life of the product, starting at the time of commercialization $(t = 0)$ and extending to the end of the planning horizon $(t = H)$,

S_t expected sales volume at time t,

P the probability that the R&D project reaches commercialization,

p_t the probability that, once commercialized, the R&D project survives into period t

r discount rate reflecting the full cost of capital, including intra-period risk .

All values appearing in formula (1) are discounted to the moment of commercialization (period $t = 0$). But the actual estimation of these values is carried out at some earlier point in time, while the product is still being developed, say at time $t = -1, -2$ or earlier. Strictly speaking, one more operation of discounting is necessary to convert the NPV in formula (1) to a monetary equivalent dated at this earlier point in time.

The calculation of the NPV of expected profits involves the following three steps:

- Estimate the life cycle of sales, and calculate the NPV according to formula (1);
- Similarly, estimate the life cycle curve of all costs, and calculate the NPV of expected costs;
- Deduct the NPV of expected costs from the NPV of expected sales revenues.

Next, use the following additional notation:

FIXED	fixed costs
VAR_t	variable manufacturing costs at time t
$R\&D_t$	R&D costs at time t

Operating costs are $FIXED + VAR_t$ and total costs are $FIXED + VAR_t + R\&D_t$. The NPV of the expected profit stream is then

$$NPV = P \times \sum_{t=0}^{t=H} p_t (S_t - VAR_t - R\&D_t) / (1+r)^t - FIXED \qquad (2)$$

Perhaps the most remarkable feature of the two formulas (1) and (2) is the all-pervasive presence of risk. There are three risk elements or probabilities present:

- The risk $1-P$ that the R&D project will never reach commercialization.
- The inter-period risk $1 - p_t$ that the project will be withdrawn from the market at the end of period $t - 1$, so that it does not survive into period t.
- The cost of capital r reflecting both the actual capital costs of the company and intra-period risk elements. The discount factor $1 / (1 + r)^t$ converts the sales along the projected life cycle S_t into present value sales $S_t / (1 + r)^t$.

Since these are all subjective risks, they are difficult to estimate and one person's assessment may differ greatly from that of another person. Furthermore, as can easily be verified by some numerical examples, the net present value NPV is quite sensitive to these risk estimates. Even small changes in the risk probabilities can cause great changes in present values.

The *internal rate of return* of an investment project is defined in the capital budgeting literature as that rate of discounting which reduces a stream of cash flows to zero. Returning to formula (2), and this time considering the rate r as an unknown rather than a known statistic, it is determined from the equation

$$P \times \sum_{t=0}^{t=H} p_t (S_t - VAR_t - R\&D_t) / (1+r)^t - FIXED = 0 \qquad (3)$$

where the fixed costs *FIXED* include all up-front capital investments. Numerical solution of equation (3) is nowadays a routine task, using widely available computer software (such as Microsoft Excel).

3. THE LIFE CYCLE OF SALES AND PROFITS

High technology products go through characteristic life cycles, starting with product development and subsequent commercialization. If a product is successful, it will thereupon enter a phase of growth, quite rapid at first, but decelerating as the product gains market share. Finally there is a phase of falling sales and eventual obsolescence, as competitors bring on line new and more sophisticated products embodying more advanced technology.

The upswing. Consider a company that is alone in its technology niche, and that faces no threats from close substitutes in the market. The rate of growth at this stage is essentially determined by the ability of the company to get its new production facilities into gear, and to build a distribution network. Sales grow approximately exponentially. However, unit costs of manufacturing a new unproven product are high. Marketing costs (advertising the new product, establishing wholesalers and export contacts, etc.) may also be considerable. Furthermore, there may be a need for follow-up investments and R&D to consolidate the technological advantage gained. In particular, the new product may embody major technological advances (such as Apollo and Sun developing the workstation concept in the early 1980s). The need for investment and R&D varies a lot from one technology to another. For instance, the technology of Dell Computer was essentially one of a new marketing channel (direct mail, with a higher level of attention to customers' needs) but with standard engineering. The result was not only lower distribution costs but also lower R&D costs.

Maturation. Eventually, as the immediate market opportunities have been seized, sales will grow less quickly. The limitations of the market are now being felt. The potential size of the market - - the size of the “niche” - - depends upon the product lines of the competitors and the technological

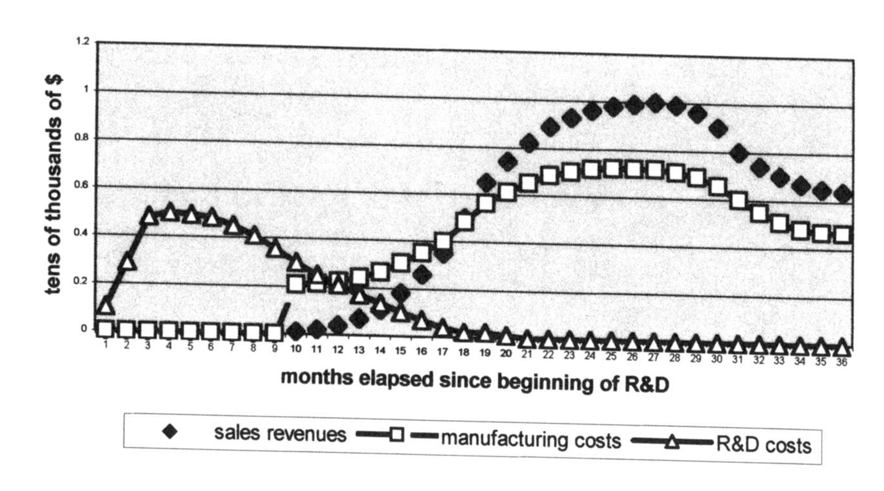

Figure 1. Sales revenues and costs during life cycle of new product

characteristics of their products. At the same time, manufacturing and marketing unit costs are coming down as a company travels down its learning curve. Most investment in real capital and R&D has been completed.

Saturation. Sales (or market share = sales relative to the total market) are stationary. Minimal costs usually exist. Presumably, the corporation has now reached the bottom of its learning curve. R&D costs can be lowered as the entire corporation adjusts from an expanding to a stationary mode. Thus although prices and margins have declined, profits are nonetheless greatest at this stage.

Decline. The downswing of the product cycle sets in when a producer is not able to keep pace with the creativity and the change of its competitors. The consumers, restlessly looking for superior purchasing alternatives, turn to more advanced product designs. As the buyers desert the product and sales dwindle, the life cycle races downhill.

3.1 The life cycle of net profit and the NPV of expected profits

What matters for the evaluation of an R&D project is not expected sales but expected profit. Profits are needed to build equity.

Perhaps the most important thing about profits is not their absolute size but rather their timing. Profits of an R&D project are needed early over the life cycle to vindicate the trust of the investors. Profits are also needed to pay back loans and advances raised during the R&D period and initial investments. The net equity position of an R&D project is typically negative during the first few years, when expenses are large and sales are still in their infancy. As a positive margin of profit slowly develops over time, the net equity position of the project will gradually improve. A milestone in the life of the project occurs when accumulating profits stretch to pay back all sunk costs, so that the net equity position of the project becomes positive. *The maturation phase of the product cycle needs to be long enough and sustained enough to generate positive net profits to cover the initial losses.* For the calculation of the life cycles of profits, see Figure 2.

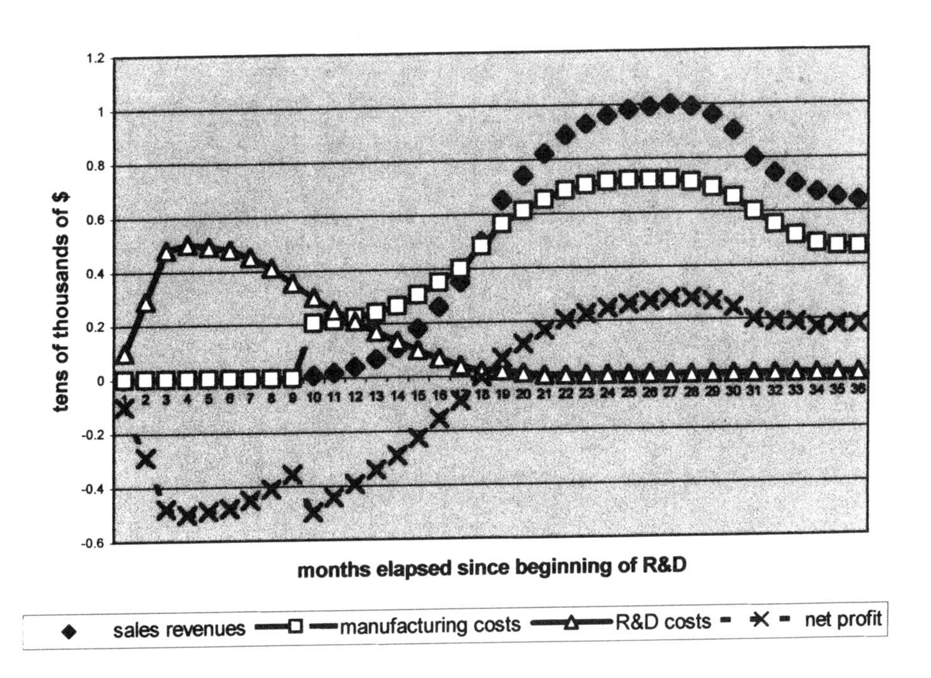

Figure 2. Calculating the life cycle of profits. See the main text.

The diagram shows the same sales revenues and costs as in Figure 1; the new feature in Figure 2 is the lower curve showing net profits as the difference between sales revenues and costs. More precisely, this calculation involves the following steps:

- Sales revenues S_t are formed as the product of sales volume and price. Both exhibit typically life cycles. While the product is still in its introductory phase, the market is small and the price needs to be set modestly. As the market strengthens, the price may be raised. Hopefully, the company is still alone in its particular niche of the market where it enjoys an evanescent position of quasi-monopoly. The price now needs to be set high enough to recoup all R&D costs, not only those attributable to this particular product but also for those others that never made it beyond the laboratory. To broaden the market even further, the price eventually needs to be lowered. Toward the end of the life span there will be intense competition, price wars, and rapidly falling prices.

- Deduct operating costs (fixed costs $FIXED$ plus variable costs VAR_t). Unit variable cost, which perhaps is 30 cents on the dollar in the startup phase, will gradually come down along the so-called learning curve.
- Finally, deduct R&D costs $R\&D_t$, which are considerable during the development stage, before startup, but gradually declining as the product gets into successful production.

The resulting curve of net profits, $S_t - FIXED - VAR_t - R\&D_t$, exhibits large losses (negative profits) during the initial phase of R&D; there will also be net losses during the beginning of the startup phase. Only later will the life curve of net profits hopefully end up in the black. Typically, profits will peak close to market saturation. During the end game the price falls faster than unit costs, so that profits decline again.

4. THE LOGISTICS DIFFUSION PROCESS

A simple mathematical representation of the diffusion of a new product is given by the so-called logistics curve. It has a characteristic S-shape, initially growing exponentially but eventually slowing down and approaching asymptotically a long-run saturation level. Use the following notation:

- A saturation level of sales (total market potential)
- $F_t = S_t/A$ the fraction of the total market potential reached at time t

The logistics diffusion process is then described by

$$F_t / (1 - F_t) = Ce^{\alpha t} \tag{4}$$

where C and α are given parameters. In words, the ratio between actual sales and potential sales increases exponentially over time. Drawn on semi-logarithmic paper, it will follow a straight line through the origin.

The projected course of sales over time S_t is determined by three parameters: A, C and α. Therefore, any three observations of the sales curve suffice to determine the entire course of the process. For instance, those three observations may taken to be

- Initial sales after commercialization, S_0.
- The growth rate of sales during the first period, $(S_1 - S_0) / S_0$
- The saturation level A.

Calculate first sales as a fraction of potential sales at the time of commercialization, F_0, and during the first period, F_1. Next, insert $t = 0$ and $t = 1$ into (4), to get

$$F_0 / (1 - F_0) = C \qquad (5)$$
$$F_1 / (1 - F_1) = Ce^{\alpha}$$

The two parameters C and α can now be solved recursively.

Example. Assume that opening sales after commercialization are $S_0 = 120$, that expected sales next year are $S_1 = 150$ and that the sales potential is estimated at $A = 200$. Sales as a fraction of the sales potential are then $F_0 = 0.6$ and $F_1 = 0.75$, respectively. Solving (4), one finds $C = 0.6/0.4 = 1.5$ and $e^{\alpha} = (1/1.5) \times (0.75/0.25) = 2$.

Sales are then given by the formula $S_t = 300 \times 2^t (1 + 1.5 \times 2^t)$. During the 10 first periods this comes out as

$S_0 = 120$, $S_1 = 150$, $S_2 = 171.4$, $S_3 = 184.6$, $S_4 = 192.0$, $S_5 = 195.9$, $S_6 = 197.9$, $S_7 = 199.0$, $S_8 = 199.5$, and $S_9 = 199.7$.

5. SCENARIO ANALYSIS

Historical background. Scenario analysis became known through the work by American think tanks such as the Hudson Institute. Under its leader Herman Kahn, the Hudson Institute used this tool in the 1970s and 1980s. In his book *The Coming Boom,* 1982, Kahn argued that scenario analysis can accomplish the following:

- Illuminate the interactions of psychological, social, political, and military factors, including individual personalities;
- Force the analyst to deal with details and dynamics that he might easily neglect if he restricted himself to abstract considerations;

- Dramatize and illustrate possibilities that might otherwise be overlooked;
- Illustrate certain principles or questions that would otherwise be ignored, lost or dismissed;
- Consider alternative possibilities and branching points;
- Overcome the terra-incognita quality of much of the present and future.

Scenarios are alternative futures but they do not reliably predict the future. Scenarios spell out some eventualities but they do not include all eventualities.

Scenario Analysis of Industrial R&D. The business world is the world of change. Perhaps the greatest fallacy of all in industrial planning is to assume that everything is going to go according to plan, as an orderly progression of existing trends. Scenarios may help the manager to consider the uncertainties of the future and things that may go wrong, or go very differently from what was originally though. Here is a list of possible favorable events, impacting upon a particular industrial R&D project:

- The government restricts the importation of the products of some of our competitors;
- Regulation or licensing practice will change to permit us to manufacture or market products from which we are barred today;
- Technical breakthroughs in the use of energy, the use of new materials;
- The economy at large improves next year.
- Possible adverse developments include:
- Competitors introduce new and better products that will compete with our own, and eventually capture market shares from us;
- Liability lawsuits.

These are all possible events, even if they may not individually be very likely.

Underestimating uncertainty can lead to strategies that neither defend against the threats nor take advantage of the opportunities that higher levels of uncertainty may provide. Managers who can expand their imaginations to see a wider range of possible futures will be better positioned to take advantage of the unexpected opportunities that will come along. Among the many tools a manager can use for strategic planning, scenario planning stands out for its ability to capture a whole range of possibilities in detail. By the identification of basic trends and uncertainties, a manager can envision a series of scenarios that will help to compensate for the usual errors in decision-making.

Porter on Scenario Analysis. Porter 1985, Ch.13, advocates the use of scenario analysis to design corporate strategy, and to discuss the future of industry, its energy needs and environmental pollution. Porter defines a scenario as an internally consistent view of what the future might turn out to be. By constructing multiple scenarios, a firm can explore the consequences of uncertainty for its choice of strategies.

Porter lists the following elements in the process of constructing industry scenarios:

- Identify the uncertainties that may affect industry structure;
- Determine the causal factors driving them;
- Make a range of plausible assumptions about each important causal factor;
- Combine assumptions about individual factors into internally consistent scenarios;
- Analyze the industry structure that would prevail under each scenario.

Converting the list of uncertain structural elements into scenarios begins by dividing them into independent uncertainties (causes) and dependent uncertainties (effects). Next, individual causes are grouped together into a set of suitable "scenario variables." An industry scenario involves plausible assumptions about each of the scenario variables.

An example: Scenario analysis of the market for multi-media. We briefly relate a study of the future market for multi-media, carried out in 1996 by Analysys Consultancy, a British consulting company (see www.analysys.co.uk). After extensive discussions with specialists in the various fields, the company defined four key scenarios as listed below. Note that each scenario consists of a confluence of many separate events, which possibly can go any way in the future but which have here been grouped into four most likely outcomes.

Other possible outcomes of combinations of individual events are suppressed. That is, this example illustrates the use of scenario analysis to focus on the most likely outcomes. The use of scenario analysis to prepare for unlikely events or surprise events is not demonstrated.

Scenario 1: *Slow Evolution*. Fixed multimedia services fail to take off in the mass market. The networked multimedia market is slow to evolve. Unsuccessful liberalization discourages market entry by service providers; failure of global standardization sustains high service and terminal prices. The attractiveness of service is limited by security fears.

Scenario 2: *"Business Centric."* The business sector embraces fixed networked multimedia services but mobile multimedia fail to attract the consumer. The multimedia revolution takes off in the business sector quite quickly, with significant innovation in service and application design. The consumer market for multimedia, however, fails to gain impetus from a dynamic business market and grows slowly. Limited liberalization discourages market entry by service providers, and limited success in development of global standards sustains high service and terminal prices.

Scenario 3: *Sophisticated Mass Market.* Consumers readily adopt feature-rich multimedia services: the Information Society has reached the mass market. Mobile multimedia services and applications make it accessible anytime, anywhere. Successful liberalization encourages market entry by service providers, and the development of global standards helps to reduce service and terminal prices. Service attractiveness is improved through a combination of high levels of IT literacy, artificial intelligent interfaces and agent technology.

Scenario 4: *Commoditized Mass Market Scenario.* The multimedia revolution has arrived. The multimedia market grows quickly, with the developments in mobile multimedia mirroring those in the fixed networks. Successful liberalization encourages market entry by service providers, and the successful development of global standards and configurable radio technologies helps to reduce service and terminal prices. The attractiveness of services is improved through the development of simple services and simple interfaces using a centralized intelligence network.

REFERENCES

Dean, J. (1951). *Capital Budgeting*, Columbia University Press, New York, N.Y.

Dean, J. (1951). *Managerial Economics*, Prentice Hall, Englewood Cliffs, New Jersey, 1951.

Kahn, H. (1982). *The Coming Boom*, Simon and Schuster, New York, N.Y..

Lapão, L.M. (1998). "Strategy under Uncertainty: Scenario Planning in the Telecommunication Business," presented at the 2nd International Conference on Technology Policy and Innovation, Lisboa.

Lorie, J.H. and Savage, L.J. (1955) "Three Problems in Rationing Capital," *Journal of Business*, Oct. 1955, reprinted in Solomon, ed. 1959.

Porter, M. (1985). *Competitive Advantage*, Free Press, New York, N.Y.

Solomon, E., ed (1959). *The Management of Corporate Capital*, The Free Press, Glencoe, Ill.

Wack, P. (1985). "Scenarios: Unchartered Waters Ahead," *Harvard Business Review*, Fall.

Prioritizing R&D Projects in the Face of Technological and Market Uncertainty: Combining Scenario Analysis and DEA

A Research Paper [1]

S. Thore and L. Lapão
Instituto Superior Técnico, Lisbon

Abstract: Assessing the priorities of a portfolio of R&D projects, uncertainty pertains not only to the narrow outcome of the product development efforts but also to the state of future technology and market conditions in general. A few alternative scenarios are spelled out and each project under each scenario is rated using data envelopment analysis (DEA). In an application using data from a large telecommunications manufacturer and distributor, a set of development projects were rated under alternative scenarios for the future fortune of the company. Each scenario was characterized by a set of technology, market and social "drivers" such as the technological progress in optical communications, the success of the planned EU common currency etc. Each individual event (single project under a particular scenario projected for a particular future ti period) was recorded as a vector of inputs and a vector of outputs. The ev were ranked using DEA. The final prioritization of the R&D projects w established calculating ordinal ranks and validating the obtained rank using the Kruskal-Wallis non-parametric test.

Key words: Telecommunications, life cycles of sales and profits, saturation logistics diffusion process, scenario analysis, data envelopme efficiency ratings over time, ordinal rankings, non-parametr Wallis test

[1] An earlier version of this paper was presented at the 18th Forecasting, Edinburgh, in June 1998.

1. INTRODUCTION

The task of managing the R&D activities of a corporation, and of prioritizing and selecting the most promising projects, involves considerations of both a technological and marketing nature. Recently, the use of data envelopment analysis (DEA) has been proposed to rate and prioritize R&D projects (see Thore and Rich in Chapter 2 in the present volume). To effect these rankings, the analyst needs data on the expected performance and costs of each project.

There are two reasons why such data are not easy to collect. One is the rapid volatility over time of most high tech projects, so that even a very promising project may have only a short life cycle. To rate projects, one therefore needs to consider their entire life cycles of performance and costs. Second, there is pervasive technological and marketing uncertainty surrounding the R&D and commercialization of most projects. How is it possible to perform the DEA calculations in the presence of such life cycle uncertainty?

The answer proposed in the present paper is a combination of DEA and "scenario analysis." (For some recent applications of conventional scenario analysis, see Schoemaker and van der Heijden, 1992, Wack, 1995, and Courtney *et. al*., 1997.) To put it simply, scenario analysis involves spelling out a few possible future scenarios in great detail without attaching any *a priori* probabilities to the likelihood of their occurrence. Instead, the final evaluation of these various scenarios is left to management. Our approach involves tracing the entire time path of each scenario over time. Each such time path takes the form of a product life cycle, with its typical upswing, maturation and decline. The "frontier" of best performance of the R&D projects thus has two dimensions: the frontier projects are best over all scenarios, and they are best over time. To prioritize the projects, we rate them across scenarios and across time periods.

The particular application to be reported here relates to X-Tel, a fictitious large international telecommunications company. Our aim is to rank a few real-life R&D projects currently under way in the areas of optical switching, fiber-optics, and satellite communications.

A few introductory remarks regarding the field of photonics and optical omputing may be helpful to the reader. The field of opto-electronics is rrently subject to rapid development, with a number of large international yers in the electronics industry searching for equipment with increased ormance and value added. For conventional chip manufacturers basing products on silicium, the objectives of development are faster nission and switching speeds and an increasing degree of parallelism. o-electronics, on the other hand, the goal is optical switching. To achieve the necessary high rates of operations per second, the technology requires optically activated switches and ultra-pure materials that prevent laser light from leaking or heating up the optical fibers.

Our scenarios (listed in Section 2) spell out in some detail a set of possible outcomes of key variables that impact directly or indirectly on the R&D efforts of X-Tel. This would be true both with reference to technological conditions in a more narrow sense and to the market conditions and more general macro-economic conditions, nationally and internationally. The scenarios involve assumptions about

- Technological issues: Direct (innovating technologies), enabling (banking) and indirect (increased need for risk experts).
- Economic issues: Economic trends and forces shaping the economy as a whole, microeconomics (competition between small, innovator companies) and forces at work or within the company itself (employee training, "intranet").
- Social dynamics: Quantitative, demographic issues (e.g. increased immigration and visible minorities) and softer issues of values, lifestyle, demand or political energy.
- Political issues: Regulatory issues (Will there be government intervention or a free competitive market? How will taxation work?)

To help model the evolution of each scenario over time, Section 2 further identifies a number of technological and societal drivers that define the future course of the various investment projects investigated. Each scenario is associated with a particular outcome of these drivers, thus determining the technological and market success of the projects.

For the purpose of the DEA calculations (Section 3), each project was characterized by its projected R&D cost (taken to be deterministic), and a vector of outputs such as expected sales or net income (uncertain. The rating of the projects is done across scenarios, pooling all possible input-output pairs, without attaching any probabilities to their occurrence. The results are displayed in a series of simple diagrams, one for each scenario considered, charting the DEA ratings of each project over time. Finally, we convert the (cardinal) efficiency ratings into ordinal ranks, and the projects are ordered by rank sums (summing over both years and scenarios).

In section 4 we turn to the intriguing question whether the obtained ordering is statistically significant rather than due to random variation. To investigate this matter, we follow Brockett and Golany (1992) and Golany and Thore (1997) using a nonparametric test procedure called the Kruskal – Wallis test. Section 5 offers some concluding comments.

2. X-TEL AND THE FUTURE OF THE TELECOMMUNICATIONS INDUSTRY: SCENARIOS FOR TECHNOLOGIES, PRODUCTS AND MARKETS

The fictitious company analyzed here is X-Tel, a large European telecommunications company that wishes to develop long range plans for its R&D and new strategic investments. The company has enjoyed rapid evolution for some time, and advances in technology intertwine with evolution in the communications industry itself. Five projects, to be listed in a moment, are being discussed by management at the current time (in 1998). All projects are to be developed in close connection with the marketing team.

The uncertainty facing a high tech industry like X-Tel is daunting. One element of uncertainty is the nature of future technology, as new communications media appear like optical electronics or the Internet. Another element of uncertainty is posed by takeovers and mergers fostered by the recent liberalization and deregulation in Europe, and the formation of big international telecommunications groups. In terms of revenues, Western Europe is still the largest market for voice communications, but the vagaries of dynamic demand are extremely difficult to predict.

The task at hand is to prioritize a few R&D projects in the area of optical electronics and satellite communications, namely the following $j=1,2,3,4,5$ projects (while illustrative of the range of R&D at X-Tel, the list is only an example of many possible R&D projects):

- *Optical data storage jukebox ($j=1$).* This project aims at developing a real optical data storage or warehouse for network management and customer contact. The project is developed together with other commercial partners and with academic institutions. The optical memory physical principium is holography. Supported by a polymer-like material, it will enable several wavelengths of recording and reading.
- *Optical switching device (ATM) ($j=2$).* This project concerns the combination of the company's own capabilities on ATM communication protocols with other company skills relating to optical switching at core networks. The switching market is predicted to continue growing, outpacing solutions based on network protocols such as ATM. This development forces vendors to continue emphasizing switch management and virtual network management tools.
- *Cellular communication amplifiers ($j=3$).* This project aims at developing a new amplifier upgrading the infrastructure of the

fixed wireless phone industry. Cellular service providers are continually looking for ways to improve the performance of their existing cellular networks. The new amplifier would be capable of providing a 10,000-fold improvement over existing technology. The product would exploit a physical phenomenon in the area of opto-electronics technology known as optical bi-stability. However, commercial application is still very much in its infancy.

- *Satellite broadband uplink ($j=4$).* The company envisages initiating satellite-based digital video broadcasts for telemedicine applications and distance learning. The project requires the development of a satellite uplink, and a satellite multiplexer working in an asynchronous transfer mode that connects the system with public networks.
- *Optical computing management system ($j=5$).* This is an internal project at X-Tel intended to capture the results from the other four projects, combining them into suitable management software, mostly for handling customer contacts Thus, it would realize the oft-prophesized convergence between communication and computing.

These are all projects of basic industrial research, and their commercialization potential is shrouded in uncertainty. In any case, the development and subsequent commercialization of them will all take several years. Therefore, we shall have to consider not only some different scenarios, but also the time development of each project up to the target year of 2005. Assuming that commercialization occurs sometimes before 2000, we shall then have six years over which to rate each project, that is, our time span covers $t = 2000, 2001, \ldots, 2005$.

Preparing for the scenario analysis to follow, we next sought to identify a set of suitable scenarios. Conducting extensive interviews with management and engineers at X-Tel, we probed issues like:

- Which will be the basic telecommunication needs in the year 2005?
- Which technologies will be available?
- What will be the real impact of the Internet?
- Which moves will the major players in the telecommunications industry make in the future?
- What will future European telecommunications markets look like, and what will be the consequences of the new EURO currency?

Based on the responses from these interview, we identified $k=1,2,3$ alternative scenarios for the future development of the company, ranging from rapid continued expansion to market contraction, namely

- *Intense international competition ($k=1$).* The telecommunications industry has recently experienced a flurry of acquisitions and mergers, resulting in the creation of giant consortia like Concertn, GlobalOne and Unisource. Under this scenario, this trend of intense competition and of a turbulent industry environment will continue unabated for some time to come.
- *Multimedia explosion ($k=2$).* The emergence of the Internet has dramatically changed the nature and opportunities of multimedia services. This includes the transmission and processing of audio, video and live TV. Under this scenario, the convergence of telecommunications and computing will accelerate, leading to seamless solutions for interaction between the user and the cyber-world.
- *Social pressure ($k=3$).* Assume, for the sake of this scenario, that the European currency unification gets into trouble and that a number of member countries leave the currency union. Consider also the possibility of additional vast unemployment and financial instability in Europe.

While painting a broad spectrum of possible outcomes, this list of scenarios nevertheless disregards many social trends, e.g. the impact of demographic change in creating new markets and the acceptability of new technologies in the workplace and at home.

This gives us 5 projects to rate, 6 time periods and 3 scenarios. Using the shorthand notation "event" to describe the possible outcome of a given project in a given year under a given scenario, there are then altogether $5 \times 6 \times 3 = 90$ events to be evaluated. For each project, there are $6 \times 3 = 18$ events to be evaluated. Based on these evaluations, the 5 projects are to be ranked and prioritized.

2.1 The life cycles of sales, costs and profits

To illustrate the procedures, we now turn to a numerical example. The outputs $r = 1,2,\ldots,s$ of the same project j in year t will all be taken as uncertain, distinguishing one possible outcome Y_{rjtk} for each possible scenario k. Three outputs will be recorded for each project:

- annual sales ($r=1$),
- annual net income ($r=2$), and
- an index of the learning achieved inside the company from the R&D effort ($r=3$).

The accumulated development cost X_j of each project j will be taken as deterministic.

Annual sales are supposed to follow the well-known logistics curve. It has a characteristic S-shape, initially growing exponentially but eventually slowing down and approaching asymptotically a long-run saturation level. Use the following notation:

- S_t expected sales volume at time t
- A saturation level of sales (total market potential)
- $F_t = S_t/A$ the fraction of the total market potential reached at time t

The logistics diffusion process is then described by

$$F_t / (1 - F_t) = Ce^{\alpha t} \tag{1}$$

where C and α are given parameters. In words, the ratio between actual sales and potential sales increases exponentially over time.

The projected course of sales over time S_t is determined by three parameters: A, C and α. Therefore, any three observations of the sales curve suffice to determine the entire course of the process. For instance, those three observations may taken to be

- Initial sales after commercialization, S_0 .
- The growth rate of sales during the first period, $100(S_1 - S_0) / S_0$ percent.
- The saturation level A.

Given these observations, the two parameters C and α are determined as follows. Calculate first sales as a fraction of potential sales at the time of commercialization, F_0 , and during the first period, F_1 . Next, insert $t = 0$ and $t = 1$ into (4), to get

$$F_0 / (1 - F_0) = C \tag{2}$$

$$F_1 / (1 - F_1) = Ce^{\alpha}$$

The two parameters C and α can now be solved recursively.

We now present projections of expected sales of each project once it has been commercialized, its expected immediate growth rate, and the eventual sales potential. Using an adaptation of the Delphi method (see Linstone and

Turoff, 1975 and Whellwright and Makridakis, 1980), we arrived at the figures listed in Tables 1-3.

Table 1. Initial sales expected in 2000 in millions of EUROS (denoted S_0 in the text)

	Scenario $k=1$	Scenario $k=2$	Scenario $k=3$
Project $j=1$	3	4	2
Project $j=2$	4	0.5	1
Project $j=3$	2	3.5	1.25
Project $j=4$	12	9	7
Project $j=5$	6	4	2.25

Table 2. Percentage growth of sales in first year, from 2000 to 2001 (with same notation, it would read $100\, S_1 / S_0 - 100$

	Scenario $k=1$	Scenario $k=2$	Scenario $k=3$
Project $j=1$	10	8	6
Project $j=2$	12	7	8
Project $j=3$	20	9	5
Project $j=4$	8	4	1
Project $j=5$	3	4	1

Table 3. Saturation sales levels (notation is A)

	Scenario $k=1$	Scenario $k=2$	Scenario $k=3$
Project $j=1$	10	8	3
Project $j=2$	12	7	4
Project $j=3$	8	12	6
Project $j=4$	40	25	16.5
Project $j=5$	12	8.5	5.25

As explained, the data listed in Tables 1-3 are sufficient to determine the parameters A, C and α for each project under each scenario. Next, we calculate the time path of sales S_t over the entire time span, for each project under each scenario.

Finally, we form projections of manufacturing costs over the planning span, assuming that initial costs (in 1998) in all instances would be 60 cents on the EURO and that through learning and earlier experience the company would be able to reduce manufacturing costs gradually. More precisely, we assumed that unit costs K would fall to 95 % of their previous level every time accumulated sales $ACCS$ double. That is, manufacturing costs are given by the formula

$$K_t = 0.60\ (ACCS_t/0.01)^{(\log 0.95/\log 2)} \qquad (3)$$

where the symbol $ACCS_t$ is used to denote accumulated sales

$$ACCS_t = \sum_{\tau=0}^{\tau=t} S_\tau \qquad (4)$$

Thus prepared, we formed annual profit by deducting R&D costs and manufacturing costs from annual sales. Total R&D costs are displayed in Table 4. In years 1998 and 1999, before commercialization occurs, there are no sales revenues and no manufacturing costs, only R&D costs (for simplicity, we booked half of total R&D costs for each of these two years). In the year 2000 and later, there are sales revenues and manufacturing costs but no R&D costs.

Table 4. Projected R&D costs, in millions of EUROs

	R&D costs, in millions of Euros
Project $j=1$	14.5
Project $j=2$	12.5
Project $j=3$	20
Project $j=4$	15
Project $j=5$	12

The costs are the same under all scenarios.

The third output of each project is an index of the expected learning and experience achieved. Please refer to Table 5.

Table 5. Projected learning achieved from each project, rated on a scale from 1 to 10

	Index of learning obtained
Project $j=1$	3
Project $j=2$	3
Project $j=3$	3
Project $j=4$	3
Project $j=5$	7

To repeat, we now have available data on three outputs (sales, profits and an index of learning) and one input (total R&D costs) for altogether 90 events (5 projects during 6 time periods, under 3 different scenarios).

3. DEA IN AN INTERTEMPORAL SETTING COMBINED WITH SCENARIO ANALYSIS

Use the following notation

$j = 1,2,\ldots, n$	the various projects of R&D and commercialization ,
$i = 1,2,\ldots,m$	the inputs of projects,
$r = 1,2,\ldots,s$	the outputs of projects,
$t = 1,2,\ldots,u$	the time periods,
$k = 1,2, \ldots, l$	the scenarios.

The given data are Y_{rjtk} and X_{ijtk}, the rth output and the ith input of project j at time t under scenario k.

We outline the basic output-oriented BCC model with intertemporal scenario analysis of all inputs and all outputs. (For the mathematical notation and formulation, cf. the standard account in Charnes, Cooper, Lewin and Seiford, 1994, p.31, see also the Mathematical Appendix to this volume.)

Each possible output-input pair, in each time period and under each scenario, is considered as a separate DMU ("decision making unit"). The task at hand is to rank all such input-output pairs, that is, to rank the projects across both time periods and scenarios.

The BBC model then reads, ranking all projects under scenario k $(k = 1,2,\ldots, l)$

$$\text{Max } \theta + \varepsilon \{\Sigma_i \, s_i^- + \Sigma_r \, s_r^+\} \tag{5}$$

subject to

$$\theta \; Y_{r0} - \Sigma_j \Sigma_t \Sigma_k \, \lambda_{jtk} Y_{rjtk} + s_r^+ = 0, \quad r = 1,2,\ldots,s$$

$$\Sigma_j \Sigma_t \Sigma_k \, \lambda_{jtk} X_{ijk} + s_i^- = X_{i0}, \quad i = 1,2,\ldots,m$$

$$\Sigma_j \Sigma_t \Sigma_k \lambda_{jtk} = 1$$

$$\lambda_{jtk} \geq 0 \text{ for all } j,t, \text{ and } k$$

where (Y_{r0}, X_{i0}) are the outputs and inputs of the project and scenario currently rated.

Program (4) rates a particular project at a particular time under a particular scenario (this combination denoted as index "0"). The unknowns λ_{jtk} are the weights to be attached to each project at each time under each scenario, the output and input slacks, s_i^-, s_r^+ respectively, and the desired efficiency rating θ indicating the possible degree of expansion in all outputs of the project rated. The parameter ε is a small (infinitesimal) number.

The results of the rankings can be displayed as a series of matrices, one for each scenario, like this

$$[\theta_{jt1}],\ [\theta_{jt2}],\ \dots,\ [\theta_{jtk}] \qquad (6)$$

See the Table below.

Table 6. Efficiency scores (the coefficients θ) under three scenarios

Scenario *k=1*

	Project *j=1*	**Project *j=2***	**Project *j=3***	**Project *j=4***	**Project *j=5***
2001	2.323	2.125	2.333	1.261	1
2002	2.26	1.92	2.333	1.202	1
2003	2.197	1.727	2.333	1.147	1
2004	2.135	1.564	2.256	1.095	1
2005	2.075	1.428	2.155	1.046	1
2006	2.011	1.297	2.05	1	1

Scenario *k=2*

	Project *j=1*	**Project *j=2***	**Project *j=3***	**Project *j=4***	**Project *j=5***
2001	2.125	2.333	2.22	1.488	1
2002	2.068	2.333	2.159	1.456	1
2003	2.015	2.333	2.099	1.426	1
2004	1.966	2.333	2.04	1.396	1
2005	1.921	2.333	1.982	1.367	1
2006	1.877	2.333	1.921	1.339	1

Scenario *k=3*

	Project *j=1*	**Project *j=2***	**Project *j=3***	**Project *j=4***	**Project *j=5***
2001	2.333	2.333	2.333	1.69	1
2002	2.333	2.333	2.333	1.682	1
2003	2.333	2.333	2.333	1.674	1
2004	2.333	2.333	2.333	1.667	1
2005	2.333	2.333	2.333	1.659	1
2006	2.333	2.333	2.333	1.651	1

We can also illustrate these results diagrammatically, see Figures 1-3. For each scenario, the efficiency ratings have been plotted over time.

Inspecting the results, we notice that project $j = 5$ is rated the best under all three scenarios. It is a solid winner: this project comes out as efficient in

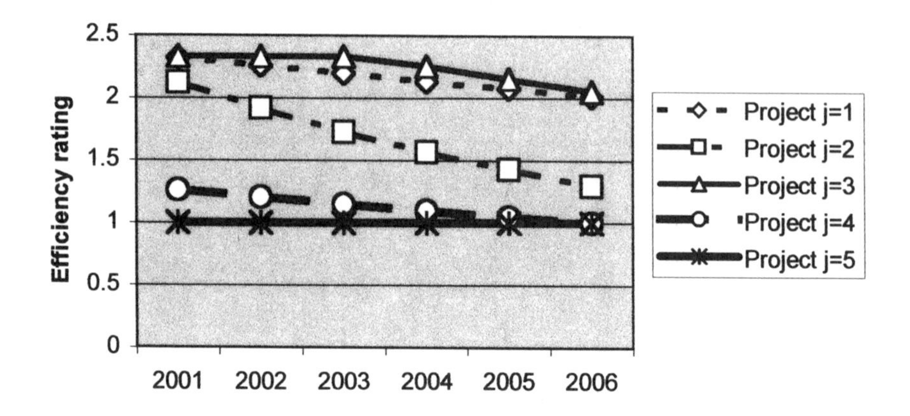

Figure 1. Scenario $k=1$: efficiency ratings over time

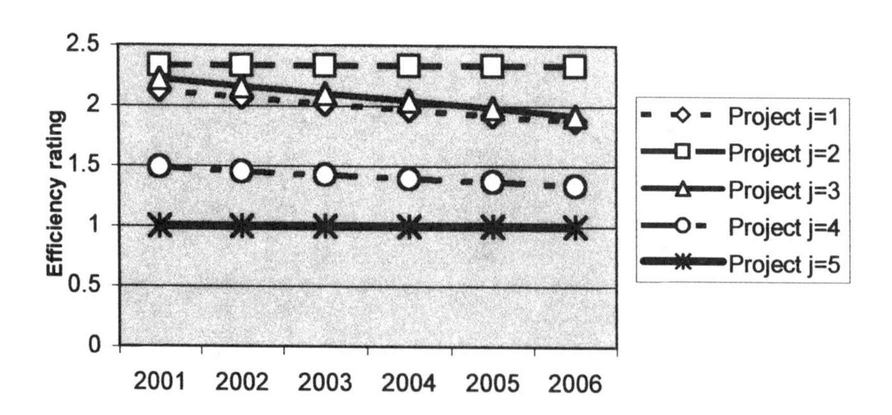

Figure 2. Scenario $k=2$: efficiency ratings over time

all time periods and under all three scenarios. There is just one more efficient single observation: project $j = 4$ in the year 2006. Project $j=4$ is the runner-up. Under all three scenarios, and in all six time-periods, it attains the second position. But which project should be ranked next, in the number three position? Under scenario $k = 1$ the answer is univocally project $j = 2$. But under scenario $k = 2$ the answer is project $j = 1$. Under scenario $k = 3$, the three projects $j = 1,2,3$ are doing equally well and would all be rated in the third position (in Figure 3, these three projects are all represented by one common line marked with squares).

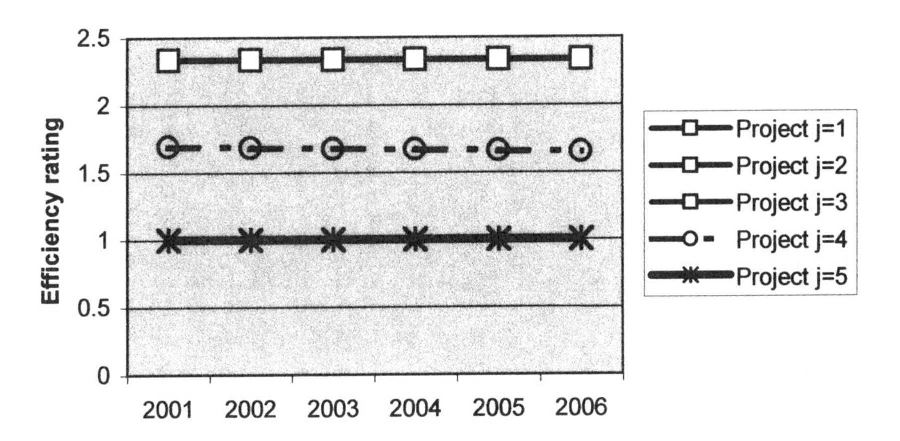

Figure 3. Scenario $k=3$: efficiency ratings over time

3.1 Ordinal rankings of the DEA scores

To make the above observations more systematic, let us now follow Golany and Thore, 1997, ranking all events (a given project ranked in a given time period under a given scenario) *ordinally*, giving the rank 1 to the lowest efficiency rating measured, and successively higher ranks for larger ratings. Thus, we replace the actual efficiency ratings in each cell in Table 4 with the corresponding rank statistic. Ties are resolved by replacing the ranks by their midpoints.

To see how this works, note that there are 19 winners with the efficiency score 1.0; their mid-rank is 1. The next events in the ranking list are

(Scenario 1, Project 4, Year 2005),
(Scenario 1, Project 4, Year 2004),
(Scenario 1, Project 4, Year 2003),
(Scenario 1, Project 4, Year 2002),
(Scenario 1, Project 4, Year 2001),

in this order. They are assigned the ranks 20,21,22,23,24, respectively. Next again is the event (Scenario 1, Project 2, Year 2006). It is assigned the rank 25. And so on. See Table 7 below. In the table, we have also entered the project rank sums under each scenario.

Table 7. Ranks of efficiency scores, organized as the three matrices $[C_{jt1}]$, $[C_{jt2}]$, $[C_{jt3}]$, respectively.

Scenario $k=1$					
	Project $j=1$	**Project $j=2$**	**Project $j=3$**	**Project $j=4$**	**Project $j=5$**
2001	63	54.5	77	24	10
2002	62	42	77	23	10
2003	58	40	77	22	10
2004	56	33	61	21	10
2005	52	30	57	20	10
2006	47	25	50	10	10
Rank sum	338	224.5	399	120	60
Scenario $k=2$					
	Project $j=1$	**Project $j=2$**	**Project $j=3$**	**Project $j=4$**	**Project $j=5$**
2001	54.5	77	60	32	10
2002	51	77	59	31	10
2003	48	77	53	29	10
2004	45	77	49	28	10
2005	43.5	77	46	27	10
2006	41	77	43.5	26	10
Rank sum	283	462	310.5	173	60
Scenario $k=3$					
	Project $j=1$	**Project $j=2$**	**Project $j=3$**	**Project $j=4$**	**Project $j=5$**
2001	77	77	77	39	10
2002	77	77	77	38	10
2003	77	77	77	37	10
2004	77	77	77	36	10
2005	77	77	77	35	10
2006	77	77	77	34	10
Rank sum	462	462	462	219	60

More generally, let the matrices of ordinal ranks corresponding to (6) be

$$[C_{jt1}],\ [C_{jt2}],\ \ldots,\ [C_{jtk}] \tag{7}$$

Finally, form the ordinal rank sums for each project

$$\textit{project 1} \quad \Sigma_t \Sigma_k C_{1jtk} \tag{8}$$

project 2 $\Sigma_t \Sigma_k C_{2jtk}$

...

project n $\Sigma_t \Sigma_k C_{ntk}$

In our present application, one obtains the grand total rank sums for the five projects currently examined displayed in the second column in Table 8. *Note that the sum total 4095 entered on the last line of Table 8 simply equals 1+2+3+4+...+90.*

Table 8. Rank sums of projects

Project	**Rank sum R_j**	**Rank sum squared R_j^2**
Project $j = 1$	1083	1,172,889
Project $j = 2$	1148.5	1,319,052
Project $j = 3$	1171.5	1,372,412
Project $j = 4$	512	262,144
Project $j = 5$	180	32,400
Total	4095	4,158,897

Ranking the projects by their rank sums R_j, we conclude that the project should be ranked in the following order: 5,4,1,2,3. But is this ranking statistically significant? We turn to this and related questions in the next section.

4. TESTING FOR STABILITY OF THE ORDINAL RANKINGS, USING THE KRUSKAL – WALLIS TEST

The question at hand is whether the obtained ranking of the projects remains stable over scenarios, and over time. We want to investigate whether it can be said, with statistical confidence, that the five projects maintain their relative position relative to each other over scenarios, and over time.

Following Golany and Thore, 1997, and Brockett, Golany and Li, 1998 we shall use a non-parametric test, the Kruskal-Wallis test to probe this matter. Brockett, Golany and Li point at two reasons why a non-parametric test is attractive. First, a non-parametric test is more consistent with the nature of DEA, being itself a non-parametric approach to the determination of the production function. Second, the statistical distribution of the DEA scores is generally not known, but the non-parametric test statistics have known statistical distributions.

The Kruskal-Wallis ANOVA test can be used to test the stability of the obtained rankings of the five projects $i=1,2,3,4,5$ over scenarios and over time. The null hypothesis is that the five projects have the same distribution throughout the $6 \times 3 = 18$ samples drawn.

Denoting the number of projects by N and the number of samples drawn by K, the test statistic H is calculated as

$$H = (12/(NK \times (NK+1))) \quad \Sigma_j (R_j^{\,2} / K) \; - \; 3(NK+1) \qquad (9)$$

where R_j is the rank sum for each individual sample. (The rank sums R_j and also their squares $R_j^{\,2}$ were listed in Table 8 above.) In the present case, one obtains

$$H = (12/(90 \times 91)) \quad (4158897/18) \; - \; 273 = 65.53 \qquad (10)$$

The test statistic is distributed according to a Chi-squared distribution with $N\text{-}1 = 4$ degrees of freedom. In this case, the calculated value 65.53 is greater than 13.277 which is the value found in a table of the Chi-squared distribution for the 0.01 confidence level. In other words, there is only a 0.01 chance that a calculated Chi-squared value would be greater than 13.277. The null hypothesis of identical efficiency rankings for all five projects must therefore be rejected.

It follows that the five projects maintained their relative efficiency positions over both scenarios and over time.

5. CONCLUSIONS: EVALUATION AND FUTURE PROSPECTS

In the pages above, we have demonstrated a procedure for rating industrial R&D projects in the face of fundamental uncertainties concerning the possible success or failure of the pursued projects, about future technology and about the future marketplace. In order to accomplish what was desired, we have combined the well-known procedures of scenario analysis with the technicalities of data envelopment analysis (DEA).

One may ask whether it is at all possible to describe deep-going structural uncertainties as a finite set of scenarios. In the example provided here, we compressed the uncertainties of R&D work in the field of optical computing and telecommunications into three alternative scenarios, ranging from a boom alternative to a static alternative. In a more detailed application, one may want to include a much longer list of possible events influencing technologies and markets, including extreme possibilities.

In any case, the standard criticism of scenario analysis applies: by focusing on a few spelled-out alternatives, it neglects

- fuzzy structural change that will only be understood clearly in retrospect,
- chaotic and unstructured change,
- the intervention into technologies and markets by agents motivated by non-rational behavior, and
- unexpected political change.

Considering these objections, one may ask whether the procedures described here are *robust* in the sense that the computed project rankings remain unchanged as the detail of the scenarios is expanded, and new possible technology or market outcomes are allowed for. It would be gratifying if such robustness could be demonstrated. Unfortunately, it is easy to imagine situations where the results would be thrown in doubt by refined analysis, if these refinements contain provisions for highly favorable or highly unfavorable outcomes that had earlier been entirely neglected.

The only answer that we can see to this dilemma is to devote much hard work to the task of defining and listing the scenarios to be considered. The list should be realistic, relevant and provide a reasonable balance between the main probabilities and statistical outliers. Perhaps one could also experiment with alternative solution methods, such as genetic algorithms.

Leaving the scenario analysis behind us, and turning now to the DEA calculations, an entirely different kind of set of problems may plague the calculations. In our account above, it turned out that the calculated rankings remained statistically stable over both scenarios and time periods. We do not know to what extent such experience will be common. More dubious situations are also possible. In fact, it is easy to imagine extreme situations where the obtained rankings are violently sensitive to the outcomes of scenarios.

For instance, a particular satellite network project could be crucially dependent upon the prior development of an up-link technology. If there is no up-link, there is no network to install. In other words, the various scenarios must *a priori* and by the nature of things be expected to generate different rankings.

There may exist ways out of this dilemma, but they will require more research. It may be possible to establish *clusters* of projects that are rated higher than others, even if there are contradictions inside individual clusters.

Or it may be possible to establish stable rankings for a *partial* list of projects, avoiding ranking some of the more controversial ones.

REFERENCES

Brockett, P.L. and Golany, B. (1996). "Using Rank Statistics for Determining Programmatic Efficiency Differences in Data Envelopment Analysis," *Management Science,* Vol. 42:3, pp. 466-472.

Brockett, P.L., Golany, B. and Li, S. (1999). "Analysis of Intertemporal Efficiency Trends Using Rank Statistics with an Application Evaluating the Macro Economic Performance of OECD Nations," mimeo April 1998.

Charnes, A., Cooper, W.W., Lewin, A.Y. and Seiford, L.M.,editors (1994). *Data Envelopment Analysis: Theory, Methodology and Applications*, Kluwer Academic Publishers, Boston .

Courtney, J., Kirkland, J. and Viguerie, P. (1997). *Harvard Business Review*, Nov.- Dec.

Golany, B. and Thore, S. (1997). "The Competitiveness of Nations," in *Impact: How IC^2 Institute Research Affects Public Policy and Business Practices*, ed. by Cooper, W.W., Thore, S., Gibson, D. and Phillips, F., Quorum Books, Westport, Conn., pp. 189-207.

Linstone, H. and Turoff, M. (1975). *The Delphi Method: Techniques and Applications*, Addison-Wesley.

Schoemaker, P. and van der Heijden, K. (1992). "Integrating Scenarios into Strategic Planning at Royal Dutch/Shell", *Planning Review*, Vol. 20:3.

Thore, S. and Rich, G. "Prioritizing a Portfolio of R&D Activities, Employing Data Envelopment Analysis," research paper printed in Chapter 2 in the present volume.

Wack, P. (1995). "Scenarios, Uncharted Waters Ahead," *Harvard Business Review*, Sept. – Oct.

Wellwright, S. and Makridakis, S. (1980). *Forecasting Methods for Management*, John Wiley & Sons, New York, N.Y.

Chapter 4

Investment Policies by Venture Capital Firms and Government Development Foundations

Editorial Introduction

Abstract: Sometimes, a private corporation will seek funding for a new R&D venture from a venture capitalist, or from a government development foundation. The operations of venture capitalist firms are described.

Key words: Venture capitalist, government development foundation, government development bank, startup companies, project evaluation, seed capital, venture deals, exit strategy

1. A NEW BREED OF INSTITUTIONS, BOTH PRIVATE AND GOVERNMENT-OWNED, THAT ARE ENGAGED IN FUNDING R&D

A *venture capital firm* is a private corporation that invests in startup companies. The venture capital industry specializes in high-risk equity investments. Many venture capitalists focus their attention on emerging high-technology corporations whose expansion is restricted by lack of equity capital. With few assets and without a proven cash flow, such corporations are often unable to raise capital from conventional sources.

In a fashion, the modern venture capital industry acts the way the classical merchant bankers, the Rotschilds, the Morgans and the Mellons, used to do. It invests equity money in fledgling companies that it takes under its wings. The venture capitalist and the merchant banker can do this through the trick of a balanced portfolio where different risk elements hopefully offset each other so that the total risk content of the venture portfolio still remains within bounds.

The venture capitalist wants to shepherd its clients to eventual disengagement and to free up its funds. The exit strategies include a larger corporation buying the startup outright, or an initial public offering (IPO) on the stock market.

The venture capital industry grew rapidly in the US in the 1980s and 1990s; it helped fund a large number of the new technologies of the high technology age, and it is a powerful driver of the ongoing business boom.

A *government development foundation* is operated by local or national government, or even by inter-government or international entities that provides funding to help promote the development of new technology. The funding may take the form of a minority equity stake slated for cancellation or write-off, or as an outright grant.

The government development foundation or *development bank* is a common tool of technology policy in many countries. Some banks were created to stimulate local or regional industrial development, often in geographical areas that are lagging behind the nation at large. Other banks were created to promote the development of new technology in particular fields of application, such as engineering, chemistry, information technology, or biotechnology.

The theme of the present chapter is that new technology is not only developed inside private companies, but also in conjunction with various institutions, private or government-owned that have been formed explicitly to fund these exploits. *The decision to fund an R&D project is not necessarily done by the party that later will commercialize it.* Rather, the funding may be provided by an R&D precursor, a planner and assessor who funds the project but lets somebody else commercialize it. Thus the chain

Funding → R&D → Commercialization

is now split up into its two constituent parts. Specialized funds-providing institutions such as venture capital firms or government development foundations cover the first of these three steps. Private corporations (usually startups, but also existing companies) would then only do the two latter steps, being relieved of the funding decision.

The separation of functions now described introduces two considerations:

- The assessment and ranking that we will be dealing with here, is an *initial* one, before the research has started, or it is one of *renewed funding,* after the initial funding has been used up. It does not include, however, the current monitoring of the research. The latter task rests with the entity that actually conducts the R&D. The renewed funding may take the form of second-round financing of the venture capital company, or of renewed research funds being provided by a government development foundation, development bank, or similar agency.

- The distinction between a project and a startup company conducting the R&D becomes fluid, because often a startup company is launched to commercialize a particular R&D venture. Often we shall end up assessing and ranking *startup companies* rather than projects. This introduces many new and additional considerations, including the financial structure of the company, its management, and maybe even its potential in the stock market. All this is very much the concern of the provider of funding. To assist in these matters, a venture capital firm will often help searching for a strategic alliance partner for the startup.

Even inside a private corporation, there may occur a separation between the funding decision and the daily management of the R&D. This happens in a large hierarchically organized corporation where a division of the corporation delegates funding to an arm of the company (like a research department) charged with actually carrying out the R&D. The division makes the initial long-term commitment, and the department is responsible for the daily supervision. The division may also intervene in the R&D process, as partial results become available, suggesting for instance an outside strategic partner. Similarly, the division may decide to spin off a particular project as a wholly owned subsidiary of the company, so that, for all practical purposes, a separate startup company is formed.

2. VENTURE CAPITALIST INVESTMENT ACTIVITY: A SURVEY OF COMMON PRACTICES

When the venture capitalist arrives at his or her office in the morning, there is a stack of business plans and other proposals waiting on the desk, each written by a prospective entrepreneur looking for the funding of a new venture. How do venture capitalist officers go about assessing and rating these projects?

A useful flow-chart of the decision process has been has been supplied by Tyebjee and Bruno (1984), see Figure 1 below. The first step of the decision process is the *deal origination*. It describes how venture capitalists learn about the various investment opportunities. Some of the deals originate as unsolicited "cold calls" from entrepreneurs. The typical response of the venture capitalist is to request the inquirer to send in a business plan. The source of other deals is through a referral process, from within the venture capital community, by prior investees and personal acquaintances, by banks, or by investment brokers.

Venture capitalists also actively search for deals, often monitoring developments in particular technologies. They attend conventions, trade shows and conferences.

The second step is project *screening*. Venture capital firms receive a large number of proposals, far more than they can possibly fund with the size of their portfolios. They use broad screening criteria to reduce the potential projects to a more manageable number for in-depth evaluation.

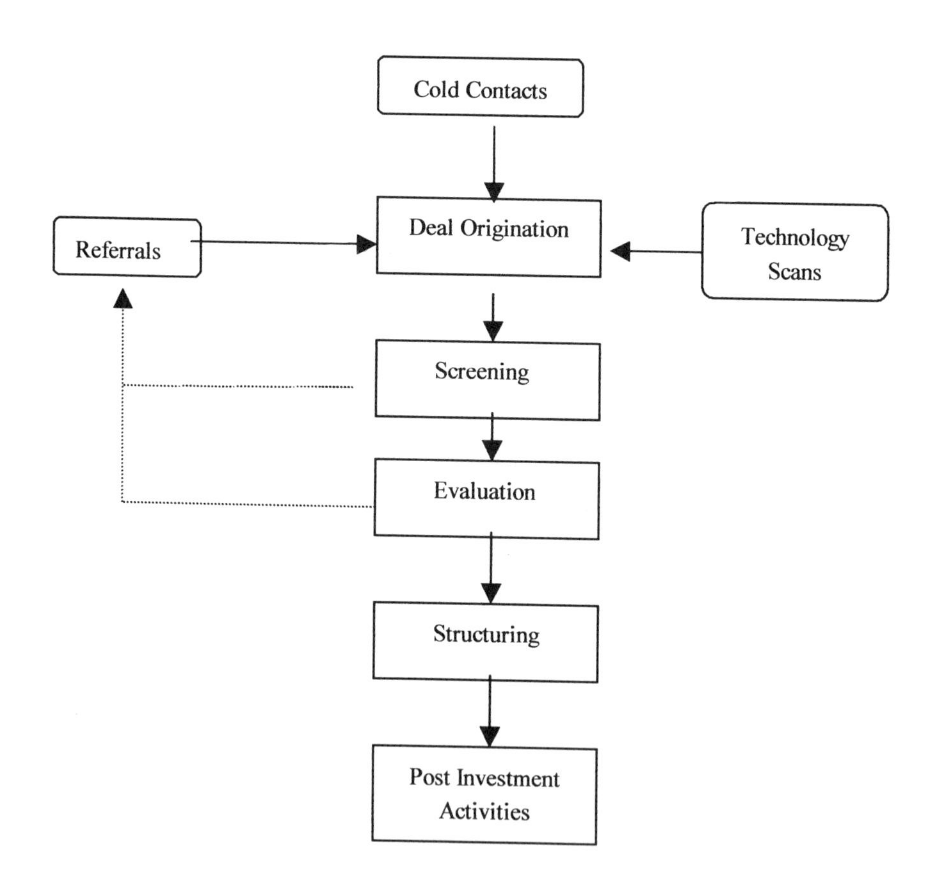

Figure 1. Decision process model of venture capitalist investment activity

They tend to limit themselves to investment areas that they are familiar with, particularly in terms of technology, product and market scope of the venture. The criteria include the following:

- The size of the investment and the investment policy of the venture fund.
- The technology and the market sector of the venture. Venture capitalist must have some familiarity with the technology or the market of the proposed venture.
- Geographic location of the venture.
- Stage of financing (the successive stages are: seed capital, startup capital, first round expansion, second round expansion).

The next step of the decision process is project *evaluation*. By the nature of things, most ventures have little, if any, operating history. Instead, the venture capitalist must rely on an assessment of the business plan, and an assessment of the ability of the founders and management team of the prospective venture. The criteria include the following:

- Market attractiveness of the new venture: the size, growth, and accessibility of the market and the existence of a market need.
- Product differentiation, determined by the ability of the entrepreneur to apply technical skills in creating a product that is unique, can deter competition through patents, and will enjoy a high profit margin.
- Managerial capabilities of the venture's founders, including management skills, marketing skills, and financial skills.
- Resistance to environmental threats, such as protection from competitive entry, protection from obsolescence, protection against downside risk, and resistance to economic cycles.
- Cash-out potential for the venture capitalist (the exit strategy).

The fourth step in the decision process is *deal structuring*. Once the venture capitalist has decided that the project is acceptable, the terms of the deal need to be spelled out and agreed to. The terms include:

- The price of the deal, that is, the equity shares that the entrepreneur will give up in exchange for the venture capital.
- Protective covenants, under which the venture capitalist can take control of the board, force a change in management or liquidate the investment by forcing a buy-back. Other covenants may entitle the venture capitalist firm to force a merger, acquisition or public offering although it holds a minority position only.

The final entry in the flow chart in Figure 1 is *post-investment activities*. Once the deal has been consummated, the role of the venture capitalist becomes one of collaborator and facilitator. While the day-to-day management of the company is left to the project management, the venture capitalist may exert informal influence in market, supplier and creditor networks. If a financial or managerial crisis occurs, the venture capitalist may intervene and even install a new management team. Finally, with an eye upon its eventual exit from the project, the venture capitalist will try to steer the company towards merger, acquisition, or a public offering.

REFERENCES

Tyebjee, T. and Bruno, A. (1984). "A Model of Venture Capitalist Investment Activity," *Management Science* Vol. 30:9, pp. 1051-1066.

Applying Data Envelopment Analysis to Evaluate the Efficiency of R&D Projects - A Case Study of R&D in Energy Technology

A Research Paper

B. Yuan and J.-N. Huang
Institute of Management of Technology, National Chiao Tung University, Taiwan

Abstract: This research uses Data Envelopment Analysis (DEA) to evaluate energy technology projects in Taiwan. Collecting empirical data from several such projects, we develop a model and an integrated framework for the evaluation of such projects. Both cross-sectional and longitudinal studies are conducted. Cross-sectional analysis is used to evaluate the efficiency of technology projects within the same year; longitudinal analysis is used to evaluate the overall trend of technology projects and the performances of cross-period technology projects that last for several years. Through cross-sectional analysis, we identify the efficiently run projects from the sub-efficient ones and determine how the latter ones might be improved. Through longitudinal analysis, we evaluate the overall trend of technology projects that last several years. Hopefully, our analysis will serve as a reference for project leaders and management who wish to monitor and control their technology projects.

Key words: Taiwan Ministry of Economic Affairs, energy technology, battery research, freezing/cooling technology, heating technology, solar energy, cross-sectional data, longitudinal data, DEA, technical efficiency and scale efficiency, returns to scale, frequency of reference (of corner points)

1. INTRODUCTION

Every year, Taiwan devotes considerable manpower and resources to the research and development of technology. What specific benefits or rewards do these huge expenditures on R&D bring the whole country and its industries? The institutions in charge of supervising and monitoring the status of government-sponsored R&D projects need to be constantly updated on their progress so that subsequent budget allocations can be arranged. Therefore, it has become increasingly important to evaluate the performance of the R&D projects, both proposed new projects and ongoing projects.

There are many ways to evaluate the results of an R&D project. The number of patents, copyrights, dissertations and technical reports that a project may generate provides some numerical information. However, beneficial effects on the investment environment in general, or future production output and profit margins cannot be easily evaluated quantitatively. And yet, these are all factors that need to be considered in assessing the attractiveness of a given R&D project. Thus, the task at hand is certainly no easy matter.

With a fair evaluation of its various R&D projects at its disposal, management would be fully informed of the progress of the projects and could compare its own performance relatively to that of other firms or other research organizations. To accomplish what is desired, we thus need to identify an efficiency indicator that takes into regard all relevant input and output factors. This is the major purpose of our research.

Traditional quantitative evaluation methods cannot cover all major indicators of inputs and outputs; in addition, expert reviews tend to be subjective. Fortunately, Data Envelopment Analysis (DEA) overcomes two drawbacks of previous methods. First, DEA can combine multiple inputs and outputs in the evaluation. Therefore, DEA is more appropriate for evaluating technology projects that involve multiple inputs and outputs. Second, DEA does not set weights in advance. The weights are determined by the model and are in this sense objective.

The purpose of our research is to use DEA to evaluate a portfolio of technology R&D projects and to explore the applicability and feasibility of this method in different time frames.

2. GOVERNMENT-SPONSORED ENERGY R&D IN TAIWAN

The Energy Technology Committee is a unit reporting to the Taiwan Ministry of Economic Affairs. Its main function is to define and implement the energy related policies of the country. The Committee is in charge of a non-profit organization called the Energy Foundation that provides funding of energy-related R&D projects in the following areas:

- saving energy, improving energy efficiency and utilization,
- developing technologies for new power sources,
- improving and/or preventing pollution,
- energy management.

The funds of the Energy Foundation come from donations by government enterprises such as the Taiwan Power Company, China Petroleum Company, etc. The total budget is 33 million US dollars covering a five-year time span. All funded projects are focused on early-stage R&D, which might be "technology-transferred" to corporations later for commercialization.

Non-profit organizations, research institutes, university professors/researchers or private corporations file the project proposals. The administrative processing and evaluation of proposals includes

- internal preliminary review;
- external review by a committee comprised of scholars and industry experts,
- final review.

Once a proposal has been approved, the Energy Foundation's fund would be its single source of budget. However, all approved proposals need to be evaluated annually in order to decide the budget allocations for the following year.

The Ministry of Economic Affairs currently utilizes the DEA approach outlined in the pages to follow for its internal review of projects. It is not yet used as a regular screening/ranking device. It serves as a supplemental tool to complement experts' on-site evaluation and opinions.

3. LITERATURE REVIEW

The methodology used in the present research is Data Envelopment Analysis (DEA), pioneered by Charnes, Cooper and Rhodes (henceforth CCR), 1978. They expanded Farrell's single output measurement (see Farrell and Fieldhouse, 1958) to the case of multiple outputs. Their original ratio formulation can be transformed into one of envelopment using the duality theory of linear programming. The CCR model has been widely used in empirical research.

The CCR developments are briefly reviewed below. (See also the editor's footnote at the end of the paper.) Assuming that there are $i = 1,...,m$ inputs and $r = 1,...,s$ outputs, and $j = 1,... n$ Decision Making Units (DMUs), the efficiency value of a particular DMU (denoted by the index "0") can be calculated from

$$\text{Max} \quad \theta = \sum_{r=1}^{s} \mu_r Y_{r0} \Big/ \sum_{i=1}^{m} v_i X_{i0} \tag{1}$$

subject to

$$\sum_{r=1}^{s} \mu_r Y_{rj} \Big/ \sum_{i=1}^{m} v_i X_{ij} \leq 1, \quad j = 1,2,\ldots,n$$

$$\mu_r \geq 0, \quad r = 1,2,\ldots,s$$
$$v_i \geq 0, \quad i = 1,2,\ldots,m$$

The DEA model is used to determine the maximum efficiency value (output/input ratio) θ of the DMU currently rated. A greater efficiency rating means that fewer (or the same) amounts of the inputs produce the same (or more) outputs. The efficiency rating is always less than or equal to one. The purpose of program (1) is to identify a set of weights μ_r, v_i that maximize θ. When the maximal value is $\theta^* = 1$ one says that the DMU is efficient. The μ_r are the weights of the outputs, the v_i are the weights of the inputs.

Model (1) is a fractional programming model. CCR transformed it into a linear programming model

$$\text{Max} \sum_{r=1}^{s} \mu_r Y_{r0} \qquad (2)$$

subject to

$$\sum_{r=1}^{s} \mu_r Y_{rj} - \sum_{i=1}^{m} v_i X_{ij} \leq 0, \quad j = 1,2,\ldots,n$$

$$\sum_{i=1}^{m} v_i X_{i0} = 1$$

$$\mu_r \geq 0, \quad r = 1,2,\ldots,s$$
$$v_i \geq 0, \quad i = 1,2,\ldots,m$$

Norming the total weight of the inputs and setting it equal to one, one sees that the desired efficiency rating θ^* equals the total weight of the outputs.

Boyd and Färe, 1984, pointed to a difficulty with the CCR model. When either of the optimal solutions μ_r^*, v_i^* is zero, the solution to (2) is degenerate in the sense that even if the efficiency value is one, too much input may still be used, and the DMU is actually inefficient. To deal with this situation, Charnes, Cooper, Lewin, Morey and Rousseau, 1985 introduced the Euclidian infinitesimal small number ε, represented in the numerical calculations by 10^{-5} or 10^{-6}, and added the constraints

$$0 < \varepsilon \leq \mu_r \qquad (2a)$$
$$0 < \varepsilon \leq v_i$$

thus making sure that the solution weights are all positive.

The dual to program (2) is

$$\text{Min } \theta - \varepsilon\left(\sum_{i=1}^{m} s_i^- + \sum_{r=1}^{s} s_r^+\right) \qquad (3)$$

subject to

$$\sum_{j=1}^{n} Y_{rj}\lambda_j - s_r^+ = Y_{r0}, \quad r=1,\ldots,s$$

$$\theta X_{i0} - \sum_{j=1}^{n} X_{ij}\lambda_j - s_i^- = 0, \quad i=1,\ldots,m$$

$$\text{all } \lambda_j,\ s_i^-,\ s_r^+ \geq 0$$

where the λ_j are weights to be attached to the various DMUs and the s_i^- and s_r^+ are input and output slacks, respectively. The desired efficiency value can now be obtained from the optimal value of the objective function in (3). If the objective function is $= 1$ and if all input slacks s_i^- and output slacks s_r^+ vanish then we say that the DMU is efficient. If these conditions are not fulfilled, the DMU is inefficient.

If the efficiency rating is less than one, the DEA model will recommend directions of adjustment of each output and each input. With the following adjusted values, a point on the efficiency frontier is reached (the asterisk denotes an optimal value)

$$X_{i0}\hat{} = \theta^{*} X_{i0}^{*} - s_i^{-*}$$
$$Y_{r0}\hat{} = Y_{r0}^{*} + s_r^{+*}$$

The CCR model assumes constant returns to scale. To allow for the possibility of increasing or decreasing returns to scale, Banker, Charnes and Cooper, 1984 proposed a model that measures so-called pure technical efficiency and scale efficiency. It is called the BCC model. Starting out from Shephard's definition of a production possibility set, BCC assumes that this set satisfies basic axioms of convexity, inefficiency, ray unboundedness and minimum extrapolation. From those four postulates it follows that

$$\lambda_j \geq 0 \text{ and } \sum_{j=1}^{n} \lambda_j = 1.$$

BCC used the axioms and Shephard's distance function to derive a model that measures pure technical efficiency, see also Caves, Christensen and Diewert 1982. It is

$$\text{Min } \theta - \varepsilon\left(\sum_{i=1}^{m} s_i^{-} + \sum_{r=1}^{s} s_r^{+} \right) \qquad (4)$$

subject to

$$\sum_{j=1}^{n} Y_{rj} \lambda_j - s_r^{+} = Y_{r0}, \quad r=1,\ldots,s$$

$$\theta X_{i0} - \sum_{j=1}^{n} X_{ij} \lambda_j - s_i^{-} = 0, \quad i=1,\ldots,m$$

$$\sum_{j=1}^{n} \lambda_j = 1, \text{ and all } \lambda_j,\ s_i^{-},\ s_r^{+} \geq 0$$

Denote the efficiency rating of program (3) by θ_{CCR}^{*} and the rating of program (4) by θ_{BCC}^{*}. BCC call θ_{BCC}^{*} the technical efficiency and they define $\theta_{CCR}^{*} / \theta_{BCC}^{*}$ as the scale efficiency. Obviously, the scale efficiency cannot exceed one.

When the scale efficiency of a DMU is less than one, a further step can be taken to decide whether it is located at a stage of increasing returns to scale or decreasing returns to scale. Using the CCR model, the criterion is (see also Nunamaker, 1985):

- $\lambda_j < 1$ implies increasing returns to scale (IRS),
- $\lambda_j = 1$ implies constant returns to scale (CRS),
- $\lambda_j > 1$ implies decreasing returns to scale (DRS).

Rather than inspecting the value of $\Sigma\ \lambda_j$ in the CCR model, it is also possible to include the constraints mentioned just now directly into the programming model. Adjoining $\Sigma\ \lambda_j = 1$ one gets the BCC model. Adjoining $\Sigma\ \lambda_j \le 1$ one gets

$$\text{Min } \theta - \varepsilon\left(\sum_{i=1}^{m} s_i^- + \sum_{r=1}^{s} s_r^+\right) \tag{5}$$

subject to

$$\sum_{j=1}^{n} Y_{rj}\,\lambda_j - s_r^+ = Y_{r0},\quad r=1,\ldots,s$$

$$\theta X_{i0} - \sum_{j=1}^{n} X_{ij}\,\lambda_j - s_i^- = 0,\quad i=1,\ldots,m$$

$$\sum_{j=1}^{n} \lambda_j \le 1, \text{ and all } \lambda_j,\ s_i^-,\ s_r^+ \ge 0$$

which fits a frontier of non-increasing returns to scale (NIRS) to the given observations. Denote the optimal value of (5) by θ_{NIRS}^*. Then

- if $\theta_{NIRS}^* = \theta_{CCR}^*$ there are increasing returns to scale,
- if $\theta_{NIRS}^* = \theta_{BCC}^*$ there are decreasing returns to scale.

4. EMPIRICAL RESEARCH

In order to evaluate and rank energy projects funded by the Taiwan Energy Technology Committee of the Ministry of Economic Affairs, our first task was to identify the inputs and outputs to be used in the DEA model. Two types of data are relevant:

- Quantitative measurements of R&D projects to build input and output indicators.
- Qualitative measures used to evaluate the performance of institutions that are in charge of R&D projects, and their direct and indirect benefits to society.

The Technology Advisory Office of the Ministry of Economic Affairs uses the following list of indicators.

Inputs:

- Manpower (with a doctor's, master's, or bachelor's degree),
- Total budget.

Outputs:

- Number of patent applications, number of patents and copyrights granted;
- Number of dissertations published, technical reports and training reports;
- Technology seminars attended, introductions and presentations at seminars;
- Technology innovations and transfers resulting from research, joint ventures;
- Number of contracted research projects;
- News coverage in media.

Screening, explicating and combining these indicators, we arrived at the following set of variables that were used for the DEA calculations:

Inputs:

- *X1* Researchers with a doctor's degree or a master's degree (persons per year),
- *X2* Researchers with a bachelor's degree (persons per year),
- *X3* Total budget in millions of dollars.

Outputs:

- *Y1* Number of patent applications,
- *Y2* Number of patents granted,
- *Y3* Number of copyrights,
- *Y4* Number of dissertations published,
- *Y5* Number of reports issued,
- *Y6* Number of technology innovations resulting from research,
- *Y7* Number of technology seminars organized,
- *Y8* Resulting technology transfers, revenue in hundreds of thousands of dollars.

The projects analyzed belonged to various areas of energy research, such as battery research, freezing/cooling technology, heating technology, and solar energy. A detailed list is provided in Table 10 (in the Table Appendix at the end of the paper). There were 41 projects in 1994, 30 projects in 1995 and 24 projects in 1996, and altogether 95 projects. But several of the projects in the two later years were continuations of earlier projects, so that there were only 54 different project titles all in all.

Both cross-sectional and longitudinal studies of the data will be presented. Cross-sectional analysis will apply to projects in 1996. Longitudinal analysis applies to projects covering the time span 1994 – 1996. We use 3 years of evaluation to identify an overall trend of the projects. Data for a single year would not suffice for that purpose.

Each year the number of R&D projects decreased (see Table 10), but the average budget of each project increased. Under such circumstances, project titles launched in different years are not truly comparable. Fortunately, a few projects (8 projects, see further below) cover all 3 years. With longitudinal analysis, we can evaluate the performance of these projects every year, and also their overall performance.

Our DEA calculations will include determining the efficiency rating of each project, and the slack variables using the CCR model. The BCC model is used to calculate the technical efficiency and the scale efficiency of the project. We also compute the "reference set" of each project, that is, the set of corner points making up the facet of the piece-wise linear frontier onto which the project is projected. Finally, solving model (5) with non-increasing returns to scale, we determine θ_{NIRS}^* and thus obtain information about the returns to scale (increasing, decreasing, or constant returns to scale).

4.1 Cross-sectional results (for the year 1996)

The results for 1996 are exhibited in Table 11. For each project, the table lists the following information:

- Overall efficiency θ_{CCR}^*
- Technical efficiency θ_{BCC}^*
- Scale efficiency $\theta_{CCR}^* / \theta_{BCC}^*$
- Efficiency of non-increasing returns model θ_{NIRS}^*
- Reference set lists the projects with positive λ_j's
- Referred times, for efficient projects the number of times the project serves as a reference point to itself or other projects
- Returns to scale, constant (C), increasing (I), or decreasing (D).

For BCC-efficient projects that are themselves corner points of the piece-wise linear frontier, the reference set is simply the project itself. For BCC-inefficient projects, the reference set is two or more corner points that together make up the linear facet onto which the project can be projected. For instance, the reference set to project C18 is C11, C16 and C19. This means that in order to obtain efficiency, project C18 has to be projected onto a linear facet that is spanned by the corner projects C11, C16 and C19.

The "referred times" statistic shows how often a given project serves as a reference point to other projects. When the statistic is greater than one, it shows that the project is a "role model" to others. Projects C11, C12, C19 and C20 were the most "popular" projects in 1996, each serving as reference points to 3 projects. What this amounts to is that some corner points of the BCC-efficiency frontier are more important than others in setting the norms of efficient behavior.

We shall also use the term "anchor projects" to denote those projects that most commonly serve as reference points to other projects. Projects C11, C12, C19 and C20 were anchor projects in 1996.

Tables 12-14 lists information on the CCR-inefficient projects: Table 12 lists the optimal slacks, Table 13 lists the projections on the CCR frontier (sometimes called "best practice") and Table 14 records the returns to scale. Some comments follow below:

- C5 was the largest of all technology projects in 1996. The evaluation result shows that this project should be downsized in terms of scale. At optimal scale, it can become efficient.
- C11 was a relatively small project. Our recommendation is to increase its scale in order to make it efficient.
- The inefficiency of C18 results from both technology and scale. An improvement of both at the same time would raise the efficiency ratings of this project.
- The source of inefficiency of projects C22 and C23 is from technology. By improving technology, they can also become efficient.

4.2 Longitudinal results

There are 95 projects for years 1994 – 1996. After conducting longitudinal analysis on these data by using the CCR model, the BCC model, and the non-increasing returns to scale model, we obtained the results exhibited in Table 15.

Inspecting the table, we see that 15 out of 41 projects in 1994 were rated CCR-efficient. So were 9 out of 30 projects in 1995 and 7 out of 24 projects in 1996. In this sense the 1994 projects performed better than the 1995 and 1996 projects, with the two latter years being about equal in terms of performance.

The entries in Table 15 under the heading "Referred times" can be used to distinguish those projects that most commonly serve as reference points to other DMUs. In Table 1 below, the most frequent reference projects are called "strong anchor projects" (more than 20 references) or "anchor projects" (10-19 references).

Among the strong anchor projects and anchor projects, A31, B4, B9 and C16 span across all three years. Project B17 spans two years. Actually, cross period projects tend to perform better than single-period projects. We can think of two reasons for this:

- projects with a longer duration are in a better position to accumulate both R&D resources and results;
- projects enjoying the continuous support of management also tend to achieve a better performance.

Table 1. Longitudinal results brought from Table 15 in the Appendix: Projects listed by reference frequencies (number of times a given project serves as reference to other projects)

Frequency category	**List of projects**
Strong anchor projects (referred to 20 times or more)	A3,A9,A17,B9,B17,C16
Anchor projects (referred to 10 – 19 times)	A31,A36,B4
BCC-efficient projects referred to 2-9 times	A4,A6-7,A12-14,A16,A18-19,A24,A26-27, A29, B5-6,B12-14,B16,B26,B28, C1,C9, C12, C21,C24
Single-reference BCC-efficient projects	A1,A30,A33,B7,B18,B20,B24,C3-6,C14
BCC inefficient projects	A2,A5,A8,A10-11,A15,A20-23,A25,A28, A32,A34-35,A37-41, B1-3,B8,B10-11,B15,B19,B21-23,B25,B27, B29-30, C2,C7-8,C10-11,C13,C15,C17,C20,C22-23

The entries in the last column of Table 15 indicate whether a project can obtain economies of scale by either increasing it (I) or decreasing it (D), or whether it is located at a position of constant returns to scale. There were 63 non-efficient projects altogether; of these, 45 projects were subject to increasing returns to scale and 18 projects to decreasing returns to scale. Breaking up these statistics by years, one finds that

- In 1994, 20 projects exhibited increasing returns to scale and 6 projects decreasing returns to scale;
- In 1995, 13 projects exhibited increasing returns to scale and 7 projects decreasing returns to scale;
- In 1996, 12 projects exhibited increasing returns to scale and 5 projects decreasing returns to scale.

With a decreasing numbers of technology projects, the scale of projects was growing larger. Actually, several of the projects grew too large and reached the stage of decreasing returns to scale. In 1996, close to half of the projects would have benefited from a reduction in size.

4.3 Across-periods results

A total of *eight* projects have a time frame that spans across all three years 1994-96. We now compare the yearly performance of these projects and see how it changes over the years.

Fuel battery system research was non-efficient in 1994 and 1995 but became efficient in 1996 (Table 2). The major improvement in 1996 was one of technology. Having reached efficiency, it served as reference to 6 other projects.

Table 2. Fuel battery system research

1994 (project A1)	1995 (project B1)	1996 (project C1)
Overall efficiency=0.847, Technical efficiency =1, Scale efficiency=0.847. Decreasing returns to scale. Inefficiency is due to scale and downsizing scale would improve efficiency.	Overall efficiency=0.565, Technical efficiency =0.661, Scale efficiency=0.855, Increasing returns to scale. The overall efficiency rating is pulled down by a low technology factor. Inefficiency is from both scale and technology.	Overall and technical efficiency =1. Serves as reference to 6 projects. Dissertation published.

The electrical motorcycle project was efficient in both 1994 and 1995 (Table 3). It served as reference to 9 other projects in 1994 and became an anchor project in 1995 (serving as reference to 18 projects). In 1996, however, the scale efficiency fell dramatically and it would have been advisable to reduce the size of the project.

Table 3. Electric motorcycle technology research

1994 (Project A6)	1995 (project B4)	1996 (project C3)
Overall and technical efficiency=1.	Overall and technical efficiency=1.	Overall efficiency =0.501, Technical efficiency=1,

1994 (Project A6)	1995 (project B4)	1996 (project C3)
Serves as reference to 9 projects.	Anchor project (serves as reference to 18 projects).	Scale efficiency=0.501. Decreasing returns to scale. The scale efficiency is quite low and operating the project on a smaller scale would increase efficiency.

Freezing/cooling and energy saving technology research was efficient in 1994 and 1995, being an anchor project in 1995 (Table 4).

Table 4. Freezing/cooling and energy saving technology research

1994 (project A19)	1995 (project B9)	1996 (project C7)
Overall and technical efficiency=1. Serves as reference to 5 projects.	Overall and technical efficiency=1. Anchor project (serves as reference to 23 projects).	Overall efficiency=0.712, Technical efficiency=0.716, Scale efficiency=0.994. The technical efficiency rating has fallen but the scale efficiency is still maintained.

Heat switch technology development was non-efficient in 1994 but climbed to the efficiency frontier in the two following years (Table 5).

Table 5. Heat switch technology development

1994 (project A22)	1995 (project B12)	1996 (project C9)
Overall efficiency=0.478 Technical efficiency =0.497 Scale efficiency=0.963 Increasing returns to scale Inefficiency is almost entirely from technology.	Overall and technical efficiency=1. Serves as reference to 6 projects.	Overall and technical efficiency=1. Serves as reference to 5 projects.

Electrical engineering energy saving and control technology is similar to the electrical motorcycle technology: it started out at the efficiency frontier but dropped to inefficiency in 1996 (Table 6).

Table 6. Electrical engineering energy saving and control technology research

1994 (project A24)	1995 (project B18)	1996 (project C15)
Overall and technical efficiency=1. Serves as reference to 7 projects.	Overall and technical efficiency=1.	Overall efficiency=0.873 Technical efficiency=0.980 Scale efficiency=0.891 Decreasing returns to scale, hence it is recommended to

1994 (project A24)	1995 (project B18)	1996 (project C15)
		operate the project on a smaller scale.

Factory energy supply systems management technology is similar to electrical motorcycle technology and electrical engineering energy saving technology (Table 7). It becomes non-efficiency unit in 1996 due to inappropriate expansion of scale.

Table 7. Factory energy supply systems management technology

1994 (project A25)	1995 (project B19)	1996 (project C13)
Overall efficiency=0.703, Technical efficiency=0.722, Scale efficiency=0.974. Increasing returns to scale.	Overall efficiency=0.797, Technical efficiency=0.806, Scale efficiency=0.989. Decreasing returns to scale.	Overall efficiency=0.824, Technical efficiency=0.835, Scale efficiency=0.987. Increasing returns to scale.

Infrared heating systems were located at the efficiency frontier each year (Table 8). The project served as reference to 9 projects in 1996.

Table 8. Infrared heating system

1994 (project A26)	1995 (project B14)	1996 (project C12)
Overall and technical efficiency=1.	Overall and technical efficiency =1.	Overall and technical efficiency=1 Serves as reference to 9 projects.

Electricity demand-monitoring technology performed well all three years, although a lack of dissertations in 1995 did not propel it to the status of a reference project (Table 9).

Table 9. Electricity demand-monitoring technology research

1994 (project A31)	1995 (project B20)	1996 (project C16)
Overall and technical efficiency=1. Anchor projects (serves as reference to 11 projects).	Overall and technical efficiency=1. Project produced fewer dissertations this year.	Overall and efficiency=1. Strong anchor project (serves as reference to 21 projects). Dissertation publication, revenues from technology transfer, new patent applications.

Summing up, we see that cross period projects improve year by year mainly due to improvement in technology. They are in a good position to accumulate resources and experience; hence they often make impressive annual strides forward. But if they are over-expanded, they may run into decreasing returns to scale.

5. CONCLUSIONS

In the pages above we have reported on an evaluation and ranking of energy projects funded in 1994-96 by the Energy Foundation, administered by the Taiwan Ministry of Economic Affairs. We used the CCR model of data envelopment analysis (DEA) to determine the efficiency ratings of projects together with the slack variables and virtual multipliers. The slack variables indicate how inputs can be decreased and how outputs can be increased at the efficiency frontier. Furthermore, we used the BCC model to split the overall efficiency rating into a pure technical efficiency and scale efficiency. Technology and scale are two separate reasons why a project can be inefficient. With these calculations at hand, management is given a tool to evaluate how the overall CCR- efficiency can be improved.

For each project we calculated the reference set of projects which together define the facet on the piecewise linear frontier onto which the project can be projected. We counted the number of times each efficient project served as a reference point for one or more other projects. The projects of the study are not evenly distributed on or below the efficiency frontier. Some corner points of the frontier serve as references more often than other corner points. We suggested the term "anchor projects" to identify those projects most commonly used as references.

The longitudinal analysis was based on an overall evaluation of each project across the three years 1994 – 1996, tracing its development year by year. We found that the 1994 projects overall had a better performance than those in 1995 and 1996, the two latter years scoring about equally well. Close to half of the projects in showed decreasing returns to scale in 1996. Their performance would have benefited from scaling them down.

From a longitudinal analysis of the eight projects that spanned all three years of study, we found that multi-period projects scored better than single-period projects. Some of them maintained efficiency ratings of 1 throughout; others made constant progress due to improvement in technology. We have attributed such progress to the accumulation of resources and experience during the course of projects.

EDITOR'S FOOTNOTE

The original mathematical notation of the authors has been changed to conform to that used throughout the present volume. See also the Mathematical Appendix.

REFERENCES

Banker, R.D., Charnes, A. and Cooper, W.W. (1984). "Some Models for Estimating Technical and Scale Inefficiencies in Data Envelopment Analysis", *Management Science* Vol.30:9, pp.1078-1092.

Banker, R.D. (1984). "Estimating the Most Productive Scale Size using Data Envelopment Analysis," *European Journal of Operational Research* Vol.17, pp.35-44.

Bowlin, W.F., Charnes, A., Cooper. W.W. and Sherman, H.D. (1985). "Data Envelopment Analysis and Regression Approaches to Efficiency Estimation and Evaluation," *Annals of Operations Research*, Vol. 2:1, pp. 113~138.

Charnes, A., Clark, C.T., Cooper, W.W. and Golany, B. (1985). "A Developmental Study of Data Envelopment Analysis in Measuring the Efficiency of Maintenance Units in the U.S. Air Force," *Annals of Operations Research*, Vol. 2:1, pp. 95-112.

Charnes, A., Cooper, W.W. and Rhodes, E. (1978). "Measuring the Efficiency of Decision Making Units," *European Journal of Operational Research* Vol.2:6, pp. 429-444.

Charnes A., Cooper, W.W. and Rhodes, E. (1979). "Short Communication: Measuring the Efficiency of Decision Making Units," *European Journal of Operational Research* Vol.3:4, p. 339.

Charnes, A. and Cooper, W.W. (1984). "The Non-Archimedean CCR Ratio for Efficiency Analysis: A Rejoinder to Boyd and Färe," *European Journal of Operations Research*, Vol. 15, pp. 333-334.

Charnes, A., and Cooper, W.W. (1985). "Preface to Topics in Data Envelopment Analysis," *Annals of Operations Research*, Vol. 2:1, pp. 59-94.

Charnes, A., Cooper, W.W., Lewin, A.Y., Morey, R.C. and Rousseau, J. (1985). "Sensitivity and Stability Analysis in DEA", *Annals of Operations Research*, Vol.2, pp. 139-156.

Charnes, A., Cooper, W.W., Lewin, A.Y., and Seiford, L.M. (1994). *Data Envelopment Analysis: Theory, Methodology and Applications*, Kluwer Academic Publishers, Boston, Mass.

Caves, D.W., Christensen, L.R. and Diewert, W.E. (1982). "The Economic Theory of Index Numbers and The Measurement of Input, Output, and Productivity," *Econometrica*, Vol.50:6, pp.1393-1414.

Färe, R.A. (1986). "Dynamic Non-Parametric Measures of Output Efficiency," *Operations Research Letters*, Vol 5:2, pp. 83-85.

Farrell, M.J.and Fieldhouse, M. (1957). "Estimating Efficiency," *Journal of the Royal Statistical Society*, Series A, General, 120:3, pp. 253-281.

Försund, F.R. and Hjalmarsson, L. (1979). "Generalised Farrell Measures of Efficiency: An Application to Milk Processing in Swedish Dairy Plants," *The Economic Journal*, Vol.89, pp. 294-315.

Försund, F.R., Lovell, C.A.K. and Schmidt,P. (1980). "A Survey of Frontier Productions and of their Relation to Efficiency Measurement," *Journal of Econometrics*, Vol.13, pp. 5-25.

Golany, B. and Roll, Y. (1989). "An Application Procedure for DEA," *OMEGA*, Vol.17:3, pp. 237-250.

Ganley, J.A. and Cubbin, J.S. (1992). *Public Sector Efficiency Measurement - Applications of Data Envelopment Analysis*, North-Holland, Amsterdam.
Lewin, A.Y, Morey, R.C. and Cook, T.J. (1982). "Evaluating the Administrative Efficiency of Courts," *OMEGA*, Vol.10:4, pp. 401-411.
Lewin, A.Y. and Minton, J.W. (1986). "Determining Organizational Effectiveness: Another Look, and An Agenda for Research," *Management Science*, Vol.32:5, pp. 514-538.
Norman, M. and Stoker, B. (1991). *Data Envelopment Analysis - The Assessment of Performance*, John Wiley & Sons, New York, N.Y..
Nunamaker, T. (1985). "Using Data Envelopment Analysis to Measure the Efficiency of Non-profit Organisations: A Critical Evaluation," *Managerial and Decision Economics*, Vol. 6:1, pp. 50-58.
Sami, E.M. and Risto, L. (1995). "Data Envelopment Analysis: Visualizing the Results," *European Journal of Operations Research*, Vol.85, pp. 700-710.

TABLE APPENDIX

Table 10. Technology projects 1994-96

1994	1995	1996
A1. Fuel battery system	B1. Fuel battery system	C1. Fuel battery system
A2. Battery energy storage		
A3. Lead acid battery		
A4.Battery testing system	B2. Battery testing system	
A5.Battery energy storage demo system		
A6. Electrical motorcycle	B4. Electrical motorcycle	C3. Electrical motorcycle
A7. Nickel hydrogen battery	B5. Nickel hydrogen battery	
A8. Electrical motorcycle battery		
A9. High EER window size air conditioner development		
A10. Distributed air conditioner development		
A11. High efficiency water cooler development		
A12. High efficiency whirl type compressor research	B6. High efficiency air conditioner development	C4. High efficiency air conditioner development
A13. Air conditioner function test technology	B7. Air conditioner components function improvement technology	C5. Air conditioner components function improvement technology
A14. Ventilation efficiency improvement technology	B8. Air conditioner system energy saving technology	C6. Air conditioner system energy saving technology
A15. Dehumidifying		

1994	1995	1996
ventilation energy saving		
A16. Ice storage air conditioner system		
A17. CFC substitute energy saving technology research		
A19. Freezing/cooling	B9. Freezing/cooling	C7. Freezing/cooling
A20. Ice storage air conditioning system		
A21. Steamer evaporation recompression technology		
A22. Heat switch technology	B12. Heat switch technology	C9. Heat switch technology
A23. Heat pipe energy saving products research	B13. Heat pipe energy saving products research	
A24. Electrical equipment energy saving control	B18. Electrical equipment energy saving control	C15. Electrical equipment energy saving control
A25. Factory energy supply system management	B19. Factory energy supply system management	C13. Factory energy supply system management
A26. Infra red heating	B14. Infra red heating	C12. Infra red heating
A27. Lighting system energy saving technology	B15. Lighting system energy saving technology	
A28. Electricity saving lighting manufacturing	B16. Electricity saving lighting manufacturing	
A29. Radiation filter multiple-layer film	B17. Radiation filter multiple-layer film	
A30. Heating technology		
A31. Electricity demand monitoring technology	B20. Electricity demand monitoring technology	C16. Electricity demand monitoring technology
A32. Industrial oven	B21. Industrial oven	
A33. Low pollution burning	B22. Low pollution burning	
A34. Sulphur/aquafortis deleting technology	B23. Sulphur/aquafortis deleting technology	
A35. Waste energy saving	B24. Waste energy saving t	
A36. Whirl liquidity bed inflammation oven		
A37. Solar energy humidifying air conditioning	B26. Solar energy humidifying air conditioning	
A38. Solar energy absorption air conditioning efficiency improvement		
A39. Interceptable solar battery technology	B28. Interceptable solar battery technology	

1994	1995	1996
A40. Marsh gas purification technology & small size generator utilization research		
A41. Synthetic fuel	B30. Synthetic fuel	
	B3. Battery energy storage demo system research	
	B10. Chemical separation manufacturing process	
	B11. Thin film separation procedure application	
	B27. Solar energy medium temperature steam system	
	B29. Marsh gas purification and electricity generation	
		C2. Battery energy storage
		C8. Evaporation procedure energy saving technology
		C10. Waste heat recycling
		C11. Heat/erosion resistant material for heat switch
		C14. Lighting system
		C17. High efficiency inflammation system
		C18. High efficiency metallic industrial oven
		C19. Fuel gas electric oven function improvement
		C20. Waste cracking
		C21. Solar energy
		C22. Solar photonics
		C23. Bio material
		C24. Ocean energy

Table 11. Evaluation results for 1996 (for interpretation, see Section 4.1)

Project	θ_{CCR}^*	θ_{BCC}^*	$\theta_{CCR}^* / \theta_{BCC}^*$	θ_{NIRS}^*	**Reference set**	**Referred times**	**Returns to scale**
C1	1	1	1	1	C1	1	C
C2	1	1	1	1	C2	1	C
C3	1	1	1	1	C3	1	C

Project	θ_{CCR}^*	θ_{BCC}^*	$\theta_{CCR}^* / \theta_{BCC}^*$	θ_{NIRS}^*	Reference set	Referred times	Returns to scale
C4	1	1	1	1	C4	1	C
C5	0.955	1	0.955	1	C5	1	D
C6	1	1	1	1	C6	2	C
C7	1	1	1	1	C7	1	C
C8	1	1	1	1	C8	1	C
C9	1	1	1	1	C9	1	C
C10	1	1	1	1	C10	2	C
C11	0.578	1	0.578	0.578	C11	3	I
C12	1	1	1	1	C12	3	C
C13	1	1	1	1	C13	1	C
C14	1	1	1	1	C14	2	C
C15	1	1	1	1	C15	1	C
C16	1	1	1	1	C16	2	C
C17	1	1	1	1	C17	2	C
C18	0.639	0.854	0.748	0.639	C11,C16, C19	0	I
C19	1	1	1	1	C19	3	C
C20	1	1	1	1	C20	3	C
C21	1	1	1	1	C21	1	C
C22	0.619	0.645	0.960	0.619	C10,C11, C12,C17, C19,C20	0	I
C23	0.795	0.797	0.997	0.795	C6,C12, C14,C20, C24	0	I
C24	1	1	1	1	C24	2	C

Table 12. Evaluation results for 1996: optimal slacks solved from the CCR program (3)

Project	s_1^-	s_2^-	s_3^-	s_1^+	s_2^+	s_3^+	s_4^+	s_5^+	s_6^+	s_7^+	s_8^+
C5	0	0	4.337	0	6.462	0	0	2.276	3.454	0	3.830
C11	0	0	0.823	0.294	1.683	0.819	0.186	0	0.323	0	0
C18	1.841	0	5.471	0	2.448	0.155	0.552	0.823	0	0	0
C22	0.724	0	0	0	0.072	0	0	1.017	1.010	0	1.056
C23	0	0	0	0	3.809	0.136	1.013	1.465	1.585	0	0

Table 13. Evaluation results for 1996: Projections of inputs and outputs on CCR frontier

Project	X1	X2	X3	Y1	Y2	Y3	Y4	Y5	Y6	Y7	Y8
C5	8.316	9.328	40.356	5.000	24.462	11.000	4.000	6.276	4.454	26.000	6.830
C11	0.866	0.578	3.046	0.294	1.683	0.819	0.186	1	0.323	2.000	1.000
C18	0.797	1.456	4.429	1.000	4.448	1.155	0.552	0.823	1.500	1.000	1.000
C22	2.96	2.476	12.378	2.000	4.072	1.000	3.000	1.017	1.010	3.000	1.056
C23	3.379	2.513	15.587	2.000	6.809	2.136	1.013	3.465	1.585	4.000	5.000

Table 14. Evaluation results for 1996: Returns to scale for non-efficient projects

Project	Overall efficiency	Technical efficiency	Scale efficiency	Recommendation for change of scale
C5	0.955	1	0.955	Decrease
C11	0.578	1	0.578	Increase
C18	0.639	0.854	0.748	Increase
C22	0.619	0.645	0.960	Increase
C23	0.795	0.797	0.997	Increase

Table 15. Evaluation results for 1996-98 (for interpretation, see Section 4.2)

Project	θ_{CCR}^*	θ_{BCC}^*	$\theta_{CCR}^* / \theta_{BCC}^*$	θ_{NIRS}^*	Reference set	Referred times	Returns to scale
A1	0.847	1	0.847	1	A1	1	D
A2	0.527	0.631	0.835	0.527	A3,A9,A17,A29, A31,B17	0	I
A3	0.829	1	0.829	0.829	A3	29	I
A4	1	1	1	1	A4	4	C
A5	0.389	0.456	0.854	0.389	A17,A24,A31,A36, B16,B17	0	I
A6	1	1	1	1	A6	9	C
A7	0.333	1	0.333	0.333	A7	3	I
A8	0.307	0.547	0.562	0.307	A3,A9,A17,A3,B17	0	I
A9	1	1	1	1	A9	23	C
A10	0.441	0.579	0.762	0.441	A3,A4,A9,A13,A18, B9	0	I
A11	0.648	0.729	0.890	0.648	A3,A17,A36, B4,B9,B26	0	I
A12	0.942	1	0.942	1	A12	2	D

Project	θ_{CCR}^*	θ_{BCC}^*	$\theta_{CCR}^* / \theta_{BCC}^*$	θ_{NIRS}^*	Reference set	Referred times	Returns to scale
A13	1	1	1	1	A13	8	C
A14	1	1	1	1	A14	4	C
A15	0.788	0.795	0.992	0.788	A14,A31, B4,B12, B16,C9	0	I
A16	1	1	1	1	A16	2	C
A17	1	1	1	1	A17	28	C
A18	1	1	1	1	A18	2	C
A19	1	1	1	1	A19	5	C
A20	0.623	0.841	0.741	0.623	A17,A19,A29,B17	0	I
A21	0.787	0.856	0.920	0.787	A3,A9, A13,B16	0	I
A22	0.478	0.497	0.963	0.478	A3,A6,A13,A16,A17, B4,B17	0	I
A23	0.743	0.748	0.994	0.743	A17,A19,A27,A31, A36,B4,B17	0	I
A24	1	1	1	1	A24	7	C
A25	0.703	0.722	0.974	0.703	A17,A24,A27,A31, B4,B17	0	I
A26	1	1	1	1	A26	2	C
A27	1	1	1	1	A27	5	C
A28	0.363	0.811	0.448	0.363	A3,A7,A17	0	I
A29	1	1	1	1	A29	5	C
A30	0.923	1	0.923	1	A30	1	D
A31	1	1	1	1	A31	11	C
A32	0.607	0.949	0.640	0.607	A3,A9,A29	0	I
A33	0.863	1	0.863	1	A33	1	D
A34	0.788	0.799	0.987	0.788	A3,A9,A17,B4	0	I
A35	0.795	0.795	1	0.795	A9,A17,A19,A24, A27,A31,A36, B13,B17,C16	0	D
A36	1	1	1	1	A36	18	C
A37	0.589	0.589	1	0.589	A9,A17,A27, A31,A36,B4,C12	0	I
A38	0.846	0.992	0.853	0.846	A17,A19,B17	0	I
A39	0.879	0.881	0.997	0.881	A24,A26,A31,A36, B9,B13	0	D
A40	0.441	0.463	0.953	0.441	A3,A6,A13,A17, B9,B17,B26,C16	0	I
A41	0.001	0.236	0.004	0.001	A3,A7	0	I
B1	0.565	0.661	0.855	0.565	A3,B9,C1,C16	0	I

Project	θ_{CCR}^*	θ_{BCC}^*	$\theta_{CCR}^* / \theta_{BCC}^*$	θ_{NIRS}^*	Reference set	Referred times	Returns to scale
B2	0.574	0.598	0.960	0.574	A3,B9,B17,C16	0	I
B3	0.849	0.947	0.896	0.849	A3,B9, C1,C16	0	I
B4	1	1	1	1	B4	18	C
B5	0.517	1	0.517	0.517	B5	2	I
B6	0.942	1	0.942	1	B6	4	D
B7	0.779	1	0.779	1	B7	1	D
B8	0.585	0.591	0.990	0.585	A3,A17,B9,B12	0	I
B9	1	1	1	1	B9	23	C
B10	0.565	0.572	0.989	0.565	A3,A9,A17,B12,B17	0	I
B11	0.596	0.619	0.963	0.596	A3,A9,A17,B17	0	I
B12	1	1	1	1	B12	6	C
B13	1	1	1	1	B13	5	C
B14	1	1	1	1	B14	3	C
B15	0.715	0.734	0.974	0.734	A9,A12,A17,B13,C16	0	D
B16	0.961	1	0.961	0.961	B16	9	I
B17	1	1	1	1	B17	21	C
B18	1	1	1	1	B18	1	C
B19	0.797	0.806	0.989	0.806	A9,B9,B14,B17,C16	0	D
B20	1	1	1	1	B20	1	C
B21	0.686	0.754	0.910	0.686	A3,A9,A36,B9,C16	0	I
B22	0.740	0.835	0.886	0.835	A6,A17,B4,B6,B9,B17	0	D
B23	0.747	0.818	0.912	0.747	A3,A9,A14,A17, B4,B17,B28	0	I
B24	1	1	1	1	B24	1	C
B25	0.826	0.835	0.990	0.835	A9,B4,B13,C16,C21	0	D
B26	1	1	1	1	B26	6	C
B27	0.623	0.837	0.744	0.623	A3,A17,A36,B9,B26	0	I
B28	0.987	1	0.987	1	B28	2	D
B29	0.664	0.706	0.940	0.664	A13,B9,B16,B17,B26	0	I
B30	0.402	0.516	0.779	0.402	A3,A31,B5,B16 C1,C16	0	I
C1	1	1	1	1	C1	6	C
C2	0.732	0.745	0.982	0.732	A36,B9, C1,C12,C16,C24	0	I
C3	0.501	1	0.501	1	C3	1	D
C4	0.822	1	0.822	1	C4	1	D
C5	0.731	1	0.731	1	C5	1	D
C6	1	1	1	1	C6	1	C
C7	0.712	0.716	0.994	0.712	A3,A6,A9,A17,	0	I

Project	θ_{CCR}^*	θ_{BCC}^*	$\theta_{CCR}^* / \theta_{BCC}^*$	θ_{NIRS}^*	Reference set	Referred times	Returns to scale
					B9,B12,C12,C16		
C8	0.615	0.634	0.970	0.615	A3,A6,A9,A17,B4,B9	0	I
C9	1	1	1	1	C9	5	C
C10	0.729	0.800	0.910	0.729	A17,A29,A36, B16,B17,B26,C16	0	I
C11	0.432	0.760	0.569	0.432	A3,A6,A13,A36,B4	0	I
C12	1	1	1	1	C12	9	C
C13	0.824	0.835	0.987	0.824	A9,A36,B9,C12,C16	0	I
C14	1	1	1	1	C14	1	C
C15	0.873	0.980	0.891	0.980	A6,A17,B4,B6,B14, B17,C16	0	D
C16	1	1	1	1	C16	21	C
C17	0.753	0.768	0.980	0.753	A3,A6,A9,A17, B4,B9,C16	0	I
C18	0.234	0.330	0.710	0.234	A3,A4,A36,B9,B16, B17,C9,C12	0	I
C19	0.710	0.812	0.873	0.710	A3,A9,A14,A24,A36, B4,B12,C9,C12	0	I
C20	0.590	0.621	0.950	0.590	A36,B4,B9,B16,B17, C16,C24	0	I
C21	0.978	1	0.978	1	C21	2	D
C22	0.414	0.433	0.956	0.414	A3,A9,A17,A36, B9,C12,C16	0	I

Chapter 5

Rating Academic Research

Editorial Introduction

Abstract: The societal production chains extending from academic research to eventual commercial applications are examined. The theory of the role of knowledge in economic development is briefly reviewed. Some common metrics to evaluate the inputs and outputs from academic research are listed.

Key words: Academic R&D, long waves, intellectual capital, leading sectors, spillover effects, technology platforms, firm-specific knowledge, bibliometric data, publications, citations, patents, licensing

1. SHOULD ACADEMIC RESEARCH BE RATED?

The chapters in this volume have dealt with ways of evaluating and ranking commercial R&D - - new products and new processes developed in commercial laboratories and destined for the commercial world ("commercialization"). This chapter looks at research activities carried out at university institutions. Some of these activities may eventually lead to commercial developments, directly or indirectly. Others may have no commercial applications at all.

One may perhaps ask whether this is a proper field of application of economic analysis. Economics deals with scarcities and the best use of scarce resources. Obviously, academic resources are scarce, both nationally and internationally. But is it legitimate to assume that academic resources should be allocated in order to optimize their returns? In any case, what constitutes the "return" to academic research? Certainly, it is not money in the pockets of the researchers. Possibly, it is fame among peers. Perhaps it is even academic glory. Fundamentally, academic achievements are driven by academic liberty - - the liberty of each individual researcher to pursue his or her ideas, irrespective of any thoughts of return.

Admittedly, we shall in this chapter be moving in the borderlands of economics. But even at the most famous academic institutions in the West, it is no longer true that R&D is driven by the scientific curiosity of researchers alone. Professional academic managers manage research. Funds are allocated, laboratories are built, and research staff is assembled, under the guidance of professional staff. In making those decisions, priorities have to be set. There are always alternative courses of action. One department or one research project may be allocated more resources, or fewer resources. In short, there is a need to evaluate and rank alternative courses of academic R&D.

2. THE ROLE OF ACADEMIC RESEARCH IN THE SOCIETAL PRODUCTION CHAINS

Students of the "long waves" in economics have traced the relationship between basic scientific discoveries and the ensuing economic development. Joseph Schumpeter (1939) believed that he could discern a pattern of clustering of innovations during the upswing of the long cycle. He saw railroads, steam and steel as "leading sectors" propelling Western economies into the long upswing of 1850-1900, and electricity, industrial chemistry and the internal combustion engine as the leading sectors of the upswing during the first part of the 20th century. Walt Rostow (1988) identified a subsequent wave spearheaded by developments in plastics, synthetic textiles, air transportation, mass consumption and tourism. The latest long wave occurred during the two last decades of the century, characterized by unparalleled progress in computers, information technology, biotech and pharmaceutical sciences.

G. Mensch (1975) investigated the time lag between advance in basic knowledge (invention) and the commercialization of such progress (innovation). His conclusion: During prolonged spells of economic stagnation there accumulates a backlog of un-exploited technological and commercial opportunities. Eventually the potential of these opportunities will break the stalemates in technology, and the flow of basic innovation will swell again.

Economists use the term "production chains" to denote the routes converting resources into intermediate products and, ultimately, into consumer goods. Commercial R&D constitutes early links in these chains, converting resources like laboratory research and existing scientific knowledge into new products and processes.

Scientific knowledge is created, or "produced," in universities, academic institutions and other locales of intellectual pursuit. The complete production chain includes the following four successive links:

- Universities and academic institutions creating basic scientific knowledge,
- R&D departments of private corporations converting basic knowledge to applied knowledge, embodied in new goods and services,
- Line production, commercializing state-of-the-art (applied) knowledge to produce intermediate and consumer goods,
- Marketing, and the building of consumer awareness.

The last link is in many ways the most important one. Ultimately, the consumers of new scientific knowledge direct and validate the efforts along the entire production chain.

The conventional distinction between basic scientific research (pursued by academia) and applied research (carried out in the industrial world) used to be its motivation: whether it was driven by scientific curiosity alone, or driven by potential sales and profits. As a corollary, academic knowledge capital used to be freely available, whereas applied knowledge would typically be commercially protected.

Once, academic research was identical to basic research, and possible commercial application was left to the commercial world. But the times have changed, and universities increasingly are involved not only in pure research, but also in "development," that is in applied research such as data processing or biotechnology. Today, academic research often lays the groundwork for subsequent commercial use (by other parties). The distinction between academic R&D and commercial R&D can still be made, of course. Academic R&D are motivated by the ambitions of academic researchers. Commercial R&D are motivated by the expectations of private companies to capture market shares.

But these lines of distinction are now becoming blurred. Today, many US universities are energetically pursuing both basic and applied research with an eye on generating income for the university, in the form of licensing fees and even in the form of outright sales of technology. The University of Texas is a good example. The mission of its Office of Technology Licensing and Intellectual Property is to facilitate the transfer of university developed technology to the public sector by licensing inventions to private industry (see the reference University of Texas). Note that the University of Texas is a state university, not a private university. Making money can be good policy for a state university too, making it possible to keep student tuition within bounds. For many years, the University of Texas used to draw huge annual incomes from oil pumped on university lands. Those days are gone. In the future, the university will need to seek income from its holdings of intellectual capital, rather than land.

Conversely, some commercial enterprises nowadays find it useful to offer the fruits of their R&D entirely free of charge to the public. This happens when developers of computer software, believing in the approach of "open computing" offer their computer codes to be freely downloaded (or, purchased at a nominal fee) by any interested party. Well-known examples are the Unix operating system (originally developed by ATT) and the Linux operating systems. The rationale behind such behavior is the attempt to set industry standards, and thus to create a potentially huge demand for follow-up hardware and software.

One of the surprising features of modern high tech capitalism is how private corporations have found it possible to move research from the academic to the commercial world. Many modern corporate startups, engaged in research, do not make money, nor are they expected to do so within any reasonable time horizon. Consider the soaring prices of biotech stock on Wall Street in the early 1990s, or the recent "dot com" mania - - the skyrocketing prices of companies operating on the Internet. Many of these companies are research companies, pure and simple, financed by the investors who bought the stock during the IPO (initial public offering). The money raised pays for the ongoing research. There is no product yet; there are no sales, no revenue. But there is hope - - hope of a scientific break-through; hope enough to keep the investors happy.

3. THE ROLE OF ACADEMIC INSTITUTIONS IN NATIONAL R&D POLICY

Even if academic R&D has no immediate commercial application, it often has direct and powerful societal impacts. Recent research results in bacteriology, in health administration, in ecology and a host of other disciplines are quickly changing the world we live in. Society at large looks at the academic centers to receive guidance, advice, and intellectual leadership. University R&D is a font of new knowledge and new technology that will benefit us all.

Precisely for this reason, the public is concerned and vociferous about how academic resources are spent, and about the priorities of academic R&D. There are powerful constituencies supporting and promoting the priorities of cancer or AIDS research, or the priorities of space research.

University administrators face the difficult task of listening to these wish lists, and translating them into university R&D priorities. In response, universities during the last 50 years have created new academic disciplines, new schools and new academic degrees. Whenever such initiatives are taken, the expected academic return from them needs to be evaluated, and compared with performance of existing academic activities.

National R&D policy is also executed directly by the US federal government, through the National Science Foundation, and in the federal research laboratories. The latter facilities include

- the National Synchrotron Light Source at Brookhaven National Laboratory,
- the Combustion Research Facility at Sandia National Laboratory at Albuquerque,
- the National Center for Electron Microscopy at Lawrence Berkeley Laboratory,
- the High Flux Isotope Reactor at Oak Ridge National Laboratory, and
- the Los Alamos National Laboratory.

The government funding of all these various institutions presumably reflects the national priorities of this research.

4. ACADEMIC R&D AND ECONOMIC DEVELOPMENT: A LITERATURE REVIEW[1]

It is widely acknowledged that new knowledge is an essential source for economic growth. There are many ways in which new knowledge, or more strictly, new technology can be created. Economists have been studying these mechanisms since Arrow's (1962) seminal work on the economic implications of learning-by-doing. Here, we will focus on the contribution of R&D, and specifically university R&D, to technology and economic growth.

There is an emerging consensus among economists that R&D needs to be dealt with as an endogenous variable in economic modeling. Just as

[1] This section reviews work surveyed in several publications by Pedro Conceição, Instituto Superior Técnico, Lisbon. Permission to use this material here is gratefully acknowledged. *Ed.*

investment is an addition to physical capital motivated by market opportunities, commercial R&D is an addition to knowledge capital that is motivated by market opportunities and future possibilities of production and sales. That is, R&D cannot be taken as a datum or some given industry trend, but must be explained.

Very broadly, one can think of two conceptual approaches to constructing such theory. One is associated with the "new" theories of growth, as proposed by Nelson and Winter (1982), Romer (1990) and Grossman and Helpman (1991). These efforts adapt neoclassical theories of growth with an aggregate production function, setting them in an evolutionary framework and modifying them to allow for monopolistic positions achieved by innovative firms, and for uncertainty in getting innovations. The other conceptual view is associated with institutional approaches developed primarily by Rosenberg (e.g. 1985, 1994) and the school of scholars affiliated with SPRU, at the University of Sussex.

Both approaches agree that R&D may be linked to economic development through mechanisms of disequilibrium, like positive feedback, path-dependence and lock-in and the possible appearance of increasing returns. The concept of a representative agent in a globally optimizing framework is no longer considered appropriate. Instead, the analytical setting is one of pervasive uncertainty, technological bottlenecks and bounded opportunities, experimental and local search behavior, and cumulative capabilities. The process of R&D and technological change is thus seen as being driven by the actions of heterogeneous agents in a nonlinear manner. This applies to both the generation and diffusion of new knowledge. Similarly, on the demand side, infrastructure and network externalities lead to self-reinforcing diffusion processes.

How do these results translate to the role of academic R&D (rather than commercial R&D) in economic growth? In order to answer this question, note that academic knowledge capital is typically both non-rival (it can be used by many persons at a time) and non-excludable (no legal power is exercised to prevent others from using it). (For these terms, see Romer, 1993.) In this sense, academic R&D is a public good.

Commercial R&D, on the other hand, is typically both rival and excludable. The processes of diffusion of new commercial knowledge unfold in spite of the attempts of private corporations to keep that knowledge private. Powerful so-called spillover effects of product development and the acquisition of new software propagate new knowledge throughout the high tech economy. A product niche established by one company quickly erodes as competitors launch improved products on the market.

It may be debated whether academic R&D is subject to quicker or slower diffusion than commercial R&D. Academic R&D is neither spurred nor fettered by transitory exclusivity positions in the market, so characteristic of commercial product development. Some academic research results have immediate and dramatic impact on economic growth; others lie dormant for a long time. In any case, the path from the academic laboratory to the marketplace may be a long and winding one, involving both follow-up academic research and commercial product development.

Myers and Rosenbloom, 1996 (building on earlier work by Kline and Rosenberg 1986) further elaborated the notion of complex interactions between general knowledge and "firm-specific knowledge." Organizational capabilities are seen as the foundations of competitive advantage in innovation. These advantages include firm-specific knowledge, communities of practice, and technology of platforms.

Firm-specific knowledge represents the accumulated learning of the organization that is pertinent to the business. This is to be distinguished from the body of generally accessible knowledge. The specific knowledge of a firm is embodied in the firm's workforce and its technology platforms, products and processes. Communities of practice are ensembles of skilled technical people with expertise on working across the organization. They span organizational divisions and provide both a repository for the firm's expertise and a medium for communication and application of new knowledge. Technology platforms are an output of a design process that provides a framework on which families of specific products and services can be created over time. A platform comprises an ensemble of technologies configured in a system or subsystem that creates opportunities for variety of outputs. (See also Conceição, Gibson, Heitor and Shariq, 1997.)

The path from academic research to commercial application of a new technology involves three consecutive steps:

- Technology transfer to the business community. Increasingly, universities themselves promote such transfers, establishing an office of intellectual property, assessing transfer opportunities, and designing transfer strategies such as licensing.
- Technology development done by the licensee, such as establishing a business plan, raising seed capital, continued protection of intellectual property, prototyping and site testing.
- Technology commercialization, finalizing the product and launching it on the market.

5. METRICS TO EVALUATE ACADEMIC R&D[2]

This chapter deals with ways of evaluating and ranking university research. The direction and funding of academic research faces growing public scrutiny. How should the limited resources of a university - - manpower resources and funding - - be employed to maximize their social and economic relevance? In trying to answer this question, one obviously needs to agree suitable metrics to assess the direction, extent, quality and success of academic research.

There is widespread agreement in the academic world that publications are the yardstick of true scholarship. Other measures of performance are important also, such as an academic instructor's teaching record.

Academic publications are of many kinds, purely scientific research reports, textbooks, and journalistic endeavors. The scientific impact of a single note in a scholarly journal may be path breaking; the impact of a large monograph in several volumes may be insignificant. Also, academic publication practice varies from one discipline to another: in medicine it is common that researchers publish a large number of brief progress notes; in economic history large treatises are common.

5.1 Metrics of R&D outputs

The set of scientific results generated by the R&D activities are conventionally measured by so-called bibliometric data on publications on citations. See for instance Narin (1987). The measures of R&D activities also include data on licenses and patented inventions.

Publications. The number of various types of academic publications commonly measures the output of university R&D. The popularity of publications as an indicator rests on the understanding that all contributions to scientific research find expression in the scientific literature. It can be argued that publications are the most valid, fair and direct way to compare the research performance of departments. Commonly, when academic staff is reviewed for promotion, a major concern is to evaluate the staff in terms of its scholarship. This includes an examination of the quality and quantity of their publications. In the same manner, it makes sense to assess the performance of an entire university, a center for R&D, or other institution, by compiling statistics of staff publications (Lindsey, 1989). The various

[2] This section is based on material surveyed by Pedro Oliveira, a Ph.D. candidate at the University of North Carolina. Permission to use this material here is gratefully acknowledged. *Ed.*

types of publications include monographs, edited books, journal articles, conference papers, master theses, Ph.D. dissertations, and other academic publications.

Some authors also take into account the number of pages of each publication. Formulas have been suggested to allow for differing page sizes and so on. The resulting metric is considered an indicator of productivity and quality, since presumably all published works reach some minimum quality. Sometimes, however, scholarly work cannot be published due to the need for industrial secrecy. When this happens, the number of publications does not give a clear picture of the real quality and productivity.

Citations. The number of citations equals the number of times a paper is referred to in subsequently published papers. It provides a measure of the impact of a paper in the scientific community; see Lindsey (1989). Citation analysis is a means of measuring research impact. Data required for the carrying out of a citations analysis can be drawn from the international databases of the Institute for Science Information (ISI). There are three such databases: the Science Citation Index (SCI), the Social Sciences Citation Index (SSCI), and the Arts and Humanities Citation Index (A&HCI).

Patents. The number of patents obtained by university researchers is a common indicator in the US and Japan (for a literature survey, see Archibugi and Piana, 1996). In Europe, it is less common that university researchers apply for patents (see the Green Book, European Commission). Under US patent law, four classes of subject matter can be patented: a process, a machine, a composition of matter, or an article of manufacture. Once an invention qualifies for one of the four classes, it must also be identified as being new and useful (that is, having novelty and utility). The number of patents is an indicator of the "utility" of R&D, understood as the potential "exploitability" of the R&D results. Nevertheless, some individuals and some corporations obviously have greater opportunities to register patents than others.

Licenses. A license is an authorization given to a company to develop, manufacture or market a process or a product. Sometimes the product has already been commercialized; in other cases it may require additional development before going to the market. Once a license has been granted, the licensee (such as a university) obtains royalty income in return. The total number of licenses granted is a reasonable indicator of the market appeal and usefulness of the R&D. Again, however, it may be noted that some individuals or corporations may have greater opportunities to license than others do (Philimore, 1988).

5.2 Metrics of R&D inputs

The indicators we are going to study are the input indicators characterizing the financial and human resources devoted to R&D. As examples, we mention

R&D expenditures. R&D expenditures are funds allocated to the development of R&D, counted from the initiation of a project to its commercialization. Due to its nature, some research is less dependent on funding than other. Nevertheless, we shall use total R&D expenditure as an indicator of input. Expenditures can be broken down by type of cost, and by source of funds. The money available for support of R&D at a state university comes from the government; in addition, private organizations and private corporations can be important sources of funding. R&D funds are raised mostly from the outside, in the form of grants or contracts. Some universities allocate their own funds to research; in the US, a significant source of funding is income from endowments.

Staff devoted to R&D. The number of staff should be converted into FTE (=full time employment equivalents). Salaries can be broken down by category of personnel, such as research fellows, post-doctoral fellows, research associates, research assistants, research technicians and other support staff. The principle here is that the analysis should cover all categories of personnel that directly contribute to R&D activities. Often, researchers do not work full time for a project, and their salaries derive from a variety of sources, which makes the estimation of the salaries and hours devoted to the project difficult.

Aggregated Metrics. Adding together the number of publications of all researchers in a department provides a rough measure of the volume or quantity of research. This simple statistic can be improved in two ways. One is to weigh each publication by a weight reflecting the supposed importance of the journal or other publication outlet. The weighted number of publications presumably indicates the immediate importance of the research results and the scope of the readership. Alternatively, each publication could be multiplied by its citation count (the number of times each publication is cited by other researchers). The citation count only becomes available one or several years after publication. It is useful for gauging the long-term impact of the publication. (For a discussion of these and other bibliometric methods of measuring the research output of academic departments, see Lindsey 1991 and Nederhof and Noyons, 1992.)

5.3 Searching for new metrics

Unfortunately, all these metrics suffer from many weaknesses. Bibliometric data can be helpful in comparing the performance of individual researchers all working inside a given academic discipline. But there are pitfalls. Some very famous researchers tend to bury their latest path-breaking research results in obscure foreign journals - - to have their research results duly acknowledged but keeping them out of reach from some of their immediate competitors.

Using bibliometric data to compare the research performance between scientific disciplines is a nightmare. Publication practices vary greatly between disciplines. Many a mathematician still dreams of publishing a brief one-page note in a journal, drawing worldwide attention. Medical research teams publishing their results often list dozens of authors, from senior administrators to young Ph.D. and M.D. candidates.

The research paper to follow, "Controlling the Efficiency of University Research in The Netherlands" by T. Garcia Valderrama and T. L.C.T. Groot reports on some very interesting new metrics of academic research developed by the Association of Dutch Universities. Essentially, the new metrics is a four-dimensional score of each individual research program, set by a committee of international evaluators of outstanding reputation. Choosing four dimensions rather than one, the committee diplomatically sidestepped the task of providing a unique ranking scale. But what a committee cannot do, the OR analyst can, using data envelopment analysis! The authors show how to convert the committee scores into a unique ranking list, and they discuss the results.

REFERENCES

Archibugi, D. and M. Piana, M. (1996). "Measuring Technological Change through Patents and Innovation Surveys," *Technovation*, Vol.16:9, pp. 451 - 468.

Arrow, K., "The Economic Implications of Learning by Doing," *Review of Economic Studies*, Vol. 28, 192, 155-173.

Conceição, P., Heitor, M.V., Gibson, D.V. and Shariq, S.S. (1997). "Towards a Research Agenda for Knowledge Policies and Management," *Journal of Knowledge Management*, Vol. 1, pp. 129- 141.

Grossman, M. and Helpman, E. (1991). *Innovation and Growth in the Global Economy*, MIT Press, Cambridge, Mass.

Kline, S.J. and Rosenberg, N. (1986). "An Overview of Innovation," in Landau, R. and Rosenberg, N., editors, *The Positive Sum Strategy: Harnessing Technology for Economic Growth*, The National Academy Press, Washington DC, 1986.

Lindsey, D. (1989). "Using Citation Counts as a Measure of the Quality of Science," *Scientometrics,* Vol. 15, pp. 189 ff.

Lindsey, D. (1991). "The Relationship between Performance Indicators for Academic Research and Funding: Developing a Measure of Return on Investment in Science," *Scientometrics*, Vol. 20, pp. 221-234.

Narin, F. (1987). "Bibliometric Techniques in the Evaluation of Research Programs," *Science and Public Policy*, April, pp. 99-106.

Mensch, G. (1979). *Stalemate in Technology: Innovations Overcome the Depression*, Ballinger Publishing, Cambridge, Mass. (German original *Das Technologische Patt*, Umschau Verlag, Frankfurt, 1975).

Myers, M.B. and Rosenbloom, R.S. (1996). "Rethinking the Role of Industrial Research," in Rosenbloom, R.S. and Spencer, W.J., editors, *Engines of Innovation*, Harvard Business School Press, 1996, pp. 209-228.

Nelson, R.R. and Winter, W. (1982). *An Evolutionary Theory of Economic Change*, Belknap Press, Cambridge.

Niederhof, A.J. and Noyons, C.C.M. (1992). "Assessment of the International Standing of University Department's Research: A Comparison of Bibliometric Methods," *Scientometrics*, Vol. 24, pp. 393 – 404.

Romer, P. (1990). "Endogenous Technological Growth," *Journal of Political Economy*, Vol..98:5, pp. 71-102.

Romer, P. (1993). "Two Strategies for Economic Development: Using Ideas and Producing Ideas," in Summers, L.H. and Shah, S., editors, *Proceedings of the World Bank Annual Conference on Development Economics 1992*, supplement to the *World Bank Economic Review,* 1993.

Rostow, W. (1988). "The Fourth Industrial Revolution and American Society: Some Reflections on the Past for the Future", in Furino, A., editor, *Cooperation and Competition in the Global Economy,* Balling Publishing Co., Cambridge, Mass. 1988.

Schumpeter, J.A. (1939). *Business Cycles,* Vols. 1-2, Mc Graw Hill Company, New York.

University of Texas, Office of Technology Licensing and Intellectual Property (OTL), see www.utexas.edu/academic/otl

Controlling the Efficiency of University Research in the Netherlands

A Research Paper

T Garcia Valderrama[1] and T.L.C.M.Groot[2]
[1]*The University of Cadiz*

[2]*Vrije University, Amsterdam*

Abstract: In order to evaluate government funding of university research in the Netherlands, the Association of Dutch Universities uses a system of periodic evaluations. Review committees of international experts assess each research program. In 1995, the Association published statistics on the performance of 90 programs in economics and econometrics during a preceding five-year period. The difficulties of statistical evaluation and assessment of academic research programs are well known. There are few objective measurements of performance. Bibliometric data, such as the number of journal articles or dissertations published, give only indirect indication of the importance of the research results. In the present case, however, the review committees of international experts were asked to evaluate each program with respect to four characteristics: scientific quality, scientific productivity obtained, relevance, and long-term viability. The assessment of each of these characteristics was expressed in a single score. Drawing on the data published by the Association, the authors have used Data Envelopment Analysis (DEA) to evaluate and rank the research programs. The results of the full study are being published elsewhere. The present paper discusses in depth the results for three typical programs.

Key words: Evaluation of academic departments, Association of Universities in the Netherlands, committee of experts, quality of research, productivity of the research team, societal and technological relevance of research, DEA metrics, fractional programming format of DEA, economies of scale

1. INTRODUCTION

The Association of Dutch Universities has developed a system of evaluation of academic research programs in the Netherlands. Review committees of international experts are asked to evaluate each program with respect to four characteristics: scientific quality, scientific productivity obtained, relevance, and long-term viability. The assessment of each of these characteristics is expressed in a single score on a five-point scale. In 1995, the Association published statistics on the performance of 90 programs in economics and econometrics during a preceding five-year period.

The aim of the present paper is to measure the efficiency and analyze the advantages of Data Envelopment Analysis (DEA) as a tool that captures the assessment by the committee of experts. We shall analyze differences of efficiency of the various programs, considering their size and the inputs used, both in terms of financial sources and the number and background of the investigators.

1.1 Applying DEA to rate the performance of academic institutions: Current state of the debate

Several authors have used DEA to compare the performance of teaching and research units (e.g. departments) at various universities, see Kwimbere (1987), Tomkins and Green (1988), Cameron (1989), Ahn and Seiford (1990), Beasly (1990), Pina Martínez and Torres Pradas (1992). The decision-making units (DMUs) normally chosen for evaluation are academic departments, together with programs and projects carried out under the auspices of the departments, both in teaching and in research, see Charnes, Cooper and Rhodes[1] (1981), Bessent et al. (1984), Diamond et al. (1990), and Land, Lovell and Thore (1993).

A difficulty encountered in applying the DEA model to rate academic performance is that data are complex and sometimes difficult to obtain; once obtained, interpretation and use of the information is often also difficult. Evaluating academic teaching programs, various authors have used one or more of the following data: size of department, number of graduating students, the qualifications of the staff of the department[2], facilities or infrastructure available (libraries, computer rooms, etc.), and financial resources[3].

[1] See also the study by Charnes and Cooper (1980).
[2] In most cases, this variable is treated as a category variable, not as a quantity
[3] See Johnes (1996) on the choice of indicators for the evaluation of British universities.

A few studies have been reported using DEA to monitor the efficiency of individual academic research activities (Johnes and Johnes, 1993). As in the case of teaching, the most significant limitation is the difficulty of measuring the quality of the research results (rather than just its quantity). The Dutch experience shows, however, that it may be possible to establish within a committee a relative consensus on the definition and assessment of research outputs.

One way to deal with quality (and other variables beyond management control) is to use category variables in DEA. Beasly (1990) describes the application of DEA using three types of category variables to classify departments in terms of quality.

A few authors have used DEA to evaluate and monitor the efficiency of a the various departments within the same university, see Ahn et al. (1989), Sinuani-Stern et al. (1994), García and Gómez (1999). In such cases, the greatest problem is finding a sufficiently wide and homogeneous sample of departments to obtain conclusive results; also, it is not easy to find quantitative indicators that successfully embrace the different research practices and policies of the various departments.

It should be clear already from this brief literature review that there is a lack of agreement on and a concern about the choice of variables for inputs and outputs. Availability of data and the specific objectives of the each study seem to be the main determinants. In our own case, many of these problems could be avoided or at least sidestepped since the panel of international experts determined the choice of the relevant indicators.

1.2 Research objectives

Compared to the studies now reviewed, we believe that we have a distinct advantage in having available quite reliable data on the quality of academic research output in the Netherlands, in addition to the common quantity indicators. Obviously, the quality evaluation of the VSNU Committee of experts is a crucial part of evaluation of academic research in the Netherlands. The central objective of our study, then, is to show how the conclusions of the committee of experts can be enhanced by the DEA rankings. We shall analyze the possible advantages offered by the DEA model, over the method of efficiency evaluation by expert committee. We shall also report the rankings of several alternative DEA models, and point out their advantages and shortcomings.

Section 2 describes a system of evaluation of university research in the Netherlands. Section 3 reviews some of the theoretical background. Section

4 explains the data used. Section 5 lists the results. Section 6 provides a general discussion. Section 7 sums up.

2. UNIVERSITY RESEARCH FUNDING AND EVALUATION IN THE NETHERLANDS

Until 1983, government funding of university research in the Netherlands was directly related to the number of students enrolled; see Groot (1988). This system made it difficult for the Dutch government to promote and manage academic research directly. In 1983 a system of *conditional financing of research* was introduced, permitting the Minister to allocate funds for research independently of the number of students enrolled. University faculties were asked to cluster their research activities in "research programs" to be financed for a limited period. Financing was conditional on the approval of these programs by faculty committees consisting of experts in the relevant fields; see Hazeu (1983), Timmermans (1984), Groot and Van de Poel (1993).

The conditional financing system made resources for research and research programs visible, thus permitting policy makers and university managers to develop research policies and to evaluate research activities. For many years, university research had been evaluated by examining the quality of research program proposals. Ten years later, a new system was introduced to evaluate the output of conditionally financed programs. Under authority of the VSNU (the Association of Universities in the Netherlands) a system of periodic, discipline-oriented evaluation of university research from an international perspective was implemented; see VSNU (1990, 1994). There were three main reasons for the evaluations: to enhance the quality of research, to inform faculty managers about the achievements of their research programs and to introduce a system of accountability to the public at large of the spending of state funds, VSNU (1994), Westerheijden (1996).

At least once every five years, a review committee assesses the research output in each academic discipline. The committee consists mainly of non-Dutch peers with an outstanding reputation in their academic field. The committee is to provide an independent assessment of each program with respect to four criteria, namely its *scientific quality*, the *scientific productivity* of the research team, the *scientific* and (where appropriate) the *societal and technological relevance* of the research, and its *long-term viability*. The committee's evaluation according to each of these criteria is expressed in a single score on a five point Likert-type scale, together with a short explanatory report. The final report of the committee is available to the public, for a typical report see VSNU (1995).

In 1993, the first disciplines evaluated were mechanical engineering, biology, psychology, history and archaeology. In 1995, an international committee of six experts with outstanding reputation evaluated the output of 90 research programs in economics and econometrics. The committee was provided with bibliometric information on each group's number of publications according to quality level of publisher (in case of books) or journal (in case of articles), based on a standardized quality ranking developed by the VSNU, see VSNU (1990). Furthermore, the committee received from each research program a so-called "self study" in which each program's objectives, research results, and resources were presented. In addition to the bibliometric information, the self studies listed five key journal articles that were regarded representative of the output of the program during the five-year period.

The evaluation procedure followed by the evaluation committee can roughly be divided into four phases.

In the first phase, two committee members studied the bibliometric information and the five sample articles of each program. They proposed an evaluation score on each of the four aspects. In retrospect, it appears that the evaluation of the five sample publications greatly influenced the scores proposed by the two evaluators.[4] In any case, the full committee would discuss the scores set by the two members.[5] The committee made a decision on the proposed scores, establishing so-called "preliminary scores".

In the second phase, a round of interviews with program directors was held in order to clarify unresolved issues. From the 90 program coordinators, 55 coordinators were invited for an interview.[6] One of the original committee members and two new members took part in these interviews.

In the third phase, the evaluation committee interviewed faculty boards on policy matters regarding the research programs administered under the conditional financing system. The general outlook of the research programs and faculty policy was discussed.

In the final phase, a draft text of the evaluation of each program was sent to the corresponding coordinator for revision of factual errors or misunderstandings. This round resulted in relatively few minor revisions.[7]

[4] This information comes from an interview with a VSNU-employee who has been actively involved in the activities of the committee.

[5] In 75 % of all evaluations of quality and productivity, the scores of the committee members differed less than one point. The evaluations of relevance and viability required discussions between evaluators and in the evaluation committee.

[6] The coordinators were brought in when either of the following two criteria was met: there were some unresolved questions, or the program had been assigned a preliminary score of 2 or less on quality and/or productivity.

[7] In 12 programs, the text was changed slightly. Only 2 out of 360 scores were changed.

The final report was handed over to the president of the VSNU on December 2, 1995.

3. DEA EFFICIENCY MEASURES

The purpose of a DEA model is to provide a measure of the relative efficiency of an organizational unit (a decision-making unit, or DMU) from the study of its inputs (resources) and outputs (results achieved). The organization may be a specific non-profit-making entity - - such as a university - - from an overall point of view, or a component part of such an entity, such as a department, a faculty or a section, or even a particular academic research project or program.

This type of comparative analysis may of course only be conducted provided the DMUs use the same kind of resources for the purposes of producing the same kind of outputs. The DEA model is based on the concept of Pareto efficiency and makes transversal comparisons between the various inputs and outputs of each DMU evaluated, and those of all the other DMUs in the study. Each DMU is evaluated by comparing it with the rest, thus obtaining an indicator of its relative efficiency.

DEA allows inputs and outputs to be measured in any quantitative way, provided homogeneity is maintained using the same units of measurement for all the DMUs. Binary variables or variables representing qualitative attributes or categories may also be included. Examples of such variables mentioned in the DEA literature are size of the DMU, length of time of operation of the production process, sundry factors related to the environment, or to the organizational hierarchy to which the DMU belongs. Also, variables outside the control of managers but impacting on the DMU's efficiency may be accounted for.

DEA uses linear programming techniques to trace a benchmark or maximum limit of efficiency derived from analysis of the most efficient DMUs, which can be considered as the maximum levels of output achievable from given inputs. Those DMUs whose levels of efficiency constitute the benchmarks are classed as efficient. The original concepts of DEA are due to Charnes, Cooper and Rhodes (1978).

We shall here follow El-Mahgary and Lahdelma (1995) in organizing the results of the basic DEA model under the following four headings:

- The efficiency ratings,
- The efficiency gaps, indicating excess uses of input or output shortfalls,
- The set of referee DMUs, constituting so-called "best practice",

- Coefficients indicating the relative importance of each efficiency indicator.

These metrics provide information on the levels of outputs and inputs that a DMU should be able to reach under conditions of efficient operation, and, by reference, those aspects of its activities that could be improved. Further, they indicate which levels of services that the DMU should be able to provide if the resources available were reduced (for example, by budget restrictions). Conversely, they also indicate the additional resources that would be required in order to meet a given increase in the demand for its services.

There are three models most frequently associated with the DEA methodology: the CCR (Charnes, Cooper and Rhodes, 1978), the BCC model (Banker, Charnes and Cooper, 1984), and the additive models (Charnes et al. 1985).

The formulation of such a model in fractional programming form (Charnes, Cooper and Rhodes, 1978) is as follows:

$$\text{Max} \quad h_0 = \sum_{r=1}^{s} \mu_r Y_{r0} \Big/ \sum_{i=1}^{m} v_i X_{i0} \tag{1}$$

subject to

$$\sum_{r=1}^{s} \mu_r Y_{rj} \Big/ \sum_{i=1}^{m} v_i X_{ij} \leq 1, \; j = 1,2,\ldots,n$$

$$\mu_r > 0, \; r = 1,2,\ldots,s \text{ and } v_i > 0, \; i = 1,2,\ldots,m$$

There are $j=1,2,\ldots,n$ DMUs to be evaluated, each one using the inputs $X_{ij} > 0$ to produce the outputs $Y_{rj} > 0$ (specifically, the DMU $j=0$ uses the inputs $X_{i0} > 0$ inputs to produce outputs $Y_{r0} > 0$). The virtual multipliers to be solved by the model are denoted μ_r and v_i .The optimization produces a set of positive or zero values of the unknowns (indicated by an asterisk). At the optimum, $h_0{*} = 1$ only if the unit evaluated is "efficient". Thus, the value of the objective function will always fall between 0 and 1 for any individual DMU studied.

To resolve program (1), it is converted into an equivalent linear form, setting the denominator equal to a constant (unity) and maximizing the numerator as follows:

$$\text{Max } h_0 = \sum_{r=1}^{s} \mu_r Y_{r0} \qquad (2)$$

subject to

$$\sum_{r=1}^{s} \mu_r Y_{rj} - \sum_{i=1}^{m} v_i X_{ij} \leq 0, \quad j = 1,2,\ldots,n$$

$$\sum_{i=1}^{m} v_i X_{i0} = 1$$

$$\mu_r \geq \varepsilon, \ r = 1,2,\ldots,s \text{ and } v_i \geq \varepsilon, \ i = 1,2,\ldots,m$$

where ε is a non-Archimedean infinitesimally small positive number. The dual of program (2) can be expressed mathematically as follows:

$$\text{Min } \theta_0 - \varepsilon\left(\sum_{i=1}^{m} s_i^- + \sum_{r=1}^{s} s_r^+\right) \qquad (3)$$

subject to

$$\sum_{j=1}^{n} Y_{rj} \lambda_j - s_r^+ = Y_{r0}, \quad r=1,\ldots,s$$

$$\theta_0 X_{i0} - \sum_{j=1}^{n} X_{ij} \lambda_j - s_i^- = 0, \quad i=1,\ldots,m$$

$$\text{all } \lambda_j, s_i^-, s_r^+ \geq 0$$

The solutions s_r^{+*} represent the outputs gaps (the amount of actual output falling short of best practice output), and similarly, s_i^{-*} represent the input gaps (actual inputs exceeding best practice inputs). If the DMU currently evaluated attains the value $\theta_0^* = 1$ and if these gaps are all zero, then the DMU is considered efficient. The parameter ε will in this case assign a value for each level of residual inefficiency, or the inefficiency estimated from the gap variables.

The efficiency rating θ_0* can be interpreted as the greatest possible equi-proportionate shrinking of all inputs which the DMU currently evaluated should be able to achieve. The rate of input savings is $(1 - \theta_0*)$.

The efficient values of the inputs and the outputs (so-called best practice) can be written

$$X_{i0}^{\$} = \theta_0 * X_{i0} - s_i^{-*} \tag{3a}$$

$$Y_{r0}^{\$} = Y_{r0} + s_r^{+*} \tag{3b}$$

Eq. (3a) shows the level of inputs which the DMU currently evaluated would achieve, were it to operate efficiently. Eq. (3b) shows the level of outputs then to be obtained.

One of the main criticisms of the model by Charnes, Cooper and Rhodes (1978) is that it calculates efficiency on the assumption of constant returns of scale. However, subsequent studies were undertaken in which this assumption was removed. Specifically, Banker, Charnes and Cooper (1984) adjoined the following restriction to program (3):

$$\Sigma_j \lambda_j = 1$$

The resulting efficiency concept is one calculated under variable returns of scale. This type of relative efficiency rating is designated as the pure technical efficiency. The efficiency of scale is then obtained as the ratio between the "overall efficiency" calculated from equation (3), and the pure efficiency, see also Banker, Chang and Cooper (1996).

The primal of the model of Banker, Charnes and Cooper (1984) is:

$$\text{Max } h_0 = \sum_{r=1}^{s} \mu_r Y_{r0} + u_0 \tag{5}$$

subject to

$$\sum_{r=1}^{s} \mu_r Y_{rj} - \sum_{i=1}^{m} v_i X_{ij} + u_0 \leq 0, \quad j = 1,2,\ldots,n$$

$$\sum_{i=1}^{m} v_i X_{i0} = 1$$

$\mu_r \geq 0, \; r = 1,2,...,s$ and $v_i \geq 0, \; i = 1,2,...,m;$
u_0 unrestricted in sign

Each of the above models seeks to determine the efficiency of a particular DMU by reference to the benchmark results set by the best observed performance ("best practice"). Thus the calculated efficiency rating will depend on the form of the benchmarks and the system of evaluation implicit in each DEA model. Furthermore, as stated by Ali et al. (1995, p. 463), the choice of the variables, as well as differences in the mathematical formulation of the models, may give rise to differences in the efficiency scores. Our treatment to follow will indeed confirm this.

In addition to the above described improvements to the model, work has also been done to get round some of the initial deficiencies in the model - for example, the treatment of variables beyond the manager's control[8], category variables and other factors difficult to quantify. Yet another aspect studied in the DEA literature is the possibility of introducing *a priori* limits on the virtual multipliers, with the aim of discriminating, in terms of importance, between the various variables to be incorporated in the model, facilitating and making more feasible the comparison between DMUs. Finally, for the non-Archimedean epsilon (ε), see Ruggiero (1996, p. 556).

In summary, the information provided by DEA for the measurement of efficiency of individual research programs (DMUs), consists of the following:

Efficiency and inefficiency scores. The efficiency rating θ_0* scored, and the difference $1 - \theta_0$* between the projected maximum feasible rating and the observed value, respectively. The DEA calculations make it possible to identify and monitor those factors that cause significant inefficiencies.

The sum total of all deviations between observations and best practice. The deviations on both the output side and the input side are added together. Mathematically, we define this metric as

$$\Delta = \sum_{r=1}^{s} (Y_{r0} - \sum_{j=1}^{n} Y_{rj}\lambda_j) + \sum_{i=1}^{m} (X_{i0} - \sum_{j=1}^{n} X_{ij}\lambda_j) \qquad (6)$$

[8] See Banker and Morey (1986a and 1986b), Kamakura (1988), Rousseau and Semple (1993).

When a DMU is inefficient, the value of Δ is greater than zero. The greater the deviations between observations and projected values, the greater will also be the value of the metric Δ.

Economies of scale, measured by the hyperplane intercept u_0^*. This metric[9] assumes conditions of variable returns to scale. Its sign, positive or negative, allows one to determine the magnitude of the returns to scale - - whether the DMU currently evaluated is operating under increasing or decreasing returns to scale. Thus, if $u_0^* > 0$, the DMU is operating under conditions of decreasing returns; if $u_0^* < 0$, it is operating under increasing returns.

The sum total of all slacks. The slacks on both the output side and the input side are added together. Mathematically,

$$\delta = \sum_{r=1}^{s} s_r^+ + \sum_{i=1}^{m} s_i^- \qquad (7)$$

where the s_r^+ and s_i^- represent the output gaps and the input gaps, respectively; see program (3).

Virtual value of all input. This is the weighted sum of all observed inputs, each input being weighted by its virtual multiplier. It is obtained as the optimal value of the denominator in the objective function in program (1). As has already been pointed out, the conventional way of solving program (1) is to norm the virtual multipliers on the input side so that the virtual value of all output equals unity.

Virtual value of all output. This is the weighted sum of all observed outputs, each output being weighted by its virtual multiplier. It is obtained as the optimal value of the numerator in the objective function in program (1).

The advantage of the DEA model, in comparison with parametric models, for the measurement of the efficiency of organizational units in the public sector such as universities is based on the following points:

- There is no market for the products and services of universities, and it is impossible to measure their true output.
- Universities have many outputs, of different types, which may take a wide variety of forms.

[9] See program (4) in the main text.

- There is uncertainty and concern about the concept of "public production," which prevents us from determining the true production function.
- DEA offers the possibility of measuring the relative efficiency of a university without the need of having pricing and cost accounting in place.
- The DEA model allows intrinsically different kinds of variables to be quantified and mixed.
- The DEA model determines weights (virtual multipliers) of each input and each output.
- The DEA model evaluates each university with reference to the behavior of the best examples observed ("best practice"), and thus permits the quantification and monitoring of the causes of relative inefficiency.

All in all, readily recognizing the limitations of the DEA model, we nevertheless find it a useful tool for the measurement of the efficiency of institutions such as universities. Caution must be exercised in making decisions based on the DEA results, however. There are methodological problems inherent in the model reducing its usefulness as an instrument of control in such complex institutions.

4. OBJECTIVES OF THE STUDY, AND DATA

Our objective is to use data envelopment analysis as an instrument of measurement of the efficiency with which research activity is performed at universities. The specific subject used for demonstrating the DEA model consists of all economic research conducted by Dutch universities over a 5-year period (comprising data on 90 individual research programs). We analyze the possible components of the measured inefficiency in each of the programs.

Our aim is to compare the possible advantages offered by the DEA model to efficiency evaluations by experts. Regardless of the outcome of this comparison, however, we accept this latter method of analysis as a crucial part of the quality evaluation of Dutch university research.

The DEA approach involves some limitations that are inherent in the methodology. They will be mentioned in due course below, and they should be borne in mind when interpreting the DEA results. Our aim is to gauge the efficiency of the 90 economic research programs investigated, considering the results from seven different versions of the DEA model, using different sets of input and output variables. (There are then seven different ways of composing the efficiency ratio determined by the DEA model, all characterized by different weights assigned to each of the input and output variables.) Different combinations of inputs and outputs were tested in order to enable us to establish the relative importance of each variable, within the overall DEA efficiency calculation.

The sample on which our study is based comprises 90 research programs conducted at the economics departments of all universities in The Netherlands. Specialists in each field identified the individual programs. The departments belong to the following 8 universities: the University of Groningen, the University of Erasmus de Rotterdam, the universities of Amsterdam and of Limburg, the University Vrije of Amsterdam, the universities of Nijmegen and of Tilburg, and the University of Agriculture of Wageningen.

4.1 Output data

As already mentioned, all data used for our study were brought from the report *Evaluation of the Quality of Research Programs in the Field of Economics at the Universities of The Netherlands*, see VSNU, 1995. We selected the output variables listed below.

Publication statistics. In the research reports, scientific output was grouped under the three headings: dissertations, books, and journal articles (including contributions to collections of papers). Dissertations were classified in three categories, depending on whether the thesis was formally supervised within the institution and whether the actual research was done within the institution. Books were classified into five categories A-E on the basis of criteria such as the reputation on the publishing house, the extent of the intended readership, and language. Journal articles are classified in a list of categories A-E. The classification is based on the extent to which the journal is refereed, an on the language of the journal. The chairmen of the Standing Committee for Research of the Faculties of Economics drew up the list. See Appendix A.

Scientific quality. The assessment of the quality of a research program depends both on the originality of the ideas and of the approach chosen and on the extent to which the results have been communicated to a relevant scientific audience. The last aspect may be inferred from the scientific impact of the ouput of the program and also from the participation and prominence of researchers from the program in relevant scientific networks.

The five-point scale used by the committee reads as follows:

5= Excellent: The research program makes important innovative contributions and is among the world's leading programs in its field.

4= Good: The program makes worthwhile contributions to its field and may contain elements of excellence.

3=Average: The contributions of the program to its field are of interest, but do not attract international attention.

2= Unsatisfactory: The program contributes marginally to its field. In needs improvement in order to contribute significantly.

1= Poor: The program's contributions to its field are insignificant. The program should be reoriented or discontinued.

Scientific Productivity. Productivity depends on the amount of scientific output produced by the research group and on the size of the research group and on the ratio between these two.

For scientific productivity the committee used the followings five-point scale:

5= Excellent: The program has a high output of scientific publications of high impact; it produces considerable numbers of PhD theses.

4= Good: The program has a regular output of scientific publications with a considerable impact; it successfully communicates its results to a relevant audience, as identified in its mission statement.

3=Average: The level of productivity is average.

2= Unsatisfactory: The program has produced some scientific output, but both number and quality of publications are below standard.

1= Poor: The program has hardly produced scientific output and the output is of marginal interest.

Relevance. In assessing relevance the committee considered three different aspects: the scientific relevance of the questions addressed within the program, the relevance of the field for the disciplines of economics, and the social relevance of the research of the group. All three aspects play a role in the assessment of the final score. In specific cases, the committee supplemented the numerical score with individual comments.

Long-term viability. The assessment of long-term viability combines aspects of past scientific performance with scientific plans for the future. It also pays regard to foreseeable developments in available personnel and facilities. The committee used the following five-point scale:

5= Excellent: The research program has a well established, leading position in its field and has clear and scientifically promising plans for the future.

4= Good: The approach of the program has been fruitful and future plans and perspectives seem healthy.

3=Average. There are some hesitations about one or more of the aspects mentioned above, but there is a fair expectation that the group can maintain or obtain an adequate position within its field;

2= Unsatisfactory. The committee has serious doubts about the program's future position in the field.

1= Poor: For a number of reasons the program should be discontinued in its present form.

4.2 Input data

The size of the research group was given in *FTE* (full time equivalents) research input. This input was subdivided according to the source of finance into

- *WP1* = time equivalents funded directly by the university,
- *WP2* = time equivalents funded by the Dutch Organization for Scientific Research NWO), and
- *WP3* = time equivalents funded by other public agencies, or private enterprises.

The research input of any researcher is only part of his/her total appointment, the difference being allocated to teaching and administrative duties.

The manpower inputs considered by the committee further include

- *AIOS* = junior staff, like PhD students/trainee research assistants, trainee design engineers, and other temporary academic staff without a PhD degree; if so desired these inputs can be broken down further by each funding source separately.
- *Others* = senior staff of a similar temporary stature.

The committee calculated simple output-input ratios, in which the number of article-equivalents was calculated relative to the size of total research input (*WP1* +*WP2*+*WP3*). For these calculations, weights were assigned to publications of different categories, with emphasis placed on the categories A-C.

Table 1. . List of DEA models solved

Models	Outputs	Inputs
Model 1	Y1. Quality	X1. *FTW* (Full time equivalents)
	Y2. Productivity	
	Y3. Relevance	

Models	Outputs	Inputs
	Y4. Viability	
Model 2	Y1. Quality Y2. Productivity Y3. Relevance Y4. Viability	X1. *WP1* X2. *WP2* X3. *WP3*
Model 3	Y1. Quality Y2. Productivity Y3. Relevance Y4. Viability	X1. *AIOS* X2. Other Staff
Model 4	Y1. Dissertations Y2. Total Books Y3. Total Papers	X1. *WP1* X2. *WP2* X3. *WP3*
Model 5	Y1. Dissertations Y2. Total Books Y3. Total Papers	X1. *AIOS* X2. Other Staff
Model 6	Y1. Dissertations Y2. Papers A Y3. Papers B Y4. Papers C Y5. Papers D Y6. Papers E Y7. Papers F Y8. Books A Y9. Books B Y10. Books C Y11. Books D Y12. Books E	X1. *WP1* X2. *WP2* X3. *WP3*
Model 7	Y1. Dissertations Y2. Papers A Y3. Papers B Y4. Papers C Y5. Papers D Y6. Papers E Y7. Papers F Y8. Books A Y9. Books B Y10. Books C Y11. Books D Y12. Books E	X1. *AIOS* X2. Other Staff

The total input of research staff was broken down in two ways: first, according to the source of financing (*WP1, WP2* and *WP3*); and second, by category (*AIOS* and Other staff). Also, considering various combinations of outputs and inputs, we were able to analyze the "simple productivity", and the "quality-adjusted productivity" of the various research programs, as defined by the VSNU committee.

Throughout, we used the input-oriented version of the DEA model, measuring both the overall technical efficiency (assuming constant returns of scale) and pure technical efficiency (assuming variable returns of scale). These two metrics enable us to determine the degree of inefficiency of any individual research program arising because the program is not operated at its most productive scale.

5. RESULTS FOR 90 ACADEMIC RESEARCH PROGRAMS

The efficiency ratings for all 90 academic research programs *RP1* - *RP90* are listed in Appendix B, using all seven Models 1-7. The calculations assume variable returns to scale. For further results from the entire study and a general discussion, see Garcia Valderrama and Groot, 2000.

Given the large amount of data of the entire study, we have here chosen to present an in-depth analysis of just a few research programs, selected because of their instructive contents. This will enable us to dig considerably deeper, illustrating some of the finer points and the advantages of the DEA model in evaluating the efficiency of research programs in general. Three programs will be discussed here; they are *RP27, RP25* and *RP24*. See the brief accounts below:

- *RP27:* This research program lies on the frontier according to both Model 1 and Model 2. Using the criteria of the international experts, *RP27*, then, is a truly efficient program. But using the bibliometric criteria (Model 4), its efficiency rating comes out as only 0.45 (see the table in the Appendix). So, here is a case where it is possible to examine in some detail the shortcomings of the bibliometric criteria.
- *RP25*: This is an example of the opposite situation: it lies on the bibliometric frontier (Models 4 and 5), but falls distinctly short of true optimality (the Model 2 efficiency rating is only 0.47).
- *RP24*: This program is moderately inefficient using the bibliometric rankings (the efficiency rating is 0.69) and slightly worse according to the experts (rating 0.66). For this reason, it is interesting to discuss the corrections that would be necessary to bring *RP24* up to the frontier.

The detailed results for the three programs are exhibited in Tables 2-10. Table 2 lists three efficiency ratings of each program model: the overall efficiency $\theta_{CCR}*$, the pure technical efficiency $\theta_{BCC}*$ and the efficiency of scale $\theta_{CCR}* / \theta_{BCC}*$.

Table 2. Selected efficiency measures, Models 1-7. See main text.

Program	Efficiency concept	Model 1	Model 2	Model 3	Model 4	Model 5	Model 6	Model 7
RP27	θ_{CCR}^*	1	1	1	0.42	0.46	0.86	0.81
	θ_{BCC}^*	1	1	1	0.45	0.47	0.93	0.85
	$\theta_{CCR}^* / \theta_{BCC}^*$	1	1	1	0.93	0.97	0.92	0.95
RP25	θ_{CCR}^*	0.45	0.46	0.48	1	1	1	1
	θ_{BCC}^*	0.46	0.47	1	1	1	1	1
	$\theta_{CCR}^* / \theta_{BCC}^*$	0.97	0.97	0.48	1	1	1	1
RP24	θ_{CCR}^*	0.55	0.66	0.57	0.67	0.63	1	1
	θ_{BCC}^*	0.55	0.66	0.58	0.69	0.65	1	1
	$\theta_{CCR}^* / \theta_{BCC}^*$	1	1	0.98	0.97	0.96	1	1

Tables 3-10 all assume variable returns to scale. (This is the formulation originally suggested by Banker, Charnes and Cooper, 1984. See program (3) above including the norming conditions (4)).

Table 3 lists the various additional efficiency indicators defined in Section 3 above, viz.

- θ_0*: Efficiency score obtained from the BCC model;
- Δ: Sum total of all deviations between observations and best practice, see eq. (6);
- δ: Sum total of all slacks, see eq. (7);
- Virtual outputs: The weighted sum of all the observed outputs;
- Virtual inputs: The weighted sum of all the observed inputs;
- u_0*: Hyperplane intercept (measuring returns of scale).

Table 3. Additional efficiency indicators, Models 1-7. See main text.

	Program	θ_0*	Δ	δ	Virtual Outputs	Virtual Inputs	u_0*
Model 1	RP27	1	0	0	0.978	1	0.22
	RP25	0.46	0.54	1.6	0.44	1	0.2
	RP24	0.55	0.44	2	0.543	1	0.12
Model 2	RP27	1	0	0	1.142	1	-0.142
	RP25	0.474	0.525	1.4	0.44	1	0.027
	RP24	0.66	0.33	2.8	0.636	1	0.026

	Program	θ_0*	Δ	δ	Virtual Outputs	Virtual Inputs	u_0*
Model 3	RP27	1	0	0	0.967	1	0.033
	RP25	1	0	0	1.92	1	-0.92
	RP24	0.5885	0.411	2	0.81	1	-0.221
Model 4	RP27	0.4571	0.543	1.04	0.377	1	0.8
	RP25	1	0	0	0.838	1	0.162
	RP24	0.6953	0.305	1.09	0.644	1	0.051
Model 5	RP27	0.471	0.529	1.01	0.515	1	-0.043
	RP25	1	0	0	1.041	1	-0.041
	RP24	0.6516	0.348	1.2	0.674	1	-0.023
Model 6	RP27	0.9356	0.064	19.7	0.725	1	0.184
	RP25	1	0	0	0.981	1	0.019
	RP24	1	0	0	1.001	1	-0.001
Model 7	RP27	0.853	0.147	14.8	0.657	1	0.196
	RP25	1	0	0	0.962	1	0.038
	RP24	1	0	0	0.915	1	0.085

We now report on the results for all seven models, one at a time.

Model 1. Program *RP27* is at the efficiency frontier, whether one assumes constant returns to scale (the CCR model) or variable returns to scale (the BCC model), see Table 2.

Program *RP25* scored an overall efficiency of 0.45 assuming constant returns of scale and 0.46 assuming variable returns. Since the latter rating is the greater of the two, the program is not being operated at its most productive scale; specifically, the efficiency of scale is 0.97. The value of u_0* is 0.20, indicating an activity operating at decreasing returns of scale; each additional unit of input used by this program would achieve less output (see Table 3).

Program *RP24* scored an overall efficiency of 0.55 assuming constant returns of scale and 0.55 assuming variable returns. In this case we obtained the same pure technical efficiency and overall efficiency, meaning that the scale efficiency is 1. The value of u_0* is 0.12, which shows that this activity is also operated at decreasing returns of scale. Each additional unit of input used would generate less output.

Model 1 makes use of the fewest number of variables. The number of inefficient variables is greater than in all other models tested (cf. Table 2).

The aggregation of input into the single variable full-time staff equivalents *(FTE)* does not allow us to determine the advantages that a breakdown into different inputs might offer. This can be seen by comparing Model 1 with Models 2 and 3, where the inputs are broken down by the sources of staff financing or by staff categories.

Table 4. Results for Model 1, variable returns to scale (BCC model)

	RP27			RP25			RP24		
Outputs & inputs	Observed	At Frontier	Virtual Multiplier	Observed	At Frontier	Virtual Multiplier	Observed	At Frontier	Virtual Multiplier
Quality	3	3	E-6	2	2.33	E-6	3	3	E-6
Productivity	3	3	E-6	2	2.33	E-6	2	3	E-6
Relevance	4	4	E-6	2	3	0.220	3	4	E-6
Viability	4	4	0.244	1	2	E-6	4	4	0.136
FTE	4.5	4.5	0.222	5	2.3	0.200	8.1	4.5	0.123

With respect to the deviations between the observed values (data) and the projected or "achievable" values (the projections on the frontier), we observe that program *RP25* suffers from gaps in quality, productivity and viability. It uses 2.7 units too many full-time staff equivalents (see Table 4). This means that there are other programs achieving better output scores and using fewer full-time staff equivalents. Program *RP24* falls short in productivity and relevance. It makes excessive use of full-time staff equivalents (equal to 3.6).

The sum total Δ of all deviations between observations and frontier values vanishes for program *RP27*, since this program is BCC- efficient. It equals 0.44 for *RP 25* and 0.54 for *RP24.*

The virtual value of all outputs is 0.98 for *RP27*, 0.44 for *RP25* and 0.54 for *RP24* (see Table 3).

Model 2. In this model, the inputs of staff equivalents are broken down by categories of financing (*WP1* and *WP3*; the category *WP2* is not used). Program *RP27* is still efficient, but both programs *RP25* and *RP24* obtain better scores regardless of the assumptions of returns to scale (see Table 2). The explanation is the increased number of inputs.

The observed outputs of program *RP25* still fall short of the frontier values of quality, productivity and viability. The major deviation in input occurs in terms of the *WP1* input, followed by *WP3*. Program *RP24* falls short of frontier productivity and relevance. The largest gap occurs for *WP1* (it equals 2.2, see Table 5), followed by the gap for *WP3* (it is 1.4).

Program *RP25* obtains a lower overall efficiency than its pure technical efficiency (Table 2). It operates under decreasing returns of scale. The virtual value of the outputs of this program is 0.440; the intercept u_0* equals 0.027 (see Table 3). Further, program *RP24* now scores a slightly greater

Table 5. Results for Model 2, variable returns to scale (BCC model)

	RP27			**RP25**			**RP24**		
Outputs & inputs	Observed	At Frontier	Virtual Multiplier	Observed	At Frontier	Virtual Multiplier	Observed	At Frontier	Virtual Multiplier
Quality	3	3	E-6	2	2.33	E-6	3	3	E-6
Productivity	3	3	E-6	2	2.33	E-6	2	3	E-6
Relevance	4	4	E-6	2	2	0.224	3	4	E-6
Viability	4	4	0.286	1	1.76	E-6	4	4	E-6
WP1	4.3	4.3	0.119	4.5	2.14	0.209	6.5	4.3	0.154
WP2	0	0	E-6	0	0	0.187	0	0	E-6
WP3	0.2	0.2	2.431	0.5	0.24	0.119	1.6	0.2	E-6

sum total of all slacks (δ) than in the preceding model, Model 1. The program is inefficient, and the inefficiency is slightly more important than in Model 1. Finally, program *RP24* is also operating under decreasing returns to scale: the intercept u_0* comes out as 0.026.

Model 3. In this case, the efficiency ratings were calculated with the inputs broken down by the professional category of the research staff (*AIOS* and Others). Programs *RP27* and *RP25* are now both BCC-efficient. The

Table 6. Results for Model 3, variable returns to scale (BCC model)

	RP27			**RP25**			**RP24**		
Outputs & inputs	Observed	At Frontier	Virtual Multiplier	Observed	At Frontier	Virtual Multiplier	Observed	At Frontier	Virtual Multiplier
Quality	3	3	E-6	2	2	E-6	3	3	E-6
Productivity	3	3	E-6	2	2	0.2	2	3	E-6
Relevance	4	4	0.029	2	2	0.76	3	4	E-6
Viability	4	4	0.213	1	1	E-6	4	4	0.202
AIOS	0.20	0.20	0.073	0	0	9.3	0.8	0.47	0.002
Others	4.3	4.3	0.229	5	5	0.20	7.3	4.3	0.137

performance of program *RP25* thus has improved (it was BCC-inefficient in Model 2). We see here the importance of the composition of the research teams, in terms of staff categories.

Looking at the individual inputs, the use of both *AIOS* and the "Other" category of staff by program *RP24* exceed best practice (Table 6). The model thus informs us that there are other programs achieving better results with less use of the two staff categories. These deviations occur in both versions of the model (constant and variable returns to scale). Also, in both versions the greater weighted inefficiency is assigned to the "Other" category.

For program *RP24*, the virtual value of all outputs is 0.81. The intercept u_0* = -0.221, indicating increasing returns to scale (see Table 3).

Model 4. This model employs three simple productivity measures as outputs: the total number of dissertations submitted, the number of articles published during a four year period, and the number of books published, over the same four years.

In the case of program *RP27*, we see that the greatest shortfalls of output occur for dissertations, while the numbers of books and reviews coincide with best practice. As to the inputs, the staff category *WP1* shows the greatest excessive use (see Table 7). Program *RP25* is BCC-efficient. The results for program *RP24* are similar to those for *RP27*.

Lastly, note that program *RP27* obtains a total virtual value of all outputs equal to 0.377. The intercept u_0*, calculated under the assumption of variable rates of return (the BCC model) is 0.80; hence this program operates under decreasing returns to scale (see Table 3). For program *RP24* the total virtual value of all output is 0.644. This program also operates under decreasing returns to scale (the intercept u_0* is 0.051).

Table 7. Results for Model 4, variable returns to scale (BCC model)

	RP27			**RP25**			**RP24**		
Out-puts & inputs	Observed	At Fron-tier	Virtual Multi-plier	Observed	At Fron-tier	Virtual Multi-plier	Observed	At Fron-tier	Virtual Multi-plier
Disser tations	1	2	E-6	0	0	E-6	1	2	E-6
Books	4	4	0.029	19	19	0.044	14	14	0.019
Papers	31	31	0.008	50	50	0.000	71	71	0.005
WP1	4.3	1.97	0.231	4.5	4.5	0.172	6.5	4.52	0.148
WP2	0	0	0.005	0	0	0.000	0	0	0.003
WP3	0.20	0.09	0.039	0.5	0.5	0.453	1.6	1.11	0.025

Model 5. In this model the output of research is reported under the same three headings as in model 4, but the aim is now to analyze the composition of the input as broken down by two professional categories of staff.

Program *RP27* scores an overall technical efficiency of 0.46, slightly less than the pure technical efficiency (see Table 2). Both for this program and for *RP24*, the greatest shortfalls of output occur for dissertations (see Table 8). Among the outputs, the number of books obtains the greatest virtual value (see the column for the virtual multiplier).

Lastly, the total virtual value of all output of program *RP27* is 0.515. For programs *RP25* and *RP24*, the same sum is 1.041 and 0.674, respectively (see Table 3). As indicated by the intercept u_0*, all three programs are operating under increasing returns to scale.

Table 8. Results for Model 5, variable returns to scale (BCC model)

	RP27			**RP25**			**RP24**		
Out-puts & inputs	Observed	At Fron-tier	Virtual Multi-plier	Observed	At Fron-tier	Virtual Multi-plier	Observed	At Fron-tier	Virtual Multi-plier
Dissertations	1	2	E-6	0	0	E-6	1	2	E-6
Books	4	4	0.022	19	19	0.021	14	14	0.011
Papers	31	31	0.014	50	50	0.013	71	71	0.007
AIOS	0.2	0.09	0.446	0	0	0.421	0.8	0.52	0.234
Others	4.3	2.03	0.212	5	5	0.200	7.3	4.76	0.111

Model 6. This time, the output of research is reported in terms of the number of articles and books published. The articles are broken down by six categories of quality, the books by five categories. This classification was made in accordance with the protocol of evaluation followed by the VSNU Committee.

Table 9. Results for Model 6, variable returns to scale (BCC model)

	RP27			**RP25**			**RP24**		
Out-puts & inputs	Observed	At Fron-tier	Virtual Multi-plier	Observed	At Fron-tier	Virtual Multi-plier	Observed	At Fron-tier	Virtual Multi-plier
Dissertations	1	1.42	E-6	0	0	E-6	1	1	E-6
Paper A	0	1.56	E-6	0	0	E-6	0	0	E-6
Paper B	0	5.43	E-6	7	7	E-6	4	4	E-6
Paper C	11	11	0.035	19	19	0.037	13	13	0.002

	RP27			RP25			RP24		
Paper D	9	13.29	E-6	16	16	0.008	16	16	0.007
Paper E	7	7	0.034	6	6	E-6	32	32	0.023
Paper F	4	6.40	E-6	2	2	E-6	6	6	0.023
Book A	0	1	E-6	2	2	0.134	0	0	E-6
Book B	1	1	0.133	1	1	E-6	3	3	E-6
Book C	1	3.27	E-6	9	9	E-6	4	4	E-6
Book D	2	2.27	E-6	6	6	E-6	4	4	E-6
Book E	0	0.95	E-6	1	1	E-6	3	3	E-6
WP1	4.3	4.02	0.211	4.5	4.5	0.153	6.5	6.5	0.120
WP2	0	0	0.047	0	0	E-6	0	0	E-6
WP3	0.20	0.19	0.462	0.5	0.5	0.623	1.6	1.6	0.139

In Model 6 and in the following Model 7, considerably more outputs are accounted for than in Models 1-5. This enables us to determine the importance of the number of dissertations, and each category of articles and books, in the calculation of the efficiency scores.

As more inputs and outputs are added, the efficiency scores may increase. Program *RP27* is still inefficient, but its ratings have increased, both in the CCR-model and the BCC model (see Table 2). It is not operating at its most productive scale. Programs *RP25* and *RP24* are both efficient.

The greatest shortfalls of outputs of program *RP27* occur for papers B and D but there are also deviations for the dissertations and for all classes of books (with the exception of books B). The program employs slightly too much of the two inputs *WP1* and *WP3* (see Table 9).

The total virtual value of all outputs of program *RP27* is 0.725. The intercept u_0^* is 0.184 (see Table 3).

Model 7. The same outputs are being considered as in Model 6, but this time the inputs are broken down into *AIOS* and "Others". The objective is to analyze the efficiency ratings of the programs with explicit recognition of the composition of the research staff.

The efficiency of program *RP27* has fallen slightly. Programs *RP25* and *RP24* are still BCC-efficient (Table 3). Among the outputs, the program assigns the greatest virtual value to papers C and E. The greatest shortfalls from best practice occur for papers A, B, D and F, and for books A and C. Smaller deviations are obtained for dissertations (see Table 10). With respect to the inputs, considerable excessive use is made of the staff category "Others."

Finally, the sum total of the virtual value of all output is 0.657. There are decreasing returns of scale; the intercept $u_0^* = 0.196$ (see Table 3).

Table10. Results for Model 7, variable returns to scale (BCC model)

	RP27			RP25			RP24		
Outputs & inputs	Observed	At Frontier	Virtual Multiplier	Observed	At Frontier	Virtual Multiplier	Observed	At Frontier	Virtual Multiplier
Dissertations	1	1.51	E-6	0	0	E-6	1	1	E-6
Paper A	0	1.72	E-6	0	0	E-6	0	0	E-6
Paper B	0	5.94	E-6	7	7	0.003	4	4	0.007
Paper C	11	11	0.027	19	19	0.020	13	13	0.017
Paper D	9	10.09	E-6	16	16	E-6	16	16	E-6
Paper E	7	7	0.029	6	6	E-6	32	32	0.020
Paper F	4	5.18	E-6	2	2	0.029	6	6	0.000
Book A	0	0.91	E-6	2	2	E-6	0	0	E-6
Book B	1	1	0.156	1	1	E-6	3	3	E-6
Book C	1	2.61	E-6	9	9	0.056	4	4	E-6
Book D	2	2.84	E-6	6	6	E-6	4	4	E-6
Book E	0	1.03	E-6	1	1	E-6	3	3	E-6
AIOS	0.20	0.17	0.511	0	0	E-6	0.8	0.8	0.046
Others	4.3	3.67	0.209	5	5	0.200	7.3	7.3	0.132

5.1 Discussion of results

Model 1, using the shortest list of outputs and inputs, provides useful information on the use of resources by the three programs. Program *RP27* is efficient; the two others, *RP25* and *RP24*, are both inefficient. Given their inputs, both programs obtain fair results, but they could improve in terms of both productivity and relevance.

Model 2 enables us to examine the structure of the inputs according the means of financing, as recorded by the VSNU committee. Our findings indicate that, given the composition of the personnel by its source of financing (*WP1, WP2,* and *WP3*), the researchers of program *RP25* need to work more intensively, and take more care in the quality of their published results. The researchers of program *RP24* would seem to need to pay more attention to the relevance of their research.

Programs *RP25* and *RP24* make excessive use of the financing categories *WP1* and *WP3*. This information could be useful in changing policy orientation, seeking increases in productivity generally, and in the quality of the published work in particular (perhaps submitting research results to scholarly journals of higher quality).

Model 3 breaks down the research inputs by categories of professional staff instead. Using the BCC model, both programs *RP27* and *RP25* are now efficient. Program *RP24* is still inefficient. Among its outputs evaluated by the committee, viability is accorded the greatest virtual value. There is some excessive use of "Other" staff. The interpretation could be that senior staff (reported under the "Other" category) is dedicating too much time to training or to the management of the program, rather than to the research itself.

Model 4 breaks down the efficiency evaluations by outputs quantified by the number of dissertations, articles and books. Program *RP27* now lapses into inefficiency, while *RP25* is efficient. Programs *RP27* and *RP24* both fall short of dissertations. Among the inputs, there is excessive use of personnel of type *WP1.* This is the personnel category more closely connected financially to the university.

All three programs generate efficient outputs of books and articles. These two output categories also score greater virtual values than the dissertations. This means that the two inefficient programs should be able to use less type *WP1* personnel, and to produce more dissertations.

Model 5 uses the same three components of output but breaks down the inputs by professional staff categories rather than by funding; the results are similar to those of the preceding model.

All programs are operating under increasing returns to scale. Also, for all programs, the virtual value of books is greater than that of other output. On the input side, the virtual value of *AIOS* exceeds that of "Other" staff. This means that there exist one or more other programs also operating under increasing returns of scale that use less staffing input of personnel in training, but producing more doctoral dissertations and publishing more work. Perhaps the information revealed by this model is the necessity to increase quality, both in the dissertation work by the *AIOS* and in the work done by the "Other" staff, training and guiding them.

Model 6 lists the outputs of papers and books by several categories of the quality of the publication outlets. This time, the two programs *RP25* and *RP24* are efficient. The most highly valued output categories (in terms of their virtual multipliers) are articles published in journals rated C (program *RP25*) and E (program *R24*) in quality.

Program *RP27* falls short of the frontier output at the high end of the quality range of all publication categories. We conclude that the poor efficiency rating of this program is due to a lack of quality of publications, and that the program would have scored better by publishing more and higher quality books.

Model 7 uses the same list of outputs, but breaks down the inputs by categories of professional qualification. The two programs *RP25* and *RP24* are efficient as before, and *RP27* is sub-efficient. For the latter program, the *AIOS* input is accorded the greatest virtual multiplier but the greater excessive use is observed for the "Other" staff category. This could be the result of the composition of output generated by the "Other" researchers who have more knowledge and experience. Papers A and B and books A and C come out as highly inefficient, confirming our previous comments that the program could improve its efficiency rating by putting more quality into the work published in reviews and books.

6. GENERAL DISCUSSION

Using the four output dimensions employed by the experts and one single aggregated input, the output factors attaining the highest (virtual) values are relevance and viability. Similar results were obtained when input was broken down by the source of financing of the research staff, or by the professional category of staff. Both productivity and viability (or at least one of these two output dimensions) need to be improved. Generally, the less efficient personnel are shown to be the *WP1* type and the "Other" staff category (although obviously there are some exceptions).

In the models oriented towards quantified measures of productivity, the most highly valued outputs tended to be books and papers. The inputs with the highest virtual values tended to be the *WP1* group of researchers. As to the professional qualification of the staff, input inefficiencies were more equally assigned to both *AIOS* and the "Others" staff category. Variations in input efficiency would clearly be a function of the composition of the results achieved by each program. It also depends on the scale of operations.

Breaking down the scientific output by quality categories, the more inefficient inputs generally were found to be personnel of the funding types *WP1* and *WP3*, and junior staff, the *AIOS*.. These are results that one would logically expect. Researchers with a direct connection to the university, and having more experience and scientific knowledge, typically generate academic output of a higher quality than others.

The present study has been oriented towards the analysis of the relative efficiency in the use of academic staff, employing a quantification of research developed by the Association of Dutch Universities. Our results are only tentative, and should be considered as a point of departure for improved calculations. Also, once all relevant factors have been analyzed, it may very well be true that the efficiency improvements suggested by the models are actually impracticable. Nevertheless, we do believe that our approach is useful for evaluating the performance of complex activities such as those carried out in the academic world. The same techniques may be used to evaluate other academic activities than research, such as teaching and internal management.

It must be remembered that, in spite of the benefits offered by the DEA model, it does present certain methodological limitations; we should therefore be cautious in interpreting the results obtained. In particular, we would like to mention:

- Our model does not perform well if there is a lack of consensus about the objectives that the various research groups should pursue. However, it does represents an improvement compared to the use single indicators.
- The DEA technique is sensitive to extreme values. There is a risk of overestimation of efficiency if the sample size is too small compared to the numbers of inputs and outputs used.
- It is necessary to select and justify the suitability of the type of model to be used, since there exist no definitive or unique solutions. Therefore, it is necessary for the analyst to define, *a priori*, those objectives that the evaluation aims to achieve and then choose the model most suitable to meet these objectives.

7. CONCLUSIONS

The advantages and limitations that the DEA model offers for the evaluation and control of efficiency in university institutions can be listed as follows:

- It is possible to use DEA to measure the relative efficiency in academic research work, in terms of its quality. Careful consideration must be given to the choice of indicators of quality to be incorporated in the model. The indicators should be developed either by consensus between the various research groupings to be compared, or, preferably, by a panel of recognized and respected independent experts. Once the development and measurement of indicators has been accomplished, we consider DEA a superior technique compared to the mere listing of the various indicators separately.
- The DEA model can represent a complementary source of information for evaluating the efficiency of bodies such as universities. Academic institutions often lack a developed system of cost accounting and management control of the various costs incurred in their activities. They also lack a method of "pricing"

of their results achieved, to set against costs in a quantitative cost-benefit analysis.

- DEA establishes a basis for the effective planning of production and use of resources. It enables the calculation of objective measures of results and compresses a large numbers of separate variables into a single indicator, thus facilitating control. A comparison of the performance of similar entities can lead the detection of causes of inefficiency, and to subsequent improvement of efficiency.
- DEA also enables standards to be established based on "best practice," (although the use of some types of values as references may lead to undesirable behavior).

REFERENCES

Ahn, T., Arnold, V., Charnes, A. and Cooper, W.W. (1989). "DEA and Ratio Efficiency Analysis for Public Institutions of Higher Learning in Texas," *Research in Governmental and Nonprofit Accounting*, Vol. 5, pp. 165-185.

Ahn, T. and Seiford, L. (1993). "Sensitivity of DEA to Models and Variables Sets in a Hypothesis Test Setting: The Efficiency of University Operations." In Ijiri,Y. (ed.): *Creative and Innovative Approaches to the Science of Management*, Quorum Books, New York.

Ali, A.I., Lerme, C.S. and Seiford, L. (1995). "Components of Efficiency Evaluations in Data Envelopment Analysis," *European Journal of Operational Research*, Vol. 80, pp. 462-473.

Banker, R.D., Changn, H. and Cooper, W.W. (1996). "Equivalence and Implementation of Alternative Methods for Determining Returns to Scale in Data Envelopment Analysis,". *European Journal of Operational Research*, Vol.89, pp. 473-481.

Banker, R.D., Charnes, A. and Cooper, W.W. (1984). "Some Models for Estimating Technical and Scale Inefficiencies in DEA," *Management Science*, Vol. 30: 9, pp. 1078-1092.

Banker, R.D. and Morey, R.C. (1986a). "Efficiency Analysis for Exogenously Fixed Inputs and Outputs," *Operations Research*, Vol. 34:4, pp. 513-521.

Banker, R.D. and Morey, R.C. (1986b). "The Use of Categorical Variables in Data Envelopment Analysis," *Management Science*, Vol. 32:12, pp. 1613-1627.

Beasly, J.E. (1990). "Comparing University Departments," *Omega: International Journal of Management Science*, Vol. 18: 2, pp. 171-183.

Bessent, A., Bessent, W., Elam, J. and Long, D. (1984). "Educational Productivity Council Employs Management Science Methods to Improve Educational Quality," *Interfaces*, Vol. 14: 6, pp. 1-8.

Cameron, B. (1989). *Higher Education Efficiency Measurement Using DEA*. Working Paper, No. 17, July, University of Melbourne, Graduate School of Management.

Charnes, A., Cooper, W.W. and Rhodes, E. (1978). "Measuring the Efficiency of Decision Making Units," *European Journal of Operational Research*, No. 2, pp. 429-444.

Charnes, A. and Cooper, W.W. (1980). "Auditing and Accounting for Program Efficiency and Management Efficiency in Not-for-profit Entities," *Accounting, Organizations and Society*, Vol. 5:1, pp. 87-107.

Charnes, A., Cooper, W.W. and Rhodes, E. (1981). "Evaluating Program and Managerial Efficiency: An Application of Data Envelopment Analysis to Program Follow Through," *Management Science*, Vol. 27: 6, June, pp. 668-697.

Charnes, A., Cooper, W.W., Golany, B., Seiford, L. and Stutz, J. (1985). "Foundations of Data Envelopment Analysis for Pareto Koopmans Efficient Empirical Productions Functions," *Journal of Econometrics*, Vol. 30:2, pp. 91-107.

Diamond, A.M. and Medewitz, J.N. (1990). "Use of DEA in an Evaluation of the Efficiency of the DEEP Program for Economic Education," *Journal of Economic Education*, Vol. 21:3, pp. 337-354.

El-Mahgary, S. and Lahdelma, R. (1995). "Data Envelopment Analysis: Viasulizing the Results," *European Journal of Operational Reseach*, Vol. 85, pp. 700-710.

García Valderrama, T. and Gómez Aguilar, N. (1999). "Factores Determinantes de la Eficiencia de los Grupos de Investigación en la Universidad," *Revista Hacienda Pública Española*, Vol. 148, pp. 131-148.

Groot, T.L.C.M. (1988). Management van Universiteiten, een Onderzoek naar de Mogelijkheden voor Doelmatig en Doeltreffend Universitair Bestuur, *Ph.D. thesis*, Wolters-Noordhoff, Groningen.

Groot, T.L.C.M. and Poel, J.H.R. van de (1993). *Financieel Management van Non-profit Organisaties*, Wolters-Noordhoff, Groningen.

Hazeu, C.A. (1983). Voorwaardelijke Financiering van Onderzoek, *Economisch Statistische Berichten*, February 16, Den Haag.

Johnes, J. (1996). "Theory and Metodology Performance Assessment in Higher Education in Britain," *European Journal of Operational Research*, Vol. 89, pp. 18-33.

Johnes, J. and Johnes, G. (1993). "Measuring the Research Performance of UK Economics Departments: An Application of DEA," *Oxford Economic Papers*.

Kamakura, W.A. (1988). "A Note on the Use of Categorical Variables in DEA," *Management Science*, Vol. 34:10, pp. 1273-1276.

Kwimbere, F.J. (1987). *Measuring Efficiency in Not-for-Profit Organisations: An Attempt to Evaluate Efficiency in Selected U.K. University Departments Using Data Envelopment Analysis*, Department of Business Administration, School of Management, University of Bath.

Land, K.C., Lovell, C.A.K. and Thore, S. (1993). "Chance-Constrained Data Envelopment Analysis," *Managerial and Decision Economics*, Vol. 14, pp. 541-554.

Pina Martínez, V. and Torres Pradas, L. (1992). "*Study on the Efficiency of Spanish University Departments of Accounting*". Communication presented to the 15th European Accounting Association Congress, Madrid, April.

Rousseau, J.J. and Semple, J.M. (1993). "Categorical Outputs in DEA," *Management Science*, Vol. 39:.3, pp. 384-386.

Ruggiero, J. (1996). "On the Measurement of Technical Efficiency in the Public Sector," *European Journal of Operational Research,* Vol. 90, pp. 553-565.

Sinuani-stern, Z., Mehrez, A and Barboy, A. (1994). "Academic Departments Efficiency via DEA," *Computers and Operations Research*, Vol. 21:5, May.

Timmermans, W.A. (1984). Rechtspositie van Wetenschappelijk (en Niet Wetenschappelijk) Personeel in Verband met de Voorwaardelijke Financiering, *Universiteit en Hogeschool*, Vol. 30:3, pp. 109-127.

Tomkins, C. and Green, R. (1988). "An Experiment in the Use of DEA for Evaluating the Efficiency of UK University Departments of Accounting," *Financial Accountability and Management,* Vol. 4:2, pp. 147-164.
Valderrama, T.G. and T.C.T.Groot (2000). "Determinant Factors for the Efficiency of University Research Programs in the Netherlands," mimeo.
Vereniging van Samenwerkende Nederlandse Universiteiten (VSNU) (1990). *Memorandum on Research Policy, University Opinions concerning Science and Research Policy and the Training of Researchers* ('Nota Onderzoeksbeleid', VSNU, in Dutch), Utrecht.
Vereniging van Samenwerkende Nederlandse Universiteiten (VSNU) (1994). *Quality Assessment of Research,* Protocol 1994, August, Utrecht.
Vereniging van Samanwerkende Nederlandse Universiteiten, VSNU (1995). *Quality Assessment of Research in Economics,* December.
Westerheijden, D.F. (1996). En Solide Basis voor Beslissingen, Effecten van Onderzoekevaluaties door de VSNU, *Research Report,* May, Vereniging van Samenwerkende Nederlandse Universiteiten (VSNU), Utrecht.

APPENDIX A. CLASSIFICATION OF BOOKS AND PAPERS

The classification system used by the VSNU committee of experts is reproduced below.

Books, Category A: Original monographs for a global market and published by well-established scientific publishing houses using a strict referee system. For example: John Wiley, Cambridge University Press, Allen and Unwin, North Holland.

Books, Category B: Monographs for the international market published by an official publishing house but with less strict criteria for quality, for example a local university press. Monographs in the Dutch language published by a well-established publishing house, minus student handbooks.

Books, Category C: Collection of articles by various international authors. Student textbooks for an international market. Officially published reports, exceeding 100 pages, for the international market. Monographs in Dutch published by less known publishing houses.

Books, Category D: Collection of articles by various authors, written in Dutch.Textbooks in Dutch for students in secondary schools and higher vocational schools. International conference proceedings (as editor). Reports in Dutch, exceeding 100 pages and published by a recognized publishing house.

Books, Category E: Reports in Dutch, not published by a recognized house. Conference proceeding in Dutch (as editor).

Papers, Category A: Outstanding publications in rigorously refereed journals.

Papers, Category B: Very good publications, mostly in in English and in rigorously refereed journals. Very good publications in rigorously refereed collections of papers, in English, like *Handbook in Economics.*

Papers, Category C: Good publications in refereed journals. Good publications in refereed collections of papers, in English..

Papers, Category D: Publications in less stringently refereed journals. Contributions to "Festschrift". Publications in collections of papers, in English. Publications in collections of papers, in Dutch.

Papers, Category E: Publications in other journals. Publications in conference proceedings.

Papers, Category F: Publications in journals not mentioned by the committee.

APPENDIX B. EFFICIENCY RATINGS OF ALL RESEARCH PROGRAMS, ASSUMING VARIABLE RETURNS TO SCALE (BCC MODEL)

Program	Model 1	Model 2	Model 3	Model 4	Model 5	Model 6	Model 7
RP1	0.16542	0.23846	0.18159	0.38978	0.33809	1	0.51250
RP2	0.16116	0.23825	0.16506	0.35009	0.35360	1	0.52214
RP3	0.08458	0.13662	0.08572	0.31801	0.30602	0.68364	0.38975
RP4	0.23571	0.28630	0.23947	1	0.65332	1	0.75797
RP5	0.30612	0.30655	0.31211	0.41919	0.44560	0.63392	0.62087
RP6	0.28567	0.38981	0.33800	0.32961	0.28476	1	0.85555
RP7	0.13157	0.14607	0.13598	0.56563	0.48233	1	0.53722
RP8	0.13219	0.13698	0.13421	0.66211	0.54147	1	0.86861
RP9	0.25139	0.32500	0.25521	0.58148	0.43091	1	0.65454
RP10	0.20873	0.24191	0.24830	0.29829	0.32402	1	0.63692
RP11	0.15108	0.17691	0.18661	0.41322	0.38082	1	1
RP12	0.15901	0.57333	0.16226	0.79970	0.34809	1	1
RP13	0.59786	0.70916	0.71330	0.66527	0.66508	0.92544	1
RP14	0.19068	0.31033	0.21519	0.14446	0.30463	0.38063	0.51019
RP15	0.19828	0.26275	0.26891	0.32507	0.35098	0.59800	0.60467

Program	Model 1	Model 2	Model 3	Model 4	Model 5	Model 6	Model 7
RP16	0.09664	0.18750	0.09692	0.40136	0.12534	0.49399	0.16295
RP17	0.37200	0.48328	0.56333	0.35450	0.58034	1	1
RP18	0.43575	1	1	1	1	1	1
RP19	0.37500	0.51190	0.47778	0.62627	0.55341	1	1
RP20	1	1	1	1	1	1	1
RP21	0.25140	0.34959	1	1	1	1	1
RP22	0.27869	0.49016	0.34933	0.72374	0.79844	1	1
RP23	0.93750	1	1	1	1	1	1
RP24	0.55556	0.66154	0.58851	0.69531	0.65160	1	1
RP25	0.46000	0.47463	1	1	1	1	1
RP26	0.44688	1	1	1	0.54348	1	1
RP27	1	1	1	0.45719	0.47107	0.93561	0.85303
RP28	0.53488	0.89333	1	0.96965	1	1	1
RP29	0.31469	0.58531	0.31967	1	1	1	1
RP30	1	1	1	1	1	1	1
RP31	0.13284	0.13946	0.13363	0.33210	0.27834	1	0.48646
RP32	0.19510	0.21475	0.26684	0.29433	0.26143	1	1
RP33	0.27558	0.34822	0.31397	0.47943	0.44665	1	1
RP34	0.31000	0.37200	0.36739	0.33287	0.34945	1	0.81476
RP35	0.21464	0.39169	0.22225	0.24012	0.14573	0.45306	0.31468
RP36	1	1	1	0.15197	0.22306	1	0.49978
RP37	0.22118	0.29325	0.24427	0.59673	0.56441	1	1
RP38	0.20311	0.20850	0.20569	0.61827	0.60503	1	0.96197
RP39	0.57500	0.89750	1	0.42813	0.40556	0.66563	1

Program	Model 1	Model 2	Model 3	Model 4	Model 5	Model 6	Model 7
RP40	0.41050	0.48678	0.44513	0.60103	0.54527	0.77182	0.71478
RP41	0.22978	0.31842	0.23440	0.34865	0.27467	0.68099	0.45194
RP42	1	1	1	0.47405	0.48547	1	1
RP43	0.31028	0.41818	0.33253	0.63161	0.65116	1	0.76582
RP44	0.38265	0.68851	0.40105	0.45035	0.43490	0.50649	0.50200
RP45	0.76160	0.76160	0.79608	1	1	1	1
RP46	0.23566	0.25735	0.23844	0.14706	0.14604	0.21965	0.20708
RP47	0.13481	0.14326	0.13957	1	0.90170	1	1
RP48	0.29151	0.30527	0.32191	0.76946	0.95863	0.92368	1
RP49	0.43396	0.67736	0.46097	1	0.91226	1	1
RP50	0.25414	0.75000	0.25700	1	0.24782	1	0.30566
RPU51	0.68438	1	0.69170	0.30848	0.24140	0.63188	0.4769
RP52	0.25128	0.34074	0.26175	0.51464	0.50216	1	0.76783
RP53	0.96677	1	1	0.15789	0.26087	0.41558	0.53697
RP54	0.63409	0.73421	0.65000	0.30714	0.38588	1	1
RP55	0.49329	0.72927	0.51679	0.38512	0.44850	0.38512	0.44850
RP56	0.62603	0.61095	1	0.80219	1	1	1
RP57	0.53210	0.57253	0.59437	0.34365	0.42641	1	1
RP58	0.05520	0.30891	0.08740	1	1	1	1
RP59	0.14134	0.19845	0.19845	1	1	1	1
RP60	0.06605	0.13992	0.08495	1	1	1	1
RP61	0.11984	0.13848	0.26460	0.83660	1	1	1
RP62	0.19801	0.22338	0.25262	1	0.67599	1	1
RP63	0.18367	0.24157	0.24157	0.46956	0.48553	1	1

Program	Model 1	Model 2	Model 3	Model 4	Model 5	Model 6	Model 7
RP64	1	1	1	1	1	1	1
RP65	0.42453	0.78962	0.50000	0.40071	0.52429	1	1
RP66	0.18579	0.21924	0.33058	1	1	1	1
RP67	0.40240	0.48947	0.41901	0.42658	0.35879	0.76104	0.60088
RP68	0.34871	0.61020	0.50909	0.32224	0.32618	0.52143	0.49753
RP69	0.19986	0.22621	0.29344	0.53288	1	1	1
RP70	0.22667	0.39867	0.23003	0.39190	0.39781	1	0.73439
RP71	0.25637	0.30951	0.26204	0.36363	0.32426	1	0.74316
RP72	0.34186	0.46357	0.34680	0.24925	0.32193	0.60465	0.66667
RP73	0.21327	0.37219	0.25455	1	0.97686	1	1
RP74	0.20691	0.29423	1	0.32400	0.30707	1	1
RP75	0.56970	1	0.88167	1	0.67011	1	1
RP76	0.20769	0.30217	0.27857	1	0.69309	1	0.92922
RP77	0.20961	0.27264	0.21250	0.53787	0.49967	1	0.75706
RP78	0.15789	0.22481	0.16320	1	0.64896	1	1
RP79	0.18559	0.18683	0.20972	1	0.66055	1	1
RP80	0.93750	1	1	0.78940	0.88210	1	1
RP81	0.24261	0.26394	0.24414	0.69852	0.59458	1	0.87525
RP82	0.14973	0.21416	0.15519	1	0.10657	1	1
RP83	0.22995	0.31552	0.23622	0.18160	0.17258	0.24154	0.21048
RP84	0.72558	0.83565	0.97669	0.76993	0.70029	1	1
RP85	0.12712	0.22165	0.17063	0.76091	0.54412	1	1
RP86	1	1	1	0.71393	0.72474	1	1
RP87	0.24064	0.24446	0.24335	0.72457	0.72099	1	1

Program	Model 1	Model 2	Model 3	Model 4	Model 5	Model 6	Model 7
RP88	0.31034	0.32612	0.31468	0.70516	0.67957	1	1
RP89	0.19291	0.21075	0.19873	0.55792	0.51396	0.83357	0.73053
RP90	0.30667	0.49178	0.42322	0.73911	0.85395	1	1

Chapter 6

Investing in IPOs in Technology Stocks

Editorial Introduction

Abstract: Markowitz' portfolio theory is reviewed. In a small textbook example, the frontier of efficient portfolios is calculated numerically. The editor demonstrates that the very same frontier can alternatively be obtained using quadratic Data Envelopment Analysis.

Key words: Initial public offering, portfolio of stocks, balanced portfolio, risk, diversification, quadratic efficiency frontier, aversion against risk, covariance matrix, quadratic programming, quadratic DEA

1. WHAT IS AN IPO?

IPOs (Initial public offerings) in the stock market offer an opportunity to the common investor to participate in the launching of new ventures and new technologies. The precise circumstances behind an IPO may vary, but usually an IPO falls in one of the following categories:

- Under the guidance and nurturing of a venture capitalist or a consortium of venture capitalists, a successful startup company has reached a critical point in its expansion, needing a considerable new injection of equity capital.
- A large corporation has decided to spin off a separate entity, charged with developing existing or new technology under a new aegis. Example: AT&T spinning off Lucent Technologies.
- Many recent IPOs in information technology and on the Internet (so-called dot-com companies) relate to startups that are still encumbered by heavy past and present development costs. Sales

and earnings are on a growth path, but there is still a long way to go before the IPO reaches positive profits.
- Finally, the IPO may be a pure research venture, such as in biotechnology. It may yet be too early to say whether the research will ever result in a marketable process or product. The IPO has no current sales, no revenues, and certainly no profit.

Equity holdings in startup technologies are always risky. Ventures held by a venture capitalist are typically quite illiquid, so that if a venture turns sour there is no way of disengaging. To the venture capitalist, the IPO commonly represents the exit of his or her engagement.

IPOs bought by an investor in the stock market are certainly also risky, but at least they are liquid and can be sold in the market over night (possibly at a loss). Essentially, this is what the IPO does: it transfers the ownership of a startup from a small group of venture capitalists with personal stakes in the management of the company to the anonymity and multitude of stock market investors.

An IPO changes the scope for evaluation and assessment of a new technology in many ways, bringing in new stakeholders with new concerns. *The link between equity funding and management is further attenuated.* As the new stock is being sold on the stock market, some of the former equity holders that used to have direct insight into the management of the company will cash out and be replaced by anonymous investors who have no direct line of communication with management. At the same time, new financial controls will be put in place and more *information about the prospects of the new company and its financial conditions will become publicly available.* This happens to satisfy the various oversight bodies that regulate conditions on the stock market, and because the company will from now on have to satisfy the unquenchable thirst for technical and financial information by the investment community.

The stock market typically has little patience. Under the former terms of equity funding, the owners would take their time, letting the new technology mature on its own terms. Now, there is a scramble for immediate results and for good news to feed the community of investment analysts. The daily price quotations of the stock will reflect the immediate concerns, hopes and anxieties of the investors. For good and for bad, the time perspective of the new venture is shortened. The stock price of an IPO is typically quite sensitive to short-term expectations. The result may be a wave of enthusiasm and attendant price increases, or a wave of gloom and falling prices.

For all these reasons, the evaluation and assessment of an IPO brings in new and difficult elements of analysis (if analysis indeed is possible), that may seem new and strange to the management team but which are common fare to investment analysts. To appreciate these new elements, we need briefly to review the theory of portfolio selection.

2. MARKOWITZ' THEORY OF EFFICIENT STOCK PORTFOLIOS

The Nobel Prize in economics in 1990 went to Harry Markowitz, William Sharpe and Merton Miller. The trio led a revolution in finance that began in the 1950s and by now has changed the world of investment brokers, bankers, and financial consultants. Markowitz defined the risk of owning securities as variance, a statistical concept, and rigorously developed the principles governing the way that portfolio variance, or risk, is affected by adding individual securities to a portfolio. The major lesson learned from this analysis is that a balanced portfolio can offer a superior return for given risk (variance) than a single individual security. This may sound like a pretty obvious proposition, but it was contrary to the accepted wisdom of an earlier era that was preoccupied with efforts to pick winners on Wall Street.

The emphasis on diversification and portfolio management is at the heart of practical investment management today. Recent innovations such as options, index funds, and program trading were all developed to heighten the efficiency of portfolio management.

H. Markowitz (1951,1956) posed and solved the problem of selecting an optimal portfolio of common stocks, striking a balance between return and risk. His analysis leads to the formulation of a quadratic programming problem with linear constraints.

Consider an investor why has available a given sum of money to be invested in $i = 1,2,...,n$ different stocks. Total return R_i on each stock can take two forms: dividends and a possible appreciation of price. Both forms of return are covered by the analysis to follow. The appreciation of price is unknown, and hence risky (the dividend may also be risky).

Let the investor invest $100\ x_i$ per cent of the portfolio in stock i. The budget constraint of the investor is

$$\Sigma_i\ x_i \leq 1 \tag{1}$$

The inequality sign in (4) may be changed to an equality sign if it is understood that there is always available one risk-free investment alternative, say for index $i = n$, which may be taken to be holding cash.

The return on the entire portfolio is

$$\Sigma_i \; R_i x_i \tag{2}$$

Since the individual returns are random, the total return (2) is also random. Next, using elementary rules for the calculation of mathematical expectation and variance of the total return, one obtains:

$$E\left(\Sigma_i \; R_i x_i\right) = \Sigma_i \; (ER_i) \; x_i \tag{3}$$

$$Var\left(\Sigma_i \; R_i x_i\right) = \Sigma_i \, \Sigma_j \; Cov\,(R_i \,, R_j) \; x_i \, x_j \tag{4}$$

where the operators E and Cov denote the mathematical expectation and the covariance, respectively. In words, the expected return equals the sum of the expected returns of the holdings of each stock. The variance equals the sum of the covariances of the returns on all pairs of individual holdings.

To estimate the expected value (3) and its variance (4), Markowitz used observations from the stock market collected over some period of time. These data reflect historic variability and historic risk. But do they present a fair representation of the expected future course of prices, and the inherent future risk of the portfolio? If the underlying probabilistic structure of stock prices remained unchanged over time, it would indeed in principle be possible to extrapolate future risk from historic risk. But prices on the stock exchange also are affected by the interpretation by stock investors of a continuous stream of new information about investments concerning such things as new technologies and new market potentials. This new information may not, even implicitly, be contained in past information. If so, there will arise systematic errors if one tries to deduce future risk from past risk.

For any given portfolio $x = (x_i \;, \; i = 1,2,...,n)$ one may compute the mathematical expectation and the variance, as given by (3) and (4), respectively. The set of all x that satisfy the budget constraint (1) and the nonnegativity condition $x \geq 0$ is the set of *feasible portfolios*. It defines a feasible region in the space of the mathematical expectation and the variance, as illustrated in Figure 1. The origin O represents the alternative where the entire portfolio is placed in cash. The mathematical expectation of the return is then zero, and the risk measured by the variance is also zero. If some part of the portfolio is placed in common stock, there will be positive risk. The mathematical expectation may increase if the choice of stocks is made reasonably wisely and if there is at least one stock that offers the prospect of its price rising. The highest mathematical expectation can be achieved by investing the entire portfolio in the one stock that holds the promise of the greatest appreciation; presumably this alternative will also entail the greatest risk (point *B* in Figure 1).

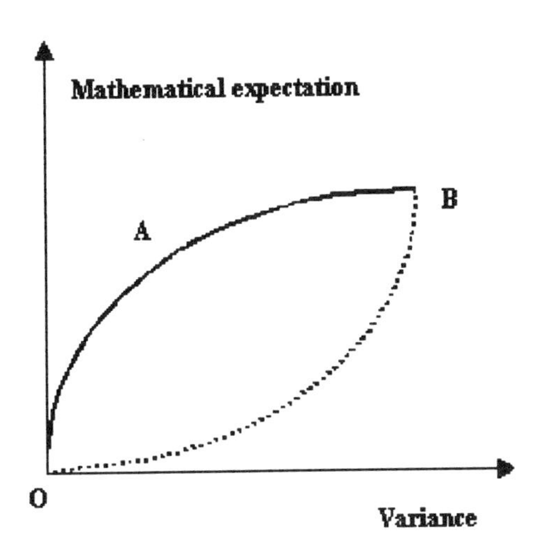

Figure 1. Locus of efficient portfolios

The region of feasible portfolios in Figure 1 is the lens-shaped region located between the solid curve *OAB* and the stippled curve. The solid curve is called the *frontier* or *efficiency frontier*. Portfolios along the frontier are *efficient portfolios*. Clearly, the investor will want to choose one of the portfolios on the efficiency frontier rather than one that is located behind it. For a portfolio to be efficient there cannot be any other portfolio which produces a higher expected return but has the same variance, or which produces a given expected return with a lower variance.

Now define the economic potential function

$$E\left(\Sigma_i\ R_i x_i\right)\ -\lambda\ Var\left(\Sigma_i\ R_i x_i\right) \tag{5}$$

where λ is a positive parameter, indicating the unwillingness of the investor to assume risk. The function (5) can be viewed as a simple utility function for the investor, the utility being calculated as the expected return on the portfolio minus an allowance for risk (measured by the variance). A large positive λ indicates substantial aversion against risk; a small λ indicates only small aversion against risk.

The optimal solution to the problem

$$\text{Max } E\left(\Sigma_i R_i x_i\right) - \lambda \, Var\left(\Sigma_i R_i x_i\right) \quad (6)$$

subject to

$$\Sigma_i x_i \leq 1 \text{ and } x_i \geq 0, \; i = 1,2,\ldots,n$$

will be an efficient portfolio. For the optimal solution must be feasible, i.e. it must lie in the feasible region (see Figure 1) and to reach the highest level of the potential function, we must clearly travel along the efficient frontier *OAB*.

Varying λ parametrically, the optimal solution to the program will trace the locus of all efficient portfolios, i.e., *OAB* itself in Figure 1. For small positive values of λ , the slope of the frontier will be quite flat and corresponds to an optimal point close to *B*. As λ becomes numerically greater, the slope becomes steeper and the optimal point moves along *BAO* toward the origin *O*.

Inserting (3) and (4) into program (6) one gets the following quadratic programming problem

$$\text{Max } \Sigma_i (ER_i) x_i - \lambda \Sigma_i \Sigma_j \, Cov\,(R_i, R_j)\, x_i x_j \quad (7)$$

subject to

$$\Sigma_i x_i \leq 1 \text{ and } x_i \geq 0, \; i = 1,2,\ldots,n$$

The first term of the maximand is linear, and the second term is a so-called quadratic form. Under weak assumptions of regularity, the quadratic form is convex. The second term of the maximand is then concave, and the entire maximand is concave. The constraint set is linear.

2.1 A numerical example

There are seven stocks, listed in the first column in Table 1. (This is one of the favorite examples of authors of textbooks in finance, studied by generations of business students.)

The returns on the seven stocks have all been calculated in per cent of an initial investment. The table lists the expected returns ER_i and the variances $Var\ R_i$.

Table 1. Data for numerical example involving seven stocks

Name	Abbreviation	Expected return	Variance
Anheuser Busch	B	0.312	0.047524
Campbell Soup	C	0.269	0.049729
Exxon	E	0.208	0.043264
IBM	I	0.202	0.037636
LTV	L	0.055	0.171396
Mesa Petroleum	M	0.175	0.2601
Teledyne	T	0.35	0.1521

Plot the data in Table 1 as in Figure 2. We notice immediately that the data points do not fall along a smooth upward sloping curve as in Figure 1.

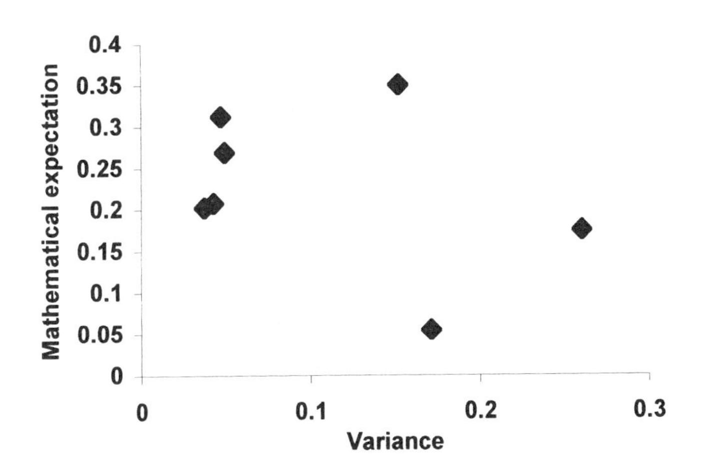

Figure 2. Numerical example: data for seven stocks

The prices that are quoted on Wall Street depend on a host of factors, such as the varying fortunes of the companies. The risk involved is only one of those explanatory factors. For instance, the company LTV (the lowest point in Figure 1) has the lowest mathematical expectation of all seven stocks, but its risk is the second largest. Teledyne has the largest expectation (the uppermost point in Figure 1).

In order to effect the Markowitz calculations, we also need the entire covariance matrix $Cov\ (R_i\ ,\ R_j\ )$ exhibited in Table 2. It is symmetric along the main diagonal. Only the lower part of the matrix is shown. The diagonal elements are the variances.

Table 2. Covariance matrix of returns for seven stocks

	A	C	E	I	L	M	T
A	0.04752						
C	0.01264	0.04973					
E	-0.00272	0.00557	0.04326				
I	0.00465	0.01255	0.01453	0.03764			
L	0.02076	0.01293	0.02928	0.02008	0.17140		
M	-0.00111	-0.01365	0.05304	0.01187	0.04198	0.2601	
T	0.00765	0.00348	0.01298	0.01438	0.05167	0.02984	0.1521

Thus prepared, we are ready to solve the quadratic program (7). Using a standard nonlinear programming code, we ran the program for a sequence of λ-values ranging from 0.05 to 30 (see Table 3, column 1). The results are listed in Table 3, columns 2-9.

With virtually no aversion against risk (the lowest λ-values), the investor buys just one stock: Teledyne, which carries the greatest expected return (0.35). With some increasing aversion against risk, the investor splits the portfolio between two stocks: Teledyne and Anheuser Busch. Already with λ = 0.4, the investor allocates slightly more than half (52.6 %) of the portfolio to Anheuser Busch.

The results for λ = 0.6 are instructive. The optimal solution is still a balanced portfolio consisting of Teledyne and Anheuser Busch, this time in the proportions 61.2 % to 38.8%, respectively. Notice that this portfolio carries much less total risk (the variance is 0.044) than the risk of any of its two constituent parts (the variances of Teledyne and Anheuser Busch, taken

Table 3. Solution to quadratic programming problem, varying parameter λ parametrically

λ	**Anheuser**	**Camp-bell**	**Exxon**	**IBM**	**Tele-dyne**	**Cash**	**Math Exp**	**Variance**
0.05					1		0.35	0.152
0.1					1		0.35	0.152
0.2	0.268				0.732		0.34	0.088
0.3	0.44				0.56		0.333	0.061
0.4	0.526				0.474		0.33	0.051
0.5	0.578				0.422		0.328	0.047
0.6	0.612				0.388		0.327	0.044
0.7	0.636				0.364		0.326	0.043
0.8	0.655				0.345		0.325	0.042

λ	Anheuser	Camp-bell	Exxon	IBM	Tele-dyne	Cash	Math Exp	Variance
0.9	0.659				0.329		0.325	0.041
1	0.636	0.053			0.31		0.321	0.038
1.5	0.568	0.176			0.256		0.314	0.032
2	0.528	0.227	0.021		0.224		0.309	0.029
2.5	0.488	0.227	0.093		0.192		0.3	0.025
3	0.461	0.228	0.142		0.17		0.294	0.023
4	0.426	0.226	0.201	0.004	0.143		0.286	0.02
5	0.399	0.214	0.218	0.046	0.123		0.28	0.019
10	0.279	0.153	0.189	0.082	0.074	0.224	0.21	0.01
15	0.186	0.102	0.126	0.055	0.049	0.483	0.14	0.005
20	0.139	0.076	0.094	0.041	0.037	0.612	0.105	0.003
30	0.093	0.051	0.063	0.027	0.025	0.741	0.07	0.001

separately, are 0.1521 and 0.047524). How can this be possible? Through the trick of a suitably balanced portfolio it is possible to create a combined investment vehicle that carries less risk than any of its individual components.

As the unwillingness to take risk increases even further, there is a point where the investor is able to lower the risk by splitting the portfolio into more than just two stocks. At $\lambda = 1$, Campbell enters the portfolio as well, and at $\lambda = 2$ so does Exxon. At $\lambda = 4$, the optimal portfolio is a mix of five stocks: Anheuser Busch (42.6%), Campbell (22.6%), Exxon (20.1%), IBM (0.4%) and Teledyne (14.3%).

There is even more to the story. With an extreme unwillingness to take on risk, the investor will eventually find even cash to be an attractive investment. The last parameter value listed in Table 3 shows a case where the investor actually holds most of the portfolio (74.1%) in cash. In so doing, the investor is able to push the joint variance of the entire portfolio down to the very minimum of 0.001. At that point, the expected return has fallen to a meager 7 percent.

Finally, the reader is asked to take a look at Figure 3 which combines the data plot of Figure 2 with the series of solutions to the quadratic programming problem now discussed. The solutions trace a smooth frontier such as the one exhibited in Figure 1. But every single individual stock except Teledyne fall behind that frontier. (Cash, at the origin, is also at the frontier.)

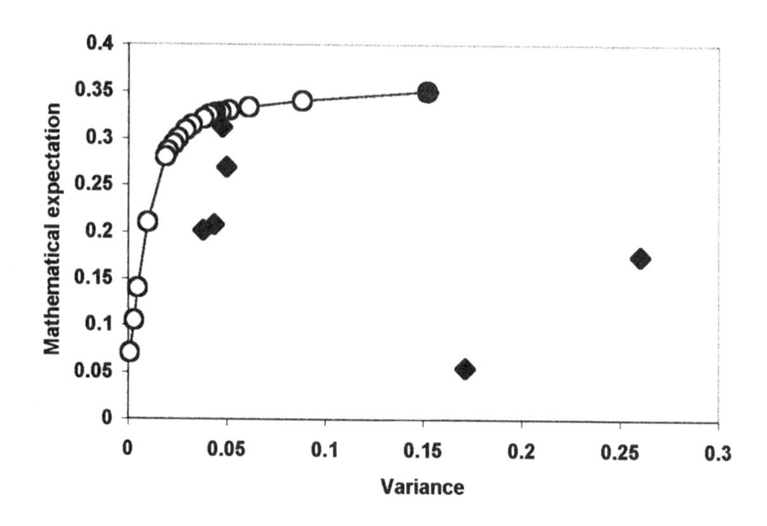

Figure 3. Range of solutions to quadratic programming problem. Legend: circles denote optimal solutions tracing the efficiency frontier; diamonds are the seven given stocks

3. CALCULATING THE FRONTIER OF EFFICIENT PORTFOLIOS BY DEA

Markowitz defined a frontier of efficient portfolios, as illustrated in Figure 1 and computed in Figure 3. Data Envelopment Analysis calculates efficient frontiers. So, is it possible to use DEA to calculate the Markowitz frontier?

The answer is in the affirmative. DEA is a general mathematical technique for computing frontiers characterized by Pareto-efficiency - - one of the most central theoretical concepts of economics, and common to both production theory and portfolio theory. It is indeed possible to employ the basic concepts and the computational procedures of DEA to calculate the Markowitz frontier.

The demonstration to follow should be particularly gratifying for those readers who have a background in finance but who might feel a bit uneasy about DEA. To persons with a thorough grounding in efficient markets and capital asset pricing, it can easily sound downright heretic to speak about inefficiencies, let alone to measure the inefficiency of individual stocks. But there is no paradox or contradiction here. DEA does not challenge the fundamental tenets of modern finance. DEA does not say anything about the effiency of markets. DEA deals with the efficiency or inefficiency of *individual stocks* and portfolios *relative to the frontier of efficient portfolios.* The possibility of such inefficiency is inherent right in the original Markowitz model. Take a look at Figure 3 again. It shows seven individual stocks, and the corresponding Markowitz frontier. One stock (Teledyne) is located on the frontier. *Six stocks are located beneath the frontier. They are inefficient.* What DEA proposes to do is to calculate an efficiency *rating* that measures the inefficiency numerically. That is all.

DEA starts out from the fundamental definition of efficiency. Consider a feasible portfolio x (satisfying the budget constraint (1) and the nonnegativity condition $x \geq 0$). Calculate the mathematical expectation

$$E^x = E\left(\Sigma_i \; R_i x_i\right)$$

and the variance

$$V^x = Var\left(\Sigma_i \; R_i x_i\right)$$

Plot the point (E^x, V^x) in (E, V) space. Let (E^0, V^0) be a single observed stock, with the mathematical expectation E^0 and the variance V^0. We want to compare this stock with the portfolio (E^x, V^x). Using standard terminology, one says that the point (E^0, V^0) in (E, V) space is *dominated* if there exists other feasible portfolios (E^x, V^x) with

$$E^x \geq E^0 \text{ and} \qquad (8)$$
$$V^x \leq V^0$$

with at least one inequality being strict.

Portfolios in the dominating set of (E^0, V^0) are clearly preferred to (E^0, V^0) because they have the same or higher expected return with the same or lower variance. If no portfolio exists that dominates (E^0, V^0), one says that (E^0, V^0) is *un-dominated.* An un-dominated portfolio is efficient.

So far, nothing new to the seasoned financial analyst. But now, there is a novel twist. Adopting a so-called "output orientation" point of view, DEA restates (8) by making use of a scalar expansion factor ϕ, as follows

$$E^x \geq \phi \, E^0 \qquad (9)$$
$$V^x \leq V^0$$

$\phi \geq 0$

Now we say that the stock (E^0, V^0) is inefficient if there exists a portfolio (E^x, V^x) such that the conditions (9) are satisfied with $\phi > 1$. But if $\phi \leq 1$ for all feasible portfolios (E^x, V^x), then (E^0, V^0) is efficient.

Using the above formulation, we can state the problem of finding the greatest value of the expansion factor ϕ as the following mathematical program:

$$\text{Max } \phi \qquad (10)$$
subject to
$$E\left(\Sigma_i \ R_i x_i\right) \geq \phi \ E^0$$
$$Var\left(\Sigma_i \ R_i x_i\right) \leq V^0$$
$$x \geq 0$$

(There is no need to consider the possibility that the optimal solution of ϕ becomes negative, since the left hand side of the inequality $E\left(\Sigma_i \ R_i x_i\right) \geq \phi \ E^0$ can never become negative. Hence, the nonnegativity condition $\phi \geq 0$ need not be explicitly included in (10).)

If the solution value ϕ * to program (10) equals 1, the stock (E^0, V^0) is efficient. If $\phi^* > 1$, the stock is inefficient. In the latter case, we will use the numerical value ϕ *as the efficiency score or efficiency rating of the stock.

Returning to our numerical example, let us illustrate by solving the DEA program for Anheuser Busch. Program (10) then reads

$$\text{Max } \phi \qquad (11)$$
subject to
$$E\left(\Sigma_i \ R_i x_i\right) \geq 0.312\phi$$
$$\Sigma_i \Sigma_j \ Cov\,(R_i, R_j)\, x_i x_j \leq 0.047524$$
$$x \geq 0$$

where the mathematical expectations $(E\ R_i)$ and the covariances $Cov\,(R_i, R_j)$ are given as in Tables 1 and 2.

The optimal solution is $\phi^* = 1.053$. Anheuser Busch is inefficient. It falls behind the frontier (as indeed we have already seen in Figure 2). Projecting it upwards, toward the frontier, one finds an efficient portfolio that consists of two stocks: Anheuser Busch itself (56.7%) and Teledyne (43.3%). The variance of that frontier portfolio is the same as that of Anheuser Busch (0.048) but the mathematical expectation is slightly greater (it is $55.7\% \times 0.312 + 43.3\% \times 0.35 = 0.328$).

Actually, this expectation is precisely 1.053 times the expectation of Anheuser Busch itself (note that $1.053 \times 0.312 = 0.328$). *The DEA efficiency rating (employing the output orientation of analysis) simply equals the maximal scalar expansion factor by which it is possible to multiply the observed mathematical expectation of the portfolio, while still maintaining the same variance.* In the case of Anheuser Busch, such enhanced mathematical return is possible, choosing an optimal balanced portfolio rather than sticking to the individual stock.

The DEA results for all seven stocks are listed in Table 4. Teledyne is efficient. The remaining stocks obtain ratings in this order (listed from better to poorer performance): Anheuser Busch, Campbell, Exxon, IBM, Mesa, LTV. Projecting the stocks upwards, onto the efficiency frontier, the dominating portfolio always contains Teledyne, either alone or supplemented by Anheuser Busch or by Anheuser Busch and Campbell.

Table 4. Optimal solutions to DEA programs, for all seven stocks

Stocks	Fraction of optimal portfolio held in A	Fraction of optimal portfolio held in C	Fraction of optimal portfolio held in T	Efficiency rating	Frontier variance	Frontier math exp
A	0.567		0.433	1.053	0.048	0.328
C	0.541		0.459	1.225	0.05	0.329
E	0.63		0.37	1.568	0.043	0.326
I	0.632	0.06	0.308	1.59	0.038	0.321
L			1	6.364	0.152	0.35
M			1	2	0.152	0.35
T			1	1	0.152	0.35

To conclude, the above demonstration is intended to explain fundamental DEA concepts in terms of standard portfolio theory. To accomplish this purpose, it was necessary to adapt the procedures of DEA to deal with a quadratic frontier rather than the normal piecewise linear one.

(The so-called multiplicative model of DEA involving a piecewise log-linear frontier is another example of nonlinearity.)

Unfortunately, the formulation (11) does little to convey an understanding of other features of DEA that explain its wide appeal. One of these features is the ability of DEA to rank units characterized by a host of indicators, both on the input and on the output side (rather than just a single input and a single output). For illustrations of these possibilities, the reader must return to the main themes of the present volume.

REFERENCES

Markowitz, H.M., "Portfolio Selection," *Journal of Finance*, Vol.7, March 1952, pp.77-91.

Markowitz, H.M., "The Optimization of a Quadratic Function subject to Linear Constraints," *Naval Research Logistics Quarterly*, Vol.3, March and June 1956, pp. 111-133.

Pricing IPOs, Using Two-Stage DEA to Track their Financial Fundamentals

A Research Paper

C. Abad[1] and S. Thore[2]

[1] *The University of Seville*

[2] *IC² Institute, The University of Texas*

Abstract: In order to assess the long run price potential of an IPO, we compute a piece-wise linear price frontier of similar stocks already present in the stock market. Drawing on so-called Fundamental Analysis of stocks (Ou, Penman, Abarbarell and Bushee, and others), stock prices are linked to underlying financial data in two consecutive steps: a predictive information link tying current financial data to future earnings, and a valuation link tying future earnings to firm value. A new procedure of two-stage data envelopment analysis is employed to fit a piecewise linear efficiency frontier to the observed data for each of these two steps. The procedure is illustrated by a numerical example, analyzing five IPOs in the Spanish manufacturing industry (and comparing them with industry performance) occurring in the years 1991-96.

Key words: Fundamental Analysis in stock valuation, fundamental variables, two-stage DEA, predictive information link, projected earnings as an un-observed intermediate variable, valuation link, residual income valuation model, manufacturing firms, initial public offering, price forecasts

1. INTRODUCTION

Preparing for an initial public offering (IPO) in the stock market, financial consultants will make a forecast of the market price that the equity issue will fetch. Based on the forecast, an initial opening price of the stock will be set. If the forecast turns out to be below the mark, the net proceeds to the corporation issuing the stock will fall short of its potential (the difference will accrue as capital gains by the initial subscribers to the IPO). If the forecast is excessive, some portion of the issue will remain unsold.

The present paper does not deal with the task of predicting the market price of an IPO, however valuable such a study would be. Our concern is normative rather than predictive. Adopting this perspective, we shall calculate the price and market value that the IPO "should" (or "could") fetch under some carefully spelled-out circumstances of optimal management and optimal market valuation. For those few corporations that are well managed and well understood by the stock market, this normative price will indeed serve as realistic market forecast. Most corporations, however, will fall short of these idealized circumstances.

The approach to be described in the subsequent begins by identifying a population of stocks already transacted on the stock market to which the current IPO can be compared. We construct a piece-wise linear efficiency frontier for this reference population. A few stocks will reach the frontier, but most stocks will linger behind it.

Our study opens in Section 2 with a brief survey of the recent so-called Fundamental Analysis of stocks, due to Ou and Penman (1989), Penman (1992), Abarbanell and Bushee (1997), and others. Fundamental analysis proceeds in two steps. The first step inspects the financial data of a corporation - - its profit-and-loss account and its balance sheet - - and aims at assessing future earnings. The second step traces the causal link from future earnings to market value. For both of these two steps, we shall adopt a normative interpretation. First, we shall calculate an efficiency frontier that traces the idealized relationship between standard financial indicators and revenues. Stocks located on the frontier are optimally well managed: they convert the various financial inputs into maximal revenues. Stocks falling behind the frontier are less well managed. Second, we shall calculate an efficiency frontier that traces an idealized relationship between various accounting variables and market value. Stocks on the frontier are optimally priced on the market. Stocks falling behind the frontier are valued less favorably.

To calculate these efficiency frontiers numerically, we employ data envelopment analysis (DEA). The idea of ranking stocks by DEA, making use of corporate financial data was suggested by Thore, Kozmetsky and Phillips (1994). See also Thore, Phillips, Ruefli and Yue (1994) and Thore (1996).

A characteristic feature of fundamental analysis is that it searches for an explanation of stock price and market value via an un-observed underlying causal factor: future earnings. Precisely because it is un-observed, fundamental analysis searches deeper, down to the financial fundamentals of the stock. The last step of fundamental analysis (associating future earnings with market value) therefore can never stand on its own. It needs the preceding first step as a prerequisite (associating standard financial indicators of the stock with future earnings). Correspondingly, we shall construct two successive DEA frontiers fitted to the statistical observations, with corporate revenues being the output variable of the first frontier, and the input variable to the second frontier. To be more precise: the idealized and un-observed revenues calculated from the first frontier are fed as inputs into the second frontier.

To represent this cascading causal mechanism mathematically, we propose in Section 3 a novel two-stage DEA format. For extensive discussions of two-stage DEA, see Charnes, Cooper, Lewin and Seiford (1994) and Sexton and Lewis (2000). Whereas conventional two-stage DEA breaks up into two separate consecutive steps that are estimated separately, the new procedure feeds the projected outputs of the first step as inputs into the second step.

Section 4 presents our key mathematical developments for the valuation of an IPO. The only data required are the current financial statements of the IPO. Given these, the first-stage frontier delivers the expected future revenues of the IPO, and the second-stage frontier delivers its market capitalization.

We next turn to empirical illustrations, employing financial data and stock market data for 32 Spanish manufacturing corporations, listed on the Madrid stock exchange during the years 1991-1996. Section 5 reports on the two-stage DEA of all 32 corporations. Five of those corporations were IPOs. Section 6 examines the DEA ratings of those five IPOs further, rating each one of them not only relative to the entire manufacturing industry but also relative to those companies - - and those companies alone - - that were already listed on the stock exchange at the time of the IPO. Section 7 carries out the proposed projections of expected future revenues and the market capitalization of each IPO. Section 8 concludes.

2. THE FUNDAMENTAL ANALYSIS APPROACH TO STOCK VALUATION

In recent years, there has been a renewed interest among accounting researchers in Fundamental Analysis. According to Penman (1992), the main idea of fundamental analysis research is to find which information projects future earnings of a corporation and its book value. Seen from the point of view of financial statements analysis, the task is to identify the information in the financial statements that does this. He argues that for projecting future earnings, it would be necessary to assess a big array of data, both data from and outside financial statements. Moreover, it would be necessary to determine the weights to be applied to each kind of information in order to estimate future earnings.

Ou and Penman (1989) performed a financial statement analysis that combined a large set of financial statement items into one summary measure indicating the direction of one-year-ahead earnings changes. They asserted that the disaggregation of financial statements provides information regarding the information content of current earnings for predicting future earnings. The information contained in financial statements is indicated by the "fundamental variables", those that analysts use for assessing firm's performance and predicting future earnings. The ratio calculations found in traditional financial texts were claimed to be important and the Ou and Penman provided a measure that summarized the information in those ratios.

Lev and Thiagarajan (1993) examined the value-relevance of a group of financial variables used by financial analysts to assess firm performance and to estimate future earnings. They found that fundamental signals have incremental value-relevance over earnings. Therefore, analysts must search for information other than current earnings in order to assess the value of the firm. They also conclude that investors use fundamental signals as indicators of earnings persistence.

Abarbanell and Bushee (1997) examined whether current changes in fundamental signals (those that had been used by Lev and Thiagarajan (1993)) are informative about subsequent earnings changes. Their results support the validity of much of the economic intuition that has been used to link current accounting information to earnings changes. Their results also suggest that analysts' forecast revisions fail to convey all information about future earnings contained in the fundamental signals.

More recently, Nisiim and Penman (1999) proposed a method of financial statement analysis for equity valuation that uses standard profitability analysis. They argued that the analysis of current financial statements is a matter of identifying current ratios as the predictors of future ratios that drive equity payoffs. The starting point for the identification of the ratios that are useful for valuation is the Residual Income Valuation Model. Under this model, equity value is determined by forecasting residual income (also called abnormal earnings), and then the task is to identify ratios that reflect economic factors that determine future residual income. By forecasting these ratios, the analyst builds a forecast of residual income.

They provide an algebra that explains how ratios sum up as building blocks of residual income.

Ohlson (1995) provided the theoretical framework for the valuation exercise. He developed an extension of the Residual Income Valuation Model in which the value of the firm can be expressed as a function of

- current book value of equity,
- the current profitability as expressed by abnormal earnings, and
- other information that modifies the prediction of future profitability.

Feltham and Ohlson (1995) showed that operating activities might yield abnormal earnings; hence, an understanding of firm value requires a forecast of future operating profitability. See also Fairfield and Yohn (2000).

Ou (1990) suggested that, in terms of financial statements analysis, the relationship between financial data and firm value is established by a causal process in two-stages:

- A "predictive information link" that ties current financial data to projected future earnings, and
- A "valuation link" that ties projected future earnings to firm value.

The purpose of Fundamental Analysis may be taken to identify hidden or implied causal factors drawn from financial accounting data, which can be used to explain the stock price. We shall assume a chain of causation is as follows:

Financial accounting data → Projected revenues → Stock price

In this causal process, the factor "projected revenues" is an intermediary causal factor. It is at the same time the estimated output of the predictive information link (Financial accounting data → Projected revenues), and the input into the valuation link (Projected revenues → Stock price). Thus, the valuation link cannot be established separately without first estimating Projected revenues.

A couple of elementary accounting relations may be invoked to identify the two links or stages, as seen within the context of the Residual Income Valuation Model and Ohlson's model. First, and simplifying, write the Market Value of a corporation as a function of Book Value and Operating Income.

Market Value = f (Book Value, Operating Income)

Given that Operating Income equals Revenues minus Operating Expenses, this can also be written as:

Market Value = f (Book Value, Revenues, Operating Expenses)

Given this, our aim in the first stage will be to use information contained in financial statements ratios in order to project Revenues. Plugging during the second stage this projection into the function *f( )* above, together with Operating Expenses and Book Value, the model finally projects Market Value.

2.1 The predictive information link

Our aim here is to identify those financial ratios that reflect the economic factors that drive future residual income. Well-managed companies are more likely to keep generating a steady stream of revenues in the future as well, and this allows us to construct the predictive information link between current accounting information and future revenues. Our assessment pictures the past record of a company, and its future earnings prospects.

Fairfield and Yohn (2000) suggest that a firm's value is a function of the expected growth and profitability of the firm. For financial analysis purposes, profitability is usually disaggregated into assets turnover and profit margin. They discuss whether disaggregating the change in operating profitability into change in assets turnover and change in profit margin provides sufficient information to calculate the change in profitability one year ahead. Their result: only the change in assets turnover provides the desired information, while the change in profit margin does not. The change in assets turnover thus emerges as a leading indicator of both changes in assets utilization and operating performance.

Given this evidence, we shall employ assets turnover (defined as revenues divided by total assets) as an indicator of future profitability. Fundamental Analysis is looking for information in financial statements that gives an indication of future profitability, and assets turnover is an indicator of future profitability.

To project the Revenues/Total Assets ratio, we conventionally assume that the firm aims at maximizing assets turnover, given its assets composition and operating expenses. The projection would then use the following inputs and outputs:

INPUTS: Accounts Receivables/ Total Assets
Inventory/ Total Assets
Fixed Assets/ Total Assets
Other Assets/ Total Assets
Operating Expenses/ Total Assets

OUTPUTS: Revenues/Total Assets

2.2 The valuation link

We have already cited the Residual Income Valuation Model to determine how the firm value is a function of both the book value of equity and the present value of future abnormal earnings. Further development of this model is due to Ohlson (1995) who introduced new assumptions regarding the time series properties of abnormal earnings. In our case, we shall assume that the value of the firm is a function of operating income and of the book value of equity (reflecting all earnings accumulated during the past).

INPUTS:
Projected Revenues
Operating Expenses
Book Value

OUTPUTS:
Market Capitalization

Additionally, one may very well use one or more indicators of price risk as an input at this stage, such as the beta coefficient of the stock.

3. A CUMULATIVE TWO-STAGE DEA MODEL

The production set of the predictive information link is simply an extended classical production function, tying the sales revenues of a corporation to its inputs like accounts receivables, other assets and operating expenses. (See Thore, Kozmetsky and Phillips, 1994 for a discussion of the mathematical structure of multi-period production functions suitable for this purpose.) The DEA frontier traces the geometrical locus of all Pareto-optimal points of the production set. Those corporations exhibit "best practice" in the industry - - the managers of those corporations are able to convert the given inputs into the desired outputs more efficiently. Corporations falling behind the frontier are less efficiently operated. The DEA efficiency rating for the predictive information link thus provides a numerical measure of the aptitude of the management team.

The production set of the valuation link has to be understood in the attenuated sense of a general input-output relationship, not necessarily dealing with physical production. Such similes are standard in the DEA literature. In the present case, it relates the Projected Revenues, Operating Expenses and the Book Value of equity to the Market Capitalization of the stock. Again, the frontier will represent "best practice" in the industry - - the management of those corporations that are able to translate a set of given financial data into the greatest values in the stock market.

The DEA efficiency rating for rating for the valuation link provides a numerical measure of the efficiency of our model in explaining the stock price. If the efficiency rating is equal to one, we can conclude that the stock market translates the listed inputs into a maximal stock price. An efficiency rating of less than one means that the inputs listed imperfectly mirror the entire expected future revenues profile of the stock, and hence its stock price. There must then exist other and unfavorable aspects to the expected future revenues profile that have not been listed as inputs.

3.1 A two-stage DEA model

The model format developed in the present paper employs two consecutive DEA models, one for the predictive information link and one for the valuation link. The two stages are cumulative in the sense that the outputs from the first link are fed as inputs into the second one. More precisely, we shall implement the two-stage causal process discussed in Section 2 in the following manner:

- First, we carry out the DEA calculations for the predictive information link,
- Second, we feed the Projected revenues (rather than observed revenues) as inputs into the DEA calculations for the valuation link.

In this manner, the explanation of stock prices is established through a two-stage process where the immediate causal factors explaining stock prices actually are un-observed, but instead calculated from an earlier DEA optimization process.

For both links, we shall use the so-called output-oriented version of DEA. For any given vector of inputs, this version calculates the maximal array of outputs that can be obtained. For the predictive information link, given any vector of observed financial ratios (see the formulas above), the model calculates the maximal ratio of Revenues/Total Assets. The Projected Assets Turnover is then used to calculate Projected Revenues. For the valuation link, given Projected Revenues and given Operating Expenses and Book Value, the model calculates the maximal Market Capitalization.

Note that for the first stage, all inputs and outputs are expressed in ratio form. All variables are scaled in relation to total assets, thus adjusting for the size of the firm. (For a further discussion of this assumption, and results for alternative DEA runs using inputs and outputs measured in absolute amounts rather than as ratios, see Abad and Thore, 2000.) Consequently, there should be present no significant economies of scale. In other words, constant economies of scale are postulated *a priori* and we shall use the so-called CCR model of DEA (Charnes, Cooper and Rhodes, 1978). For the second stage, we allow for the possibility of variable returns to scale and, hence, the BCC model of DEA (Banker, Charnes and Cooper, 1984) will be used.

To sum up, the objective of the two-stage DEA model to determine the Pareto-optimal stock price of each company that would take hold if

- management were as able as that of the best-managed companies in the industry, and
- the market were willing to accord the stock a price as high as that accorded to the highest flyers in the market.

The idea of splitting the DEA procedure into two or more consecutive steps over time has been around for some time. There is an extensive discussion of various multi-stage DEA procedures in the last chapter of Charnes, Cooper, Lewin and Seiford (1994). Under the heading of "hybrid modeling" (*ibid.*, pp. 431-434), these authors made the following observations:

- The number of output variables in the first stage need not be equal to the number of input variables in the second stage. For instance, there can be additional output variables from the first stage that are not fed into the second stage. Similarly, all input variables into the second stage need not be brought from the outputs of the first stage.
- It is perfectly possible to mix input-oriented and output-oriented versions of DEA For instance, the first stage may be input oriented and the second stage may be output oriented.
- One may also mix the form of the DEA model used at each stage. For instance, one may form a CCR model (constant returns to scale) at the first stage and a BBC model (variable returns to scale) at the second stage.

- The authors also discuss the possibility of using a DEA procedure with three stages rather than two: an introductory stage, an intermediate stage and a final stage.

In order to narrow down the discussion, we now present the mathematics of a two-stage DEA model. As already explained, we shall choose an output-oriented CCR formulation for the first stage and an output-oriented BCC formulation for the second stage. Use the following notation:

There are $j=1,\ldots,n$ stocks. For each stock j, the inputs into the first stage X_{ij} , $i=1,\ldots, m$ and the outputs from the first stage Y_{kj} , $k \in K_1 \subset K$ are recorded .The index k runs over all elements in the set K_1, which is the set of all outputs from the first stage. The inputs into the second stage are written Y_{kj} , $k \in K_2 \subset K$. This time, the index k runs over the elements of the set K_2, which is the set of all inputs into the second stage. The sets K_1 and K_2 are not necessarily identical: the set K_1 may contain elements that are not fed into the second stage; similarly, the set K_2 may contain elements that were not brought from the first stage. The set $K_1 + K_2 = K$ is the set of all variables that are either outputs from the first stage or inputs into the second stage, or both. The outputs from the second stage are written Z_{rj}, $r=1,\ldots,s$.

For the first stage, consider the output-oriented CCR model

$$\text{Max } \psi + \varepsilon\Big(\sum_i s_i^- + \sum_{k \in K_1} s_k^+ \Big) \tag{1}$$

subject to

$$\psi Y_{k0} - \sum_j \lambda_j Y_{kj} + s_k^+ = 0, \quad k \in K_1$$

$$\sum_j \lambda_j X_{ij} + s_i^- = X_{i0}, \quad i = 1,\ldots,m$$

$$\lambda_j \geq 0, \quad j = 1,\ldots,n$$

For the second stage, consider the output-oriented BCC model

$$\text{Max } \psi + \varepsilon\Big(\sum_{k \in K_2} s_k^- + \sum_r s_r^+ \Big) \tag{2}$$

subject to

$$\psi Z_{r0} - \sum_j \lambda_j Z_{rj} + s_r^+ = 0, \quad r = 1,\ldots,s$$

$$\Sigma_j \lambda_j Y_{kj} + s_k^- = Y_{k0}, \quad k \in K_2$$
$$\Sigma_j \lambda_j = 1$$
$$\lambda_j \geq 0, \; j=1,\ldots,n$$

Programs (1) and (2) together form a conventional two-stage or "hybrid" DEA model, of the type discussed by Charnes, Cooper, Lewin and Seiford, ibid. We have illustrated the two-stage procedure schematically in Figure 1. The figure features three axes

- A f irst stage input *X*,
- A first stage output (second stage input) *Y*
- A second stage output *Z*

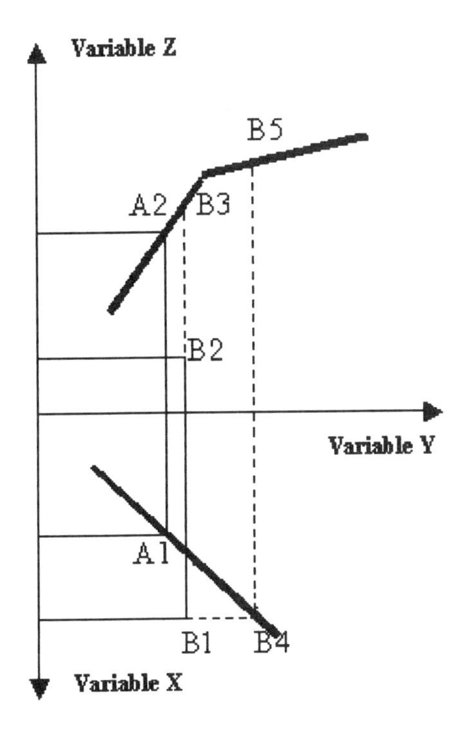

Figure 1. Two-stage DEA procedures illustrated. See the text

Events during the first stage are illustrated in the southeast quadrant of the diagram; events during the second stage are illustrated in the northeast quadrant. We have plotted two observations, *A* and *B*.

The first observation is represented as *A1* in the first stage quadrant, and as *A2* in the second quadrant. *A* happens to lie on both the first-stage frontier and the second-stage frontier. (The two frontiers have been drawn with thick lines). The second observation *B* is represented as *B1* in the first stage quadrant, and as *B2* in the second-stage quadrant. This observation is inefficient at both stages.

Following the procedures of conventional two-stage output-oriented DEA, the two observations would be projected on the frontiers as follows. For the first stage, *A1* is already located on the frontier and *B1* projects onto point *B4*. For the second stage, *A2* is also already located on the frontier while *B2* would be projected onto point *B3*.

3.2 A novel two-stage cumulative procedure

We now expand on programs (1)-(2) in a manner that is motivated by the sequential reasoning of the analysis of stock fundamentals. Remember that the fundamentals of the first stage provide a kind of "hidden" explanation of the stock valuation in the second stage that the second-stage variables alone cannot generate. That is indeed the very essence of the idea of the stock "fundamentals." In order to explain the stock valuation it just is not enough to look at the second-stage stock characteristics. One needs to dig deeper in the causal structure, uncovering the underlying first-stage accounting performance.

To accomplish this cumulative explanation from the first stage to the second, we propose a novel feature, feeding the projected outputs from the first stage as inputs into the second stage. Using Figure 1 as an illustration again, we now feed the first-period projected output of the B-observation as the input into the second stage. That is, we feed the input of *B4* into the second stage, and the projected result is *B5*.

In terms of the variables of fundamental analysis, the second-stage valuation link relates the projected future revenues of a stock to its observed market capitalization. Those calculated future revenues, coming out of the first stage DEA model, are obtained as a frontier projection. In other words, the observed market value is causally brought back to an unknown and hidden entity: projected future revenues.

Turning to the general case and the mathematical treatment, note that the projected outputs of the first-stage program (1) are

$$Y^*_{k0}, \quad k \in K_1$$

where the asterisk denotes the optimal solution to program (1). Next, we feed these projected outputs as inputs into the second-stage program (2)

$$\text{Max } \psi + \varepsilon\left(\sum_{k \in K_2} s_k^- + \sum_r s_r^+\right) \tag{3}$$

subject to

$$\psi Z_{r0} - \sum_j \lambda_j Z_{rj} + s_r^+ = 0, \quad r = 1,\dots,s$$

$$\sum_j \lambda_j Y_{kj} + s_k^- = Y^*_{k0}, \quad k \in K_1 \cap K_2,$$

$$\sum_j \lambda_j Y_{kj} + s_k^- = Y_{k0}, \quad k \in K_2 - (K_1 \cap K_2),$$

$$\sum_j \lambda_j = 1$$

$$\lambda_j \geq 0, \quad j = 1,\dots,n$$

(The notation $K_1 \cap K_2$ means the intersection of the two sets K_1 and K_2, that is, the set of all indices k that serve as both outputs from the first stage and inputs into the second stage. The set $K_2 - (K_1 \cap K_2)$ is the set of all inputs into the second stage that were not outputs from the first stage.) The novel feature in program (3) is the set of constraints

$$\sum_j \lambda_j Y_{kj} + s_k^- = Y^*_{k0}, \quad k \in K_1 \cap K_2,$$

These constraints feed the projected outputs Y^*_{k0} from stage 1 as inputs into stage 2, rather than the observed inputs Y_{k0}, $k \in K_1$.

4. DEA MODEL FOR PROJECTING THE STOCK PRICE OF AN IPO

The procedure for making a projection of the stock price of an IPO now to be described, requires only one set of data: current financial information for the IPO to be used as inputs into the predictive information link. The first stage of the DEA model will then calculate the frontier expected future revenues of the stock. Next, feeding these expected revenues (and data on Operating Expenses and Book Value) as inputs into the valuation link, the second stage of the DEA model will calculate the projected frontier stock price.

In order to accomplish what is desired, one simplifying assumption is needed: the DEA models for each of the two consecutive steps of analysis must use one single output only. This is indeed how we have already arranged things. The account of the two steps given in Section 2 above listed one output for the predictive information link (the ratio of Revenues to Total Assets) and one output for the valuation link (the Market Capitalization).

The procedure is actually quite simple. Fit the piece-wise linear first-stage frontier to the existing stocks, as before. There is only one output variable: projected future revenues. Mark off the financial inputs of the IPO, and calculate the projected future revenues located on the frontier. Next, feed this projection together with other observed inputs into the second stage. Fit a piece-wise second stage frontier, as before. Calculate the market capitalization of the stock located on the frontier.

For a geometrical demonstration, revert to Figure 1. Fit the two piece-wise linear frontiers to the industry. Next, let the observation *B* represent the IPO to be analyzed. Only the first-stage input of observation *B* is known, but its first-stage output is not known. The exact location of point *B1* can therefore not be plotted. What can be done, however, is to project it onto the frontier, to point *B4*. Next, feed point *B4* as an input into the second stage and project it onto the second-stage frontier. The result is point *B5*. This is the final forecast.

The required mathematical developments are as follows. There are $j=1,\dots,n$ stocks. This is the population of existing stocks, already quoted on the stock market. In addition, let $j=n+1$ be the IPO to be rated.

The inputs into the first stage are X_{ij}, $i=1,\dots,m$. Denote the single output from the first stage by simply Y_j. This output is fed as an input into the second stage; in addition, there may be other inputs into the second stage written Y_{kj}, $k \in K_2$. The single output from the second stage is written Z_j.

For the first stage, consider the model

$$\text{Max } \psi + \varepsilon\left(\textstyle\sum_i s_i^- + s^+\right) \tag{4}$$

subject to

$$\psi Y_0 - \textstyle\sum_j \lambda_j Y_j + s^+ = 0,$$

$$\textstyle\sum_j \lambda_j X_{ij} + s_i^- = X_{i0}, \quad i = 1,\dots,m$$

$$\lambda_j \geq 0, \quad j=1,\dots,n$$

$$Y_0 = a$$

The index $j = 0$ now no longer denotes a stock already present in the stock market, but instead the IPO $j=n+1$. The first-stage inputs of the IPO are the X_{i0} , $i = 1,2,...,m$. The output observation for the IPO is not yet known. Instead we simply plug in an arbitrary small positive number, say $a > 0$, $a < min\ (Y_j\ , j = 1,2,...,n)$. Our procedure is then as follows: Solving program (4), we will find that the point $(X_{i0}\ ,\ i = 1,2...m;\ a\ )$ is located below (actually, far below) the CCR frontier. In particular, it will certainly not be a corner point of the CCR frontier. Next, project this point onto the frontier, calculating so-called "best practice" first-stage output obtained as $\Sigma_j \lambda_j^* Y_j$. This is the desired projection of the revenues of the IPO.

The second stage program now reads

$$\text{Max } \psi + \varepsilon(\sum_{k \in K_2} s_k^- + s^+) \tag{5}$$

subject to

$$\psi Z_0 - \Sigma_j \lambda_j Z_j + s^+ = 0,$$

$$\Sigma_j \lambda_j Y_{kj} + s_k^- = Y^*_{k0},\ k \in K_1 \cap K_2,$$

$$\Sigma_j \lambda_j Y_{kj} + s_k^- = Y_{k0},\ k \in K_2 - (K_1 \cap K_2),$$

$$\Sigma_j \lambda_j = 1$$

$$\lambda_j \geq 0,\ j=1,...,n$$

$$Z_0 = b$$

Program (5) is adapted from the output-oriented BCC program (2). The output observation for the IPO is not known. Instead we plug in an arbitrary small positive number, say $b > 0,\ \ b < min\ (Z_j\ , j = 1,2,...,n)$. Solving program (5), we will find that the point $(Y_{k0}\ ,\ k \in K_2\ ;\ b)$ is located far below the BCC frontier. It is certainly not be a corner point of the CCR frontier Project the point onto the frontier, calculating best-practice second-stage output $\Sigma_j \lambda_j^* Z_j$. This is the desired projection of the market capitalization of the IPO.

Theorem 1. Starting out from the fictitious point $(X_{i0}\ ,\ i = 1,2,...,m;$ $a)$ and projecting it onto the first-stage frontier, we have found the point $(X_{i0},\ i = 1,2,...,m;\ \Sigma_j \lambda_j^* Y_j\ )$. This is the same projection as the one that would have been obtained from the full observation $(X_{i0}\ ,\ i = 1,2,...,m,\ Y_0)$, had that first-stage output Y_0 of the IPO been known. Similarly, starting out from the fictitious point $(Y_{k0},\ k \in K_2\ ;\ b)$ and projecting it onto the second-stage frontier , we found the point $(Y_{k0},\ k \in K_2\ ;\ \Sigma_j \lambda_j^* Z_j)$. This is the same projection as the one that would have been obtained from the full observation $(Y_{k0},\ k \in K_2\ ;\ Z_0)$, had those second-stage inputs and outputs of the IPO been known

The proof is immediate and is omitted.

5. DATA DESCRIPTION AND INDUSTRY RESULTS

The numerical exercises reported in this paper make use of statistical data for Spanish manufacturing firms quoted on the Madrid stock market. The accounting information was taken from the database Auditorías de Sociedades Emisoras published by the Comisión Nacional del Mercado de Valores (the Spanish Securities and Exchange Commission). It contains the normalized financial statements for companies listed on the Madrid Stock Exchange. The stock market information was extracted from the database Extel Financial Company Analysis Service.

Spanish accounting regulations require the parent company of a group to disclose both consolidated financial statement for the group and individual financial statements for the parent as a single firm. The database Auditorías de Sociedades Emisoras includes both consolidated and individual information. We decided to focus on the consolidated accounting information, given the existing evidence that it is the consolidated information that is being taken into account when valuing the stocks of parent companies. (Abad *et al.*, 2000, found evidence that for Spanish firms the consolidated information is more value-relevant than the parent company disclosure alone. Moreover, interviews with Spanish financial analysts reveal that valuations of the parent company are based on the group rather than the individual accounts, unless the parent company's activities are highly differentiated from the rest of the group. See Larrán and Rees, 1997.)

The variables used as inputs and outputs for both stages were listed and defined as follows:

- Inventory
- Accounts Receivables
- Fixed Assets = fixed tangible assets + fixed intangible assets
- Other Assets = financial investments + deferred expenses +cash + others

- Total Assets = inventory + accounts receivables + fixed assets + other assets
- Operating Expenses = cost of goods sold + personnel expenses + depreciation + change in provisions + other operating expenses
- Revenues = sales + other operating income
- Book Value = capital + retained earnings
- Market Capitalization = firms' market capitalization in the Madrid Stock Exchange

The DEA calculations require a population of corporations (the DMUs of the analysis) that ideally should be homogenous in terms of common management practices. To obtain a sufficiently great number of observations, we grouped all manufacturing firms together (as opposed to services, utilities and primary products). The number of manufacturing firms in the database Auditorias de Sociedades Emisoras was 47 firms in 1991, 48 firms in 1992, 47 firms in 1993, 49 firms in 1994, 49 firms in 1995, and 58 firms in 1996. Dropping firms with lacking information on one or several variables, we ended up with 28 firms in 1991, 29 firms in 1992, 28 firms in 1993, 29 firms in 1994, 29 firms in 1995, and 30 firms in 1996.

The two-stage DEA developed in the present paper ranks the performance of each stock relative to each of the two frontiers calculated:

- A first-stage frontier for the predictive information link, indicating the maximal assets turnover;
- A second-stage frontier for the valuation link that indicates the maximal capitalization and stock price.

Table 1. Number of efficient firms at each stage

Year	1st stage	2nd stage	Both stages
1991	11	6	3
1992	11	5	2
1993	12	4	2
1994	12	6	3
1995	12	7	5
1996	9	4	3

For each company, we have determined whether it is located on the best-practice frontier for the first stage, on the best-practice frontier for the second stage, or on both frontiers, over a number of years. As it turns out, it is possible to identify a group of firms that consistently stay on the efficiency frontier (in either of the stages) over time. The numbers of efficient companies in each year are given in Table 1.

A novel feature of our two-stage DEA model is the fact that projected or best-practice outputs from the first stage are fed as inputs into the second stage. Actual revenue for all DMUs and projected or best-practice revenue from the first stage calculations are shown in Table 2. Projected revenue and actual revenue are the same for firms that are efficient in the first stage. Efficiency ratings for both stages are shown in Table 3.

For first stage inefficient firms, projected revenue is higher than actual revenue, since we are calculating the projected output that the firms could have obtained, provided they used inputs as efficiently as the best managed companies in the industry. This implies that it is more difficult for these companies to reach efficiency in the second stage. The reason is that we are using projected, and thus enhanced revenue as input; one of the input figures is consequently greater that the observed one. In this way, we are taking into account information from the first stage solution in order to run the second stage DEA. The efficiency rating achieved by a company in the second stage

Table 2. Actual and projected revenues, in billions of pesetas

Firm	Revenues 1991		Revenues 1992		Revenues 1993		Revenues 1994		Revenues 1995		Revenues 1996	
	Actual	Projected	Actual	Projected	Actual	Projected	Actual	Projected	Actual	Projected	Actual	Projected
1	17.5	24.7	12.1	19.9	10.6	16.5	16.7	20.0	26.1	28.1	51.5	52.7
2	40.9	40.9	37.7	37.7	35.3	35.3	29.2	29.2	24.1	24.1	2.9	5.4
3	223	268	171	216	111	154	85.5	102	37.0	42.1	37.6	43.5
4	42.0	45.0	39.6	39.9	31.4	31.4	34.4	34.4	29.3	29.3	40.9	40.9
5	10.2	10.8	8.2	8.9	7.4	8.2	5.4	6.9	48.4	48.4	44.2	45.1
6	-	-	-	-	-	-	-	-	-	-	13.9	13.9
7	15.9	16.1	16.7	17.4	15.8	16.2	17.1	17.1	17.6	18.0	19.2	19.4
8	49.0	49.0	55.9	55.9	57.8	57.8	69.7	69.7	83.6	85.0	91.3	92.4
9	32.8	32.8	37.2	37.2	32.6	34.6	24.7	27.1	21.5	23.4	23.7	27.2
10	45.5	45.5	43.3	43.3	46.7	46.7	55.5	59.4	117	123	104	104
11	25.4	26.1	23.5	23.5	26.0	26.0	27.8	29.0	33.9	34.0	33.9	34.5
12	47.5	47.5	48.5	49.0	47.4	48.6	49.6	51.4	50.9	51.4	50.8	57.6
13	28.6	30.5	38.3	39.5	35.4	36.8	40.1	40.8	41.4	41.4	-	-
14	75.9	83.8	65.2	67.7	63.6	67.9	68.3	71.5	75.7	83.9	15.7	19.8
15	654	654	704	704	673	673	788	788	783	783	822	822
16	36.6	36.6	43.2	43.2	48.4	48.4	50.7	50.7	56.3	56.3	58.5	58.5
17	19.9	23.7	15.9	19.5	18.9	21.5	29.9	30.4	33.0	33.2	31.7	35.3
18	5.1	6.9	4.5	5.8	-	-	-	-	-	-	-	-
19	59.1	65.2	44.7	52.4	44.6	49.9	38.0	38.6	42.2	42.2	42.9	46.9
20	16.5	16.5	12.5	12.8	16.8	16.8	18.8	19.5	15.9	16.7	15.8	17.3
21	17.4	18.4	18.0	19.5	24.8	27.7	30.6	32.7	38.6	45.5	41.6	50.0
22	36.5	38.1	40.3	44.3	43.7	51.1	49.0	58.3	61.4	69.2	56.8	67.4
23	32.0	32.0	33.5	33.5	39.6	39.6	45.1	45.1	47.8	48.5	50.5	52.5

Firm	Revenues 1991		Revenues 1992		Revenues 1993		Revenues 1994		Revenues 1995		Revenues 1996	
24	-	-	7.9	8.2	8.6	8.6	9.8	9.8	11.5	11.5	14.2	14.2
25	5.2	5.8	8.3	9.0	4.8	5.2	5.3	6.0	6.2	6.6	6.2	6.9
26	248	248	288	288	310	310	379	379	395	395	465	465
27	51.8	53.7	55.6	56.0	57.3	60.5	58.7	60.7	61.3	66.6	65.8	73.4
28	-	-	-	-	-	-	29.5	29.5	31.2	31.2	34.1	35.0
29	459	472	545	545	490	501	628	628	677	677	724	724
30	33.3	33.3	35.0	35.0	30.6	30.6	35.9	35.9	39.4	39.4	42.2	42.5
31	128	136	147	152	144	154	157	165	157	167	163	177
32	-	-	-	-	-	-	-	-	-	-	19.4	19.4

is in fact influenced by its relative performance in the first stage. The underlying reasoning is that for valuing a company it is not enough just to look at its earnings figure. It is also necessary to gauge how the firm is performing relatively to the others in generating those earnings.

Looking at the results, it can be seen that twenty-five firms are situated either on the best-practice frontier for the first stage or the best-practice frontier for the valuation stage at some point in time (see Table 3). The remaining seven firms (firms 1, 3, 14, 17, 21, 22, and 27) are consistently inefficient year after year.

Looking at the results, it can be seen that twenty-five firms are situated either on the best-practice frontier for the first stage or the best-practice frontier for the valuation stage at some point in time (see Table 3). The remaining seven firms (firms 1, 3, 14, 17, 21, 22, and 27) are consistently inefficient year after year.

The success stories. Firms 15 and 16 are efficient in both stages during all six years. In terms of individual outputs, firm 15 has the highest assets turnover and the highest market capitalization over the years analyzed.

Firm 16 ranks in the third place in terms of market capitalization in the first three years and in the second in the remaining years.

Mixed results. Firm 26 is efficient in terms of management practices in all six years, and 30 is also efficient for the first five years, but none of these two firms achieve the best-practice frontier for the valuation stage in any year. Firm 2 is also only efficient in the first stage for the period 1991-1995, but then is no longer considered as well managed and becomes

Table 3. DEA ratings at each stage

Firm	Revenues 1991		Revenues 1992		Revenues 1993		Revenues 1994		Revenues 1995		Revenues 1996	
	Actual	Projected	Actual	Projected	Actual	Projected	Actual	Projected	Actual	Projected	Actual	Projected
1	1.41	6.85	1.64	11.9	1.56	3.02	1.20	2.86	1.07	2.90	1.02	4.05
2	1.00	7.90	1.00	4.79	1.00	16.4	1.00	7.40	1.00	6.64	1.85	1.00
3	1.20	4.17	1.26	10.3	1.39	8.20	1.19	4.15	1.14	5.53	1.16	8.05
4	1.07	1.74	1.01	1.00	1.00	1.32	1.00	1.22	1.00	1.00	1.00	1.21
5	1.06	4.89	1.08	2.75	1.10	1.00	1.29	1.00	1.00	5.41	1.02	3.73
6	-	-	-	-	-	-	-	-	-	-	1.00	2.09
7	1.01	5.34	1.04	3.33	1.02	5.26	1.00	3.58	1.02	4.12	1.01	3.96
8	1.00	1.49	1.00	2.26	1.00	2.58	1.00	2.99	1.02	5.32	1.01	4.05
9	1.00	7.20	1.00	7.89	1.06	14.5	1.10	4.16	1.09	1.00	1.15	2.02
10	1.00	4.30	1.00	3.49	1.00	4.51	1.07	2.44	1.05	2.62	1.00	2.99
11	1.03	3.51	1.00	3.95	1.00	5.15	1.05	4.83	1.01	4.90	1.02	5.11
12	1.00	3.23	1.01	4.22	1.03	4.45	1.04	4.02	1.01	5.52	1.14	7.24
13	1.07	1.37	1.03	1.26	1.04	3.53	1.02	3.28	1.00	3.11	-	-
14	1.10	7.41	1.04	8.28	1.07	4.02	1.05	4.26	1.11	4.97	1.27	1.89
15	1.00	1.00	1.00	1.00	1.00	1.00	1.00	1.00	1.00	1.00	1.00	1.00
16	1.00	1.00	1.00	1.00	1.00	1.00	1.00	1.00	1.00	1.00	1.00	1.00
17	1.19	6.39	1.23	7.29	1.14	6.66	1.02	5.69	1.01	4.46	1.11	5.40
18	1.36	1.00	1.28	1.00	-	-	-	-	-	-	-	-
19	1.10	12.3	1.17	24.2	1.12	33.3	1.02	1.00	1.00	1.00	1.09	1.56
20	1.00	1.00	1.02	1.82	1.00	2.68	1.04	3.67	1.05	3.50	1.09	6.66
21	1.06	2.14	1.08	2.54	1.12	3.66	1.07	4.65	1.18	8.18	1.20	9.38
22	1.04	1.73	1.10	3.53	1.17	5.13	1.19	4.11	1.13	3.92	1.19	5.04
23	1.00	1.20	1.00	2.02	1.00	1.54	1.00	2.11	1.02	2.97	1.04	2.70
24	-	-	1.03	1.20	1.00	1.58	1.00	1.00	1.00	1.00	1.00	1.03
25	1.12	1.00	1.09	1.00	1.08	1.00	1.13	1.00	1.07	1.00	1.13	1.51
26	1.00	5.96	1.00	4.70	1.00	5.60	1.00	3.63	1.00	4.33	1.00	5.11
27	1.04	3.97	1.01	4.80	1.06	11.6	1.03	5.95	1.09	8.36	1.12	10.1
28	-	-	-	-	-	-	1.00	7.38	1.00	8.52	1.03	12.8
29	1.03	2.97	1.00	2.03	1.02	1.15	1.00	1.25	1.00	3.52	1.00	3.15
30	1.00	2.73	1.00	4.42	1.00	5.91	1.00	6.62	1.00	6.00	1.01	8.82
31	1.06	1.00	1.04	1.48	1.07	1.84	1.05	1.81	1.06	2.03	1.09	1.98
32	-	-	-	-	-	-	-	-	-	-	1.00	1.00

efficient in the valuation stage in the last year. On the contrary, firm 25 is on the frontier for the second stage in most of the years (not including 1996) but never achieves an efficiency rating equal to one during the first-stage calculations. Even though we feed the projected (and thus enhanced) sales in the first stage as inputs into the valuation stage, the performance of firm 25 in the market stage is never good enough to reach full efficiency.

Additional insight can be gained by looking at the market-to-book ratio of those companies that are consistently efficient or consistently inefficient. Firm 16 consistently ranks among the top three firms in terms of market-to-book ratios and firm 15 among the top eleven firms. Firm 32 enters the stock market in 1996 with a very high market-to-book ratio, reaching efficiency in both stages right away.

The laggards. The market-book-ratios for those firms that never achieve the best-practice frontier are less than one. There are only two exceptions to this observation: firms 1 and 3 in years 1993, 1994, and 1995 and firm 27 in 1994. The market value apparently reflects the fact that these companies are far from the best-managed companies in the industry.

Finally, when looking at the ranking of firms in terms of size, it is not possible to infer any clear relationship between size and efficiency; in fact, most of the largest companies are inefficient in both stages.

6. RATING THE IPOS: A ROUND OF EX POST RESULTS

As mentioned, the population of manufacturing stocks quoted on the Madrid stock exchange during the years 1991-96 includes five IPOs. (For the purpose of our calculations, we define an IPO as occurring in the first year for which accounting information for a new stock listed on the exchange becomes publicly available. As an IPO grows, it will sometimes first provide accounting information as a single firm and later file consolidated statements).

This section provides some detailed *ex post* results for these five IPOs, using the complete data records available. The data include the recorded revenues and market capitalization of the IPOs.

In addition to the standard DEA calculations, we also report on a set of modified DEA calculations, rating each IPO no longer in relation to all manufacturing stocks *but just in relation to all non-IPO stocks.* Mathematically, this amounts to solving

$$\text{Max } \psi + \varepsilon(\textstyle\sum_i s_i^- + s^+) \tag{6}$$

subject to

$$\psi\, Y_0 - \Sigma_j\, \lambda_j\, Y_j \;\; + s^+ = 0,$$

$$\Sigma_j\, \lambda_j\, X_{ij} \;\; + s_i^- = X_{i0}\,, \;\; i = 1,\ldots,m$$

$\lambda_j \geq 0,\; j=1,\ldots,n$ and $\lambda_j = 0$ for all IPO stocks

for the first stage, and

$$\text{Max } \psi + \varepsilon\Big(\sum_{k \in K_2} s_k^- + s^+ \Big) \tag{7}$$

subject to

$$\psi\, Z_0 - \Sigma_j\, \lambda_j\, Z_j \;\; + \;\; s^+ = 0,$$

$$\Sigma_j\, \lambda_j\, Y_{kj} \;\; + s_k^- \;\; = Y^*_{k0}\,, \;\; k \in K_1 \cap K_2\,,$$

$$\Sigma_j\, \lambda_j\, Y_{kj} \;\; + s_k^- \;\; = Y_{k0}\,, \;\; k \in K_2 - (K_1 \cap K_2)\,,$$

$$\Sigma_j\, \lambda_j \; = 1$$

$\lambda_j \geq 0,\; j=1,\ldots,n,$ and $\lambda_j = 0$ for all IPO stocks

for the second stage. In simple words, this is to treat the IPOs as a set of truly new observations distinct from the earlier ones and keeping the performance of the IPOs and the existing stocks apart in the ratings. Existing stocks are rated only in relation to each other, and no existing stock is rated in relation to an IPO. The IPOs are rated only in relation to the existing stocks, and not in relation to other IPOs (or to itself).

Speaking in geometric terms, the possibility then presents itself that the IPO observation lies above the efficiency frontier to the existing stocks - - that the IPO is "hyper-efficient". Should that happen, the efficiency rating ψ^* solved from programs (6) and (7) will then be less than one.

Starting our calculations with the year of 1991, Ebro Agricolas Compania de Alimentacion (firm 31) made its debut on the stock exchange that year. Referring to Table 3, we see that its efficiency rating for the production stage was 1.06 - - in other words, it was slightly CCR inefficient. The reference firms were firms 8, 16 and 23 with the optimal λ weights

$\lambda_8 = 0.234,\; \lambda_{16} = 0.313,\; \lambda_{23} = 0.216$ (and all other λ's $= 0$).

Since the weights add up to less than unity, the company operated under increasing returns to scale at its introduction on the exchange. In the second stage, the company was BCC efficient.

Dropping Ebro from the set of permissible reference companies (setting $\lambda_{31} = 0$ in programs 6 and 7), the results for the first stage obviously remain the same, but the efficiency rating for the second stage now is 0.760, meaning that this stock is "hyper-efficient" relative to the existing stocks. The projected market capitalization of Ebro, located along the efficiency frontier of the existing stocks, would have been only 76 % of the actual market capitalization! Here is a strong indication that this stock was greatly overpriced at the time of its IPO.

The DEA calculations for Ebro for the subsequent years (Table 3, 1992 - 1996)) indicate a company that was reasonably well managed every year, although it never achieved full efficiency (the DEA ratings for the predictive information link stay in the interval 1.04 - 1.09). The ratings for the market stage during the subsequent years varied over the interval 1.480 - 2.031 indicating that the stock price was still far below the frontier projection.

Actual events in many ways bear out the results of our analysis. The stock lost more than half its value right away during 1992. Later it recuperated slowly. The net annualized result over the time period studied nevertheless came in at a loss of 8.8% per annum.

Moving on to the year 1992, Azkoyen (firm 24) enters the statistics this year. (The company actually had its IPO in 1991 but has filed consolidated statements since 1992.) Its efficiency rating for the production stage that year was 1.03 -- quite close to CCR efficiency. The reference firms are 8, 9 and 16 with the weights

$$\lambda_8 = 0.343,\ \lambda_9 = 0.206,\ \lambda_{16} = 0.377,\ \lambda_{30} = 0.037 \text{ and all other } \lambda\text{'s} = 0.$$

The weights add up to slightly less than unity; hence, the company operated under increasing returns to scale at its introduction on the exchange.

The efficiency rating for Azkoyen for the valuation stage was 1.20. This indicates that the IPO price was 20 per cent below the prices fetched by comparable stocks.

The DEA calculations the following years indicate a very well managed company (Table 3). The efficiency score for the production stage was equal to 1.000 all four years 1993-1996, indicating a frontier assets turnover ratio. The DEA rating for the market stage was 1.105 in 1992 and 1.583 in 1994, indicating a stock price still falling behind its potential. During the two last years, the company stayed at the market frontier with the stock price faithfully mirroring the shifting potential of the industry.

Actual events confirm the encouraging DEA prognosis. The stock price of Azkoyen more than doubled right away in 1993, and continued to grow strongly in 1994. It fell back in 1995 but doubled again in 1996. The net annualized result was a growth of 62.9% per annum, the second best performance of all stocks in the entire industry.

There were no IPOs in 1993. The following year, 1994, Omsa Alimentacion (firm 28) enters our statistics. (The company actually had its IPO in 1992 and has filed consolidated statements since 1994). This company seems to have had excellent management. Revenues were close to, or equal to, efficiency in every year following the IPO (the DEA rating for the predictive information link was 1.000 in 1994-95 and 1.027 in 1996.

Dropping Omsa from the set of admissible reference companies in 1994, solution of program (6) with $\lambda_{28} = 0$ yields the efficiency rating 0.968. In other words, OMSA is slightly hyper-efficient relative to the existing stocks. The reference firms are 2, 23 and 26 with the weights

$$\lambda_2 = 0.390,\ \lambda_{23} = 0.077, \text{ and } \lambda_{26} = 0.492.$$

The weights add up to 0.959, indicating increasing returns to scale.

The efficiency rating for Omsa for the valuation stage in 1994 comes out as 7.38, which seems to indicate that this stock was greatly under-priced at the time of its IPO (the frontier price would have been more than seven times the actual price). The calculations for the following years indicate a continuing huge gap between the actual market price and its frontier potential. The ratings for the market stage for the 1995 and 1996 come out as 8.52 and 12.75, respectively.

Yet, this IPO did not fare well. Its stock price fell by 19 % in 1995, and continued to fall in 1996. Our calculations do not reveal the root cause of this malaise. Obviously, the market had access to some bad news depressing the stock price that our own calculations have failed to register.

There were no manufacturing IPOs in the year of 1995. In 1996, there were two: Miguel y Costas (firm 6) and Telepizza (firm 32). Miguel y Costas had its IPO in late 1996. Carrying out the standard DEA calculations, we obtain an efficiency rating of 1.00 for the production stage. Next, dropping Miguel y Costas and Telepizza from the set of permissible reference companies, the rating of Miguel y Costas falls to 0.900. The reference firms are 5, 11, 23, and 26 with the weights

$$\lambda_5 = 0.214,\ \lambda_{11} = 0.047,\ \lambda_{23} = 0.630, \text{ and } \lambda_{26} = 0037.$$

The weights add up to 0.928, indicating increasing returns to scale.

The Madrid stock market, however, seems greatly to have underestimated the potential value of this stock, arriving at a stock price that fell more than half short of its potential. Miguel y Costas' efficiency rating for the valuation stage is 2.09. The reference firms are 2 and 32, with the weights $\lambda_2 = 0.401$ and $\lambda_{32} = 0.599$ respectively. As it so happens, the reference firm 32 is the other IPO that same year. Dropping both IPOs from the reference set, the rating of Miguel y Costas falls to 1.78. The reference firms now are 2 and 24, with the weights

$\lambda_2 = 0.194$ $\lambda_2 = 0.401$ and $\lambda_{32} = 0.599$

respectively.

Telepizza went to the market in November, 1996. Telepizza is a chain of pizza restaurants that also provide pizza delivery. It was born in 1988 and has had a significant growth: from 2 restaurants and 85 employees in 1988, to 590 restaurants and 22900 employees in 1998. Its sales have grown from 7,782 millions pesetas in 1988 to more than 31,000 millions pesetas in 1998.

Telepizza is rated as efficient in both the production and valuation stage. Dropping Miguel y Costas and Telepizza from the set of permissible reference companies, the rating for the production stage drops to 0.506. In other words, actual revenues of Telepizza are almost twice their (frontier) potential. There is just one single reference company: firm 29 with the weight $\lambda_{29} = 0.350$. Since this single weight is less than 1, there are increasing returns to scale.

The rating for the valuation stage drops dramatically, to 0.085, indicating that the IPO price of Telepizza was more than 10 times greater than its frontier price! In other words, this company would seem to be wildly overpriced at the time of its IPO. The set of reference companies still consists of a single firm, this time firm 2.

One may speculate that there is a connection between these observations for the production and valuation stage. Was it perhaps because the revenues of this stock so greatly exceeded their long-run potential that the IPO price was bid up so dramatically?

7. PRICING THE IPOS: THE EX ANTE FORECASTS

We are now ready to return to the task of forecasting the price and the market capitalization of an IPO. For each of the five IPOs under study, we assume that only the input variables to the DEA calculations at each stage are available. The task is to forecast the outputs.

More precisely, we assume that the following financial ratios have been observed for the first stage calculations: accounts receivables, inventory, fixed assets, other assets, and operating expenses, all calculated as a ratio of total assets. But the output variable revenues/assets is not available. Instead, a projection of this ratio is to be made. Further, the following inputs for the second stage calculations have been observed: operating expenses and book value. But the actual market capitalization is not available. Instead, the projected market capitalization is to be estimated.

Turning to the mathematical machinery developed in Section 4, it so happens that the desired *ex ante* projections are already at hand. This follows from the following

Theorem 2. The optimal projected output $\Sigma_j \lambda_j {}^*Y_j$ obtained from the first-stage program (6) actually is identical to that calculated from program (4). The optimal projected output $\Sigma_j \lambda_j {}^*Z_j$ obtained from the second-stage program (7) is identical to that calculated from program (5).

The proof is immediate, noting that the envelopes defined by the two sets of programs are actually identical. In the one case, the IPO under consideration has been assigned arbitrary low outputs (a and b, respectively) to make sure that it lies well below the first-stage and second-stage envelopes. The other IPOs are not even participating in the calculations (4) and (5). In the other case, all IPOs have been excluded from the reference sets to begin with. The resulting envelopes are the same.

Now refer to Table 4. Column (i) lists the IPOs. Column (ii) lists the results from the first stage projections, projecting the observed revenues/total asset ratio onto the envelope that spans all existing stocks at the time of the IPO (but excluding the IPO itself). The figure in column (iv) is the projected revenues/total assets ratio multiplied by total assets. Column (vi) gives the results from the second stage projections, again excluding the IPO from the set of permissible reference stocks.

Beginning with *Ebro*, remember that this firm was first-stage inefficient at the time of its IPO (in 1991). Consequently, whether Ebro is included in the DEA calculations or not, the first stage envelope is actually the same.

Table 4. Results of IPO projections

(i) IPO	(ii) Projected ratio revenues/ total assets	(iii) Actual ratio revenues/ total assets	(iv) Projected revenues, billions of pesetas	(v) Actual revenues, billions of pesetas	(vi) Projected capitaliz'n, billions of pesetas	(vii) Actual capitaliz'n, billions of pesetas
Ebro, 91	0.874	0.822	135.7	127.6	86.87	114.37
Askoyen, 92	1.203	1.165	8.19	7.94	4.63	3.88
Omsa, 94	2.133	2.204	28.58	29.53	56.34	7.64
Miguel y Costas, 96	0.835	0.927	12.47	13.85	22.68	12.78
Telepizza, 96	1.022	2.021	9.79	19.37	3.58	42.07

The projections are then also the same, and the projected revenue for Ebro listed in Table 4 coincides with the projected revenue listed in Table 2. The projected revenue of 135.7 million pesetas is a bit more than actual revenues. For the second stage, our calculations showed that Ebro is located at some considerable distance above the efficiency frontier (it was hyper-efficient with an efficiency rating of 0.760). Its projected frontier capitalization was only 86.87 million, well below the actual figure.

Azkoyen was inefficient during both stages for 1992. It does not matter whether Azkoyen is included in the set of permissible reference stocks or not: the results of the DEA runs for both stages are the same. Projected revenues are 8.19 million, the same figure as that reported in Table 2. The projected capitalization is 4.63 million.

Omsa entered the stock market above the 1994 frontier of existing stocks (it was slightly hyper-efficient). The projected frontier revenues of 28.58 million fall below actual revenues. In the second stage, Omsa was strongly inefficient. The projected market capitalization of 56.35 million exceeds the actual figure by almost 8 times.

Miguel y Costas comes out as being located above the first-stage 1996 frontier of existing stocks (it was hyper-efficient). Projected frontier revenues of 12.47 million fall below actual revenues. In the second stage, Miguel y Costas falls behind the peer frontier. Its projected market capitalization of 22.68 million is almost twice its actual value.

Telepizza was the second IPO in 1996. It presents the remarkable spectacle of being launched above both the first-stage frontier and the second-stage frontier. Projected frontier revenues of 9.79 million were about half actual revenues. Its projected market capitalization of 3.58 million is less than a tenth of the value assigned by the stock market.

8. CONCLUDING REMARKS

In the pages above, we have shown how it is possible to give the recent ideas of Fundamental Analysis of the valuation of stocks a precise mathematical content, using two-stage data envelopment analysis (DEA). Fundamental analysis reconstructs the intrinsic value of a stock in two stages: In the first instance it searches the profit-and-loss statement and the balance sheet to gauge the earnings potential of the stock. In a second and final stage it establishes a relationship between the earnings potential (together with other data) and the market price. DEA fits an "envelope" or frontier to each of these stages. Each frontier is piece-wise linear and it is fitted to span the "best" stocks in the industry. These stocks are termed "efficient." Others lie behind the frontier. They are inefficient.

In the first-stage calculations reported here, the revenues/assets ratio of each stock was compared to a number of underlying financial ratios, such as the ratio of accounts receivables, inventory, and fixed assets, to total assets. Efficiency in this first stage is a measure of outstanding management. Inefficiency means that the mentioned ratio falls short of what other comparable stocks achieve, so that the stock falls below the frontier spanning the industry. In the second-stage calculations, the capitalization of each stock was compared to the projected revenues (obtained from the first stage), the book value of equity and operating expenses. Efficiency at this stage means an outstanding evaluation by investors in the stock market. Inefficiency means that the price falls short of what other comparable stocks have reached, so that the stock falls below the capitalization frontier.

DEA is sometimes termed a "one-sided" estimation technique, meaning that all observations lie on the frontier or on one side of the frontier: below it. (Statistical regression analysis is "two-sided" because observations lie on both sides of the fitted regression relationship.) There is much to be said for such an approach in financial studies, where the analyst (and investor) is searching for optimally performing stocks and the maximization of returns on a portfolio. Fundamental analysis will then relate the performance of a given stock to the frontier of the entire industry to which it belongs (or some other suitable subset of stocks quoted on the stock exchange). Efficient stocks have only other efficient stocks as peers and do not stand back to any stock. An inefficient stock is related to the superior performance of a few "reference stocks" that define the linear facet on the frontier. Projecting the inefficient stock onto this facet, one finds the hypothetical best performance that the stock should have achieved, had it performed at par with the efficient ones.

This analysis may seem reasonable enough, investigating a set of established stocks. But the idea of one-sidedness certainly cannot apply to the case of IPOs on the stock market. There is no reason why an initial public offering should be contained by a frontier estimated to fit the existing stocks. An IPO may be highly successful, breaking the pattern of the existing stocks. An IPO may enter the stock market above the frontier - - on the other side of the frontier.

There are two ways of evaluating such an event. In both cases, the inputs into the calculations are the financial ratios brought from the balance sheet of the IPO, its book value of equity and its operating expenses. One evaluation is ex ante, the other is ex post:

In many instances, the analyst may desire to make an early forecast of the revenues and the capitalization of an IPO that will hold once it is launched on the stock market. As explained in the paper, the forecast of the revenues potential of the stock is obtained by projecting the financial ratios onto the first-stage frontier. Next, the forecast of the market capitalization and the price is obtained by projecting the projected revenues potential, the book value of equity and operating expenses onto the second-stage frontier. The details of the calculations were illustrated using data for five IPOs on the Madrid stock exchange during the years 1991-1996.

Once the ex post data on revenues and market capitalization are known, the performance of an IPO relative to the industry frontier may be gauged. Three of the five IPOs that we investigated (see Table 4) turned out to fall behind the frontier. Their stocks were inefficient and under-valued, relative to what other comparable stocks in the industry were able to achieve. Two of the five IPOs fell above the frontier. Those stocks were hyper-efficient and over-priced, relative to what other comparable stocks were fetching.

REFERENCES

Abad, C., García-Borbolla, A., Garrod, N., Laffarga, J., Larrán, M. and Piñero, J. (2000): "An Evaluation of the Value Relevance of Consolidated versus Unconsolidated Accounting Information: Evidence from Quoted Spanish Firms," *Journal of International Financial Management and Accounting*, Vol. 11:3, pp. 156-177.

Abad, C. , Thore, S, and Laffarga, J. (2000) "Fundamental Analysis of Stocks by Two-Stage DEA," presented at the INFORMS 2000 Annual Meeting in San Antonio, Texas.

Abarbanell, J.S. and Bushee, B.J. (1997): "Fundamental Analysis, Future Earnings and Stock Prices," *Journal of Accounting Research*, Vol. 35:1, pp. 1-24.

Abarbanell, J.S. and Bushee, B.J. (1998): "Abnormal Returns to a Fundamental Analysis Strategy," *The Accounting Review*, Vol. 73:1, pp. 19-45.

Banker, R.D., Charnes, A. and Cooper, W.W. (1984): "Models for Estimation of Technical and Scale Inefficiencies in Data Envelopment Analysis," *Management Science*, Vol. 30:9, pp. 1078-1092.

Charnes, A., Cooper, W.W., Lewin, A.Y. and Seiford, L.M. (1994): *Data Envelopment Analysis: Theory, Methodology and Applications*, Kluwer Academic Publishers, Dordrecht.

Charnes, A., Cooper, W.W. and Rhodes, E. (1978): "Measuring the Efficiency of Decision Making Units," *European Journal of Operational Research*, Vol. 2:6, pp. 429-444.

Farfield, P.M. and Yohn, T.L. (2000): "Using Asset Turnover and Profit Margin to Forecast Changes in Profitability," Working paper, Georgetown University.

Feltham, G. and Ohlson, J. (1995): "Valuation and Clean Surplus Accounting for Operating and Financial Activities," *Contemporary Accounting Research*, Vol.11:2, pp. 689-731.

Larrán, M. and Rees, W. (1997): "Forecast Accuracy and Practices in Spain". Paper presented at the European Accounting Association Annual Congress, Graz, Austria.

Lev, B. and Thiagarajan, S.R. (1993): "Fundamental Information Analysis," *Journal of Accounting Research*, Vol. 31:2, pp. 190-215.

Nissim, D. and Penman, S.P. (1999): "Ratio Analysis and Equity Valuation". Working paper, Columbia University.

Ou, J.A. (1990): "The Information Content of Non-earnings Accounting Numbers as Earnings Predictors," *Journal of Accounting Research*, Vol. 28, pp. 144-163.

Ou, J.A. and Penman, S.H. (1989): "Financial Statement Analysis and the Prediction of Stock Returns," *Journal of Accounting and Economics*, Vol. 11, pp. 295-329.

Ohlson, J. (1995): "Earnings, Book Values and Dividends in Equity Valuation," *Contemporary Accounting Research*. Vol.11:2, pp. 661-87.

Penman, S.H. (1992): "Returns to Fundamentals," *Journal of Accounting, Auditing and Finance*, No.7, pp. 465-483.

Salinas-Jiménez, J. and Smith, P. (1996): "Data Envelopment Analysis Applied to Quality in Primary Health Care". *Annals of Operations Research*. Vol. 67, pp. 141-161.

Sexton, T. R. and Lewis, H.F. (2000): "Two-Stage DEA: An Application to Major League Baseball". Working paper. State University of New York at Stony Brook

Thore, S., Kozmetsky, G. and Phillips, F. (1994): "DEA of Financial Statements Data: The U.S. Computer Industry". *Journal of Productivity Analysis*. Vol. 5, pp. 229-248.

Thore, S., Phillips, F., Ruefli, R.W., and Yue, P. (1996): "DEA and the Management of the Product Cycle: The Computer Industry," *Computers and Operations Research*, Vol. 23:4, pp. 341-356.

Thore, S. (1996): "Economies of Scale, Emerging Patterns, and Self-Organization in the U.S. Computer Industry: An Empirical Investigation Using Data Envelopment Analysis," *Journal of Evolutionary Economics*, Vol. 6:2, pp. 199-216.

Chapter 7

Monitoring the Dynamic Performance of a Portfolio of R&D Projects over Time

Editorial Introduction

Abstract: The task of monitoring a portfolio of R&D projects over time is discussed. The so-called "window analysis" of DEA is briefly explained.

Key words: Time-lines, entry band, exit band, window analysis, productivity, peer group

1. TIME-LINES OF R&D PROJECTS

This chapter deals with the task of monitoring and assessing the performance of a portfolio of R&D projects over time. Once a project has been accepted for research and development, it will be evaluated intermittently - each quarter, say.

Figure 1 illustrates the time lines of three projects, Project *A*, *B* and *C*. The vertical scale measures the efficiency rating scored by each project, at the end of each of the eight quarters 2002: I-IV and 2003: I-IV. These ratings refer to some suitable input-oriented DEA model, so that the rating 1.0 indicates efficiency and ratings less than 1.0 indicate sub-efficiency.

Along the vertical scale three time bands have been marked off, with an upper (shaded) band covering efficiency ratings from 1.0 - 0.8, and a lower (also shaded) band encompassing ratings equal to 0.3 or less. The upper band defines an "entry range" of projects: no project will be initiated with an efficiency rating less than 0.8. The lower band indicates the "exit range" of projects: projects dipping down into this range will be terminated. The numerical ranges are examples only; actually, more sophisticated ways of screening initial projects and terminating projects will be discussed in a moment.

Project *A* is an ongoing project, covering all eight quarters. The efficiency ratings of project *A* are quite good, most of the time staying in the entry range (0.8,1) and reaching efficiency in three quarters: 2002:I and 2002:IV and 2003:IV. There is a brief episode in quarter 2001: I when the rating dips down into the mid-band, but the ratings recover immediately in the next quarter.

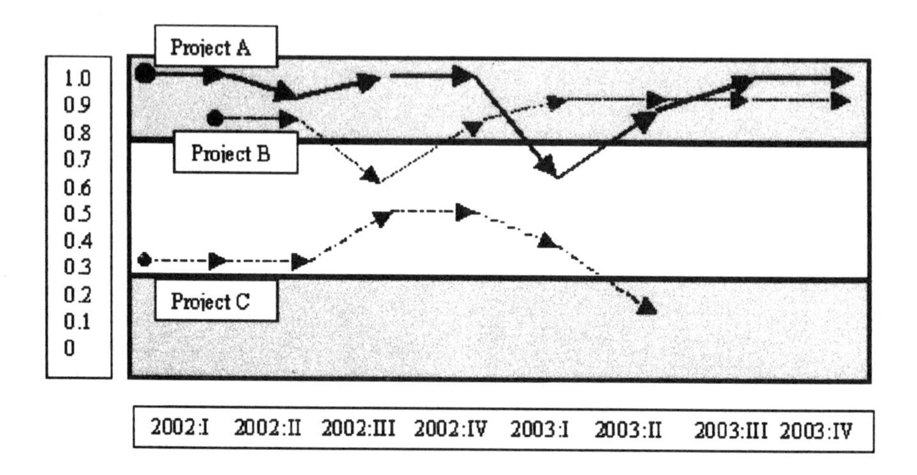

Figure 1. Time-lines of several R&D projects

Project *B* is initiated in quarter 2002:II. It suffers a shaky start, however, and dips down below the entry range already in quarter 2002:III. From then on, it is smooth sailing. The project reaches the score 0.9 in quarter 2003:I and stays there throughout the remainder of the year.

Project *C* is an existing project that may have been going on for some time; it is not doing well. Its efficiency score is lurching along at the bottom of the mid-range of scores, just barely keeping clear of the termination territory. There is a blip of improvement in the two quarters 2002:III and 2002:IV but from then on, it slips downhill again. The project breaks into the exit range in quarter 2003:II and is terminated.

These three imaginary examples should suffice to invoke the flavor of the argument of the present chapter. Up to now, the discussion in the present volume has exclusively dealt with the assessment and prioritization of a portfolio of R&D projects *A, B, C, D, E, F,...* at some given point in time, that is, at some vertical cut along the time line in Figure 1. Our present task is to discuss the performance of the projects over time, that is, tracing one or several of the time lines in Figure 1.

Insisting on a pure time series approach, one might try to rate the performance of a single project compared to its own performance in all past time-periods. Examining the performance of project *A*, one would then compare its performance A_t in time period *t* with its performance in earlier time periods, say A_{t-1}, A_{t-2}, A_{t-3},...

A moment of afterthought, however, reveals that a mixed cross-section/time-series approach is rather to be preferred. To rate project *A*, one needs to compare its present A_t to both its own time history A_{t-1}, A_{t-2}, A_{t-3}, ... and to the performance of all other projects, that is, to the time profile B_t, B_{t-1}, B_{t-2}, B_{t-3},... and also to the profile C_t, C_{t-1}, C_{t-2}, C_{t-3},... and so on. In order to spot a candidate for termination (see the exit range in Figure 1), it is certainly not sufficient to examine only the continued performance of the R&D project compared to itself. To cancel a project, one needs to establish that its current performance fails to live up to that of other and more successful projects.

2. WINDOW ANALYSIS

One way of establishing a mixed cross-section/time-series evaluation, much used in the DEA literature, is so called window analysis. A "window" is a sequence of consecutive time-periods. All observations of R&D projects falling within the time window are treated as separate observations. The performance of each project is rated relative to all observations in the window. Next, the window is moved step-wise forward in time and the ratings are repeated.

For instance, using a window of three time-periods and rating project *A*, one would compare its present A_t with its immediate precursors A_{t-1}, A_{t-2} and also with the performance of all other projects during the last three time-periods, that is, to the time profiles $\{B_t, B_{t-1}, B_{t-2}\}$, $\{C_t, C_{t-1}, C_{t-2}\}$, and so on. Next, moving the window one time-period ahead in time, one would compare A_{t+1} with its precursors A_t, A_{t-1} and also with the profiles $\{B_{t+1}, B_t, B_{t-1}\}$, $\{C_{t+1}, C_t, C_{t-1}\}$, etc. In this fashion, each project is analyzed several times with slightly different comparison sets.

The results of a window analysis for a particular project, say project *A*, might be exhibited as in the table below (adapted from Charnes, Cooper, Lewin and Seiford, 1994, p. 59):

Table 1. Results of window analysis with three-months window

Month 1	Month 2	Month 3	Month 4	Month 5	Month 6	Month 7
1.00	1.00	1.00				
	1.00	0.98	0.95			
		0.99	0.96	0.93		
			0.94	0.96	1.00	
				0.97	1.00	1.00

Translated to the present context, the table shows the DEA efficiency scores for a given R&D project, say project *A*. The first row lists the three scores obtained from the first window, covering the months (1,2,3). The second row lists the scores obtained from the window encompassing the months (2,3,4), etc. In this particular example, project *A* stays efficient during the three first months, but there is a weakening of performance in months 4 and 5. Later, in months 6 and 7, the project bounces back to efficiency again.

As illustrated by this example, window analysis enables the analyst to

- Test the stability of the efficiency ratings;
- Detect trends and seasonal effects in the efficiency performance of individual projects;
- Analyze time-lagged effects of specific variables;
- Allow for variable number of projects, e.g.., as a result of new entrants or discontinued projects;
- Flag possible errors in the data;
- Further distinguish efficient projects by the consistency of the their scores.

(This list is adapted from Charnes, Cooper, Golany, Learner, Phillips, Rousseau, 1994, p. 153.)

3. SEQUENTIAL PRODUCTIVITY MEASURES

In the standard DEA calculations, the score of a given project is determined comparing its performance to that of all members of a comparison group or reference group to which it belongs. The comparison group of projects includes the project itself. The highest attainable score is 1.00, meaning that no comparison project performs better than the one currently analyzed.

In dynamic analysis, new data are collected at regular time intervals. Typically, one wants to evaluate the renewed performance of a given project, comparing it to all former observations (including former observations of the project itself). In the common fashion of DEA, the comparison group includes the new data just collected. Suppose that new data relating to time period $t+1$ are just in. Rating project A_{t+1} and using a window of three time periods, the comparison group is $\{A_{t+1}, A_t, A_{t-1}\}$, $\{B_{t+1}, B_t, B_{t-1}\}$, $\{C_{t+1}, C_t, C_{t-1}\}$, etc. The highest attainable score is 1.00, which means that no data - - neither former data nor any data just collected - - yield better results than the ones now analyzed.

An alternative approach would be to exclude the new data from the comparison group, determining how project A_{t+1} scores relative to the group $\{A_t, A_{t-1}, A_{t-2}\}$, $\{B_t, B_{t-1}, B_{t-2}\}$, $\{C_t, C_{t-1}, C_{t-2}\}$, etc. In this case, the highest attainable score could be *greater than* 1.00, meaning that the new performance exceeds the results scored formerly. The efficiency rating would thus provide a measure of the increased *productivity* of project *A* in time period $t+1$. See further Thore, Kozmetsky, Phillips, 1994.

4. THE PEER GROUP

Evaluating and ranking the performance an R&D project always involves the comparison of a given project at a given time, say project A_t, to the performance of a list of some other projects, past or present. This *peer* group may contain not only all currently proposed projects (or some subset of them) but also other projects from which valuable experience can be gained. It could include past projects that have already been moved from the laboratory to the market and which were successfully commercialized. It could include model projects at other laboratories or installations, or even projects carried out by other companies, presently, or at some other time.

The research paper to follow illustrates how one can include past successful ventures into the peer group, and how this group evolves dynamically as new projects are moved from the laboratory to the market.

Suppose that the task is to evaluate and rank the projects *A,B,C,...* as before. Let data be available on these projects and also on the performance of a list of already commercialized projects *K,L,M,...* As projects are moved from the laboratory to the market over time, the list *K,L,M,...* expands dynamically.

REFERENCES

Charnes,A., Cooper, W.W., Golany, B., Learner, D.B., Phillips, F.Y., and Rousseau, J.J. (1994): "A Multiperiod Analysis of Market Segments and Brand Efficiency in the Competitive Carbonated Beverage Industry," in *Data Envelopment Analysis: Theory,*

Methodology and Applications, ed. By Charnes, A., Cooper, W.W., Lewin, A.Y., and Seiford, L.M., Kluwer Academic Publishers, Boston, pp. 145-166.

Charnes, A., Cooper, W.W., Lewin, A.Y. and Seiford, L.M. , editors (1994): *Data Envelopment Analysis: Theory, Methodology and Applications*, Kluwer Academic Publishers, Boston.

Thore, S., Kozmetsky, G. and Phillips, F. (1994): "DEA of Financial Statements Data: The US Computer Industry," *Journal of Productivity Analysis*, Vol.5, pp.229-248.

Evaluating a Portfolio of Proposed Projects, Ranking them Relative to a List of Existing Projects

A Research Paper

S. Thore and F. Pimentel

Instituto Superior Técnico, Lisbon

Abstract: The paper discusses the use of Data Envelopment Analysis (DEA) to rank the relative efficiency of R&D projects, when information is available on both earlier projects already carried out and a set of new proposed projects. Each proposed project may then be measured in (at least) two different ways: its performance relative to the other proposed projects, and its performance relative to the projects already carried out. To illustrate the calculations an application is discussed, rating the performance of a series of proposed student residence halls in Lisbon, Portugal. The proposed housing units are ranked among themselves, and in relation to existing housing units in the city.

Key words: Reference projects, dynamic rankings, hyper-efficiency, bisection technique, order of completion of projects

1. INTRODUCTION

In an earlier study in the present volume, Thore and Rich (see Chapter 2 *supra*) discussed the use of Data Envelopment Analysis (DEA) to rate the R&D activities of a corporation. Examples were brought from Baker Hughes, a Texas company developing high technology systems for oil drilling., and from NASA aeronautics investments. These examples all involved various proposed new technologies and investments, rating them relative to each other.

To support evaluations of proposed new systems of this kind, management often has available information about the performance of earlier projects as well. Some of the past projects were terminated, and were never carried out. Others, however, may have been realized and may be currently in operation. The data for these earlier projects can provide valuable benchmark information for the assessment of proposed new ones.

In principle, there will then exist *two* efficiency frontiers: the frontier of new projects and the frontier of existing past projects. A suggested new project can then be rated in two different ways: relative to other new projects, or relative to the existing past projects. Note in particular that it is of course perfectly possible (and indeed desirable) that a given new project is located *above* the frontier of the old projects.

The application to be discussed below rates a series of proposed student residence halls (identified as the decision-making units or DMUS of DEA), comparing them both with each other, and with the existing student residences. It may be argued, of course, that the latter kind of comparison must always be flawed, because the new housing units would presumably use modern building technology and state-of-the-art design, whereas the existing units may be dated and obsolete. On the other hand, the proposed building plans may be too rosy and optimistic, whereas the information from the existing halls reflects demonstrable experience. It may serve as a valuable reality-check to rank the proposed projects relative to their progenitors.

The methods outlined in the present paper are suggested to be of general relevance for the rating of R&D projects and investments in many different applications. The "projects" are the student residence halls, both proposed new halls and existing ones.

To measure the attractiveness of student residence halls, we shall construct several utility indices. One form or other of utility measures cannot be avoided when the performance of the individual projects to be ranked is in the nature of a subjective estimate of intangible benefits. Examples of such benefits are the value that a student places on close vicinity to campus, the access to shopping facilities and other amenities, etc.

Often, DEA dispenses with the need to formulate a utility function. This happens when the multi-output DEA replaces the evaluation of a single-index utility. In other applications, however, the breaking up of a global utility function into its constituent arguments does not obviate the need for spelling out the utilities of those separate arguments. In the particular example studied here, the specification of the various dimensions of student preferences of their housing needs still leaves the analyst with the challenge of defining a utility function for each of these dimensions separately.

Section 2 examines a plan for building new student residence halls in Lisbon, Portugal. Section 3 presents the basic DEA model when there are two classes of projects to be ranked: proposed new projects, and already existing ones. Whereas the ranking of the proposed projects alone can be effected by the standard DEA model, the rating of the proposed projects relative to the existing ones involves some mathematical modifications. Only existing projects will now be permitted to enter as "reference" projects (corner points of the polyhedron of feasible projects). In the common manner, efficient projects will have efficiency rating of one. Using an output-oriented version of DEA, sub-efficient projects will have ratings greater than one (given the inputs, it is possible to expand all outputs equi-proportionally by a factor greater than 1). Sub-efficient projects lie behind the efficiency frontier to the existing projects. This time, however, there is a third possibility. A proposed new project may also be *hyper-efficient*, obtaining an efficiency rating less than one. Hyper-efficient projects lie *above* the efficiency frontier of the existing projects.

Only hyper-efficient projects will be slated for selection. But from here on, there is a parting of the ways. One possibility is simply to rank the projects by their *ex ante* efficiency ratings, and to suggest that the projects be completed in this order. Section 4 looks at another possibility: a step-wise procedure completing the projects one by one, at each step moving the latest completed project from the set of contemplated new projects to the set of existing projects. At each new step, the remaining project with the highest hyper-efficiency rating is selected.

Section 5 concludes.

2. EVALUATING PROPOSED STUDENT RESIDENCE HALLS IN LISBON

This paper reports on a proposal for a series of new student residence halls in Lisbon, Portugal, developed by the Instituto Superior Técnico, see Gabinete de Estudos e Planeamento, 1997.

Some of the questions that the proposal tried to answer were these:

- How many student rooms in the city should be provided altogether?
- How many new student residences should be built?
- Where in the city should the new residences be located?
- Which should be the proportion between single rooms and double rooms?

Eighteen possible locations for the new halls $J_1 = \{1,2,...,18\}$ were identified, in addition to the seven halls $J_2 = \{19,20, ...25\}$ that already exist today. The suggested locations include various places in the city where student residences could reasonably be built or bought.

To assist in the selection process, four fundamental points of view (FPsV, see Chapter 1 in the present volume) $r = 1,2,3,4$ were identified:

- Easy access to and from the proposed student hall to the university. This variable was calculated as the time spent by students during the rush hour commuting from the proposed residence to campus. For some residences, the travel route allowed for on-going plans of subway expansion.
- Integration with local community. This criterion reflects the balance between the various community functions of each possible residence. From this point of view, a good location is a residential area with easy access to parks and green belts, to commerce and services, all in desirable proportions. A specialist in urban studies was asked to carry out the evaluation.
- Urban surroundings. Evaluates the morphological characteristics of the urban space, reflecting the design and the state of conservation of the buildings.
- Protection and security. For this criterion, we used an index developed by the university security police, reflecting criminal statistics collected from the various proposed residence locations.

To quantify each of the criteria now listed, we used the bisection technique described in the Chapter 1 in the present volume. This technique

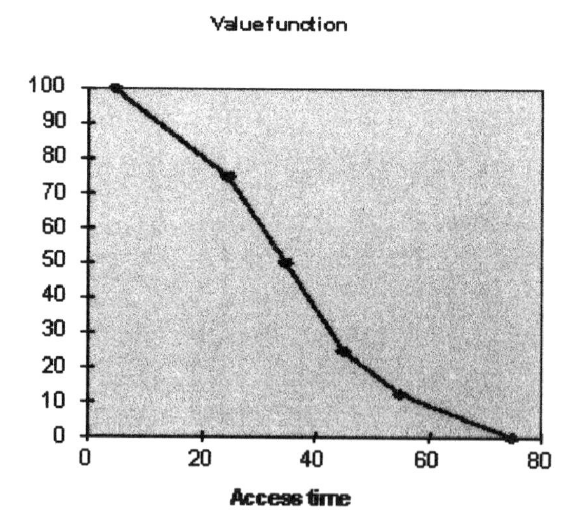

Figure 1. Value function of the criterion "Accessibility"

converts data such as access times or crime statistics into a utility function reflecting the subjective views of the policy-maker. As an illustration, we show in Figure 1 below the utility function used to evaluate various commuting times between a student hall and campus (criterion $r = 1$ above). The function ranges from 100 (best performance, with an access time of only 5 minutes) to 0 (worst performance, access 75 minutes). Intermediate points along the curve are plotted to reflect the subjective advantages and disadvantages of reduced or prolonged commuting times. For instance, the first bisection of the value function yielded an access time of 35 minutes. This means that a reduction in access time from 75 minutes to 35 minutes was deemed as attractive as a reduction from 35 minutes to 5 minutes. Additional bisections produced the remaining points illustrated in Figure 1.

Utility indices for the other three performance indicators were constructed in the same manner.

On the input side, we collected data on the average building costs per square meter of area at each residence site. In the case of already existing residence halls, the historical construction cost was calculated. For proposed sites, the expected acquisition or construction cost was estimated.

3. MATHEMATICAL DISCUSSION

Motivated by the present application, we start out from the so-called output-oriented BCC model of data envelopment analysis. See Program (A15) in the Mathematical Appendix to the present volume, amended as discussed in Section A3 in the same appendix. In this fashion, we make sure that a point on the frontier would be labeled efficient only if both all output and input constraints are tight at a point of optimum. The resulting program reads

$$\text{Max } \psi 0 + \varepsilon \left(\sum_{i=1}^{m} s_i^- + \sum_{r=1}^{s} s_r^+ \right) \tag{1}$$

subject to

$$\sum_{j=1}^{n} X_{ij}\lambda_j + s_i^- = X_{i0}, \quad i=1,\dots,m$$

$$\psi 0\, Y_{r0} - \sum_{j=1}^{n} Y_{rj}\lambda_j + s_r^+ = 0, \quad r=1,\dots,s$$

$$\sum_{j=1}^{n} \lambda_j = 1, \text{ and all } \lambda_j,\ s_i^-, s_r^+ \geq 0$$

The task at hand is to rate the performance of $j = 1,2,\ldots n$ "decision making units" (DMUs), to be identified in a moment as the various projects of R&D and investment to be rated. Program (1) rates a particular DMU ($j=0$). The unknowns are the weights λ_j to be attached to each DMU, the output and input slacks s_r^+, s_i^- respectively, and the desired efficiency rating $\psi 0$ indicating the possible degree of expansion in all of DMU_0's outputs. The data parameters for the model are Y_{rj} and X_{ij}, the rth output and i^{th} input of DMU_j, respectively, and ε, a small (infinitesimally small) number. Using conventional terminology, we shall refer to the weighted sums

$$\sum_j Y_{rj}\lambda_j \ ,\ r = 1,2,\ldots,s \tag{2}$$

as "best practice outputs," and to

$$\sum_j X_{ij}\lambda_j \ ,\ i = 1,2,\ldots,m \tag{3}$$

as "best practice inputs." In simple words, program (1) -(3) determines the efficiency rating θ as the maximal possible rate of equi-proportional expansion of all outputs, while ensuring that

- best practice outputs (2) do not fall short of observed outputs,
- best practice inputs (3) do not exceed contracted inputs.

The optimal $\psi 0 = \psi 0^*$ determined in the manner now described is the inverse value of the rating which can be determined by the input-oriented BCC model. Sub-efficiency in the output-oriented model means that more outputs can be obtained with the same inputs; in the input-oriented model it means that less inputs can be used to obtain the same outputs. In the common manner, the inclusion of the convexity constraint $\sum_j \lambda_j = 1$ in the BCC model permits the presence of increasing returns to scale, constant returns to scale, or decreasing returns to scale. Geometrically, each linear facet of the piece-wise linear efficiency frontier may have a negative intercept, a zero intercept, or a positive intercept at the origin. (The so-called CCR model, which does not feature the convexity constraint, requires constant returns to scale throughout.)

Assume now that the set of all DMUs $J = \{1,2,...n\}$ is divided into two subsets:

- a set of proposed new R&D and investment projects J_1
- a set of already existing and completed projects J_2

with $J = J_1 + J_2$. Several rankings then suggest themselves, such as rating just the new projects by themselves (selecting $j \in J_1$ in program (1)), rating just the old projects (selecting $j \in J_2$), or rating both new and old projects together (selecting $j \in J$).

Rather than comparing and ranking a set of proposed projects with each other, it is for many purposes more natural to compare them with the existing investment projects instead. Deciding whether a particular new project should be undertaken, the first question that a decision-maker will pose is certainly not how it would fare relatively to other proposed projects. The essential issue is rather whether the new project will represent an improvement over the existing investments already been carried out. Initiation of projects that are expected to fall short of what is already available in the marketplace must be out of the question.

One of the purposes of the present paper, then, is to investigate the case when the proposed projects are ranked only in relation to the old ones, that is, when

$$\lambda_j = 0 \text{ for } j \in J_1. \tag{4}$$

Adjoining relation (4) to program (1) and solving, there are three possibilities:

- the DMU currently rated is said to be *efficient*, when $\psi_0^* = 1$
- the DMU is said to be *sub-efficient*, when $\psi_0^* > 1$
- the DMU is said to be *hyper-efficient*, when $\psi_0^* < 1$.

In the first case, the project rated lies on the efficiency frontier spanning the old projects. In the second case, it lies below this frontier. The project may be an old sub-efficient project, or it may be a new proposed one dominated by the old ones. In any case, it represents a step backwards and it should not be realized. The third case, finally, offers the possibility of starting something new that outperforms the old. This project lies above the old frontier. The task at hand is now to rank the hyper-efficient projects.

3.1 Empirical results

Proceeding as now explained, we rated both the proposed new residence halls $j = 1,2,...,18$ and existing halls $j = 19,20,...,25$ with respect to the four criteria $r=1,2,3,4$. Denote the resulting indices Y_{1j}, Y_{2j}, Y_{3j} and Y_{4j}, $j = 1,2,...,25$. As mentioned earlier, the sole input into the selection process was taken to be the average building costs per square meter of area at each residence site. Denote the input variable X_j, $j = 1,2,...,25$.

We start the calculations by solving the standard DEA program (1-3) pooling all residence halls together, both proposed and existing ones. The results are exhibited in Table 1 below.

Table 1. Rankings and reference halls

Student halls	**Pooling all halls together**		**Rating the proposed halls in terms of the existing ones**	
	Efficiency score	**Reference halls**	**Efficiency score**	**Reference halls**
hall 1	1.386	8,19	1.319	19,23
hall 2	1.386	8,19	1.319	19,23
hall 3	1.386	8,19	1.319	19,23
hall 4	1.386	8,19	1.319	19,23
hall 5	1.386	8,19	1.319	19,23
hall 6	1	6	0.846	19,21
hall 7	1.339	8,19,20	1.331	19,20,21
hall 8	1	8	0.865	19,21,23
hall 9	1	9	0.9	20,21
hall 10	1.337	8,19,21	1.318	19,21,23
hall 11	1	11	0.882	19
hall 12	1.032	6,16,19	0.985	19,20,21
hall 13	1.263	6,16,19,20	1.207	19,20,21
hall 14	1.064	14	0.929	19,23
hall 15	1.159	6,8,16,19,21	1.08	19,20,21
hall 16	1	16	0.934	19,20,21
hall 17	1	17	0.934	19,20,21
hall 18	1.125	18	1.051	19,20,21
hall 19	1	19		
hall 20	1	20		
hall 21	1	21		
hall 22	1.35	6,9,16		
hall 23	1.05	8,19,21		
hall 24	1.05	8,19,21		
hall 25	2.437	8,19		

A few authors have looked at the problem of ranking the efficient observations themselves, emerging from the DEA calculations. One obvious approach is to count the number of times each efficient observation serves as a reference for other observations. Inspecting the results listed in column (3), we find that

- hall 6 serves as a reference 3 times,
- hall 8 serves as a reference 9 times,
- hall 9 serves as a reference 1 time,
- hall 11 serves as a reference 1 time,
- hall 16 serves as a reference 4 times,
- hall 17 serves as a reference 1 time.

The winner is hall 8. It is a role model for precisely half of all new projects investigated.

Unfortunately, one is treading on thin ice here. The measure now indicated can easily be badly contaminated. Consider a hypothetical DEA application where all non-efficient observation points happen to project onto a single facet of the efficiency frontier. The corner points of that facet will then all show up as winners. All other corner points of the efficiency frontier will have only themselves as reference points. In other words, the frequency measure discussed now often will say more about the particular configuration of observations relative to the frontier, than about the relative merits of the frontier points themselves.

To find a better alternative, turn to columns (4) and (5) in Table 1. These columns list the results from ranking the new residence halls in terms of the existing ones only. Column (3) shows the optimal ψ *obtained from solving program (1)- (4); column (5) lists the reference halls with positive weights $\lambda_j > 0$. Note that for each residence, the optimal ψ * reported in column (3) is less than the optimal ψ * reported in column (2). Both program (1) and the same program adjoining relation (4) are maximization programs and the latter program contains additional constraints; hence, the optimal value of the latter cannot exceed the optimal value of the former.

Inspecting the scores listed in column (3), we can divide the proposed halls into three classes:

- Proposed student halls that are *efficient*, with $\psi^* = 1$. No hall happens to fall in this category.
- Proposals that are *subefficient*, with $\psi^* > 1$. Halls 1-5, 7, 10, 13, 15, 18 fall in this category.
- Proposals that are *hyper-efficient*, with $\psi^* < 1$. These are halls 6, 8-9, 11-12, 14, 16-17. Among them, hall 6 attains the most attractive score (the lowest optimal ψ * value).

The hyper-efficient halls are candidates for actual completion. They are *better* than the already existing halls. Note that all hyper-efficient proposals were earlier (in column 1) rated as efficient.

The winner of them all is hall 6. It has an efficiency ranking of $\psi^* = 0.846$ relative to the two existing halls 19 and 21. This means that proposal 6 should be compared with the weighted "best practice" performance of halls 19 and 21. But this "best practice" is in terms of the old student halls only, and it falls short of the proposed hall 6 by *100 – 84.6 = 15.4* percent.

4. A DYNAMIC PROCESS OF SELECTING ONE PROPOSED PROJECT AT A TIME

Introducing an explicit time perspective in the analysis, we shall now posit that in the first instance one single new project is to be selected for adoption, followed by a second one and so on. *At each stage of this decision sequence, the proposed projects are re-examined relatively to the existing ones, and the one with the most attractive score (the lowest ψ^* value) is chosen for construction.* Thus, a dynamic order of construction is established, removing one project at a time from the set of proposed projects and adjoining it to the set of adopted projects.

In the first instance, it might be conjectured that the order of projects established in this dynamic fashion would be identical to the order indicated by the original pre-construction DEA ratings. As we shall see in a moment, however, this proposition is not always true.

To investigate these matters, we return to our assessment of the proposed student residences in Lisbon. Inspecting again the results reported in Table 1, we see that *hall 6 will be the first residence slated for construction*. Next,

Table 2. DEA results after completion of residence hall 6

Student halls proposed for construction	Rating the proposed halls in terms of the existing ones (now including hall 6)	
	Efficiency score	**Reference halls**
hall 1	1.319	19,23
hall 2	1.319	19,23
hall 3	1.319	19,23
hall 4	1.319	19,23
hall 5	1.319	19,23
hall 7	1.331	19,20,21
hall 8	0.865	19,21,23

Student halls proposed for construction	Rating the proposed halls in terms of the existing ones (now including hall 6)	
	Efficiency score	Reference halls
hall 9	0.900	6,20
hall 10	1.318	19,21,23
hall 11	0.882	19
hall 12	1.028	6,19
hall 13	1.262	6,19,20
hall 14	0.929	19
hall 15	1.131	6,19,21
hall 16	0.982	6,19.20
hall 17	0.988	6.19
hall 18	1.111	6,19,20

remove hall 6 from the set J_1 (the set of proposed residences) and adjoin it to the set J_2 (the set of completed residences). Carrying out the same calculations as before, one this time obtains the results reported in Table 2.

Table 3. DEA results after completion of residence halls 6,8,11,9, in this order

Student halls proposed for construction	Rating the proposed halls in terms of the existing ones (now including halls 6,8,11 and 9)	
	Efficiency score	Reference halls
hall 1	1.386	8,19
hall 2	1.386	8,19
hall 3	1.386	8,19
hall 4	1.386	8,19
hall 5	1.386	8,19
hall 7	1.339	8,19,20
hall 10	1.337	8,19,21
hall 12	1.028	6,19
hall 13	1.202	6,9,19,20
hall 14	1.064	8
hall 15	1.158	6,8,19,21
hall 16	0.982	6,9,19
hall 17	0.988	6,19
hall 18	1.111	6,9,19

Inspecting Table 2, we see that hall 6 now in a number of instances has entered the set of reference halls, see halls 9, 12-13 and 15-18. This is what we should expect: the newly built residence will immediately serve as one of the reference points for the next round of construction.

At this stage, there are five hyper-efficient residences, 8-9,11,14,16-17. Among them, residence 8 scores most favorably with the rating $\psi^* = 0.865$. Residence 8 thus is obtained as the next candidate for construction. Going back to the initial rankings in Table 1, column 3, we see that it was already at the outset ranked as the second-best option, with the very same score $\psi^* = 0.865$.

We now continue the dynamic process of constructing one residence at a time, always picking the hyper-efficient residence with the most favorable ψ^* rating. Space does not permit the reporting of the details of these steps; suffice it to note that the subsequent selections will be 11 and 9, in this order. That is, the order coincides with the initial rankings in Table 1, column 3, where these residences obtained the scores $\psi^* = 0.882$ and $\psi^* = 0.9$, respectively.

So far, the dynamic order of construction has coincided with the initial order. Checking with Table 1, column 3 again, the next candidate for construction would be expected to be residence 14, which originally obtained the score $\psi^* = 0.929$. Now, however, an exception occurs. Refer to Table 3 listing the DEA scores *after residences 6,8,11,9 have been built, in this order*. At this stage, the efficiency rating for residence 14 turns out to be $\psi^* = 1.064$, that is, this residence is not even hyper-efficient any longer. Instead, residence 16 with $\psi^* = 0.982$ now is being presented as a candidate for construction.

Students of dynamic analysis will not be surprised by this result. Solutions to intertemporal static economic models rarely coincide with the dynamic path actually followed by an economic system over time.

The task of monitoring the performance of a portfolio of projects thus falls more heavily on the DEA analyst than one might have expected. It is not sufficient not rank the projects just initially, or at some suitable regular intervals. The entire portfolio needs to be re-assessed each time a new project is selected.

5. CONCLUDING COMMENTS

It is probably wrong to limit the assessment of investment or R&D projects to proposed new projects only. The performance of earlier projects already completed should provide an important source of benchmark data.

It is true, or course, that many proposed new projects involve advanced technology that may not easily compare with the existing one. On the other hand, the record of the past may sometimes serve as a helpful correction to many lofty dreams for the future, bringing the assessments of the engineering and commercialization possibilities in better contact with the real world.

One obvious and immediate way of incorporating both new and existing projects in the DEA analysis is to pool them together into one single population, rating the performance of each project relative to the entire pool. Adopting this approach, not only will the sample population be of mixed origin, containing both new and existing projects; also the "best" or frontier performance will typically be mixed, being some (linear) combination of both new and old projects.

The alternative procedure demonstrated in the present paper keeps the population of new projects and the population of old projects apart. The frontier performance of each new project is written as a linear combination of the old ones only. This is a more natural way of looking at things when projects are large and expensive and take a long time to complete. The relevant question then is how a new project might improve upon the performance of the already existing ones. Since only one new proposal (or only a few of them) may be slated for completion, it would in any case be rather academic to ask how a new project would perform relative to a bunch of other new projects.

Posing the rating problem in this manner, some modifications of the conventional DEA model are necessary. All projects may now be divided into three classes: sub-efficient projects (lying behind or below the old frontier), efficient projects (spanning the old frontier), and hyper-efficient projects (lying above the old frontier). Only the hyper-efficient projects would be recommended for completion and the winning candidate would be the project with the greatest θ–rating, using an input-oriented DEA model (the lowest ψ-rating, using an output-oriented model).

Once the most attractive new proposal has been adopted, and the first new student hall has been built, there is the intriguing possibility of repeating the rankings in the same fashion. This time, the set of existing halls has been increased by one hall, and the set of new proposals has been reduced correspondingly. The winner is the *next* candidate for construction.

Economists have since long recognized that optimal solutions of intertemporal models do not necessarily hold up the light of dynamic analysis. Barring any unexpected interceding events, the decision-maker will go for the solution for the very first time period. The remaining optimal multi-period time path, however, may forever remain a figment of earlier planning. Even absent new information, the dynamic time path will in general not follow the intertemporal one.

Translating these general observations to the present case, the conclusion emerges that even a careful initial analysis of a portfolio of R&D projects can never replace the need for regular and recurring monitoring of the portfolio over time. Actually, a number of unexpected events can make such re-evaluations necessary:

- The initiation and adoption of new projects that add to the population of new projects;
- Changing prospects of projects currently being developed;
- The completion of ongoing projects, removing them from the set of current projects, and moving them to the set of existing projects;
- The termination of new projects;
- Changing prospects of existing projects;
- The termination of old projects.

To exemplify how the methods outlined in the present paper may be applied to analyze such dynamic events within the framework of DEA, consider the last item on this list: the termination of old projects. Suppose that in addition to building new student halls, the possibility has also been raised of selling, razing, or otherwise disposing of the most inefficient existing hall. In this context, one would be looking for the *bottom rungs* rather than the top rungs in the ranking list.

One obvious possibility is to pull down an existing student hall and to build a new one in its place, on the same site. Also such a combined strategy of action can easily be accommodated and analyzed, using the same extended DEA formats.

REFERENCES

Gabinete de Estudos e Planeamento (1997): *Projecto de Criaçao de Residencias Universitárias do IST. Parte 1,* Instituto Superior Técnico, Lisboa.

Goodwin, P. and Wright,G. (1991): *Decision Analysis for Management Judgment*, Wiley.

Pimentel, F. and Oliveira, P. (1997): *Projecto de Criaçao de Residencias Universitárias do IST. Parte 2: Estudo de Apoio à Decisão,* Gabinete de Estudos e Planeamento, Instituto Superior Técnico, Lisboa, April.

Chapter 8

Assessing the Efficiency of R&D Projects in the Face of Resource Constraints

Editorial Introduction

Abstract: In a classical piece of work, Martin Weingartner back in 1963 showed how it is possible to pose the problem of allocating a given budget between a number of investment or R&D projects as a problem of zero-one programming.

Key words: Capital budgeting, indivisible projects, integer programming, zero-one programming, binary variables, mutually exclusive projects, contingent projects

1. RANKINGS VERSUS RESOURCE ALLOCATION

What is the purpose of the DEA rankings? The answer is almost always that the analyst would like to know how well the decision units under investigation (the DMUs) actually perform, and how this performance could be improved. If there is some kind of management policy intent in the background, it is to advise lagging units: to pinpoint excessive use of inputs and output shortfalls. The task of the DEA analyst is not to blame or to punish: it is to help by identifying fruitful areas for additional management attention.

Questions of allocation of scarce resources rarely enter these considerations. Theoretically, management might in some instances shuffle global resources around, increasing the allocations to the high-performance units and starving the low performers. But in most cases, this is simply not possible. Analyzing the performance of public schools in a big city, for instance, it is easier said than done to switch resources from the well-endowed schools in the suburbs to lagging inner-city units.

And yet, these are precisely the kind of questions that loom over most instances of ranking of R&D projects. R&D resources are scarce - - they are scarce in a commercial setting, and they are scarce even at a well-endowed university engaged in basic research. The ultimate aim of the DEA rankings is typically not just to determine the efficiency scores of the various projects currently considered, but also to find out how resources should be allocated between alternative projects. At the solution point, some projects would be allocated whatever they need. Others might have to be squeezed for funding. Others again would be terminated (or never launched in the first place).

How can one combine the conventional DEA ratings with such issues of allocation? This is the theme of the present chapter.

2. CAPITAL BUDGETING BY ZERO-ONE PROGRAMMING

Neoclassical economists assumed routinely that the purchase and use of all goods - - consumer goods and capital goods alike - - were "divisible" so that they could be continuously adjusted up to some equilibrium point. In the case of investment and capital theory, these assumptions lead to the concept of a schedule of the marginal product of capital, illustrating how increasing volumes of capital invested in some given project would gradually lead to a falling rate of return. A company considering several projects should pursue each project up to the point where the rate of return on all projects was the same. If one were to ask a 1940s economist how the optimal allocation of a given sum of money between a set of alternative investment projects were to be carried out, the answer would be that the company should travel down its rate of return curve, expanding investment in each and all projects *pari passu* (a favorite Latin term of the times) until the sum total of all investments exhausted the available budget. All projects able to reach the equilibrium rate would be carried out. There could be no ranking of projects. They would be all equally attractive, all yielding the same equilibrium rate.

Once capital is recognized as being indivisible or "lumpy," however, the neoclassical theory breaks down. Historically, the idea of indivisibilities is a fairly recent one in economics. To deal with lumpiness in economics, some entirely new mathematical machinery is needed. That new tool is integer programming - optimization problems where the unknowns cannot be continuously adjusted but only take a finite number of discrete values.

The first economist to consider capital budgeting of indivisible projects was Martin Weingartner. His pioneering study, *Mathematical Programming and the Analysis of Capital Budgeting Problems* (Weingartner, 1963) made use of the so-called "cutting planes" techniques of integer programming developed a couple of years earlier by Gomory (see Gomory, 1958).

The general class of programming problem solved by Gomory was standard linear programming with the additional requirement that some or all of the variables in the solution take on only integer values. Briefly, the cutting plane approach involved the addition of linear restrictions supplementary to those of the original linear programming problem that cut away part of the original feasible region, without disturbing the original feasible integer points. By successive cuts Gomory was able to produce in a finite number of steps a new linear programming problem whose optimal solution was in integers. The new restrictions are generated during the computational process and do not necessarily have any economic interpretation.

The basic capital budgeting model treated by Weingartner involves a financial officer considering $j = 1,2,...,n$ alternative and independent investment projects, stretching over a time span of $t = 1,2,...,T$ time periods. The net present value of all revenues and costs associated with each project j is denoted b_j. The cost of each project in time period t is c_{tj} ; the available budget ceiling in the same time period is C_t. Weingartner then writes the mathematical program

$$\text{Max } \Sigma_j \; b_j x_j \tag{1}$$

subject to

$$\Sigma_j \; c_{tj} x_j \le C_t, \quad t = 1,2,...,T$$

$$0 \le x_j \le 1, \; x_j \text{ integer}, \; j = 1,2,...n$$

There is one unknown x_j for each project j, a kind of switching variable which is either switched on (the project is accepted, $x_j = 1$) - - or it is switched off (the project is not accepted, $x_j = 0$). Such a variable is also called a "zero-one variable" or a binary variable. In simple words, the program instructs the financial officer to maximize the combined net present value of all projects subject to a budget constraint in each time period.

2.1 Numerical example[1]

Consider three projects *A,B* and *C*, each of which can start now or one year from now. Projects starting now will have subscript 1 and those starting a year later will have subscript 2. The stream of cash flows (in thousands of dollars) generated by each of the projects is tabulated below.

Table 1. Example involving six alternative and independent investment projects

	Project A1	Project A2	Project B1	Project B2	Project C1	Project C2
Year 1	-200	0	-300	0	-250	0
Year 2	125	-200	175	-300	150	-250
Year 3	125	125	175	175	150	150
Year 4	125	125	175	175	150	150
Year 5	0	125	0	175	0	150
NPV	110.9	100.8	135.2	112.9	123	111.8

The last figure in each column is the net present value (NPV) of the project in that column, using the discount rate *0.10.* Note that each project requires a payment in the first period, and then produces a positive return for exactly three years. From this it is clear that the projects, if accepted, will be in danger of producing a negative cash flow only during the first two years.

Suppose that the firm has budget constraints (in thousands of dollars) of *300* and *375* for years 1 and 2, and it wants to know which of the six projects it can accept without exceeding its budgets in the first two years. Define the following zero-one variables

- x_1 = accept project A_1
- x_2 = accept project A_2
- x_3 = accept project B_1
- x_4 = accept project B_2
- x_5 = accept project C_1
- x_6 = accept project C_2

Since these variables can take on only values 0 and 1, the interpretations of their values is that the corresponding statement is true when the value of the variable is one and false if it is zero. Using this, we can set up the following zero-one programming model of the firm's decision problem:

[1] The numerical example is reproduced from Thompson and Thore, 1992, pp. 140-141.

$$\text{Max } 110.9\,x_1 + 100.8\,x_2 + 135.2\,x_3 + 122.9\,x_4 + 123\,x_5 + 111.8\,x_6$$

subject to

$$200\,x_1 + 300\,x_3 + 250\,x_5 \leq 300$$

$$-125\,x_1 + 200\,x_2 - 175\,x_3 + 300\,x_4 - 150\,x_5 + 250\,x_6 \leq 375$$

and all the unknowns x_1 through x_6 being binary variables.

Notice that the coefficients of the projects have had their signs changed compared to the way they appear in the table. That is because the first period payment appears on the left hand side of the first constraint so that if the corresponding project is accepted its cost is subtracted from the first period budget of *300*. On the other hand, the second period receipts appear with negative signs on the left hand side of the second constraint so that if the corresponding project is accepted its second period receipt is added to the second period budget of *375*. In this way such receipts can be immediately reinvested in the second period.

As late as the early 1980s, the numerical solution of even small integer programming problems was difficult. Today, standard computer packages are available to solve a variety of mathematical programming problems, including zero-one programming. Numerical solution gives[2]

$$x_3 = x_4 = x_6 = 1$$
$$x_1 = x_2 = x_5 = 0.$$

The optimal objective value is *369.9*. In other words, the optimal solution is to accept projects B_1, B_2 and C_2.

2.2 Dependency and independency between projects

Weingartner also showed how it is possible to handle the presence of various kinds of project dependencies by further constraining the zero-one variables x_j, $j=1,2,\ldots n$ in program (1). He discussed the following cases:

[2] An easy-to-use software package for mathematical programming is GAMS (general algebraic modeling system) which includes a solver (called "ZOOM") for integer programming problems. See Thompson and Thore, 1992, which includes a diskette with GAMS software.

- *Mutually exclusive projects*, so that only one in a group of projects is permitted to be carried out. Suppose that the group of projects $j \in J$ are mutually exclusive, where J is a subset of $j=1,2,...n$. Mathematically, this is accomplished by adjoining the constraint

$$\sum_{j \in J} x_j \leq 1$$

to program (1). For instance, if the alternatives for each project type A, B and C in the previous example are mutually exclusive, one adds the constraints
$x_1 + x_2 \leq 1$, $x_3 + x_4 \leq 1$, and $x_5 + x_6 \leq 1$. At most one of the two zero-one variables in each of these constraints can then equal one.

- *Contingent projects*, so that the realization of one project is dependent on the prior realization of another project. If project m is desirable only if project k is adopted, but not otherwise, one writes the constraint $x_m \leq x_k$. If project k is rejected, then, necessarily, project m is also rejected.

Group contingencies can be handled in a similar fashion. For instance, if the two projects $j=1$ and $j=2$ both depend on the prior realization of project $j = 3$, one writes $x_1 + x_2 - 2x_3 \leq 0$. If project 3 has not been carried out, one must then have $x_1 = x_2 = 0$ and none of the two projects 1 and 2 can be carried out.

REFERENCES

Gomory, R.E. (1958): "Outline of an Algorithm for Integer Solutions to Linear Programs," *Bullletin of the American Mathematical Society*, Vol. 64, Sept., pp. 275-278.

Thompson, G.L. and Thore, S. (1992): *Computational Economics: Economic Modeling with Optimization Software*, Scientific Press, South San Francisco, Calif.

Weingartner, H.M. (1963): *Mathematical Programming and the Analysis of Capital Budgeting Problems*, Prentice Hall, Englewood Cliffs, New Jersey.

On the Ranking of R&D Projects in a Hierarchical Organizational Structure subject to Global Resource Constraints

A Research Paper

B. Golany[1] and S. Thore[2]

[1]*Technion, Israel*

[2] *IC[2] Institute, the University of Texas*

Abstract: The problem of evaluating a portfolio of R&D projects is not only to rank the projects but also to find the necessary resources to see the projects through development and eventual commercialization. We discuss ways of arranging a set of two-stage DEA calculations in a hierarchical organizational structure where headquarters allocates resources to departments and each department operates a portfolio of R&D projects. Assuming that projects are indivisible, we formulate a zero-one programming model for the allocation of resources to them. Finally, we construct a global DEA program covering the entire organizational hierarchy that combines rankings with a set of global resource constraints.

Key words: Hierarchical organization, divisions, departments, matrix of resource use, two-stage DEA, intermediate causal factor, goal focusing, indivisibilities, zero-one programming, global program, couplings, decomposition of a linear program

1. INTRODUCTION

The task of managing a portfolio of R&D projects includes the repeated evaluation of individual projects (both ongoing projects and proposed new ones) and the allocation of resources to them. Specifically, once the performance of an ongoing project has been assessed, the question immediately presents itself whether sufficient (or excessive) resources have been committed to it in the past, and earmarked for it in the future. Similarly, once the performance of a proposed new project has been assessed, the question is whether it should be adopted, and if so, the amount of resources that should be committed to it now, and in the future.

The present paper deals with the interplay of these kinds of decisions in a large organizational structure, where some overarching body controls the resources, and R&D decisions are delegated via research departments to individual managers. The overarching body could be the office of the Vice President for R&D in a commercial company, the R&D office at a research university, or the ministry of government-supported industrial research. In such situations, routines for hierarchical evaluation and control need to be developed, and then delegated from the center to the research departments. These routines should be flexible enough to allow for the termination (= withdrawal of resources) of projects that fall below expectations, and for the acceleration (=injection of additional resources) of break-through projects. That is, whereas the aims of R&D management are the enhancement of project performance at the bottom level of the R&D organizational structure, the means of policy are laid down through resource allocations at earlier levels.

The mathematical technique of Data Envelopment Analysis (DEA) is an obvious tool for evaluating the performance of a number of R&D projects. However, it was never designed to control the amount of resources used. In most DEA applications, there is the tacit understanding that resources will always be forthcoming to support the DMU's (decision making units), whether they are operating at their actual scale or at some calculated frontier level. Calculating the "best practice" of hospitals or banks (to cite just two of the most common areas of application), it is always understood that enough doctors, hospital beds, operating theaters, or deposits, bank clerks and handling facilities somehow are available. It would take only a slight change of management perspective, however, to ask how some given global availability of resources should be delegated and allocated. Certainly, in cases of R&D management, this question immediately presents itself.

Cook *et al.*, 1998, dealt with the adaptation of DEA to rank units belonging to an organizational hierarchy. They discussed various methods of grouping such DMUs and proposed ways to evaluate and rank groups of DMUs belonging to the hierarchy. Our own work brings in additional dimensions relating to questions of the hierarchical channeling of resources flowing from the top to the bottom in the hierarchy.

Section 2 describes the nature of the two intertwined problems of ranking and resource-control, as they would be encountered in a large organizational structure of R&D projects. Section 3 introduces the basic DEA formulations, ranking some subset of projects (such as all projects belonging to a given department).

In Section 4, we suggest adapting the method of multi-stage DEA to portray the successive sequence of rankings in a hierarchical structure with two levels: "divisions" and "departments." The divisions delegate resources to the departments, such as capital and labor. We formulate a two-stage DEA model, where in the first stage the performance of the departments is ranked in their ability to generate general support conducive to the research effort inside the department. The second-stage DEA ranks the performance of projects inside a given department. The factor "departmental support" is an intermediate causal factor. It is at the same time the estimated output of the first-stage departmental production of support, and the input (together with individual project inputs) into second-stage project developments.

Section 5 embeds the conventional DEA rankings inside a global resource-constrained program with binary (accept /do not accept) variables. The programming format includes a goal-programming feature, seeing to it that the efficient projects are accepted first, and that later projects are carried out in the order of decreasing efficiency.

Sometimes, management may decide to *scale down* an R&D project rather than discontinuing it. Section 6 investigates the ranking of projects that are not necessarily indivisible, so that a department may accommodate its resource constraints by operating one or several projects on a scale less than one. To the standard system of DEA programs - - one for each project - - we may then simply adjoin a set of global couplings laying down the overall resource constraints.

Section 7 sums up.

2. A HIERARCHICAL STRUCTURE FOR THE RANKING AND CONTROL OF R&D PROJECTS

It may be instructive at the outset to illustrate the kind of intertwined performance assessment and resource allocation problems that we presently have in mind. For this purpose, consider a typical situation in some government office running a large R&D organization charged with the development of new technologies and equipment. The office oversees the allocation of resources to a large number of projects of different size, duration, cost and impact. We want to extend the conventional concept of project control "actual versus plan" to both

- a hierarchical vertical setting (project control being delegated from an upper organizational level to a lower one), and

- a horizontal setting (projects located at the same organizational level).

A major task of the organization is to allocate resources to government-owned companies and to oversee contracts with private corporations. These business units operate on a second level of control, reporting to the main office but in their turn supervising the performance of their various divisions (see Figure 1.)

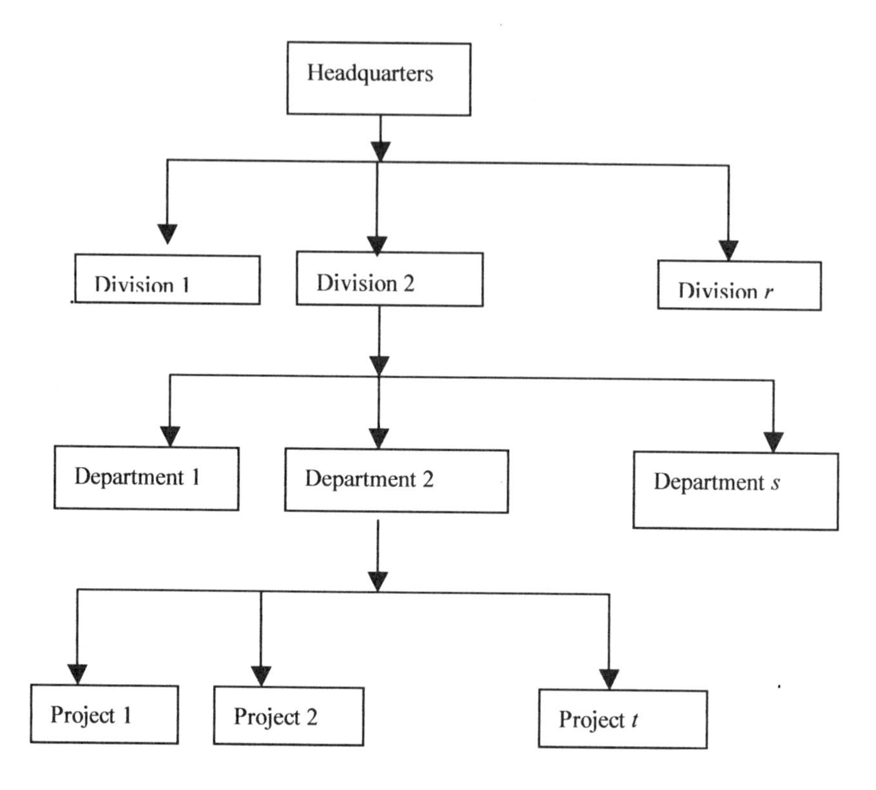

Figure 1. Hierarchical structure of organizations of defense-oriented R&D

The flow of funds through the hierarchy is initiated at the top. It takes two forms: government funds, and revenues from customer-ordered research. These funds are first controlled on a divisional level and next on a departmental level. At each level, some resources are set aside for "internal consumption", that is, as overheads; the remainder is passed on down the hierarchy to lower levels of the organization. Examples of overheads at the divisional level are personnel training, maintenance of existing facilities and the construction of new facilities, developing knowledge in various basic scientific areas. These are crucial activities for the long-term (10-20 years) objectives of the division, maintaining its technological leadership.

A crucial issue is the efficiency of resource allocation. That question has at least two aspects:

- Do the mid-level units take enough (too little or too much) resources for their own use vis-à-vis the amounts that they pass on?
- Is the allocation of resources by a mid-level unit to its lower level units done efficiently?

Let us use the generic term "departments" for the organizational entities below the level of divisions. The chunk of resources allocated from a "division" to a "department" goes through a similar process of evaluation and allocation, only that the horizon relevant for the overhead activities carried out by the department is shortened to 5-10 years. Again, these activities could be: sending employees to courses, building test equipment or facilities that might be used by various projects, performing control activities to verify compliance of the projects with external regulations, etc.

The planning and execution cycle of individual R&D projects is typically 2-5 years. So, at the bottom level, the scenario is the conventional settings of DEA -- we have $N(d)$ projects under the jurisdiction of the d-th department. We shall assume that the projects are close enough to make comparison among them legitimate. To evaluate and rank them, we may employ any one of the DEA models that we find appropriate.

Following Cook *et al.*, 1998 we are also interested in the evaluation of the various departments reporting to each division head. The purpose of such rankings could be to find out, for example, how well the departments have allocated their resources. We might even be interested in rating the divisions themselves in decreasing order of priority. However, the small numbers of departments (and even smaller number of divisions) precludes any ordinary DEA for such purposes. Instead, one would have to rely on an aggregation that starts at the lowest level of the hierarchy, or to develop special models to do it. (For the use of non-parametric methods to find out whether there are any systematic differences between groupings of DMUs, see Brockett and Golany 1996 and Golany and Thore, 1997a.)

Cook *et al.* also discussed situations when there are several criteria (called "attributes") for grouping the DMUs into a hierarchy. These issues do not seem to be of interest for our application, since our hierarchy is always stable (once a particular project is assigned to a department, it stays there).

2.1 Inputs and outputs

It is typically easy to identify the various individual projects in terms of the inputs that they use - - engineering hours of different kinds, equipment, laboratory facilities available at the right time and knowledge capital (basic and applied). Sometimes, however, it is difficult to express and quantify the amount of output. This happens because the R&D objectives of the organization are aimed to enhance technological leadership at the national level and are definitely not for profit.

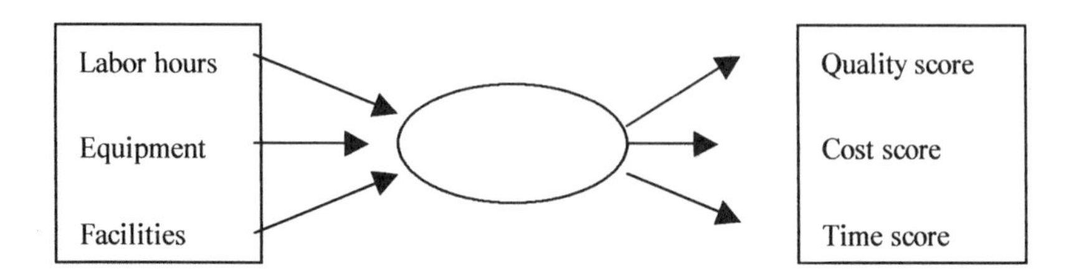

Figure 2. Inputs and outputs of R&D project

Thus, we shall use subjective performance ratings of projects to measure the outputs. Using these output scores is essential in bridging the gaps that exist among projects in different technological areas (e.g., software and hardware projects). Figure 2 lists three performance ratings:

- Quality = the gap between the original engineering specifications and actual performance. Obviously, there are many dimensions to this concept, and each one of them may be weighted by an a priori weight.
- Cost = gap between original expected product unit cost and currently estimated unit cost (according to the blueprint).
- Timeliness = target number of days to completion minus estimated time to completion. These time estimates should include reasonable estimates of technical uncertainties, and uncertainty about the future market (including uncertainty about moves by competitors, national and international).

The resource use and performance of the R&D projects are allocated and monitored by the management of the departments (see Figure 1). We now discuss how this information is communicated, reported and processed upwards along the hierarchy. The division manager is not concerned with the resource use of individual projects; instead, he will develop control routines for the total use of resources by each department, preparing a table like Table 1 below.

Table 1. Matrix of use of resources across departments

	Electric engineering hours	Mechanical engineering hours	Optical engineering hours	Computer engineering hours	Equipment	Facilities
Dept 1						
Dept 2						
...						
Dept *s*						

We can imagine that one such table is prepared for each division, and sent to the headquarters (see Figure 1). Presumably, these tables will assist management at the divisional and headquarters level to see to it that the actual use of resources complies with some master plan for allocation of resources. What does this master plan look like? We shall return to this question, but already now it must be noted that the master plan should typically be flexible enough to permit transfer of resources between divisions. It would rarely take the form of a master matrix of type Table 1 with goal figures for each cell. Presumably, however, in the short run the column sums of the table are given and fixed.

3. PRELIMINARY DISCUSSION OF DEA

The problem at hand blends two problems of a different and even in many ways conflicting nature: the ranking of a group of projects in terms of their performance, and the allocation of scarce resources to these projects. These objectives can easily become conflicting, because it is of little help to assess the priority of a project if there are no resources, or incomplete resources, available to realize it.

We first discuss the application of DEA to rank the projects. There are three possible ways of doing this:

- either on a completely decentralized basis, letting each department head rank its own projects, and those only,
- pooling the projects belonging to each division, and establishing a master ranking for each division across its various departments,
- pooling all projects in the entire organization, establishing a master ranking across all departments and all divisions.

Let us use the index $j = 1,2,...,N$ to denote the master list of projects when all projects of the entire organization are pooled. Further, let $\{j \in A\}$ be some subset (either a department or a division) of the master list $\{1,2,...,N\}$. In the common manner, the inputs or resources are denoted X_{ij}, $i = 1,2,...,m$

and the outputs or performance indicators Y_{rj}, $r = 1,2,...,s$. Let k denote the specific project currently being evaluated.

We choose the output-oriented version of the BCC model, since the present concern is with determining the maximal frontier performance of each R&D project, given its inputs. Furthermore, to simplify, we assume that the solution to the DEA program always delivers an un-dominated point on the efficiency frontier, i.e. with zero output and input slacks.

Ranking project k relative to its peers within the subset A only, the DEA program reads

$$\text{Max } \psi_k \tag{1}$$

subject to

$$\psi_k Y_{rk} - \sum_{j \in A} \lambda_{jk} Y_{rj} \leq 0, \qquad r = 1,2,...,s$$

$$\sum_{j \in A} \lambda_{jk} X_{ij} \leq X_{ik}, \; i = 1,...,m$$

$$\sum_{j \in A} \lambda_{jk} = 1, \text{ and } \lambda_{jk} \geq 0, \; j \in A$$

where ψ_k is the efficiency rating of project k and λ_{jk} , $j \in A$ are the weights of other projects to be used when forming its best practice output $\sum_{j \in A} \lambda_{jk} Y_{rj}$ and its best practice input $\sum_{j \in A} \lambda_{jk} X_{ij}$.

On the other hand, evaluating the same project relative to all projects in the master list (the third possibility listed above), the set $j \in A$ in program (1) should be replaced by the full list $j \in \{1,2,...,N\}$.

For subsequent use, we also note an alternate formulation of the conventional DEA program that brings together and embeds all individual ranking problems inside a single aggregate program. It is

$$\text{Max } \sum_{k \in A} \psi_k \tag{2}$$

subject to

$$\psi_k Y_{rk} - \sum_{j \in A} \lambda_{jk} Y_{rj} \leq 0, \qquad r = 1,2,...,s \text{ and } k \in A,.$$

$$\sum_{j \in A} \lambda_{jk} X_{ij} \leq X_{ik}, \; i = 1,...,m \text{ and } k \in A,$$

$$\sum_{j \in A} \lambda_{jk} = 1, \; k \in A,$$

$$\lambda_{jk} \geq 0, \; j,k \in A$$

The aggregate objective function in (2) is the sum of all the individual efficiency ratings, all of which are to be determined under the set of conventional constraints for each research project evaluated. There are yet no "couplings" (in the sense of decomposition theory) tying the individual DEA programs together. The aggregate program therefore breaks up into the N conventional DEA programs of type (1).

4. EXPLORING HIERARCHICAL STRUCTURES BY MULTI-STAGE DEA

To explore the interplay among levels of the hierarchy, we turn to the use of multi-stage formulations of DEA. The idea of splitting the DEA procedure into two or more consecutive steps over time has been around for some time. There is an extensive discussion of various multi-stage DEA procedures in the last chapter of Charnes, Cooper, Lewin and Seiford, 1994. Under the heading of "hybrid modeling" (ibid., pp. 431-434), these authors made the following observations:

- The number of output variables in the first stage need not be equal to the number of input variables in the second stage. For instance, there can be output variables from the first stage that are not fed into the second stage. Similarly, all input variables into the second stage need not be brought from the outputs of the first stage.
- It is possible to mix input-oriented and output-oriented versions of DEA For instance, the first stage may be input oriented and the second stage may be output oriented.
- One may also mix the form of the DEA model used at each stage. For instance, one may form a CCR model (constant returns to scale) at the first stage and a BBC model (variable returns to scale) at the second stage.
- The authors also discuss the possibility of using a DEA procedure with three stages rather than two: an introductory stage, an intermediate stage and a final stage.

Independently of the work by Charnes *et al.*, 1994, Färe and Grosskopf (1996) initiated a modeling effort aimed at multi-stage DMUs. Lothgren and Tambour (2000) later implemented their theoretical foundation. These authors explored multi-stage units where some outputs from one stage feed as inputs into subsequent stages. In our work we also investigate the impact of such intermediate factors but we do so in a structure of one-to-many controls (i.e., hierarchical trees) rather than the one-to-one structure that was used by Färe and his colleagues.

Let us focus on two successive levels of the hierarchy, say department and projects. Assume the department receives capital (K) and labor (L) from the division. It leaves K_0 and L_0 for its own use and allocates the rest to its relevant projects. That is,

$$\sum_{j \in A} K_j + K_0 = K, \text{ and} \qquad (3)$$
$$\sum_{j \in A} L_j + L_0 = L$$

(where A denotes the department). The department uses its K_0 and L_0 to generate an output that we shall call its "support level" and denote by S_0. This output is then used as an input (resource) by the projects within the department. The departmental support level can be expressed in terms of qualified support personnel, test equipment, and other means that the department is making available to its projects.

The chain of causation may be depicted as unfolding over two consecutive periods or "stages," in the following manner:

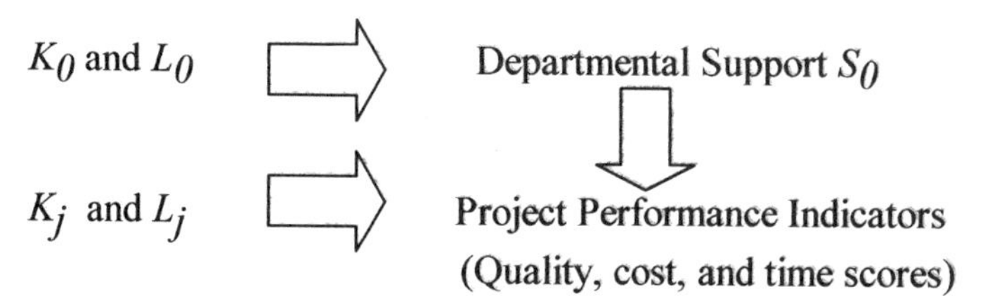

Figure 3. Causal structure of two-stage model

In this causal process, the factor "Departmental Support" is an intermediate causal factor. It is at the same time the estimated output of the first-stage departmental production of support, and the input (together with individual project inputs) into second-stage project developments. Furthermore, S_0 is not split into several components each serving a particular project. Instead, we assume that all the project receive the same amount of support (S_0). The rational behind this assumption is that S_0 is typically composed of qualitative elements such as knowledge, reputation, etc. that are difficult to split into pieces.

Now, we can evaluate the performance of the department and its projects in several ways:

- *Separate evaluation of each level*: run a DEA model for the department (in comparison to like departments) with two inputs (K_0 and L_0) and one output (S_0). Then, run a DEA to evaluate the projects across several departments where each project has three inputs (K_j, L_j and S_0) and three outputs (those depicted in Figures 2 or 3).

- *Aggregate evaluation*: for each department, aggregate the three output scores of its relevant projects (e.g., this can be done using a weighted average of the projects' scores where the dollar values of the projects serve as weights). Then, run a DEA only at the aggregated departmental level with the two inputs K and L, and the three aggregated project performance indicators as outputs. Notice that the intermediate factor S_0 does not play a role in this evaluation.

The first possibility offers a more detailed analysis. We may find situations, in which the department level performed well, producing an adequate level of support that was later wasted by some or all of the projects. Alternatively, we may encounter situations in which the department uses too much capital and labor to produce its support level, and yet the individual projects are able to overcome this handicap, generating significant output scores. In any case, a separate evaluation may guide the department in deciding on the proportion of resources it should leave for itself.

The aggregate evaluation, on the other hand, does not care how the department uses the resources as long as the outcome is deemed efficient, in terms of the eventual success of the R&D projects. This approach will be useful to evaluate whether the department was given enough, too much or too little resources to match with its eventual projects scores.

We now turn to the mathematical formulation for the separate evaluation, presenting it as a two-stage DEA. For simplicity, we shall stick to an output-oriented BCC formulation for both stages. Use the index $d = 1,2,\dots,D$ to denote the master list of all departments (across divisions) of the entire organization, and let $\{h \in V\}$ be a subset of "like" departments in the master list $\{1,2,\dots,N\}$.

For the first stage, the task is to rank the performance of the departments in producing the support levels. To evaluate the performance of a specific department $h = u$, one solves the program (analogous to program (1))

$$\text{Max } \psi_u \tag{4}$$

subject to

$$\psi_u S_u - \sum_{h \in V} \lambda_h S_h \leq 0,$$

$$\sum_{h \in V} \lambda_h K_h \leq K_u,$$

$$\sum_{h \in V} \lambda_h L_h \leq L_u,$$

$$\sum_{h \in V} \lambda_h = 1, \text{ and } \lambda_h \geq 0, \quad h \in V.$$

In simple words, program (4) seeks to maximize the expansion or enlargement factor ψ subject to the conditions that each of the expanded output indicators cannot exceed best practice output, and that the actual use of the two inputs capital and labor cannot fall short of best practice use.

For the second stage, the task is to rank projects across departments. As before, denote the set of projects to be ranked by A. Evaluating the performance of a specific project $j = k$, one solves

$$\text{Max } \psi_k \tag{5}$$

subject to

$$\psi_k Y_{rk} - \Sigma_{j \in A} \lambda_{jk} Y_{rj} \leq 0, \quad r = 1,2,\ldots,s$$

$$\Sigma_{j \in A} \lambda_{jk} K_j \leq K_k,$$

$$\Sigma_{j \in A} \lambda_{jk} L_j \leq L_k,$$

$$\Sigma_{j \in A} \lambda_{jk} S_j \leq S_k,$$

$$\Sigma_{j \in A} \lambda_{jk} = 1, \text{ and } \lambda_{jk} \geq 0, \; j \in A.$$

This time, the DEA program seeks to maximize the expansion or enlargement factor ψ subject to the conditions that the expanded departmental support cannot exceed best practice departmental support, and that the actual use of the three inputs capital, labor and departmental support cannot fall short of best practice use.

Programs (4) and (5) together form a two-stage or "hybrid" DEA model, of the type discussed by Charnes, Cooper, Lewin and Seiford, *ibid.*

Pursuing the separate evaluation further, additional in-depth analysis may be suggested. First, one may want to define and measure the support factor – probably on a qualitative rather than a quantitative scale. Second, one may want to investigate whether the support factor should be considered as a cumulative rather than a periodic factor. It probably makes more sense to view support as a cumulative factor where a project may enjoy department capabilities that were built over a long period that precedes the period under evaluation. In that case, the output at the department level would be the change in the value of its support between the end of last period and the end of the present period. The input to each of the relevant projects would be the cumulative support value associated with the department.

5. ALLOCATING SCARCE RESOURCES BY ZERO-ONE PROGRAMMING

Perhaps the most natural way to conceptualize the problem of allocating scarce resources throughout the hierarchical organization is to think of it as being carried out in two successive steps:

- first, the task of evaluating and ranking the R&D projects,
- second, the task of allocating resources to them, based on these rankings.

If this dichotomy is accepted, the first part of the analysis is carried out by DEA, as already described (Section 3). The second part of the analysis involves allocating resources to individual projects in the order of their rankings, as long as the available resources so permit.

For instance, assume that one first decides to pool all R&D projects inside each division (that is, across departments) and establishes one ranking list for each division. Furthermore, assume that headquarters have allocated a fixed budget of resources to each division. The task then facing the division manager is to allocate his budget between departments, letting each department carry out its projects in the order of their rankings, until it runs out of resources.

In order to facilitate this procedure, we shall first reorder the projects so that the efficient projects are listed first and the inefficient projects follow them, in the order of monotonically increasing efficiency coefficients $\psi \geq 1$. (In the case of ties, one may just leave the original order unchanged.)

As before, let $j = 1,2,...,N$ be a master list of all projects (across divisions) and let $j \in A$ represent the projects of division A. Next, reorder the projects by their divisional rankings so that

$$\psi_1^* \leq \psi_2^* \leq \ldots \leq \psi_j^* \leq \ldots \leq \psi_{N(A)}^*, \quad j \in A \tag{6}$$

where $N(A)$ is the number of projects in the division, and the asterisk in the common manner denotes the optimal value.

Imagine that a divisional head uses the following simple step-wise rule of allocation of resources to departments and to projects. First, resources to all efficient projects are allocated. Then, one by one, proceeding in the order of the efficiency ratings (6), resources are allocated to inefficient projects, as long as the global availability can accommodate them. When the first resource limit is encountered, allocation of resources stops; this and all subsequent projects are discontinued (terminated). (This is by no means the only possible rule of allocation of scarce resources; we can think of several possible variations on or modifications of this rule.)

To spell out in mathematics what has now been said, define the binary variables z_j, $j \in A$ where each z_j can take only one of two values, viz.

- $z_j = 1$ indicating that the project will be carried out, with the full amount of its required resources allocated to it,
- $z_j = 0$ meaning that the project will not be carried out, with no resources allocated to it.

The limited availability of divisional resources may then be written as

$$\sum_{j \in A} z_j X_{ij} \leq R_i, \quad i=1,2,\dots, m \tag{7}$$

where R_i is the availability of resource i (provided by headquarters). If one or several resources are not globally constrained, the corresponding upper limit may be taken to be an arbitrary and sufficiently large positive number. So, formally, we can always assume that all resources are constrained by (7).

The rule of step-wise allocation of resources to projects by division A in the order of monotonically increasing efficiency ratings may then be expressed as follows:

$$z_1 \geq z_2 \geq \dots \geq z_j \geq \dots \geq z_{NA} \quad , j \in A \tag{8}$$

Since the z_j's can only take on the two values 1 and 0, the list (8) will start off with all accepted projects, for which $z_j = 1$. At cut-off, the z-value will drop from 1 to 0, and the corresponding relation in (8) will hold as strict inequality. Finally, for all non-accepted projects, the z_j values are all 0.

As one proceeds down the list of increasing efficiency coefficients, the aim is to exhaust the global availability of resources, that is, to exhaust the slack in the global resource constraint (7). To accomplish it, we construct a so-called goal-focusing program, calculating total penalties

$$\sum_i M_i (R_i - \sum_{j \in A} z_j X_{ij}) \tag{9}$$

where M_i is the unit penalty for non-use of resource i. In the common manner of goal programming and goal focusing, the unit penalty is a non-Archimedean transcendental, reflecting the relative priority of the goal. It may not be possible to drive total penalties down to zero, but at least one wants to make the total penalties (9) as small as possible.

The entire globally resource-constrained program now reads

$$\text{Min } \sum_i M_i (R_i - \sum_{j \in A} z_j X_{ij}) \tag{10}$$

subject to

$$\sum_{j \in A} z_j X_{ij} \leq R_i \quad , i = 1,2,\ldots, m$$

$$z_1 \geq z_2 \geq \ldots \geq z_j \geq \ldots \geq z_{NA} \quad , j \in A$$

$$z_j = 0 \text{ or } 1, \quad j \in A$$

To sum up, program (10) determines a stepwise exhaustion of the divisional resource constraints. The exhaustion is effected via the zero-one accept/reject variables z_j and a goal-focusing feature.

Actually, the optimal solution to (10) remains the same for any positive unit penalties M_i , so that one may simply put all $M_i = 1$. It is easy to see why. As one moves step-wise along the ranking priority (8), the zero-one variables are switched on (that is, $z_j = 1$), one by one. The only thing that matters in evaluating yet another project in the ranking order is whether it, too, in its entirety can be accommodated by the available resources. If it can, the total resource slack will be reduced further by switching the zero-one variable for that next project to $z_j = 1$.

To see the full power of the goal-focusing approach, we now make a slight change in the assumptions. Instead of the "hard" resource limitations (7), suppose that the division head may - - if pressed - - be able to bargain with headquarters, coming by some additional resources. That is, replace (7) by the "soft" goaling mechanism

$$\sum_{j \in A} z_j X_{ij} + d_i - e_i = R_i, \quad i = 1,2,\ldots,m \tag{11}$$

where d_i and e_i are both nonnegative and $d_i e_i = 0$, that is at least one of the two deviations must equal zero. A positive d_i means some slack under-utilization of resources, as before. A positive e_i means some injection of additional resources above the existing allocation.

Both deviations are associated with penalties. The unit penalty for non-use of a resource is written M_i as before; the unit penalty for excessive use is written N_i .Now the entire programming problem reads

$$\text{Min } \sum_i M_i d_i + N_i e_i \tag{12}$$

subject to

$$\sum_{j \in A} z_j X_{ij} + d_i - e_i = R_i, \quad i = 1,2,\ldots, m$$

$$z_1 \geq z_2 \geq \ldots \geq z_j \geq \ldots \geq z_{NA} \quad , j \in A$$

$$d_i, e_i \geq 0, , \quad i = 1,2,\ldots, m$$
$$z_j = 0 \text{ or } 1, \quad j \in A$$

Model (12) may be used to portray a variety of institutional settings inside the organizational hierarchy involving bargaining situations where divisions may actually exceed their allocation of resources, counting on the headquarters to come up with the shortfall. The result is more flexibility in the entire system, with a potential to accommodate R&D breakthroughs and accompanying increased needs for resources when occurring.

5.1 A numerical example

Consider a small example with one input, one output, and 6 projects, as exhibited in Table 2.

Table 2. Data for numerical example

Project	Input X_j	Output Y_j
$j=1$	1	1
$j=2$	2	2
$j=3$	2.5	1
$j=4$	3	2.5
$j=5$	5	2
$j=6$	6	3

The optimal frontier is shown in Figure 4. Projects $j = 1,2,4,6.$ are located on the frontier; projects $j = 3,5$ fall behind it.

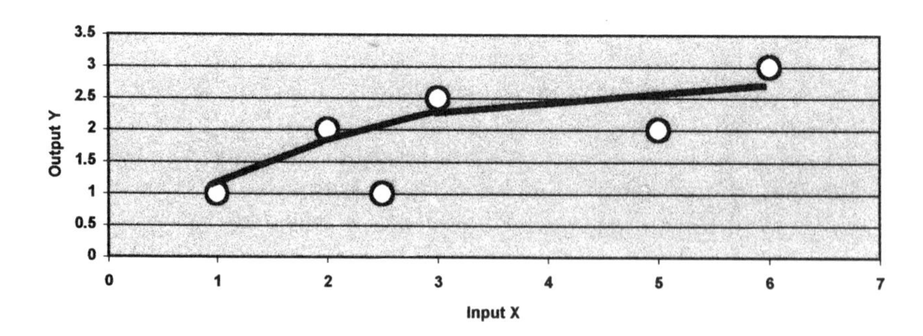

Figure 4. Numerical example

The result is listed in Table 3 below. Note that the efficiency rating for the subefficient projects is greater than unity, in the common fashion of the output-oriented DEA.

Table 3. Results of conventional output-oriented DEA

Project	ψ^* **score**	**Best Input** $\sum_j \lambda_j X_j$	**Best Output** $\sum_j \lambda_j Y_j$
$j = 1$	1	1	1
$j = 2$	1	2	2
$j = 3$	2.25	2.5	2.25
$j = 4$	1	3	2.5
$j = 5$	1.417	5	2.833
$j = 6$	1	6	3

Reordering the projects in terms of falling efficiencies (increasing ψ_1^* scores) we get the order *1,2,4,6,5,3*. Project 3 is the loser.

Next, assume now the presence of a global resource constraint, limiting total best practice input to *16* units (rather than the *19.5* units employed in the solution displayed in Table 2). Program (10) then reads

$$\text{Min} \quad M(16 - z_1X_1 - z_2X_2 - z_4X_4 - z_6X_6 - z_5X_5 - z_3X_3) \qquad (13)$$

subject to

$$z_1X_1 + z_2X_2 + z_4X_4 + z_6X_6 + z_5X_5 + z_3X_3 \leq 16,$$
$$z_1 \geq z_2 \geq z_4 \geq z_6 \geq z_5 \geq z_3.$$
$$z_j = 0 \text{ or } 1, \quad j = 1,2,3,4,5,6$$

where M is a suitable large positive number.

The solution, of course, is $z_1 = z_2 = z_4 = z_6 = 1$ and $z_5 = z_3 = 0$. Projects *1,2,4* and *6* will be carried out, with a total resource use of *12* units. Projects *5* and *3* will not be carried out. There will be *4* units of resources left unused.

But is this really sound advice? Would it not be smarter to permit project *3* to go ahead, after all? It uses up only 2.5 units of resources, and the combined resource use of the package of projects *1,2,4,6* and *3* would only be *14.5* units, still within the total budget of *16* units.

The dilemma that one confronts here is one of trading off performance against budget availability. Is it right to sacrifice performance in order to squeeze projects inside an available budget? There seems to be no general answer to this question.

6. COMPROMISING BEST PRACTICE IN THE PRESENCE OF GLOBAL RESOURCE CONSTRAINTS

It is easy to extol the virtue of keeping the DEA ranking procedure separate from the task of allocating scarce resources. Management should be offered a clean and unadulterated estimate of the true performance of each project. Can we also expect the project optimally to be carried out that way, in a situation of tight resources and an overall need to economize on their use? Perhaps it would be wiser to make allowance for such scarcities already in the DEA rankings themselves?

The alternative is to modify the DEA calculations up-front to allow for the presence of a set of global resource constraints. We now show how this can be done. The starting point is the embedded master version of the conventional DEA calculations, program (2), to which we adjoin the global constraints

$$\Sigma_{k \in A} \ (\Sigma_{j \in A} \ \lambda_{jk} X_{ij}) \leq R_i, \quad i = 1,2,\ldots, m \tag{14}$$

The expression inside the parenthesis in (14) in the common manner stands for "best practice" inputs. Constraint (14) states that the sum total of all best-practice inputs must be accommodated by the global resource availability R_i. In other words, best practice for each R&D project is now adjusted or compromised to allow for the presence of these global constraints.

We now form a global master program consisting of the individual DEA programs - - one for each project - - and adjoining the couplings (14):

$$\text{Max } \Sigma_{k \in A} \ {}_{+}\psi 1 \tag{15}$$

subject to

$$\psi_k Y_{rk} - \Sigma_{j \in A} \ \lambda_{jk} Y_{rj} \leq 0, \qquad r = 1,2,\ldots,s \text{ and } k \in A,.$$

$$\Sigma_{j \in A} \ \lambda_{jk} X_{ij} \leq X_{ik}, \ i = 1,\ldots,m \text{ and } k \in A,$$

$$\Sigma_{j \in A} \ \lambda_{jk} = 1, \ k \in A,$$

$$\Sigma_{k \in A} \ (\Sigma_{j \in A} \ \lambda_{jk} X_{ij}) \leq R_i, \quad i = 1,2,\ldots, m$$

$$\lambda_{jk} \geq 0, \ j,k \in A$$

The solution to program (15) ranks the R&D projects, and allocates resources to them, in one sweep.

Invoking standard theory of decomposition of linear programs (see e.g. the text Thompson and Thore, 1992), the master program (15) may be decentralized into individual programs, one for each project $k \in A$. Various decentralization methods are possible, but common for them all is the delegation of some kind of information or constraint from the master program to the individual programs. In other words, these individual programs will take the form of the standard DEA program *and* some additional information delegated from the master.

As is well known (see e.g. Golany and Thore, 1997b), any kind of additional (binding) mathematical constraint imposed upon the standard DEA format results in a modified efficiency frontier. Considering the outcome for an individual project, there are three possibilities:

- the project will be allocated its full need of resources, and the globally constrained
- best practice coincides with the unconstrained practice;
- the project will be curtailed and will be operated on a lower scale;
- the project will be dropped altogether.

The first and the last of these three alternatives we have already encountered using zero-one variables (Section 5). The middle alternative is new and may appear unsettling. Note in particular that there is no guarantee that inefficient projects only will be trimmed to satisfy the global constraints. Even projects located on the efficiency frontier may be compromised.

6.1 Numerical example

To illustrate, we return to the numerical example discussed in Section 5.1. Consider again the data exhibited in Table 2. This time, adjoin to the set of regular DEA programs a global constraint limiting the total resource use to 16 units. Program (15) then reads

$$\text{Max } \psi_1 + \psi_2 + \psi_3 + \psi_4 + \psi_5 + \psi_6 \tag{16}$$

subject to

$$\psi_k Y_k - \Sigma_j \lambda_{jk} Y_j \leq 0, \quad k = 1,2,3,4,5,6$$

$$\Sigma_j \lambda_{jk} X_j \leq X_k, \quad k = 1,2,3,4,5,6$$

$$\Sigma_{j \in A} \lambda_{jk} = 1, \quad k = 1,2,3,4,5,6$$

$$\Sigma_{k \in A} (\Sigma_{j \in A} \lambda_{jk} X_j) \leq 16$$

$$\lambda_{jk} \geq 0, \quad j,k = 1,2,3,4,5,6 .$$

The new solution is exhibited in Table 4. Note that the new solutions for the first 4 projects are identical to the old ones. But the solutions for the two projects $j = 5$ and $j = 6$ are different:

- Project $j = 5$ is now downscaled to use a slightly smaller input, only 4.5 units rather than the 5 units used before. Notice that best-practice output is still located on the old frontier (the thick black line in the figure). It comes out as 2.75 units.

Table 4. Results of globally resource-constrained DEA

Project	ψ^* score	Best Input $\sum_j \lambda_j X_j$	Best Output $\sum_j \lambda_j Y_j$
$j = 1$	1	1	1
$j = 2$	1	2	2
$j = 3$	2.25	2.5	2.25
$j = 4$	1	3	2.5
$j = 5$	1.375	4.5	2.75
$j = 6$	0.833	3	2.5

- Project $j = 6$, the most input-intensive project of all projects, is curtailed quite drastically, down to 3 units of input - - only half of its old resource use. But best-practice output is still located on the old DEA frontier. It is 2.5. The best-practice point for this project now actually coincides with the actual performance of project $j = 4$. So, the result for this project demonstrates that *even efficient projects may be curtailed.* Note also that the efficiency rating of project $j = 6$ is now only 0.833, that is, it is less than unity. Here is a clear signal that the global resource constraint intervenes in the old DEA program and displaces the old best practice point.

The above discussion assumes that all six projects will actually be carried out. As we have seen, it requires a scaling down of project $j = 6$. Whether such downscaling is technically possible, or not, is another matter.

7. CONCLUDING REMARKS

As we have had reason to point out several times, ranking projects and allocating resources to them are two different things. Actually, these two procedures can easily appear to be mutually contradictory: in the first instance, one might believe that the ranking of projects should be carried out without regard to the availability of resources to carry them through.

Conversely, economists have studied the task of allocating resources to projects for more than half a century, without ever asking for a ranking of those projects.

And yet, what meaning is there to rank projects if resources are not available to see them through the required development in the laboratory and the subsequent commercialization?

To sort out the various issues involved, we found it useful (in Section 4) to examine the twin problems of rankings and allocation of resources inside a hierarchical organization consisting of "divisions" and "departments." Each division allocates resources such as capital and labor to its various departments. Each department ranks and prioritizes a number of R&D projects. To model this sequence of events, we formulated a two-stage DEA model. In the first stage, the departments compete for resources from the divisions, and convert the resources obtained into "departmental support" such as research facilities, in-house knowledge and expertise. Each department makes its support available to all its projects. In the second stage, and drawing upon the support received, the R&D projects of each department are rated.

A baffling issue that we wrestled with in Section 5 was that of "indivisibilities." Are R&D projects indivisible, or is it possible to operate them on a smaller or a larger scale? If a department is running out of resources but there are still some projects awaiting initiation, is it then possible to operate them on a scaled-down level?

Formally, one can always deal with such a situation by identifying a few realistic levels of operation of a given research project, and defining each such level as a separate project. Proceeding in this manner, all projects are indeed "indivisible". The proper mathematical technique of dealing with them is zero-one programming.

Rather than scaling down a project, management may decide to extend its time horizon and let it run over a few more months or even a few more years. There may be several advantages to be gained by keeping projects on the "back-burner" as it were. Issues of technical feasibility may take some time to establish, and in the meanwhile management may get some breathing time to set aside necessary resources for the subsequent commercialization.

Taking a somewhat different tack, we demonstrated in Section 6 a kind of grand synthesis, fusing the DEA ranking technique with considerations of resource availability. The idea here was to build resource availability directly into the ranking technique. The result was a linear master program with "global" constraints (the resource constraints). If the global constraints are not binding, the master program breaks up into the standard DEA calculations, one for each DMU. But if one or several global constraints do bind, the DEA calculations have to be modified. A new set of efficiency scores are obtained, reflecting the alternate priorities that would hold in a world that pays due regard to the existing resource scarcities.

Adopting this approach, there is no longer any conflict between ranking and resource allocation. All projects ranked can be realized with the available resources. But as we saw, there is a price to be paid for such analytical nicety. The modified rankings may severely punish some otherwise efficient projects that use up large amounts of scarce resources.

REFERENCES

Brockett, P.L. and Golany, B. (1996): "Using Rank Statistics for Determining Programmatic Efficiency Differences in Data Envelopment Analysis," *Management Science*, Vol. 42, pp. 466-472.

Charnes, A., Cooper, W.W., Lewin, A.Y. and Seiford, L.M. (1994): *Data Envelopment Analysis: Theory, Methodology and Applications*, Kluwer Academic Publishers, Dordrecht.

Cook, W.D., Chai, D., Doyle, J. and R. Green, R. (1998): "Hierarchies and Groups in DEA," *Journal of Productivity Analysis*, Vol.10, pp. 177-198.

Färe, R. and Grosskopf, S. (1996) *Intertemporal Production Frontiers With Dynamic DEA*, Kluwer Academic Publishers, Dordrecht.

Golany, B. and Thore, S. (1997a): "The Competitiveness of Nations," *in IMPACT: How IC2 Institute Research Affects Public Policy and Business Practices*, ed. by Cooper, W.W., Thore, S., Gibson, D. and Phillips, F., Quorum Books, Westport, Connecticut.

Golany, B. and Thore, S. (1997b): "Restricted Best Practice Selection in DEA: An Overview with a Case Study Evaluating the Socio-Economic Performance of Nations," *Annals of Operations Research*, Vol. 73, pp. 117- 140.

Lothgren, M. and Tambour, M. (1999): "Productivity and Customer Satisfaction in Swedish Pharmacies: A DEA Network Model," *European Journal of Operational Research*, 115, pp. 449-458.

Thompson, G.L. and Thore, S. (1992): *Computational Economics: Economic Modeling with Optimization Software*, Scientific Press, South San Francisco, Calif.

PART II

ENVIRONMENTAL CONCERNS

Chapter 9

The Environmental Impact of New Products
A Tutorial

S. Thore and P.C. Ferrão
Instituto Superior Técnico, Lisbon

Abstract: Negative externalities of goods may arise both from their production, their use by the consumers, and from the disposal of waste. The concept of life cycle assessment (LCA) of a good is explained, tracking the environmental impacts of a good along its entire life cycle. Some elementary linear programming models of industrial production are presented, illustrating the possible presence of environmental goals laid down on resource use, on consumer demand, or on environmental impacts. The corresponding dual programs are formulated, featuring excise taxes to be imposed on harmful releases into the environment (rather than direct constraints)

Key words: Negative externalities, property rights, life cycle assessment, the greenhouse effect, eco-profiles, environmental goals, excise tax, environmental impact coefficients, shadow prices of resources

1. NEGATIVE EXTERNALITIES OF TECHNOLOGY

The advances in technology during the last centuries have gone together with an extensive destruction of the environment. Lately, a wealth of scientific knowledge has been accumulated regarding the effects of pesticides and herbicides on the ground water, the effects of chlorofluorcarbons (CFCs) on the ozone layer surrounding the globe, and the long-run effects of the burning of tropical rain forests.

The problem of negative environmental impacts of technology, use of resources, and the disposal of harmful substances and products is that the true cost of such effects does not appear in the profit-and-loss calculation of the individual company. The cost of disease and other harms is borne by workers, consumers, or even by people who participate neither in the production nor the consumption of the product in question. These are so-called "external costs" or negative "externalities". Whenever such costs are present, the conventional profit and loss calculation of a technology gives an erroneous picture of the true cost to society. There is a discrepancy between the profit calculation of the individual producer and for society as a whole

Negative externalities occur or are exacerbated when no *property rights* have been defined to resources like air or water. No property owner will claim recompense when a polluter releases toxic substances into the environment. The market price paid by the polluter for discharging the toxic substances is zero.

Restoring the environment and safeguarding it offers tremendous technological challenges. In a society that is willing to accord environmental repair work a high priority, there will also emerge incentives to develop new environmental technology. There is money to be made from converting waste to energy, and from building refrigerators using helium or natural gas as coolants. Harnessing solar, and wind energy can be highly profitable. There are consumers willing to pay for the cleaning up the beaches and the designing and building of attractive resorts. Producing and selling organic food is big business nowadays.

2. LIFE CYCLE ASSESSMENT OF ECONOMIC GOODS

Life cycle assessment (LCA) is a technique of assessing the environmental impacts associated with a product or service, during its life cycle. The life cycle covers the entire time span from the extraction primary resources employed for manufacturing the good to the end of its useful life and its disposal.

Figure 1 illustrates the principal phases of the life cycle. The blocks of the diagram represent processes or actions; between the blocks flows energy or products. Reading the diagram from the left to the right, one follows the conventional production chain from resources to the use of the finished product and the eventual disposal of it. Two feedback loops are illustrated: the reuse of goods returning the discarded product to the distribution block, and recycling and the return of the discarded product as input into production.

As an example of the life cycle, consider the manufacture, distribution and consumer use of wine and beer bottles. The main raw material in the glass mills is silicon sand. The needed electric power is provided by an electric utility. The electric utilities burned coal or oil and discharged sulfur and other pollutants into the air. Should these negative impacts be included in the balance sheet? For any given study, the analyst has to decide how far back upstream in the production chain it is desired to track the effects. Somewhere, the line has to be drawn between endogenous and exogenous factors.

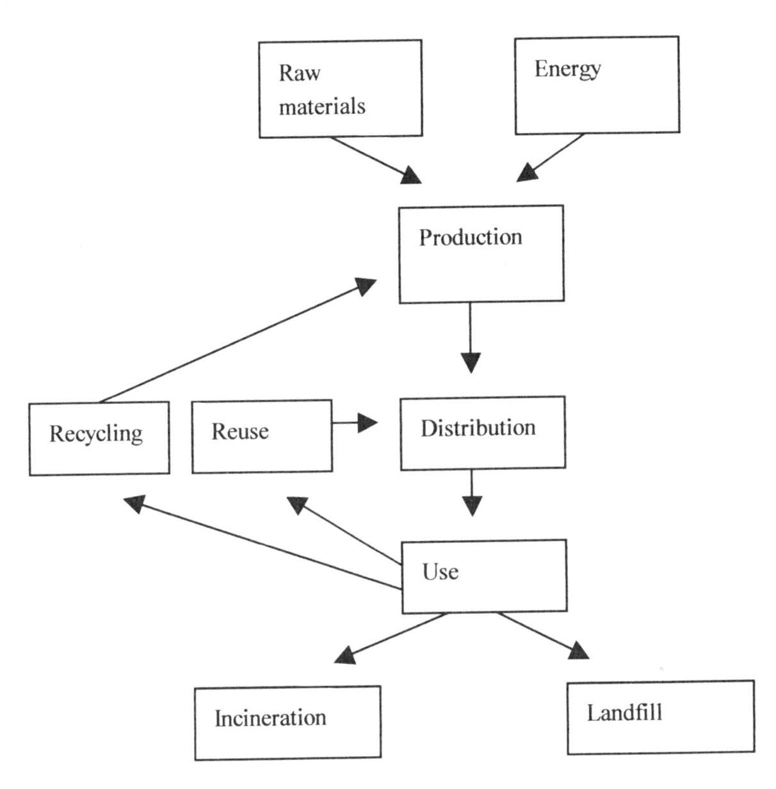

Figure 1. Life cycle of economic goods illustrated.

Once the glass bottles have been manufactured, they are transported from the glass mills to the wine and beer bottlers. Actually, transportation is an important feature at every link of the logistics chain; it is not shown in Figure 1. Also, there is use of energy and discharges into the air. Next, the final consumer product is distributed to warehouses and supermarkets, eventually to be sold to the consumers. What happens to the glass bottles after they have been used? Some bottles may be collected and cleaned (using inputs like water and detergents), others are collected and recycled back to the glass mills, and the remainder ends up in the landfills.

Life Cycle Assessment aims at giving an accounting of all these environmental impacts; both the withdrawals from nature and the disposals back into nature. Ideally, all impacts should be quantified, both in physical units and in terms of harm done (and possible benefits provided). Only then is it possible to provide a final judgment of the true environmental costs of the product.

2.1 Major categories of environmental impacts

There are different ways of systematizing the various discharges into the environment. One is to record the chemical substances released, such as CO_2, NO_2, SO_2, CO, methane, chlorine, lead, and so on. For each substance, the actual release will be compared with the total "critical" volume beyond which some particular damage will occur, such as destruction of the ozone layer of the earth, cancer, or lead poisoning. As long as the actual volume is well below the critical volume, there is no immediate cause for concern. But if current releases push the concentration of some chemical substance at a given geographical location close to the critical level, a warning bell should be sounded.

Often it is attractive to list the environmental negative impacts directly in terms of the kind of damage done to the environment. The damage includes

- The greenhouse effect
- Thinning of the ozone layer
- Acid rain
- Eutrophication (dying lakes and waterways)
- Smog (= smoke + fog)
- Pesticides
- Lead and other heavy metals
- Cancer in humans
- Exhaustion of non-reproducible natural resources
- Solid residuals.

Carbon dioxide is part of a fine-tuned global ecological balance. Humans breathe in oxygen and breathe out carbon dioxide. Combustion engines burn hydrocarbons and release CO_2. All green plants and microorganisms do the opposite: through photosynthesis they convert carbon dioxide back into hydrocarbons and oxygen. This global balance has been disrupted for some time. The burning of fossil fuels and of tropical rain forests spews more CO_2 into the air than the dwindling reservoir of green plants is able to break do again. The result is a pyramiding of carbon dioxide levels in the atmosphere. This is the greenhouse effect: increasing levels of greenhouse gases trap more heat from the sun inside the atmosphere. The average temperature rises - - global warming.

According to the current trend, the average temperature of the globe increases by approximately 0.2 degrees Celcius every 10 years. By 2050, the winters in the North and West of Europe should be about 5 degrees warmer, and the summers in Southern Europe about 4 degrees warmer. The geographical areas most vulnerable to such change are precisely those that have the least capacity of adapting. The warming will be most intense at high latitudes; the world's grain belts will become drier, and rises in the sea level will affect people living in deltas and low-lying coastal areas.

Ozone is formed in the stratosphere when oxygen is exposed to solar ultraviolet radiation. The ozone layer blocks most of the radiation from reaching lower atmospheric levels and the Earth's surface and is thus important for the existence of life on Earth. Exhaust from high-flying aircraft damages the layer; so do the propellant freon and other hydrocarbons containing chlorine and fluorine (CFCs). In 1987 the US government signed the Montreal Protocol banning CFCs by the end of the century and several international conferences have later reaffirmed the goal of discontinuing the use of CFCs, but worldwide implementation is still lacking.

Acid rain develops as the burning of fossil fuels pours millions of tons of sulfur and nitrogen into the air. Most of these emissions are from power stations and the steel industry. In contact with air, sulfur and nitrogen are oxidized to form sulfuric and nitric acids. An acidic haze is formed. When it rains, the droplets pass through the haze and acid rain falls to the earth. Winds carry acid clouds over great distances. Acid rain kills forests and lakes and rivers. Acid rain is a major problem in the United Kingdom, the Low Countries, Germany, Poland, Chechia and Slovakia.

Eutrophication (decay) of lakes and waterways occurs as a result of excessive fertilization in agriculture. It involves a buildup of excessive concentrations of nutrients, in particular of phosphates and nitrates. The growth of algae is stimulated (even to the point of algae "bloom"). Increased levels of organic matter and of microorganisms lower the oxygen content in the water, causing higher organisms to die. The ecological balance is disrupted. Eventually, all biological life in the afflicted waterways dies. Eutrophication is common in the waterways of the Low Countries, in parts of Germany, and in northern Italy (the Po river basin).

Smog is community-wide polluted air. It describes the pall of automotive or industrial origin that lies over my cities. There are at least two distinct types of smog: sulfurous smog (winter smog) and photochemical smog (summer smog). Sulfurous smog results from high concentrations of sulfur oxides in the air and is caused by the combustion of sulfur-bearing fuels. It is aggravated in the presence of dampness and high concentration of suspended particulate matter (SPM) in the air. Photochemical smog requires neither smoke nor fog. It is caused by photochemical reactions in the lower atmosphere prompted by hydrocarbons and nitrogen oxides emitted by automobiles and other sources. The atmosphere becomes lightly brownish;

there is reduced visibility, plant damage, irritation of the eyes and respiratory distress.

Pesticides are man-made products used to combat agricultural pests. The main categories of pesticides are insecticides, herbicides, fungicides and disinfectants. Most of them are not broken down when released into nature, and thus eventually enter the ground water and the food chain. The contamination of the water table is a serious problem in the European Union and about 65 percent of the regions exhibit concentrations above the maximal recommended levels. The toxic effects of pesticides present in the water and in foods are still debated. Small amounts of toxaphene and many other common insecticides cause tumors in mice. Small doses of the herbicide dioxin cause rhesus monkeys to stop their production of red and white blood cells.

Table 1. Eco-profile of glass bottles in the wine and beer industry. The reference unit is a quantity of glass capable of packaging 1000 liters of fluids. Source: Ferrão, 1998.

Category of environmental impact	**Units**	**Reusable bottles**	**Non-reusable bottles (recycled or ending up in landfills)**
The greenhouse effect	Kilograms of CO_2	487	888
The ozone layer	Kilograms of CFC11	1.16×10^3	4.51×10^3
Acid Rain	Kilograms of SO_2	6.43	9.02
Eutrophication	Kilograms of PO_4	0.79	1.03
Carcinogens	Kilograms of B(a)P	1.7×10^3	2.0×10^3
Sulfurous smog	Kilograms of suspended particular matter	1.28	1.49
Photochemical smog	Kilograms of C_2H_4	1.06	1.51
Energy	MegaJoules	8200	16000
Heavy metals	Kilograms of Pb	2×10^3	24×10^3
Solid residuals	Kilograms	42.6	88.7

Many heavy metals are poisonous to man. Lead, cadmium, arsenic and mercury belong to this category. Lead intervenes with the biosynthesis of blood in the human body and it attacks the nervous system. A major lead pollutant used to be leaded gasoline. Cadmium affects the kidneys. Cadmium is present in many fertilizers. Mercury causes cerebral damage. Even mercury fillings in teeth are dangerous.

2.2 Eco-profiles

One way to sum up the Life Cycle Assessment of a product and its impacts on the environment is to establish a cross-reference table between the various chemical substances released and the subsequent harmful effects. Continuing our example of the LCA of glass bottles that are used in the wine and beer industry, turn to Table 1 that lists the environmental impacts of glass bottles providing packaging for 1000 liters of fluid contents.

Perhaps the most important lesson of the table is that any given product typically has a broad range of impacts on the environment. Also, the table gives a good indication of the kind of environmental savings that can be obtained by reusing glass bottles.

3. A MATHEMATICAL CLASSIFICATION OF ENVIRONMENTAL IMPACTS

Assuming linear production technologies, we provide a brief classification of the environmental impacts of production and demand. The starting point is a simple activity-analysis type model of the production activities of a corporation. (See e.g. Thompson and Thore, 1992, Chapter 5.) Use the following notation

- x is a column vector of unknown activity levels operated by a company, each activity representing an alternative method of production;
- w is a column vector of supplies of resources, assumed fixed and given (like endowments of nature);
- A is a matrix of input coefficients; each element denotes the quantity of a resource required to operate an activity at unit level, the vector of requirements of the various inputs is then Ax;
- B is a matrix of output coefficients; each element is the quantity of an output obtained when an activity is operated at unit level, the vector of quantities of the various outputs obtained from production is then Bx;
- p is a row vector of prices of outputs, the market value of all output produced by the company is then pBx.

The task of maximizing the total revenues of the company, subject to the given availability of resources can then be written as the simple linear programming problem

$$\text{Max } pBx \qquad (1)$$
$$\text{subject to } Ax \leq w, x \geq 0.$$

3.1 Environmental impact on resources

Many environmental concerns relate to the excessive extraction of scarce minerals, crude oil, or ground water. These are depletable and non-reproducible resources. Once the existing deposits have been exhausted, they are gone. Considerations of national security (strategic materials) or economic independence (oil) may suggest that a nation should not dip too deeply into such stocks. Perhaps some buffer should be set aside for possible use in the future.

Ground water is in many instances a public good rather than a private good, and its price (essentially the unit-drilling and pumping cost) may grossly underestimate the true opportunity cost of it to society. A lowering of the water table may occur as the result of excessive use of water, or unsuitable land developments (golf courses); it may also take place as a result of environmental changes prompted by actions of man such as deforestation and urban growth.

Other resources can in principle be restored, such as fish in a lake or even fish in the oceans. But such restoration is costly and it takes time. If the reproducible resource is a private good, such as a salmon river owned by a private landowner, the market price of it should in principle reflect the cost of conservation and prudent management. But if the resource is a public good and no ownership of the resource is defined, such as in the case of the air in a big city, there is no market price that can signal the scarcity of the resource. The competitive economy will adjust as if the supplies of it were inexhaustible. One needs to implement a system of local management to protect and to clean up the air in cities or polluted lakes.

In model (1) above, the concerns now discussed translate into questions whether corporations should be free to make use of the entire supply of resources w available to them or whether society somehow should intervene, formulating a column vector of goals w^{GOAL} and imposing the restrictions

$$Ax \leq w^{GOAL} \tag{2}$$

(Goals may not necessarily be formulated for all resources. Formally, one may then put the corresponding elements of w^{GOAL} equal to the available supply itself.) In the first instance, we shall assume that these goals w^{GOAL} are "hard" upper limits, which may not be violated by the company. Later we shall also deal with "soft" goals that may be violated, but at a cost.

The linear programming problem of the corporation, earlier written as (1), now takes the form

$$\begin{aligned} &\text{Max } pBx \\ &\text{subject to} \\ &Ax \le w \\ &Ax \le w^{GOAL},\ x \ge 0. \end{aligned} \tag{3}$$

3.2 Environmental impacts of the operation of production activities

Sometimes the current inputs into production processes pose grave dangers to workers, or even to the community at large. Herbicides and pesticides used in agriculture contain toxic elements that may find their way into the food chain eventually or enter the ground water. One of the first synthetic pesticides was DDT, which accumulates to lethal levels in the food chain, killing birds and fish. DDT was banned in the US in 1972.

In order to fight the war against pests and weeds on the farms, the chemists have developed ever larger, stronger and more varied doses of poison. In 1980 there existed about 35000 different kinds of products for fighting insects, weeds, and fungi. Foresters, utility work crews, rice growers and ranchers use herbicides to eliminate brush and weeds. (For further discussion and references, see Thore 1995, Chapter 8.)

In other instances, outputs of technologies have undesired side effects. Consider the industrial use of fossil fuels (natural gas, oil, or coal) for production and for transportation. All technology using energy generated from the burning of fossil fuels wreaks damage to the environment. Each of these fuels involves long networks of exploration, extraction, distribution and marketing. Each fuel requires its own combustion technology, delivering a unique mix of outputs, kilowatt-hours together with carbon dioxide, carbon monoxide, sulfur and a plethora of other byproducts with long complicated chemical names.

All conventional forms of generating energy result involve damage to the environment. The burning of fossil fuels is associated with the greenhouse effect and acid rain. Hydroelectric power typically requires the rerouting of rivers and huge geographical engineering. Only solar power, wind power and other "alternative" sources of energy leave the environment unencumbered.

Yet other examples can be quoted when the concern does not necessarily relate to the release of unwarranted or dangerous substances into the environment, but to other potential dangers associated with technology. Some production technology involves small risks of very serious accidents, such as nuclear technology or the transportation of oil in single-hull tankers.

In all examples now mentioned, public opinion has asked whether corporations should be at liberty to operate these various technologies at will, or whether society should impose limitations on activities that entail harmful consequences. Returning to model (1), one shortcut way of representing such intervention would be to lay down goals on the operation of agricultural and industrial activities, say x^{GOAL} and insist on restrictions of the type

$$x \leq x^{GOAL} \tag{4}$$

(Goals may not necessarily be formulated for all activities. Formally, one may then put the corresponding elements of x^{GOAL} equal to a very large positive number.)

The linear programming problem of the corporation then reads

$$\begin{aligned} &\text{Max } pBx \\ &\text{subject to} \\ &Ax \leq w \\ &0 \leq x \leq x^{GOAL}. \end{aligned} \tag{5}$$

Note in particular that such constraints (a more fanciful word is "industrial policy") may actually, if properly designed, serve the role not only of deterring corporations from employing harmful technology but inducing them to switch to new and more environment-friendly technology. To see how this works, it is enough to consider the mathematical (if not the political) possibility that some harmful technologies are entirely banned and the engineers are left with the task of designing new technologies that would replace the banned ones.

3.3 Environmental impacts of consumer demand

In the public debate, the private corporation often becomes the whipping boy, accused of all the environmental sins of our material civilization. But some of the most serious culprits are common men and women, the consumers of all the bounty of modern technology.

Examples of consumer products that harm the environment are everywhere to be found. To see this, one needs only to ask the question what happens to an everyday consumer good after it has been used or used up. It then starts a long and zigzagging journey back to nature, as pollution in the air, in the water, in the forests, or accumulating in the landfills.

Use the notation d to denote the column vector of consumer demand for the products of the corporation. If prices are left free to clear markets, consumer demand will equal industrial output:

$$d = Bx \tag{6}$$

Now, to stave off the harmful effects of excessive demand, society may be interested in curtailing demand for the most harmful products, insisting on limitations of the type

$$Bx \leq d^{GOAL} \tag{7}$$

(Goals may not necessarily be formulated for all consumer demand. Formally, one may then put the corresponding elements of d^{GOAL} equal to a very large number.) The linear programming model then reads

$$\begin{aligned} &\text{Max } pBx \\ &\text{subject to} \\ &Bx \leq d^{GOAL} \\ &Ax \leq w, \ x \geq 0. \end{aligned} \tag{8}$$

One of the purposes of model (8) may be to study the conditions under which it is possible for society to stimulate the *recycling* of consumer products, thus limiting the harmful effects on the environment.

4. ENVIRONMENTAL IMPACT COEFFICIENTS

Given a vector of economic activities x, one may calculate the environmental impact of these activities by multiplying each activity with one or several impact coefficients. A crude way of accomplishing this is to lump all environmental burdens together in a single measure, such as Kilograms of Hazardous Waste and Toxic Release Emissions as defined in the Resource Conservation and Recovery Act, subtitle C (see the National Biennial RCRA Hazardous Waste Report 1993).

Much to be preferred, however, is to spell out a detailed list all wastes and emissions, such as emission of various greenhouse gases, of poisonous metals etc. See the discussion in Section 2 above. Let E be a matrix of environmental impact coefficients; each element is the quantity of a particular waste or emission produced when an activity is operated at unit level. The quantities of the various hazardous discharges resulting from production are then $H = Ex$. (For such matrix representation, see e.g. Heinungs, 1997 and Hendrickson, Horvath, Joshi and Lave, 1998.)

Impose now policy restrictions on the hazardous discharges, say

$$H \leq H^{GOAL} \tag{9}$$

This relation can be seen as mathematically equivalent to (4), and the resulting linear program can be written as program (5) as before. Or, explicitly, one would have

$$\begin{aligned} &\text{Max } pBx \qquad (10)\\ &\text{subject to}\\ &Ax \leq w\\ &Ex \leq H^{GOAL}, x \geq 0. \end{aligned}$$

5. ENVIRONMENTAL CONSTRAINTS VERSUS ENVIRONMENTAL EXCISE TAXES

When policy-makers try to grapple with environmental problems two alternative approaches to policy usually present themselves:

- Direct regulation. Examples: Government regulation of automobile carburetors and exhaust systems, and regulation of exhaust systems in electric power stations and the steel industry. The licensing of new pharmaceutical products by the Food and Drug Administration.
- Environmental fees or taxes (so-called excise taxes). Examples: Excise taxes on motor oil (financing the collection of dirty and spent motor oil), environmental fees on levied on glass bottles used for beer or wine (stimulating recycling), taxes on tobacco, parking fees in cities. Another interesting example is the proposed carbon-dioxide tax (to be levied on all industrial processes that involve combustion releasing carbon dioxide into the atmosphere).

From a political and administrative point of view, these two approaches work in very different ways. Yet, in a certain sense, they can be seen as mathematically equivalent. Direct regulation induces producers to modify their economic behavior by imposing constraints on their linear programming problem (see Section 2 above). Excise taxes, when correctly assessed, cause mathematically equivalent adjustments of producer behavior *on the dual side of the linear programming problem.*

To understand this, it suffices to note that the dual variable of an environmental constraint can typically be interpreted as an excise tax designed to implement the constraint. Why? The dual variable of a resource constraint in a producer linear programming problem (its "shadow price") can always be interpreted as the highest price that the producer would be willing to pay to acquire one more unit of the constrained resource. (For the economic interpretation of dual variables, see Thompson and Thore, 1992.) The dual variable of an environmental constraint, limiting the use of a resource, is the highest surcharge above the free market price that the producer would be willing to pay for the constrained resource. Apparently, an excise tax equal to this surcharge would cause the producer to adjust equivalently.

To develop the argument in slightly more detail, consider the dual program corresponding to (1), viz.

$$\begin{aligned} &\text{Min } qw \\ &\text{subject to } qA \geq pB,\ q \geq 0. \end{aligned} \tag{11}$$

The letter q is used here to denote a row vector of dual variables, denoting the shadow prices of the resources. Using (11) as a starting point, it is then easy to write down the dual formulations of the various environmentally constrained programs listed in Section 2. For instance, the dual to program (3) reads

$$\begin{aligned} &\text{Min } qw + \tau w^{GOAL} \\ &\text{subject to } (q + \tau) A \geq pB,\ q \geq 0. \end{aligned} \tag{12}$$

where τ is a row vector of excise taxes. To interpret (12), note first that if no goal constraint has been imposed on a resource, so that the resource goal equals the available supply, the excise tax levied on that particular resource is zero. But if the goal is less than the available supply, the excise tax is positive.

In words, program (12) instructs the producer to minimize the value of all available resources, adding the excise tax to the market price on the actual use of each resource. The producer should minimize this value subject to the constraint that no activity must be operated at a loss. By the dual theorem of linear programming, program (3) and program (12) are mathematically equivalent. The other direct linear programming formulations listed in Section 2 have similar duals, and the equivalence of the direct and the corresponding dual formulations can be demonstrated throughout.

In practical terms, equivalence means that it is usually possible to find an excise tax solution to environmental problems. This should not surprise because as we have pointed out, negative externalities (such as negative environmental impacts) arise when property rights have not been defined. Some economic agents can then make use of scarce factors without paying their full price. The "full price" would have included payment for those scarcities that have no owner (like paying for the use of air or water to pollute). The excise tax *simulates* the payment that would have been charged by such a fictitious owner.

This does not necessarily mean that the government steps in as the nominal owner of those scarcities for which property rights have not been defined. Sometimes it is possible for the government to set up institutional frameworks that lets the free market mechanism take over both the calculation and the collection of the environmental tax. One way to accomplish this is to issue tradable permits, like the sulfur emission allowances traded by electric utilities in the US. The institutional framework was defined in the Clean Air Act of 1990. Electric utilities that make extra-deep pollution cuts get credits that they can keep or sell to other power plants. The resulting market price of the pollution permit equals the shadow price of the pollution constraint. (See further Thore, 1995, pp. 133 ff.)

REFERENCES

Erickson, P. (1994): A Practical Guide to Environmental Impact Assessments, Academic Press, Boston.

Ferrão, P.C. (1998): Introdução à Gestão Ambiental: A Avaliação do Ciclo de Vida de Produtos, IST Press (Instituto Superior Técnico), Lisbon.

Heijungs, R. (1997): *Economic Drama and the Environmental Stage*, Ph.D. dissertation, Netherlands Research School for the Socio-Economic and Natural Sciences of the Environment, Rijksuniversiteit Leiden.

Hendrickson, C., Horwath, A., Soshi, S. and Lave, L. (1998): "Economic Input-Output Models for Environmental Life-Cycle Assessment," *Environmental Science &Technology*, pp. 184A- 191A.

Thompson, G. and Thore, S. (1992): *Computational Economics: Economic Modeling with Optimization Software*, Scientific Press, South San Francisco.

Thore, S. (1991): *Economic Logistics: The Optimization of Spatial and Sectoral Resource, Production and Distribution Systems*, Quorum Books, Westport, Connecticut.

Thore, S. (1995) *The Diversity, Complexity, and Evolution of High Tech Capitalism,* Kluwer Academic Publishers, Boston. Also published on the Internet, see www.ic2.org

US Environmental Protection Agency (1993): *National Biennial RCRA Hazardous Waste Report* (Based on 1989 Data), US Government Printing Office, Washington D.C., February.

Chapter 10

A New Mathematical Programming Format for Activity Analysis and the Life Cycle of Products

Editorial Introduction

Abstract: The main concepts of Koopmans' activity analysis are surveyed.

Key words: Environmental burdens, activity analysis, invisible hand, complementary slackness, intermediate goods, activity networks, budding, cross-fertilization

1. THE IMPACT OF NEW PRODUCTS AND PROCESSES ON THE ENVIRONMENT

Environmental considerations transcend the perspective of the single corporation. They bring into focus the views of many other stakeholders in the research, development and commercialization activities of corporations, such as the consumers, and local and central government.

The interplay (sometimes positive but mostly negative externalities) between a product and the environment is not limited to the purchase and use of the finished good alone. Tracing the vertical production chain backwards, there is at each step of the prior logistics process an exchange with the environment: during the manufacture and distribution of semi-finished parts and other intermediate goods, and certainly during the exploitation and use of natural resources and materials.

The environmental burdens imposed on society by an act of consumption are sometimes much greater in earlier production steps than in later ones. (Lead poisoning from direct contact with lead batteries is a fairly rare event. Lead poisoning in the lead mines is a serious problem.)

Once the product has been consumed, new environmental problems often present themselves. Waste has to be disposed of, often causing serious pollution of the air, of the groundwater, and other environmental resources.

New processes and products often call for a reconfiguration of existing production chains, replacing former technologies and distribution patterns by new ones. The results can be the alleviation of some environmental burdens and the imposition of new ones. For instance, advances in biotechnology that lead to the rapid growth of salmon farms has reduced the threat that the wild salmon will become extinct from over-fishing. At the same time, new environmental problems present themselves by the pollution of the seawater surrounding the salmon farms.

A generation of new processes and products aim directly at dealing with environmental problems by recovering used consumer or producer goods, and returning them to the production chain by *reuse* (of the good itself) or *recycling* (of its component parts). As a result, there will be introduced loops in the underlying production chains. These loops in the product flow will have environmental impacts as well. Furthermore, alternative regimes of reuse and/or recycling are often possible so that the environmental impacts are subject to some societal control.

Under these perspectives, the evaluation of a set of R&D projects suddenly becomes a very complex story. For each single new product considered, the entire vertical production and subsequent disposal chain has to be drawn. The commercial returns of the product have to be compared with the accumulated environmental effects over its entire life cycle. The comparison has to be carried out under alternative environmental policy regimes.

The economic analysis of the configuration and structure of entire vertical production chains is called *activity analysis*, developed by T. Koopmans in 1951. The present editorial introduction provides a brief recap. The two research papers following it develop a kind of "life cycle activity analysis," tracing the environmental impacts over the entire life cycle of the product.

2. ACTIVITY ANALYSIS

Following Koopmans, production is modeled through elementary processes called activities. Each activity requires certain inputs and produces certain outputs. The activities are chained together to cover an entire vertical production process ranging from the employment of scarce primary inputs (labor and raw materials) to the manufacture of final outputs.

Activity analysis covers a larger part of an economy than does an industry model, because it traces the vertical production chain back to the use of scarce primary inputs. Consider for instance all production chains that lead to the manufacture of an automobile. Following the production chain backwards, the automobile industry is dependent upon deliveries from the steel industry; the steel industry is dependent upon delivers from the mining industry. Also, the automobile industry is dependent upon deliveries from the tire industry; the tire industry depends upon rubber production (synthetic and natural). Automobiles also contain quite advanced digital computer equipment; the computer industry depends upon the computer chip industry, etc. Each industry along these chains may consider the supply prices of the preceding industries as given and known. When we reach the initial link of the chain (mining, natural rubber, computer chip knowledge) the supplies are limited by the natural resources of the country.

We model the activities of an economy using the following notation:

$i = 1,2,...,m$ is the index of the primary resources,
$j = 1,2,...,n$ is the index of activities,
$k = 1,2,...,r$ is the index of final outputs,
$x = (x_1, x_2, ..., x_n)$ is the (column) vector of (unknown) activity levels,
$d = (d_1, d_2, ..., d_r)$ is the (column) vector of (unknown) final demand,
$w = (w_1, w_2, ..., w_m)$ is the (column) vector of (given) supplies of primary resources
$p = (p_1, p_2, ..., p_r)$ is the (row) vector of (given) output prices,
$A = [a_{ij}]$ is the $m \times n$ matrix of input coefficients, where a_{ij} is the quantity of resource i required when activity j is operated at unit level,
$B = [b_{ij}]$ is the $m \times r$ matrix of output coefficients, where b_{ij} is the quantity of output k produced when activity j is operated at unit level.

The basic idea of activity analysis is the following: Given the endowment vector w of primary resources, how shall the economy choose to operate its productive activities to maximize the resulting vector of final outputs? To answer this question we observe first that the set of feasible combinations of final demand, d, is defined by the following set of constraints:

$$\begin{aligned} d - Bx &\leq 0 \\ Ax &\leq w \\ d, x &\geq 0 \end{aligned} \quad (1)$$

The first constraint says that demand d is constrained by the output vector Bx. The second constraint says that the resources used, Ax, should be at most equal to the available amounts of primary resources. The third constraint requires the two unknowns d and x to be nonnegative.

The solution set of the final outputs d of (1) is a polyhedral convex set. A polyhedral convex set is a convex set spanned by a finite number of points, as illustrated in Figure 1. The figure is a two-dimensional representation of an m-dimensional space; the horizontal and the vertical axes represent two final goods that both lay their claims on the endowments of primary resources.

A point $d^{(1)}$ is said to dominate d if $d_k^{(1)} \geq d_k$ for $k = 1,2,\ldots,r$ with at least one inequality being strict. Observe that point E in Figure 1 is dominated by B and F is dominated by both B and C. Point G is not dominated, but is infeasible, because it does not satisfy (1), hence is not of interest. The set of un-dominated feasible points is called the *efficiency frontier* and is indicated by the points A,B,C,D and the thick lines connecting them. Clearly, the economy will want to choose one of the points on the efficiency frontier because such points are un-dominated.

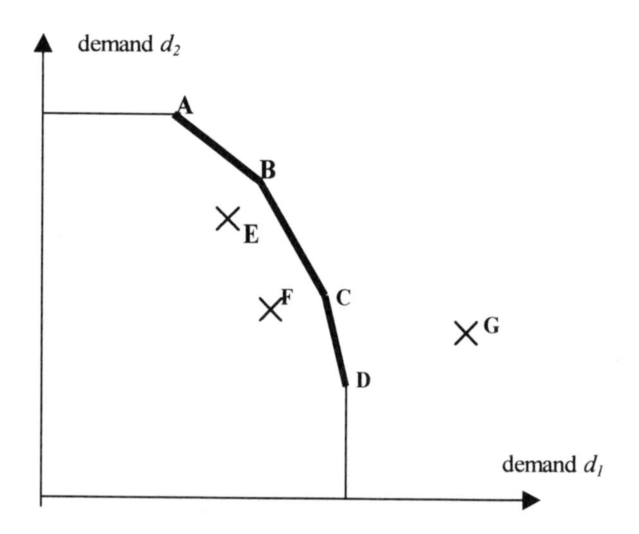

Figure 1. Efficiency frontier illustrated.
Legend: ABCD = efficiency frontier, E and F inefficient points, G infeasible

How does an economy make a choice of one of the points on the efficiency frontier at which to operate? There are various ways of approaching an answer to this question. Koopmans' own treatment (1951, 1957) makes use topological properties of convex cones. Following the pioneering contributions by Charnes and Cooper (1961), we shall here prefer to draw on the machinery of linear programming. In this fashion, the theoretical developments of Koopmans convert into a powerful tool for empirical calculations.

Given a demand price vector $p>0$, consider the linear program (2) below:

$$\begin{aligned} &\text{Max } pd \\ &\text{subject to } d - Bx \le 0 \\ &Ax \le w, \\ &d, x \ge 0 \end{aligned} \tag{2}$$

Observe that the constraints of (2) are just those that we have already listed in (1). Program (2) examines all feasible points that satisfy the constraints and selects the particular vector of final demand d that maximizes the value of demand.

Who is the master planner who would formulate and solve program (2)? As will now be explained, a competitive free economy behaves *as if* there existed a master planner who solves program (2). Using the famous term of Adam Smith, we may term the master planner the "invisible hand."

The prices established by the invisible hand can be identified as the dual variables corresponding to (2). Denote the duals as follows:

$u^F = (u_1{}^F, u_2{}^F, \ldots, u_r{}^F)$ is the (row) vector of dual variables of the final goods,

$u^P = (u_1{}^P, u_2{}^P, \ldots, u_m{}^P)$ is the (row) vector of dual variables of the primary resources.

The dual program then reads:

$$\begin{aligned} &\text{Min } u^F w \\ &\text{subject to } u^F \ge p \\ &- u^F B + u^P A \ge 0, \\ &u^F, u^P \ge 0 \end{aligned} \tag{3}$$

In simple words, the dual program (3) instructs us to minimize the imputed value of all primary resources subject to two constraints: the imputed price of any final good cannot fall short of its fixed demand price, and the imputed revenues of operating any activity cannot exceed its imputed costs.

Using the imputed prices as market prices, we note that all markets will be in equilibrium. For, by the theorem of complementary slackness in linear programming, the following two results are established on the primal side of the problem:

- *The markets for final goods clear*. If at the point of optimum a positive imputed price of a final good is established, there will be equality between the consumer demand and total sales by the managers of the activities (equilibrium in the markets for final goods).

- *The markets for primary resources clear.* If at the point of optimum a positive imputed price of a primary resource is established, there will be equality between total purchases of the managers of the activities, and the resource supply (equilibrium in the markets for primary resources).

Furthermore, by the same theorem, on the dual side:

- *All profits from the distribution of final goods are wiped out.* If at the point of optimum of program (2) the consumers demand a positive quantity of a final good, there will be equality between the fixed demand price and its imputed price.
- *All manufacturing profits are wiped out.* If at the point of optimum of program (2) an activity is operated at a positive level, the imputed revenue of operating the activity must equal its imputed cost (in other words, the net profit vanishes).

Also, by the fundamental theorem of linear programming, the value of the primal program must equal the value of the dual program. In words: the optimal value of consumers' purchases must equal the imputed value of all primary resources.

The fundamental theorem of linear programming ties the solution of the direct program and the dual program to a particular saddle point existing in the space of all direct and all dual variables. The four sets of mathematical conditions of complementary slackness listed a moment ago uniquely define the saddle point. More precisely: The conditions of complementary slackness are said to form a (linear) *complementarity problem.* The saddle point is mathematically equivalent to the solution of the complementarity problem (see e.g. Cooper and Thore, 1991, Theorem 2.3)

To sum up, the invisible hand solves both the direct program (2) and the dual program (3). All markets are in equilibrium. As the result of market competition, all profit disappears. The dual variables determined by program (3) are the competitive market prices.

3. INTERMEDIATE GOODS

Intermediate goods are both inputs and outputs, being produced at an earlier stage of the production chain and eventually used (up) at a later stage of the chain. Expanding on our notation, let A^P and A^I denote the matrices of primary input coefficients and intermediate input coefficients, respectively; and let B^F and B^I denote the matrices of final output coefficients and intermediate output coefficients, respectively. Note that the net output of intermediate goods $(- A^I + B^I)\ x$ (outputs minus inputs) must vanish. Program (2) should then be amended to read

$$\begin{aligned} &\text{Max } pd \\ &\text{subject to } \ d - B^F x \ \leq 0 \\ &(A^I - B^I)\ x \ = 0 \\ &A^P x \qquad \leq w, \\ &d, x \ \geq 0 \end{aligned} \tag{4}$$

There is now one market condition for each type of goods: final goods, intermediate goods and primary goods. Each market condition will have a dual variable, and at the point of optimum, the dual variable for each market will signify its competitive market price. All markets are in equilibrium. All managers of activities will break exactly even.

4. ACTIVITY NETWORKS

The classification of goods and services into primary, intermediary and final provides a first approximation of the vertical dimension of an industry. Beyond that, an inspection of the particular inputs and outputs of individual activities may reveal that some activities must precede others, and that other activities again may have to be operated at a later stage in time. The unit input coefficients and the unit outputs may imply an ordering of goods and activities in terms of antecedents and postcedents.

To describe these hierarchies, we shall now make use of the concept of a *network* of flows. It is a commonplace to use the network model to represent the physical transportation of a commodity from one location to another. The packaging, the measures, and the characteristics of the good transported remain the same along the path of transportation, from the supply points to the points of ultimate demand. In a so-called *generalized network*, some transformation of the commodity flowing along each link of the network may occur, changing the physical characteristics of the commodity. The format of a generalized network enables us to trace the production chains as an intermediate good travels along the path from the supply of primary goods and services to the distribution of the final consumer good to the supermarket or other sales outlet. These production chains may sometimes span the entire globe. Consider the chain that brought the tea leaves harvested in Assam into the tea bag in your morning cup of tea, or coffee beans from Colombia to your cup of decaffeinated coffee.

We shall use the network model to describe the flow of intermediate goods inside the activity analysis format. The *influxes* into the network are the use of resources and other primary goods. The *effluxes* from the network are the delivery of final goods for consumption. Use the notation

$i,j \in I$ stages of intermediate production or shipments,
G graph of the network
c_{ij} unit costs (production and shipping costs) along link (i,j),
t_{ij} amount of flow leaving node i en route for node j

Let $t = [\, t_{ij} \,]$ be the (column) vector of all flows along the network. There are as many elements in this vector as there are links in the network. Let $c = \{ c_{ij} \}$ be the (row) vector of all unit costs along the links. The vector product ct then denotes the sum total of all production and shipping costs accruing along the network.

The configuration of the graph G defines what happens to the flow t as it passes through the network. In particular, it uniquely defines the *vector of net effluxes (effluxes minus influxes)* exiting the network. Write this vector Mt (where M is the so-called "incidence matrix" of the network). These effluxes, in their turn, are delivered as final goods for consumption. In other words, the net effluxes Mt must equal the net output of intermediate goods $Mt = (- A^I + B^I)\, x$.

The programming model (4) now reads

$$
\begin{aligned}
&\text{Max } pd - ct \\
&\text{subject to } \; d - B^F x \le 0 \\
&(A^I - B^I)\, x + Mt = 0 \\
&A^P x \le w, \\
&d, x, t \ge 0
\end{aligned}
$$

For further developments dealing with the joint treatment of manufacturing activities and distribution, refer to the undergraduate textbook Thompson and Thore (1992, Chapter 17, "Activity Analysis"). See also Thore (1991, Chapter 4), a graduate text.

5. INNOVATIONS IN INDUSTRY NETWORKS

Product development and the commercialization of new products modify the configuration of the production chains, introducing new nodes (new intermediate or final goods) or new links (new activities).

Typically, product development leads to hierarchical growth in the production chains. New layers of nodes and links are added. Indeed, "high technology" can suitably be defined as the technology of long and hierarchical production chains delivering products possessing ever more varied consumer attributes.

As new manufacturing or marketing links are added to the network, others are removed for closure. New nodes and new links entail setup costs (development and investment costs). Nodes and links to be closed down also entail costs, usually in the form of obsolete capital and capital losses.

The two terms "budding" and "cross-fertilization" have been suggested (see Thore, 1998) to reflect the organic growth of the production hierarchy.

Budding can be said to occur in a production chain when the breeding of new links and nodes adds one or several new hierarchical layers downstream. The adoption of an initial technology may set the stage for subsequent product development and innovation. Any one given vintage of technology will eventually be superseded by even more advanced technology. Consider, for instance, the technology chain: dial telephone, touch-tone telephone, cordless telephone, fiber-optic cables. The graph of the chain buds as new links and new nodes are added hierarchically.

Budding forms a causal succession of technologies, with each new successful commercialization putting in place a stepping stone from which further advancement can proceed. New technologies are raised on the shoulders of the achievements of the preceding ones.

Cross-fertilization in a production chain occurs when two or several former entirely separate activities - - each with its existing sub-hierarchies - -are brought together to deliver new intermediate or final goods. Whereas budding is the archetype of product development and gradualism, cross-fertilization represents the leap into the unknown, the dramatic technological discontinuity, and the true innovation. Consider a few examples: the fax machine (cross-fertilization of digital data technology, telecommunications and copy machines), commercial satellites launched from airplanes (cross-fertilization of rocket technology, aviation, and satellite technology) and the artificial heart (cross-fertilization of electro-mechanical engineering, blood technology, and surgery.)

Although cross-fertilization in the network typically leads to dramatic changes, such changes always occur in an orderly and structured fashion, preserving the sub-hierarchies that are merged together via the new links and new nodes. The introduction of commercial overnight mail services (Federal Express) required the setting up of a combined system of customer mail pickup and delivery, the operation of aircraft, establishment of a national airport hub, and development of information systems to track packages. All these separate technologies existed before, but were now coordinated into a singled packaged product, and sold via aggressive marketing. The result was a strongly hierarchical system of technologies.

Cross-fertilization can lead to entire strings of new activities being set up, bridging nodes in the production chains in the economy that seemingly had only a distant relevance to each other. Deep-sea oil drilling has brought us the drill-ship, a curious combination of maritime shipbuilding, and drilling and seismic exploration technology. The exploration of space has spawned entire industries engaged in the manufacture of mechanical robots, the utilization of solar power, the development of new ceramics and alloys, rocket technology, electronics, and others. But all these new technologies and new products can easily be identified in terms of their sub-technology ancestry.

Viewed from the perspective of the evolutionary processes now indicated, the Koopmans schema obviously represents a stark simplification, resting on conventional assumptions of economic statics with fixed and given technologies.

REFERENCES

Charnes, A. and Cooper, W.W. (1961), *Management Models and Industrial Applications of Linear Programming*, 2 Vols., Wiley & Sons, New York, N.Y.

Cooper, W.W. and Thore, S. (1991), "Some Elements of Saddle-Point Theory," in Thore, S., *Economic Logistics: The Optimization of Spatial and Sectoral Resource, Production, and Distribution Systems*, Quorum Books, Westport, Connecticut 1991

Koopmans, T. C. (1951), editor, *Activity Analysis of Production and Allocation*, John Wiley, New York, N.Y.

Koopmans, T.C. (1957), *Three Essays on the State of Economic Science*, McGraw Hill, New York, N.Y.

Thompson, G.L. and Thore, S. (1992), *Computational Economics: Economic Modeling with Optimization Software*, Scientific Press, South San Francisco, Calif.

Thore, S. (1991), *Economic Logistics: The Optimization of Spatial and Sectoral Resource, Production, and Distribution Systems*, Quorum Books, Westport, Conn.

Thore, S., "Innovation in an Industry Network: Budding, Cross-Fertilization, and Creative Destruction," in J.E. Aronson and S. Zionts, eds., *Operations Research: Methods, Models, and Applications*, Quorum Books, Westport, Conn., 1998.

Activity Analysis with Environmental Variables and Recycling: An Example from the Portuguese Water Bottling Industry

A Research Paper

by S. Thore and F. Freire

Instituto Superior Técnico, Lisbon

Abstract: The standard mathematical programming formulation of activity analysis, due to Charnes and Cooper, 1961, is extended to embrace the presence of environmental "bads" such as pollution and waste products destined for landfills. Special attention is given to the presence of loops in the production chains such as those occurring when the packaging materials of consumer goods are recycled and reused. The possibility of stimulating recycling and reusing by appropriate environmental fees is examined. An application from the Portuguese bottled water industry is described. Some used and discarded bottles are recycled (the glass is crushed and used as raw material for the manufacture of new bottles), others are cleaned and used again; the remainder ends up in landfills. A numerical prototype is solved and discussed. The scope for environmental policy is discussed, comparing direct environmental controls with a goal programming model implemented by environmental fees

Key words: Life cycle analysis, activity analysis, environmental goods, environmental impact coefficients, bottled water industry, recycling, reutilization, recovery, pollution, landfill, input-output table, EU, direct regulation, environmental fees, fiscal incentives

1. INTRODUCTION

In the pages to follow, a mathematical programming format will be developed to analyze the environmental impacts of production with discharges of waste and other byproducts detrimental to the environment. The possibilities of reduction of such discharges through recycling and through taxation and environmental fees aimed at encouraging recycling and reutilization will be studied. A numerical example of the calculations is provided, brought from the Portuguese industry of bottled water.

Our work builds bridges between economics and operations research on the one hand and engineering and environmental sciences on the other. One such bridge connects input-output analysis and environmental life cycle analysis of products (LCA). The purpose of the latter is to study the environmental impacts of a product from the "cradle" to the "grave". Past life cycle effects are calculated as the totality of all environmental effects that are located upstream in the production sequence. Future life cycle effects are calculated as the downstream environmental effects. Much effort is currently being spent in engineering and environmental sciences to collect the necessary data, to write software and to make the LCA calculations. From the point of view of the economist, these calculations are particular instances of input-output analysis, see Leontief's own early work of 1970 and later discussions such as Lave, Cobas-Flores, Hendrickson and F.C. McMichael, 1995 and Hendrickson, Horvath, Joshi and Lave, 1998. Our own contribution below formalizes these interconnections as applied to an instance of production with recycling and reutilization. Recovery introduces closed loops in the production sequences, so that downstream outputs are returned as inputs upstream.

Another bridge ties mathematical programming formulations of activity analysis to the environmental impacts of activities. T. Koopmans, 1957, developed the basic concepts of activity analysis. Early formulations were not suitable for numerical solution (see Koopman's discussion, *ibid.* pp. 96 ff.), since it was usually assumed that there were as many commodities as there were activities, so that the resulting system of equations had a non-singular solution. A major step was the reformulation of activity analysis as a linear program, permitting any number of activities and any number of commodities, see A. Charnes and W.W. Cooper, 1961. As the field of activity analysis more recently was extended to engineering and environmental sciences, however, the formal treatment regressed again to simple matrix calculations, see e.g. Ayres 1994, and Heijungs 1996. The mathematical programming associations were lost. A major purpose of our own work is to reestablish these connections, providing standard linear (and nonlinear) programming formats for the calculation of environmental impacts.

Koopmans distinguished three classes of goods: primary goods (resources or inputs), intermediate goods and final goods (outputs). Our present purpose is to extend this well-known activity analysis format to include one more category of goods: environmental goods (a better name would be environmental "bads") such as pollution of the water, air, soil and so on. There are (in general) no markets for such goods, so that no market balancing conditions can be formulated for them. Instead, environmental targets will be formulated reflecting the stance of a policy-maker. Furthermore, in order to follow the environmental effects of a manufactured product over its entire life, we shall no longer consider consumption as a final and ultimate state; instead, the life cycle is traced to include the possible reprocessing, reuse, or recycling of the product, including waste disposal and landfill.

We begin in Section 2 with a brief mathematical statement of activity analysis with environmental goods. Section 3 describes the application brought from the Portuguese bottled water industry. Section 4 discusses the scope for environmental policy in the industry, as seen in the light of the activity analysis program and its dual. Direct environmental constraints and environmental fees are compared. Various measures are discussed aimed at influencing the shadow prices of the environmental goods, and encouraging the recycling of glass and the reutilization of bottles. Section 5 provides a numerical example. Section 6 sums up the results.

2. MATHEMATICAL ANALYSIS

Use the following notation:

x is a column vector of unknown activity levels;

A is a matrix of input coefficients; each element denotes the quantity of an input required to operate an activity at unit level;

B is a matrix of output coefficients; each element is the quantity of an output obtained when an activity is operated at unit level;

c is a row vector of unit costs of operating the various activities, it is known and given (these are unit costs to be reckoned above the use of inputs already included in the A matrix);

w is a column vector of supplies of primary resources, in the first instance it will be assumed to be known and given;

d is a column vector of final demand, it is known and given.

Conventionally, the list of goods is partitioned into three classes: inputs of primary goods (P), intermediate goods (I), and final goods (F). Correspondingly, matrix A becomes partitioned into A^I and A^P, matrix B becomes partitioned into B^I and B^F.

Standard activity analysis can be written as the linear programming problem (see Charnes and Cooper 1961, Chapter IX, see also Thore 1991 and Thompson and Thore 1992, Chapter 17):

$$\begin{array}{lll} \min cx & & (1) \\ \text{subject to } -A^P x & \geq & -w \\ (-A^I + B^I)\, x & = & 0 \\ B^F x & \geq & d \\ x \geq 0 & & \end{array}$$

The format (1) will here be extended in two ways: First, a new category of goods is called "environmental goods" (actually, more literally, environmental "bads") will be distinguished: pollution of the air, the water, the soil and so on. Second, many packaged consumer products will now be considered as intermediate goods rather than final goods. Treating them as intermediate goods makes it possible to trace the subsequent fate of the packaging (recycling, reuse or waste destined for the landfill). Instead, final consumption is a service delivered by the packaged product.

The list of goods is now partitioned into four classes: inputs of primary goods (P), intermediate goods (I), final goods (F) and environmental goods (E). Correspondingly, matrices A and B become partitioned into

$$\begin{aligned} A &= (-A^P,\ -A^I,\ 0\ ,\ 0\ ) \\ B &= (\ 0\ ,\ B^I\ ,\ B^F,\ -B^E\ ). \end{aligned}$$

Conventionally, one enters the A-coefficient of each input with a minus sign and the B-coefficient of each output with a plus sign. Furthermore, there is the new convention that the B-coefficient of each output of an economic "bad" is entered with a minus sign.

Although less common, there are also instances when economic activities generate environmental benefits. Examples are the incineration of harmful waste, and the planting of new forests helping to absorb excessive levels of carbon dioxide in the air. For these and other measures aiming at improving the environment, see the Kyoto protocol. The B-coefficients of such environmentally beneficial outputs should be entered with a plus sign.

Format (1) is then replaced by

$$\begin{array}{lll} \min cx & & (2) \\ \text{subject to } -A^P x & \geq & -w \\ (-A^I + B^I)\, x & = & 0 \\ B^F x & \geq & d \\ -B^E x & \geq & -g \\ x \geq 0 & & \end{array}$$

where g is a vector of environmental goals set by a policy-maker.

For subsequent use, denote the (partitioned row vector of) dual variables corresponding to program (2) by

$$u = (u^P, u^I, u^F, u^E). \tag{3}$$

The u's are the shadow costs (shadow values) of primary resources, intermediate goods, final goods, and environmental “bads”, respectively.

2.1 Environmental impact coefficients

In the account above, the environmental concerns of the policy-maker were represented as (maximum) targets above which the release of economic “bads” was not permitted to occur. An alternative approach is that of environmental impact coefficients. We explain this approach and we demonstrate that, with proper specifications, the two approaches are actually mathematically equivalent.

Define V as a row vector of the environmental “impact” of each activity x. The impact must be measured in some standard units, such as an environmental impact index. It could even be measured in dollars. We shall return to this issue in a moment. The total environmental impact of all activities featured in model (1) is now Vx. The environmental impact programming formulation corresponding to (2) is

$$\begin{aligned} &\min Vx \\ &\text{subject to } -A^P x \geq -w \\ &(-A^I + B^I)\, x = 0 \\ &B^F x \geq d \\ &x \geq 0 \end{aligned} \tag{4}$$

In words, program (4) aims at minimizing the total environmental impact, while drawing upon the supplies w to meet final demand d.

There exists a direct mathematical relationship between the two programs (2) and (4). Choosing the environmental impact coefficients V suitably, the two formulations are mathematically equivalent. See the Appendix.

3. THE PORTUGUESE BOTTLED WATER INDUSTRY: STRUCTURE, REUSE AND RECYCLING OF BOTTLES

The bottled water industry fills tapped spring water on glass, PVC (polyvinyl chloride) or PET (polyethylene terephthalate) bottles, and sells them to households, restaurants, bars and hotels. In Portugal, a considerable section of the market is made up by demand by tourists. Several of the springs are located in the northern mountain areas of Portugal. The water is sold in bottles of 0.25 liters, 0.33 liters, 0.5 liters, 1.5 liters and 5 liters. Collection of used glass is practiced over the entire country. Characteristic green metal containers are placed everywhere, also in the countryside. Collection of PVC or PET bottles occurs only in the large cities.

The bottling is carried in locations immediately adjacent to the springs. In the case of glass bottles, the bottling company buys empty bottles from a glass mill, or it can fill spring water on used and cleaned bottles. The glass mill, in its turn, manufactures bottles from scratch (the main raw material is silicon sand), or from recycled crushed glass. The bottling company, using road transport and regional warehouses typically also handles the distribution from the springs to the consumer. There are in Portugal about 17 independent bottling companies filling and distributing spring water. The six largest companies are Centralcer, Vidago, Spadel, Kas/Areiro, Sumolis and Àguas de Carvalhelos, with a market share of about 79% in 1994. Most companies own more than one brand. For example, Centralcer owns the brands Luso and Cruzeiro. Others, Vidago for example, are better considered to be a group of companies owning several distinct brands: Pedras Salgados, Melgaço, Salus-Vidago, Caramulo, S. Lourenço, Ladeira de envedos, Água viva. In addition, an important segment of the market is covered by imported spring water, mainly from France (Evian and Vichy).

The logistics of the industry is further illustrated in Figure 1 that is adapted from a large study presently conducted by the junior author. To simplify the figure, only one type of bottles is illustrated: glass bottles of a standard size of 0.25 liters. The figure features both the vertical dimension of the industry (the production chains from glass mills to consumption and landfills) and the spatial dimension (regional distribution). Reading the diagram from top to bottom, the following nodes are recognized in the logistics flow:

Node #1: Raw materials for glass production,
Node #2: Recycled raw glass,
Node #3: New empty bottles,
Node #4: Returned and cleaned bottles,

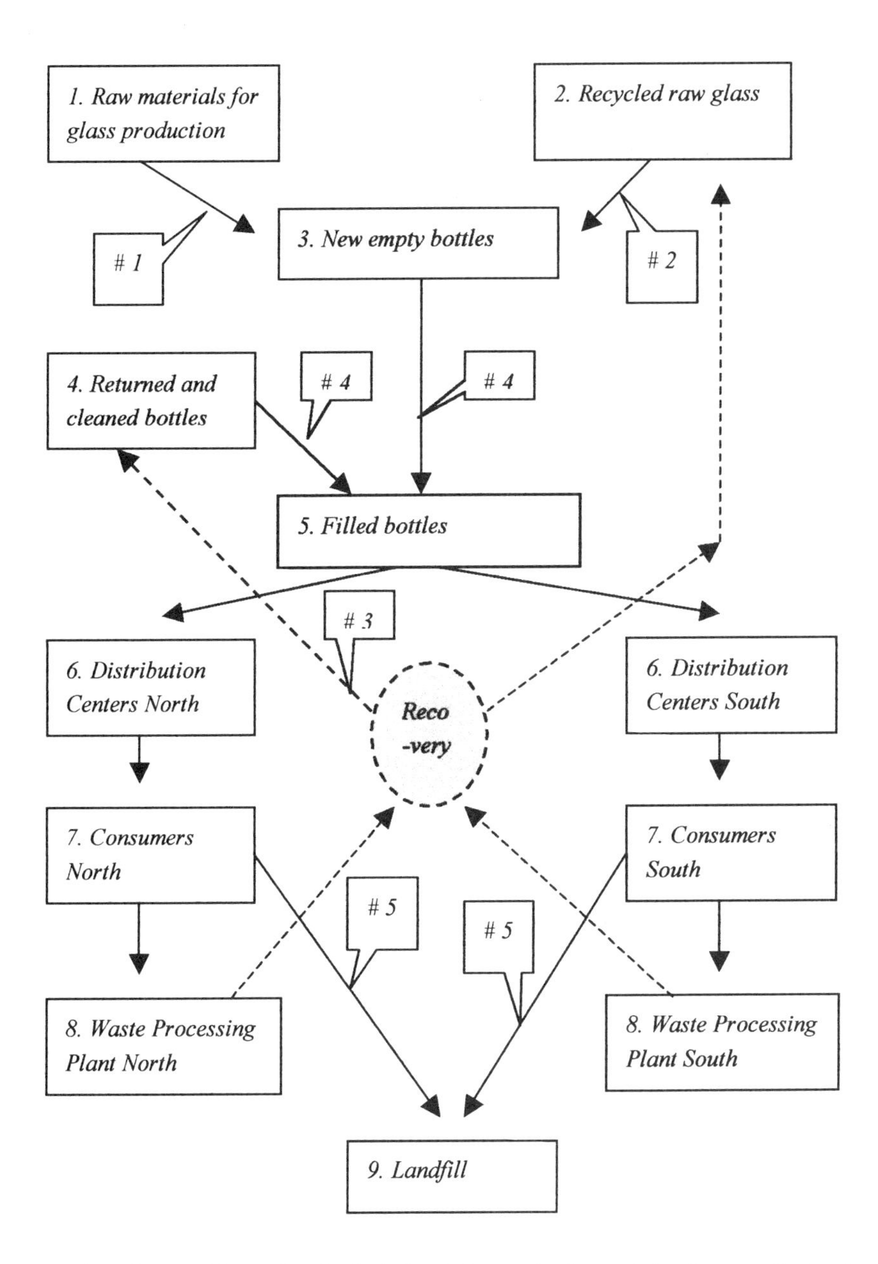

Figure 1. Flow diagram illustrating the logistics of the production and distribution of bottled water in Portugal

Node #5: Filled bottles (filled with spring water at the bottling plants),
Nodes #6: Distribution centers, North and South,
Nodes #7: Consumers, North and South,
Nodes #8: Waste collection and processing plants, North and South,

Node #9: Landfills.

The arrows in the diagram show the direction of the logistics flow. Note the loops feeding flow back from nodes 8 and 9 to nodes 2 and 4 (stippled lines in the diagram).

Thus prepared, we now outline a simple activity analysis model, highlighting the recovering activities but suppressing the regional aspects of the production and distribution. We distinguish the following list of goods:

- Primary goods (P): raw materials for glass manufacture, energy, spring water tapped from the wellhead;
- Intermediate goods (I): new empty bottles, recycled bottles (to be crushed and re-smelted), returned bottles (to be cleaned), filled bottles;
- Final goods (F): consumption services delivered by the final product;
- Environmental goods (E): pollution, landfill.

There are five activities as listed below. They are all listed as operated at unit level.

Activity #1: Manufacturing one glass bottle from raw materials;

Activity #2: Manufacturing one glass bottle from recycled glass (and from other raw materials);

Activity #3: Cleaning one returned glass bottle;

Activity #4: Filling one glass bottle with spring water;

Activity #5: Consuming one bottle of spring water.

The outputs of activities #1 and #2 flow into node 3. The output of activity #3 flows into node 4. The outputs of activity #4 flow into node 5. The outputs of the activities #5 are consumer services (spring water consumed) and used bottles flowing into node 9.

Notice that the act of consuming the final manufactured and distributed product is treated as an "activity." This corresponds to treating the purchased and consumed bottle of spring water as an intermediate rather than a final good. Instead, the final good in this system is the consumption service delivered by the distributed product. This is analogous to the approach used in environmental life cycle analysis, in which the subject of the study is the function provided by the product and not the product itself. This approach is implicitly taken into account by our extended activity analysis model resulting from the consideration of the entire life cycle of the products

Next, consider Table 1, listing all input and output coefficients of the system (the coefficients of the matrices A and B). The partitioned matrices A and B are exhibited in the table as follows. The three first rows of Table 1 form the matrix $-A^P$. The next four rows are $- A^I + B^I$. The next single row is B^F .The two last rows constitute $- B^E$. A brief list of the five activities follows:

- Activity #1. In producing the output of one new empty bottle, inputs of energy (a_{11}) and raw materials (a_{21}) are required. At the same time, there is an output of an economic "bad": air pollution (b_{91}).
- Activity #2. Producing the output of one new empty bottle using recycled materials instead (a_{52}), inputs of energy (a_{12}) and some additional raw materials (a_{22}) are required. Presumably, there is less air pollution (b_{92}) this time.
- Activity #3. Cleaning one returned bottle, inputs of energy (a_{13}) are required. Since a cleaning operation is now included, there may be significant pollution (b_{93}).
- Activity #4. Filling one empty bottle, inputs of energy (a_{14}) and spring water from the wellhead (a_{34}) are required. There may be some air pollution (b_{94}).

Table 1. Extended input-output table exhibiting environmental effects

Goods and "bads"	Activity #1	Activity #2	Activity #3	Activity #4	Activity #5
Primary (P)					
1.Energy	$-a_{11}$	$-a_{12}$	$-a_{13}$	$-a_{14}$	0
2.Raw materials	$-a_{21}$	$-a_{22}$	0	0	0
3.Spring water	0	0	0	$-a_{34}$	0
Intermediate (I)					
4.Empty bottle	$+1$	$+1$	$+1$	-1	0
5.Recycled glass	0	$-a_{52}$	0	0	$+b_{55}$
6.Returned bottle	0	0	-1	0	$+b_{65}$
7.Filled bottle	0	0	0	$+1$	-1
Final (F)					
8.Consumption	0	0	0	0	$b_{85}=+1$
Environmental (E)					
9. Pollution	$- b_{91}$	$- b_{92}$	$- b_{93}$	$- b_{94}$	0
10. Landfill	0	0	0	0	$- b_{10,5}$

- Activity #5. As stated in the main text earlier, the purchase of the filled and distributed bottle and the final act of consumption are treated as an activity. The input is one filled bottle. The immediate output is the consumption service delivered by the bottle ($b_{85} = +1$). In addition, we need to exhibit what happens to the empty bottle. There are three possibilities: it can be recycled back to the bottle manufacturer, it can be returned back to the bottle filler for reuse; or it will end up on the landfill

In the case of collecting, crushing and recycling the glass, it will be assumed that $100b_{55}$ percent of all bottles are returned for recycling. Similarly, we assume that $100b_{65}$ percent of all bottles are returned for cleaning and reuse. These are all bottles returned to the collecting points. It does not follow, however, that the same quantities will actually be used as inputs for recycling and reuse. If the bottling plants chose to demand fewer returned bottles than what is offered them, the difference will eventually end up in the landfill anyhow. We shall return to this issue momentarily.

4. ENVIRONMENTAL POLICY FOR THE PORTUGUESE BOTTLED WATER INDUSTRY

Environmental policy in Portugal must be seen within the context of the European Union. We briefly review recent EU directives in the fields of water, packaging and packaging waste management and bio-diversity, see also Pearce, 1998.

The EC Packaging and Packaging Waste directive was finalized in December 1994. In its final form, the directive may be summarized as follows. The objectives are:

- to reduce the overall impact of packaging on the environment by reducing packaging at source,
- to eliminate harmful materials in packaging waste, maximize the recovery of packaging waste for re-use, recycling, composting and energy recovery, and minimize the quantity going to final disposal (land-fill); and
- to bring national policies on packaging and packaging waste closer together to remove obstacles to trade and competition.

The directive covers all types of packaging in the European Union — industrial, commercial, office, shop "or any other level". Within six and half years of adoption of the directive (five from implementation by national law):

- 50-65% of packaging, by weight, must be recovered where recovery includes any activity which confers economic value on the waste (i.e. recycling, re-use, energy),

- 25-45% of packaging by weight must be recycled, with a minimum of 15% of each material (paper, aluminum, steel, plastics) being recycled.

These targets are relaxed for Greece, Ireland and Portugal who must attain at least 25% recovery by the five-year deadline, or achieve the targets for the rest of EU by 2005.

The directive is clear in indicating that re-use and recycling are "preferable in terms of environmental impact" to other forms of recovery and to disposal. This hints at the so-called "waste hierarchy" which has gained credence in European policy discussions on waste management. The waste hierarchy sets out a ranking of waste management options. The ranking, from the best to worst, is source reduction, re-use, recycling, composting, energy recovery, and landfill.

Pearce, 1998 points out that no LCA has yet been carried out to justify the lower rankings given to energy recovery compared to recycling and re-use. The "hierarchy" depends critically on geographical conditions and the nature of the electricity generating system. For instance, energy recovery from incineration is assumed to have a higher priority than electricity generation. But the precise magnitude of these advantages obviously depends on the kind of electricity system that is in place.

With reference to model (2) and the format Table 1, we distinguish below several categories of environmental policy measures for the Portuguese bottled water industry. These range from prohibitive measures (direct regulation and various kinds of environmental fees) to putting in place incentives aimed at encouraging recycling of glass and bottles.

4.1 Direct regulation

We begin by discussing the environmental goals entered in the vector g in program (2). These are upper limits laid down by central or local government specifying the maximal permitted release of air pollution, water pollution, landfill and other environmental bads. The first prerequisite for such regulation is that the government monitor present industry practice and collect statistics of current release on the level of individual plants. These would be the kind of environmental impact surveys such as those drawn up for projected large highway or building projects in Portugal, but with the difference that they would relate to existing pollution sources rather than potential new ones.

Next, acceptable goals would be established, presumably after consultations with health authorities, biological experts, conservationists etc. To be meaningful for operational purposes, those goals would have to be broken down into regional goals, or even goals for individual plants. They would need to be specified for detailed environmental pollution categories, such as the release of greenhouse gas emissions released from the manufacturing of glass bottles, and from transportation.

The December 1997 Kyoto protocol covers six categories of greenhouse gases: Carbon dioxide (CO_2), methane (CH_4), nitrous oxide (N_2O), hydrofluorocarbons (HCFCs), perfluorcarbons (PFCs) and sulphurhexafluoride (SF_8). They are all aggregated on the basis of their global warming potential for a time horizon of 100 years. Furthermore, the European union is aiming at a 8% emission reduction during the period 2008-2012, compared to the emission of the member states in a reference year (1990/1995)

Assuming, for the sake of the argument, that detailed plans like these can be translated into a vector of goals g, the question still remains: how would the government see to it that the promulgated regulations are actually implemented? There is no ready answer to this question in a free market economy such as Portugal's. On a less ambitious scale, however, there is scope for considerable direct regulation, such as inspections and controls of industrial combustion techniques, controls of hazardous waste, minimum standards for landfills, etc. In program (2) modifying or actually eliminating some existing activities, or introducing new government-mandated activities can mimic such partial measures.

4.2 Environmental fees

An intriguing alternative approach of government policy is to charge environmental fees on the release of environmental bads, thus setting up monetary incentives designed to prod producers and/or consumers to limit their polluting practices.

In order to see how this would work, consider again the vector of dual variables (3) corresponding to program (2). We now discuss how the shadow costs of environmental bads, denoted u^E, can be interpreted as a system of environmental fees. The fees are designed to implement the environmental goals g. In other words, rather than aiming for these goals by direct regulation, the alternate route exists of setting up incentives that would cause the economic actors (bottling plants, distributors and consumers) to reach for these goals voluntarily.

The dual program to (2) reads

$$\text{Max} - u^P w + u^F d - u^E g \tag{5}$$

subject to

$$-u^P A^P + u^I(-A^I + B^I) + u^F B^F - u^E B^E \leq c$$

$$u \geq 0$$

There is one constraint in program (5) for each activity. In the case of manufacturing activities (manufacturing bottles, cleaning them and filling them), it states that the shadow value of a bottle ($u^F B^F$) cannot exceed the cost of operations. The costs include current manufacturing costs (c), costs of energy and raw materials ($u^P A^P$), costs of intermediate goods such as recycled or returned bottles (u^I $(A^I$ - $B^I)$) and the shadow cost of environmental releases ($u^E B^E$). Furthermore, by complementary slackness, if such an activity is operated at a positive level, the shadow value of the bottle must equal these costs. In the case of consumption activities, it states that the shadow value of the consumption service plus the shadow value of the recycled or returned bottle cannot exceed the shadow cost of the purchased bottle plus the shadow cost of environmental releases. Again, if the consumption activity is operated at a positive level, these shadow values must equal these costs.

The rules now mentioned remain fictitious as long as no mechanism has been put in place that would persuade the bottlers and consumers alike to include the shadow environmental costs in their calculations. One way to implement them is for the government to actually collect these costs as environmental fees. This requires two things: first, that the government forms program (5), solves it, and determines the shadow costs u^E, and, second, that some kind of assessment and collection procedure is instituted.

Yet another means of collecting the environmental fees, very much debated recently, is for the government to issue pollution permits and to auction these off in a free market. Electric utilities in the US buy and sell permits to release sulfur in the air. The allowances are traded at the Chicago Board of Trade. The contract unit of trading is defined as 25 one-ton sulfur dioxide emission allowances. For an account, see e.g. Thore, 1995 pp.134 ff. Similar plans have been drawn up for the global issuance and trading of carbon dioxide pollution permits, see Manne and Richels, 1991.

4.3 Fiscal incentives designed to stimulate recycling

We now discuss the possibilities for the government of encouraging substitution between activities, so that the industry to a greater extent relies on recycling of glass and bottles, and less on thee manufacture of new bottles (obviously, such substitution will reduce the amount of glass sent to the landfills).

Mathematically speaking, the optimal operation of the industry is determined in two steps:

- first, by the constraint set of program (2) which spells out all feasible production points (the so-called set of feasible solutions), and,

- second, by identifying the particular feasible production point (or points) which minimize the minimand of total current costs (the efficient point).

Changing parametrically the vector c of current operating costs, substitution between activities will in general take place. The new optimal point will be a new frontier point of the set of feasible solutions. Actually, by systematically changing the vector c (referred to by Charnes and Cooper, *ibid.* p.308 as a "spiral method"), it is possible to trace the entire efficiency frontier of the feasible solution set.

Government policies that impact on the relative current operating costs of the industrial activities can then, if chosen suitably, bring about desired substitutions in the industry. Examples of measures that will promote an increased reliance on recycled glass and bottles include:

- subsidies paid to industrial operations of recycling glass or cleaning used bottles,
- excise taxes levied on the manufacture and sale of new bottles,
- instituting a system of cash deposits to be paid by consumers, returnable upon collection and recycling of the bottle (already in place in Portugal) or increasing these cash deposits,
- environmental fees placed on the use of landfills.

The purpose of these measures and others like them is to influence the relative cost of activities, making recycling a more attractive option.

As pointed out, recovering (recycling and reusing) is often limited by insufficient industrial capacity. The general public may be willing to collect and return more recyclable material and more returnable bottles than the industry is able to process. In model (2), the market relations for intermediate goods

$$(-A^I + B^I)\,x \quad = \quad 0 \tag{6}$$

may then have to be written as inequalities

$$(-A^I + B^I)\,x \quad \leq \quad 0 \tag{7}$$

permitting some collected and recycled material to remain unused.

At the moment, the industrial capacity for recycling is more than sufficient in Portugal. A few episodes have even been reported in the press of glass mills importing recycled glass from Spain. The direction of the inequality sign in (7) then has to be reversed.

The complete model now reads

$$
\begin{aligned}
&\min cx && (8)\\
&\text{subject to } -A^P x \geq -w\\
&(-A^I + B^I)\, x \leq 0\\
&B^F x \geq d\\
&-B^E x \geq -g\\
&0 \leq x \leq X
\end{aligned}
$$

where X is a vector of upper (capacity) bounds.

In order to stimulate recycling, the government may now institute policies that will encourage the building of more recycling capacity X_2 (using recycled glass to manufacture bottles) and X_3 (cleaning recycled bottles for reuse). A variety of government programs are possible, including direct cash subsidies for such construction.

5. A NUMERICAL EXAMPLE

The numerical example to follow illustrates model (8) above, with the slight modification that the three resources can be acquired as desired, at constant and given marginal costs $q = (q_1, q_2, q_3)$. In geometric terms, the supply curves of the resources are then horizontal (given supply prices) rather than vertical (given supplies). Including the total cost of resources in the minimand, program (8) reads as shown in Table 2 below.

The three first constraints in the table state market relations for the three resources: energy, raw materials and spring water at the wellhead: the actual withdrawal of each resource cannot exceed its availability. The next four constraints state market clearing for the four intermediate goods: empty bottles, recycled glass, returned bottles and filled bottles. The clearing relations for recycled glass and for returned bottles have been entered as inequalities, since actual recycling may fall short of the glass and bottles returned to the collection points. The 8th constraint is a single market relation for final demand. The two following constraints state the environmental constraints imposed on the two environmental "bads": pollution and landfill waste. A policy-maker lays down target figures (g_9 and g_{10}) for the maximal environmental damage. Finally, there is a capacity constraint for each industrial activity.

Table 2. Linear programming model for numerical example

Min								
c_1x_1	$+c_2x_2$	$+c_3x_3$	$+c_4x_4$		$+q_1w_1$	$+q_2w_2$	$+q_3w_3$	
subj to								
$-a_{11}x_1$	$-a_{12}x_2$	$-a_{13}x_3$	$-a_{14}x_4$		$+w_1$			≥ 0
$-a_{21}x_1$	$-a_{22}x_2$					$+w_2$		≥ 0
			$-a_{34}x_4$				$+w_3$	≥ 0
x_1	$+x_2$	$+x_3$	$-x_4$					$=0$
	$-a_{52}x_2$			$+b_{55}x_5$				≤ 0
		$-x_3$		$+b_{65}x_5$				≤ 0
			x_4	$-x_5$				$=0$
				x_5				$\geq d_8$
$-b_{91}x_1$	$-b_{92}x_2$	$-b_{93}x_3$	$-b_{94}x_4$					$\geq -g_9$
				$-b_{10,5}x_5$				$\geq -g_{10}$
x_1								$\leq X_1$
	x_2							$\leq X_2$
		x_3						$\leq X_3$
			x_4					$\leq X_4$

$x_1, x_2, x_3, x_4, x_5 \geq 0, \; w_1, w_2, w_3 \geq 0$

The numerical example that follows refers to a large Portuguese company, bottling and distributing spring water under its own brand name. To protect the company, the data have been adjusted so that they reflect typical rather than actual operations. The *A* and *B* matrices (see above) are given by

$$-A^P = \begin{pmatrix} -0.5 & -0.4 & -0.2 & -0.3 & 0 \\ -2 & -0.3 & 0 & 0 & 0 \\ 0 & 0 & 0 & -0.8 & 0 \end{pmatrix}$$

$$-A^I + B^I = \begin{pmatrix} 1 & 1 & 1 & -1 & 0 \\ 0 & -0.8 & 0 & 0 & 0.25 \\ 0 & 0 & -1 & 0 & 0.30 \\ 0 & 0 & 0 & 1 & -1 \end{pmatrix}$$

$$-B^F = \begin{pmatrix} 0 & 0 & 0 & 0 & 1 \end{pmatrix}$$

$$-B^E = \begin{pmatrix} -3 & -2.5 & -1.5 & -2 & 0 \\ 0 & 0 & 0 & 0 & -0.45 \end{pmatrix}$$

The vector of current operating costs is $c = (12,10,0.5,0.3,0)$. Marginal costs of supplies are $w = (3,2,18)$. Consumer demand is $d_8 = 5.4E+5$. The environmental goals are $(g_9\ ,\ g_{10}) = (25E+5,\ 2E+5)$. The vector of industrial capacities is $X = (2E+5,\ 0.8E+5,\ 0.8E+5,\ 10E+5)$ (The number 10E+5 is large enough to make sure that consumption is not capacity-constrained.)

The resulting solution is listed in Table 3. The capacity limit on the activity x_2 (manufacturing bottles from recycled glass) is binding; the capacity limits on the other activities are not binding. None of the two environmental goals is binding.

Table 3. Solution to numerical example

Origins of bottles		**Destinations of bottles**	
Bottles manufactured from scratch	$x_1 = 1.055E+5$	Bottles collected for recycling of glass	$0.8\, x_2 = 0.640E+5$
Bottles manufactured from recycled glass	$x_2 = 0.800E+5$	Bottles cleaned and reused	$x_3 = 0.795E+5$
Cleaned bottles	$x_3 = 0.795E+5$	Bottles ending up in landfill	$x_5 - 0.8\, x_2 - x_3 = 1.215E+5$
Sum bottles	$x_4 = x_5 = 2.650E+5$	Sum bottles	$x_5 = 2.651E+5$

As a result of the capacity constraint on recycling of collected glass, some collected glass bottles are never used, see below:

- Collected and crushed glass bottles, intended for renewed manufacturing of bottles: $0.25\, x_5 = 0.663E+5$,
- Collected and crushed glass bottles actually used as inputs: $0.8\, x_2 = 0.640E+5$,
- Difference, eventually ending up in landfill: 0.023E+5.

The total volume of bottles sent to the landfill can be broken down as follows:

- Bottles immediately sent by the consumers to the landfills: $0.45\, x_5 = 1.193E+5$,
- Bottles intended for recycling but rejected by bottle manufacturers: $0.25\, x_5 - 0.8\, x_2 = 0.023E+5$,
- Bottles intended for reuse but rejected by bottle cleaners: $0.30\, x_5 - x_3 = 0$,
- Sum bottles ending up in landfills: 1.216E+5.

Next, we list the dual solution. The dual variables as $u_1 = 3$, $u_2 = 2$, $u_3 = 18$, $u_4 = 17.5$, $u_5 = 0$, $u_6 = 16.4$, $u_7 = 33.10$, $u_8 = 28.18$, $u_9 = 0$, $u_{10} = 0$, $u_{11} = 0$, $u_{12} = 5.7$, $u_{13} = 0$, $u_{14} = 0$. Using these values, one can break down the value of a bottle of spring water in the hands of the consumer as exhibited in Table 4.

It remains to discuss the scope for environmental policy in this model. We first examine the two goals (g_9, g_{10}) = (25E+5, 2E+5) imposed as upper limits on air pollution and landfills, respectively. Actual discharges are only

Table 4. Breakdown of value of one bottle of spring water in the hands of the consumer

Direct and shadow costs of one bottle		**Shadow values of one bottle**	
Currents costs of energy and spring water at tap	$0.3\,u_1 + 0.8\,u_3 = 15.3$	Imputed market price paid by consumer	$u_8 = 28.18$
+ Current filling costs	$c_4 = 0.3$	+ Shadow value of recycled glass	$0.25\,u_5 = 0$
+ Shadow cost of manufacturing empty bottle	$u_4 = 17.5$	+ Shadow value of reused bottle	$0.3\,u_6 = 4.92$
= Sum costs of one bottle of spring water	$u_7 = 33.1$	= Sum shadow value	$u_7 = 33.1$

(11.66E+5, 1.193E+5) respectively, so that the formulated goals are very generous and far above actual discharge levels. It may look tempting to the analyst to lower the goals sufficiently to make them binding. Some experimentation shows that this does not work at all, however. The problem then becomes infeasible. This goes to illustrate the theme developed in Section 3 above: in order to make environmental policy operational, quite specific policy measures need to be taken that stimulate recycling directly. In the small model formulated here, it just is not enough for the government to clamp down with global environmental decrees and to leave it up to the economic actors to find ways of adjusting. (In large models with many alternative technologies available for each activity, there will exist margins for the economic actors to carry out the necessary technical substitutions.)

The obvious way of promoting recycling in the present model is for the government to encourage the building of more recycling capacity. Remember that the dual variable of the recycling capacity constraint $x_2 \leq 0.8E{+}5$ came out as $u_{12} = 5.7$. In the standard manner of interpreting dual variables, this value can be seen as the highest price that the recycling factory would be willing to pay to build (or purchase) one additional unit of capacity. For the government to induce the factory to build this additional capacity, it needs to offer a building subsidy of at least $u_{12} = 5.7$ per unit of new capacity built.

6. CONCLUDING REMARKS

Today's society faces the need to reduce negative environmental life-cycle impacts of many products. Appropriate environmental policy is needed when the production and/or consumption of a product generates negative external economies detrimental to the environment. Unfortunately, there is no consensus among economists or policy-makers of how an optimal mix of environmental measures and regulation should be brought together. It does not make things easier that most environmental studies are strongly region and product dependent.

The purpose of the present work has been to unify two separate approaches to the study of industrial processes and the environment:

1. *Activity analysis*, due to Koopmans, 1957 breaks down all resource-extracting, manufacturing and distribution activities in a given industry into a list of unitary "activities", each requiring a number of "inputs" and generating a number of (intermediate or final) "outputs." The "level" of operation of each activity is determined to enable the industry to deliver the bill of final goods that consumer demand.

In further developments by Charnes and Cooper, 1961 activity analysis was written on the format of linear programming, enabling the analyst to incorporate detailed modeling of the production chain of the industry, such as representing it as a logistics network of production and distribution.

2. *Life Cycle Analysis* (LCA) is a more recent approach designed to account for the environmental consequences of a product, tracking its total environmental impact both upstream and downstream along the production chain. The impacts upstream include pollution and waste generated during resource extraction and production of raw materials and intermediate products. Environmental impacts downstream are future pollution and waste arising from final distribution, consumption and disposal.

Bringing these two approaches together, we extended the classical Koopmans format of activity analysis to encompass the standard LCA accounting of environmental effects. The mathematical programming formulation was extended to include considerations over the entire life cycle of products in two ways. First, a separate category of goods called "environmental goods" was added to Koopmans model. Second, the entire production chain of a product was accounted for, both upstream (from the "cradle" of the product) and downstream (to its eventual "grave"). The programming formulation enabled us to include the presence of loops in the production chain associated with the recovery of products (recycling, reusing, etc).

An application from the Portuguese bottled water industry was described. Several types of environmental policy were discussed, ranging from prohibitive measures to incentives aimed at encouraging the recycling of glass and the reuse of bottles. A simple numerical example was solved and discussed. The results obtained demonstrate the potential of our combined approach, imbedding the conventional LCA in a programming framework, thus bringing the power of linear programming concepts to bear on the analysis, such as the availability of the shadow prices (dual variables) of all constraints. Examples are quantification of the costs associated with the limitations imposed by environmental legislation. We discussed how the desired environmental targets could be achieved either through direct emissions restrictions placed on the pollutants, or by suitably designed eco-taxes.

Further results applying mathematical programming techniques to analyze environmental management and policy in a large model of the Portuguese table water industry will be presented in the doctoral dissertation of the junior author.

APPENDIX

As mentioned briefly at the end of Section 2 above, there exists a simple mathematical relationship between the activity analysis format with environmental goods, program (2) and the environmental impact formulation, program (4). The precise relationship is spelled out in the following

Theorem 1. Choosing the environmental impact coefficients $V = c + u^E B^E$, the formulation (3) is actually mathematically equivalent to the target formulation (2).

Proof. The theorem follows immediately from the fact that the two saddle points

$$\min_{x \geq 0} \max_{u \geq 0} \; cx + u^P (A^P x - w) + u^I (A^I - B^I) x + \\ + u^F (- B^F x + d) + u^E (B^E x - g) \qquad \text{(A1)}$$

corresponding to program (2), and

$$\min_{x \geq 0} \max_{u \geq 0} \quad Vx + u^P (A^P x - w) + u^I (A^I - B^I)x + u^F(- B^F x + d) \qquad \text{(A2)}$$

corresponding to program (4) will then coincide. (See for instance W.W. Cooper and S. Thore, "Some Elements of Saddle-Point Theory", Chap.2 in Thore, 1991.) Q.E.D.

The coefficients $V = c + u^E B^E$ are measured in dollars. They are obtained as the sum of the current manufacturing costs c and all environmental costs. Each environmental cost is calculated as the product of an environmental input coefficient (such as a volume of polluting substances released per unit of operating an activity), and its shadow cost.

REFERENCES

Ayres, R.U. (1994), "Life Cycle Analysis: A Critique," *Resources, Conservation and Recycling*, Vol. 14, pp. 199 – 223.

Charnes, A. and Cooper, W.W. (1961), *Management Models and Industrial Applications of Linear Programming*, Vols. I-II, John Wiley & Sons, New York, N.Y.

Heijungs, R. (1997), *Economic Drama and the Environmental Stage*, Ph.D.dissertation, University of Leiden..

Hendrickson, C., Horvath, A., Joshi, S. and Lave, L. B. (1998), "Economic Input-Output Models for Environmental Life-Cycle Assessment," *Environmental Science and Technology*, April, pp. 184A- 191A.

Koopmans, T. (1957), *Three Essays on the State of Economic Science*, Mc Graw-Hill, New York, N.Y.

Lave, L.B., Cobas-Flores, E., Hendrickson, C.T. and McMichael, F.C. (1995), "Using Input-Output Analysis to Estimate Economy-Wide Discharges," *Environmental Science and Technology*, V
ol. 29:9, pp. 420-426.

Leontief, W.W. (1970), "Environmental Repercussions and the Economic Structure. An Input-Output Approach," *Review of Economics and Statistics*, Vol. 52, pp. 262-271.

Manne, A. and Richels, R. (1991), "Global CO2 Emission Reduction – the Impacts of Rising Energy Costs," *The Energy Journal*.

Pearce, D. (1998), "Environmental Appraisal and Environmental Policy in the European Union," *Environmental and Resource Economics*, Vol. 11:3-4, pp. 489-501.

Thompson, G. and Thore, S. (1992), *Computational Economics: Economic Modeling with Optimization Software*, Scientific Press, South San Francisco, Calif.

Thore, S. (1991) *Economic Logistics: The Optimization of Spatial and Sectoral Resource, Production and Distribution Systems*, Quorum Books, Westport, Conn.

Life Cycle Activity Analysis: A Case Study of Plastic Panels

A Research Paper

F. Freire[1], E. Williams[2], A. Azapagic[2], R. Clift[2], G. Stevens[2] and W. Mellor[2]

[1] *Instituto Superior Técnico, Lisbon*

[2] *University of Surrey, UK*

Abstract: Life Cycle Activity Analysis (LCAA) combines classical Activity Analysis with environmental Life Cycle Assessment (LCA). It provides a structured approach to economic and environmental optimization of the entire supply chain of products, processes or services. LCAA considers all activities from "cradle to grave" including alternative methods of production, distribution, reuse and recovery. This paper builds on the previous work by the authors and applies the LCAA approach to assess alternative end-of-life options for plastic components used in electronic equipment. The environmental and economic consequences associated with these end-of-life options, such as remanufacturing, mechanical recycling, feedstock recycling and incineration, are evaluated for the entire supply chain and opportunities for closing the material loop are highlighted. A mathematical programming model is formulated and solved numerically to determine the optimal supply chain configurations for several scenarios. Solutions are proposed which reduce both environmental and economic impacts when compared to current practice.

Key words: Activity analysis, life cycle assessment, environmental goods, foreground and background of analysis, environmental impact categories, indirect environmental burdens, scenarios, loops in the production flow, plastic panels, end-of-life options, recovery, recycling, reuse, disposal

1. INTRODUCTION

Environmental burdens always occur in conjunction with flows of substances, materials and products through the economic system. Several methods have been developed to study such physical flows and, in particular, to assess the associated environmental impacts and they include Life Cycle

Assessment (LCA), Substance Flow Analysis (SFA) and environmental Input-Output Analysis (IOA). Each of these methods serves a different but related purpose. For example, the purpose of LCA, which is one of the tools used in this work, is to study the environmental aspects and potential impacts of a product, process or service throughout its life cycle, from raw materials acquisition though production, use and disposal (ISO, 1997). This extended system boundary sets LCA apart from other related methods as it provides a full picture of human interactions with the environment. If coupled with economic analysis, LCA can provide a powerful decision-aid tool for an integrated economic and environmental assessment of the material and product supply chains.

This indeed is the departing point of this work: the authors believe that the reconciliation of economic and environmental (and social) priorities is paramount for a more sustainable world. However, to facilitate this on the practical level it is necessary to develop the appropriate approaches and tools that would help decision-makers understand the trade-offs between these disparate criteria in different situations. This need has also been recognized by a number of other authors and this has resulted in the development of various approaches that attempt to integrate physical, environmental and economic models. Some of these approaches combine LCA and optimization approaches to identify optimum solutions and in this way they also create a bridge between engineering, environmental science, economics and operations research. The following are some examples of these approaches:

Bloemhof-Ruwaard, et al. (1995) classified the interactions between operations research and environmental management under the twin headings of "supply chain modeling" and "environmental chain modeling". As in LCA, the supply chain comprises the extraction of raw materials, production, distribution, use of goods and waste collection. In the environmental chain, emissions and waste are transported and transformed, resulting in water, air and soil pollution with damaging effects to the environment. Daniel *et al.* (1997) developed also a related approach.

The concept of a "material-product (M-P) chain" was suggested by Opschoor (1994) and Kandelaars (1998). It is defined as a system of linked flows of materials and products supporting the provision of a certain service. The objective is an integrated model-based analysis of resource and pollution problems for policy-making. The economic modeling of M-P chains combines elements of physical flows and economic allocation. The analysis includes static or dynamic optimization, simulation and partial equilibrium analysis.

Azapagic (1996) and Azapagic and Clift (1995, 1998, 1999a) developed a multi-objective systems optimization approach to facilitate identification and choice of optimum solutions that simultaneously satisfy environmental and economic criteria. This methodology was applied to a number of industrial case studies, including boron products (Azapagic and Clift, 1999b) and Scotch whisky (Azapagic et al., 2000).

MATTER (Materials Technologies for Greenhouse Gas Emission Reduction) is a dynamic linear programming model, originally developed as a tool for the analysis of macro-economic energy systems. See Gielen (1998, 1999). The joint project of five Dutch institutes, coordinated by the Dutch Energy Research Foundation (ECN), extended it to materials system analysis from "cradle to grave". It consists of an integrated energy and materials system model for Western Europe used for the analysis of greenhouse gas emission reduction strategies.

Following the thrust of a more holistic approach to systems analysis, this paper presents an extended optimization-based approach – Life Cycle Activity Analysis (LCAA). LCAA combines mathematical programming of Activity Analysis with the LCA methodology. Koopmans (1951, 1957) developed Activity Analysis (AA). For this pioneering work, Koopmans received the 1975 Nobel Prize in economics (shared with I. Kantorovich). However, the original formulation, (Koopmans, 1957), was not well suited for numerical solution, since it assumed that there were as many commodities as activities, and that the resulting system of equations had a non-singular solution. A major step was the reformulation of AA as a Linear Programming (LP) problem, permitting any number of activities and any number of commodities, see Charnes and Cooper, (1961).

Activity Analysis can be viewed as a tool of partial economic analysis modeling for the representation of an industry or a sector of the economy, providing a mathematical format suitable for the representation of an entire vertical production chain (Thore, 1991). More recently, Heijungs (1996, 1997) recognized the conceptual similarities between LCA and classical Activity Analysis (AA) and observed that Life Cycle Inventory is an extension of AA, both being “commodity-by-industry analysis”, generally seen as superior to other forms of inter-industry analysis (Heijungs, 1996); however no connection between mathematical programming and LCA was made. Thus, a major purpose of LCAA discussed here is to highlight how this connection can be established, using extended mathematical programming formats of AA for integrated economic and environmental analysis of the life cycle of products.

For example, whenever products can be manufactured in alternative ways, distributed through alternative marketing channels, reused or recovered, there exists scope for choice and for controlling the environmental impacts. By combining the LCA approach with mathematical programming techniques, it is possible to represent these options explicitly along the whole supply chain and to solve for optimal economic (e.g. production levels or profit) and environmental performance (e.g. environmental impacts and allocation of resources).

The classical formulation of AA distinguishes three classes of goods: primary goods (natural resources, materials or labor), intermediate goods (outputs which serve as inputs into subsequent activities) and final goods (outputs). LCAA extends the concept of linear activities to embrace mass and energy fluxes over the entire life cycle of products. In particular, the proposed LCAA model includes one additional category: "environmental goods", representing primary resources (material or energy drawn directly from the environment) and emissions of pollutants and the disposal of waste (discarded into the environment without subsequent human transformation). These are in the LCA terminology known as environmental burdens. These environmental "goods" can be further aggregated into categories of resource usage and environmental impacts, such as global warming, ozone depletion etc. The purpose of such aggregation is two-fold. Firstly, it interprets the environmental burdens included in the output table in terms of environmental problems or hazards. Secondly, by aggregating a large set of data in to a smaller number of impact categories it simplifies the decision-making process.

The LCAA approach offers the following advantages:

- LCAA is a numerical technique, requiring the use of advanced mathematical programming software. The software used in this work is GAMS (General Algebraic Modeling Software) (Brooke *et al.*, 1998).
- LCAA explicitly recognizes the possibility of alternative ways of production (e.g. using raw or recycled materials), alternative distribution channels, and alternative reuse or recovery processes. In other words, there are mathematical degrees of freedom present in the model format, and the purpose of the programming model is to determine the optimal choices at each stage of the logistics chain.
- LCAA incorporates advanced techniques for representing environmental goals in the model, in the so-called Goal Programming. These goals do not need to be absolute targets but can be a set of ordinal priorities, laid down by decision- or policy-makers. Goals can also be ordered in hierarchies, with sub-goals in several layers. In this manner, LCAA allows for realistic modeling of the goal-based process.

Through the LCA approach, individual environmental burdens are brought together under environmental impact categories, such as global warming, acidification, etc. Using LCA terminology, this is equivalent to

Life Cycle Impact Assessment (LCIA) (ISO, 1998). However, unlike in LCA, there are mathematical degrees of freedom present in the LCAA model, because vectors of individual environmental burdens associated with alternative activities may translate into the same aggregated impacts. The optimizing format makes it therefore possible to determine the optimal levels of individual environmental burdens (and associated vector of activity levels) that are commensurate with a given set of goals in terms of environmental impact categories.

Varying the numerical assumptions of the model (and varying the goals or the priorities parametrically), LCAA can be used to generate a set of scenarios to be presented to the policy-maker. In this manner a series of "what if?" questions can be addressed and answered.

The theoretical groundwork for LCAA was laid in Thore and Freire (1999) (see the preceding paper in the present volume). That paper presented an activity analysis format augmented with environmental variables, and provided a numerical example brought from the bottled water industry in Portugal. Further developments were presented in Freire *et al.* (2001) and in an application to used tires (Freire *et al.*, 2001).

One of the goals of the present paper is to expand the LCAA programming format further, pursuing the production chains both upstream (all the way from the "cradle") and downstream (to the "grave") by explicitly considering the "eco-profile" of the primary goods (materials, products and energy from other product-systems). The eco-profile lists all environmental burdens accumulated from the prior upstream processing of the primary products themselves. In so doing, account is explicitly made of both the direct (associated with the activities) and indirect (associated with primary goods) impacts of the system. Like in other life-cycle studies, it is useful to use the concepts of "foreground" and "background" systems (e.g. Clift *et al.*, 1999, 2000). This helps to distinguish between unit processes of direct interest in the study, and other operations with which they exchange materials and energy. The foreground may be defined as the endogenous part of the production chain, which includes the set of processes whose selection or mode of operation is affected directly by decisions of the study. The background denotes the exogenous parts of the production chain, comprising all other processes that interact directly with the foreground system, usually by supplying material or energy to the foreground or receiving material and energy from it. This concept is illustrated in Figure 1. In this way, the LCAA format accounts not only for the environmental burdens of processes in the foreground but also for impacts in the background. Thus, the total environmental impacts are calculated over both the endogenous and the exogenous part of the life cycle. The foreground and background concepts are also useful in setting goals and targets which can be attached to both variables in the foreground and in the background.

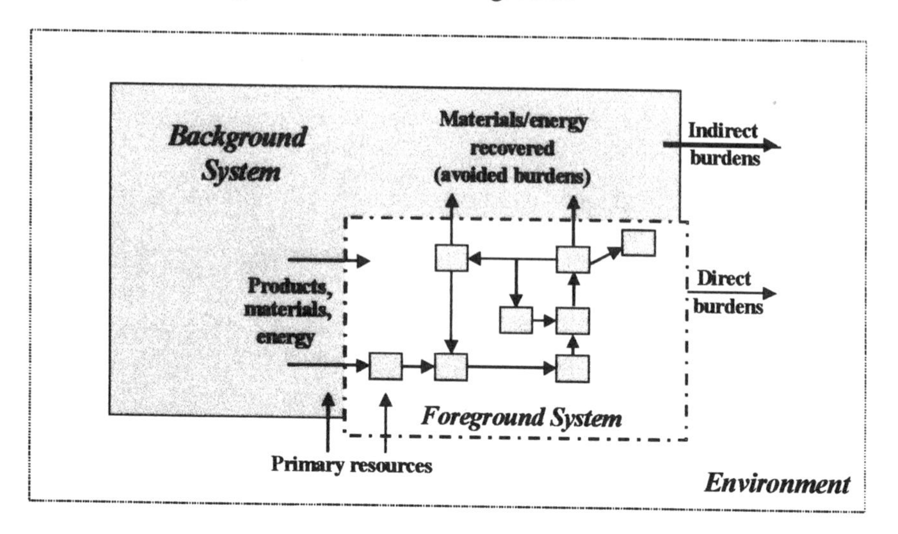

Figure 1. Foreground and background systems

Furthermore, LCAA provides a general optimization framework for the modeling of reuse and recovery of products, leading to loops in the life-cycle chain. It permits materials and energy to be recovered both inside the foreground (closed-loop) and between the foreground and the background (open-loop). In earlier publications (e.g. Freire *et al.* 2001), the possibility of closed-loops in the intermediate or final stages of the production chains was considered. Here, the approach is also applied to allow for the presence of open loops that recover goods in the foreground, supplying them to other chains in the background. In addition, the recovery of materials or energy in the foreground may displace activities in the background system, leading to the avoidance of environmental burdens that would otherwise have been generated. This is known as the "avoided burden" approach (e.g. Clift and Doig, 1996) and that can also be expressed explicitly within LCAA.

To illustrate how this extended LCAA approach can aid closing of material loops while satisfying both environmental and economic objectives, the case study of recovery and re-manufacturing of plastic photocopier panels is presented. This work represents an extension of research carried out under the auspices of the CHAMP project (CHAin Management of Polymers) at the University of Surrey. The project has developed a novel mathematical framework (Mellor et al., 2001) to model integrated chains of materials, including product design, reuse and recovery.

The paper is organized in four sections, including this introduction. Section 2 provides the mathematical background and gives an overall view of the LCAA methodology. Section 3 describes the main characteristics of the life cycle of plastic panels to be assembled into photocopiers, including post-use recovery processes. Five scenarios with both current and future reuse and recycling practices are formulated and solved. The results of the scenarios are presented and discussed. Section 4 offers some concluding remarks.

2. MATHEMATICAL ANALYSIS

2.1 Model development

This section presents the LCAA modeling development. We begin with a standard activity analysis format augmented to include life-cycle environmental burdens into the model (see the earlier paper by Thore and Freire printed in the present volume):

$$\begin{aligned}
&\min \quad cx + qw && (1)\\
&\text{subject to} \quad -A^P x + w \geq 0\\
&(-A^I + B^I)x = 0\\
&B^F x \geq d\\
&(A^E - B^E)x \geq -g\\
&x, w \geq 0
\end{aligned}$$

where cx represents the total costs of operating the activities x and qw is the total cost of primary goods. A and B are matrices of input and output coefficients, respectively. The letter w represents a column vector of supply levels of primary goods, such as material and energy from the background system. The superscripts P, I, F and E represent primary, intermediate, final, and environmental goods, respectively. Primary goods are inputs of products, material and energy produced in the background. Intermediate goods are outputs that serve as inputs into subsequent activities, either in the foreground or in the background. Final goods are the functional outputs delivered by the distributed and purchased products, the production of which is the objective of the economic system under study. Environmental "goods" or interventions are flows of materials or energy drawn from or discarded into the environment without subsequent human transformation. By convention, the input coefficients (A-coefficients) have a minus sign and the output coefficients (B-coefficients) are assigned a positive sign. Consequently, matrices A and B become partitioned into:

$$A = (-A^P, -A^I, 0, -A^E) \qquad (2)$$

$B = (0, B^I, B^F, B^E)$

The model (1) minimizes total costs, which comprise the costs of operating activities and of primary goods. For present purposes, it is assumed that the prices of all primary goods are known and constant. The crucial feature of formulation (1) is the constraint $(A^E - B^E)x \geq -g$, which requires the environmental burdens $(-A^E + B^E)x$ not to exceed a vector of environmental goals g set for example by a policy- or decision-maker.

As discussed in the introduction, the model adopts the concept of the foreground and background systems (see Figure 1). The foreground is modeled in some explicit detail: the production activities themselves, and the conversion of intermediate goods into final goods, i.e. the set of processes whose selection or level of operation can be affected directly by decisions in the study. The background comprises the exogenous flows of the model, i.e. the supplies of primary goods. A sufficient (but not necessary) condition for a good or goods to be in the background is that the exchange with the foreground takes place in a homogenous market, where the particular plants supplying them cannot be identified (Clift *et al.*, 1999).

The flow diagram in the foreground system in Figure 1 represents the flows of intermediate goods. Final goods are new or reused products delivering the same function. The two closed loops in the foreground return the post-use goods to the distribution and production chains: an inner reuse loop sends the goods to collection and further reuse, and an outer recycling loop returns the materials making up the final goods back to the re-manufacturing chain. In addition, goods can be recycled to the background (open loop recycling).

The environmental 'goods' or interventions arising from the foreground (i.e. from the operations which are being modeled directly) are termed *direct burdens*. They include the direct emissions from operating the activities (e.g. combustion, chemical reactions, thermal treatments, long-term leachate emissions from landfill etc.) and from the transportation of intermediate goods. The resource usage and emissions arising from the background activities are termed *indirect burdens;* they are caused by the changes in the demand of products, materials and energy in the foreground. The indirect burdens can be described by generic industry data, obtainable from commercial or public life cycle inventory databases. Direct burdens on the other hand are process-specific and must be sourced from the manufacturers in the foreground.

Using this terminology, the programming format (1) at present only features direct environmental burdens $(-A^E + B^E)x$ arising from processes present in the foreground. In addition, however, indirect environmental burdens may have accumulated in the background, upstream in the production chain, during the earlier processing, manufacture and transportation of primary goods. The indirect burdens will be discussed later in this section.

In order to convert model (1) into a true life cycle activity analysis (LCAA) format, the following two steps are necessary. The first step includes into the model the total accumulated environmental burdens of products over their entire life cycle, including the indirect environmental burdens of primary goods arising in the background. Thus, the total environmental burdens arising over the life cycle of the products are equal to the sum of the foreground (direct) burdens and the background (indirect) burdens, that is $(-A^E + B^E)x + Dw$, where Dw is a vector of environmental effects arising from the background. The environmental goal-condition in (1) must therefore be amended as shown below:

$$
\begin{aligned}
&\min \quad cx + qw && (3)\\
&\text{subject to } -A^P x + w \geq 0 \\
&(-A^I + B^I)x = 0 \\
&B^F x \geq d \\
&(A^E - B^E)x - Dw \geq -g \\
&x, w \geq 0
\end{aligned}
$$

The second step involves expanding the possibilities for reuse and/or recovery of products. As mentioned above, such loops in the production chain can take two forms:

- recovery entirely in the foreground (closed loop) and
- recovery from the foreground to the background (open loop).

Materials and energy recovered in the foreground, which are also inputs to the activities in the foreground (closed loops), may lead to the avoidance of environmental burdens. This is the case when burdens associated with foreground activities that are displaced by the recovery processes are higher than the burdens of the recovery itself. The opposite is also possible: material loops may sometimes lead to higher environmental burdens, i.e. a worse environmental performance overall. This can happen when the recovery of used products and materials by itself imposes considerable burdens.

A product that is recovered and exchanged with the background system will always be treated as an intermediate good. The usual assumption (Clift *et al*., 2000) is that the recovery of materials and/or energy in the foreground does not affect the demand for goods and services in the background (except for materials and energy supplied to the foreground activities). Therefore, the market balances for intermediate goods which were defined in (1) as *(-*

$A^I + B^I)x = 0$ have to be amended to $(- A^I + B^I)x - y = 0$, where y is a column vector of unknown levels of recovery of intermediate goods; zero entries indicate recovery entirely in the foreground, positive entries indicate recovery supplied from the foreground to background.

In the case of recovery entirely in the foreground, the mass balance reads: - *intermediate inputs* + *intermediate outputs* = *0*. In the case of recovery from the foreground to the background, the mass balance becomes:

-intermediate inputs + *intermediate outputs* – *recovered goods returned to the background* = *0*.

Adopting these assumptions, the total environmental burdens are then equal to the sum of the foreground (direct) burdens and the background (indirect) burdens minus the avoided burdens, that is: $(B^E - A^E)\, x + Dw - Dy$.

Regarding economic considerations, when recovery or reuse occurs entirely in the foreground, no additional net revenues or costs accrue, since these economic flows have already been taken into account in the activity analysis format. However, when intermediate goods are recovered back to the background and thus 'exported' to the exogenous part of the model, it is necessary to account for the net revenue (or net cost) py, collected in the foreground, where p is a vector of unit prices of recovered goods. Here, p is assumed to be known and to represent average prices of recovered goods. (Alternatively, marginal prices or price sensitive functions could be used, describing the price elasticity of recovered goods. The latter extension would cause the model to change from a linear to non-linear one.) Combining these changes to accommodate recovery of goods, one obtains the extended LCAA format:

$$
\begin{aligned}
&\min \quad cx + qw - py \qquad\qquad (4)\\
&\text{subject to} \quad -A^P x + w \geq 0\\
&(-A^I + B^I)x - y = 0\\
&B^F x \geq d\\
&(A^E - B^E)x - Dw + Dy \geq -g\\
&x, y, w \geq 0
\end{aligned}
$$

Further extensions to the basic model (4) are possible. For example, transportation and shipping of goods between various locations may be accounted for in all parts of the supply chain. The basic programming format still applies, treating each transportation link as a separate activity, with its own inputs and outputs (Freire *et al*., 2001). Moreover, if the time-profile of activities is important, the model may be developed into a multi-period one.

All variables then need to be dated, and the market balances in each time period need to be defined explicitly.

2.2 Environmental life cycle impact assessment

The B^E and $-A^E$ matrices constitute an inventory table, summing up the outflows and subtracting the inflows of environmental "goods" associated with the economic activities. In LCA, this is part of Inventory Analysis.

Flows of substances are recognized as environmental problems only when they pose problems to the environment and society. Thus, there is an intrinsic value-bound aspect to the definition of an environmental problem (Heijungs, 1997). To deal with this, it is necessary to establish scientific relationships between pollutants and a set of environmental impact categories, such as the greenhouse effect, acidification or ozone layer depletion. Similarly, there is a relationship between resource extraction and various depletion problems. Hence, the impact categories can be defined in terms of damage to the environment by pollutants in air, water or soil and by the depletion of available natural resources. In LCA terminology, aggregation of environmental burdens into impact categories is carried out in the Impact Assessment phase.

Using the same notation as in section 2.1, the vector of environmental burdens $E(i)$ is equal to the sum of all direct and indirect burdens minus the avoided burdens: $E(i) = (B^E - A^E)x + Dw - Dy$, where i represents individual environmental burdens. The individual burdens can be aggregated into a set of environmental impact categories according to the expression:

$$I(j) = F(j,i) \cdot E(i)$$

where $I(j)$ is a vector of environmental impact categories j and $F(j,i)$ is a matrix of relative impact coefficients (for example, the global warming impact coefficients of greenhouse gases are expressed relative to CO_2, whose coefficient is defined as unity).

The goal-oriented expression in models (3) and (4) may then be reformulated into:

$$F(j,i) \cdot [(A^E - B^E)x - Dw + Dy] \geq -g'$$

where g' is a vector of goals defined directly in terms of environmental impact categories:

$$g' = F(j,i) \cdot g$$

More advanced formulations are also possible by treating the vector of individual environmental goals g as an unknown rather than as a given parameter, as proposed in Freire *et al.* (2001). This means searching out an optimal combination of individual goals – i.e. an optimal combination of individual environmental burdens – possibly trading-off one individual burden against another while still satisfying the goals defined for the impact categories. The programming formulation (4) then becomes:

$$
\begin{aligned}
\min \quad & cx + qw - py && (5)\\
\text{subject to} \quad & -A^P x + w \geq 0 \\
& (-A^I + B^I)x - y = 0 \\
& B^F x \geq d \\
& (A^E - B^E)x - Dw + Dy + g \geq 0 \\
& F(j,i)\, g \leq g' \\
& x, y, w, g \geq 0
\end{aligned}
$$

which is a linear program with the unknowns x, y, w and g.

2.3 Dual programming formulation

The dual program corresponding to (5) is

$$
\begin{aligned}
\max \quad & u^F d - vg' && (\\
\text{subject to} \quad & -u^P A^P + u^I(-A^I + B^I) + u^F B^F + u^E(-A^E + B^E) \leq c \\
& u^P - u^E D \leq q \\
& -u^I + u^E D \leq -p \\
& u^E - vF(j,i) \leq 0, \\
& u, v \geq 0.
\end{aligned}
$$

where u^P, u^I, u^F, u^E and v are the dual variables of model (5). They may be interpreted as the shadow prices of primary, intermediate, final and environmental goods and of the environmental impact goals, respectively. The dual model (6) aims to maximize the shadow value of the final goods calculated net of the shadow costs of environmental impact goals. The constraints have the following interpretations:

- The first constraint states that the imputed cost of operating an activity at unit level cannot exceed its direct cash cost. The imputed shadow cost consists of four components: the shadow cost of the participating primary, intermediate and final goods and environmental shadow costs: $+ u^E(-A^E + B^E)$. By complementary slackness, it follows that if the activity is operated, the constraint will actually be an equality.

- The second constraint can be written as $u^P \leq q + u^E D$. It states that the shadow cost of a primary good cannot exceed its market price plus the environmental shadow cost. If a quantity of the primary good is bought, this will be an equality.
- The third constraint can be written as $p + u^E D \leq u^I$. It states that the shadow value of an intermediate good exported to the background cannot fall short of its market price plus its imputed environmental shadow costs. If a quantity is exported to the background, equality holds.
- The last constraint reading $u^E - vF(j,i) \leq 0$ states that the shadow cost of an individual environmental burden (u^E) cannot exceed the imputed cost of the environmental goal in the corresponding impact category, $vF(j,i)$. If a particular individual environmental burden occurs, then equality will hold. Thus, if the shadow cost of a corresponding environmental impact goal (v) has a positive value then the shadow cost of the environmental burden (u^E) is also positive.

According to the dual theorem of linear programming, the optimal value of the primal program equals that of the dual program:

$$cx + qw - py = u^F d - vg' \tag{7}$$

This means that total net cash costs (obtained by adding together the cash costs of operating activities and of purchasing primary materials, but deducting cash revenues obtained from selling recovered goods to the background) plus the shadow costs of environmental impact goals equal the shadow value of the final goods.

The dual variables determined by program (6) can be interpreted as the shadow costs of the primary, intermediate and final goods. It is assumed that all markets will be in equilibrium and the shadow costs of the goods represent competitive market prices, i.e. the price the economic system should be willing to pay to obtain one unit more of the commodities they measure. Concerning the shadow costs of environmental impact goals (v), these can be interpreted as environmental fees or excise taxes. This means that rather than aiming for environmental goals directly, the alternative would be to introduce environmental fees designed to implement the environmental goals g'.

The mathematical models presented in this section assume linearity, which is acceptable when the life cycle of the product being modeled involves only marginal changes in the activity levels of the operations being considered. However, if specific aspects of the life cycle are acknowledged as nonlinear, then non-linearity has to be introduced and defined mathematically in an appropriate manner.

3. APPLICATION OF LCAA: THE CASE STUDY OF PLASTIC PANELS

Due to various drivers, including "take-back" legislation, many companies recognize the need to reduce resource consumption and improve waste management. An increasing number of manufacturers accept the responsibility of taking back products for reprocessing and for the post-use management of the constituent materials. This overall concept is known as "Extended Producer Responsibility" and in the European Union this forms part of integrated product policy. It includes the possible reuse of products and recycling of materials. As a consequence, the distribution and reverse logistics of such products has to be redesigned to include the new recovery and end-of-life options. Important changes will need to occur in society to comply with new policy targets. In many cases, a paradigm shift has to take place in the way products are being designed, used and disposed of.

At the same time, the dynamics of the consumer product markets puts pressure on manufacturers to shorten the commercial life cycle of products (the cycle from market introduction to obsolescence). This is particularly true for electronic products. The rapid introduction of shorter commercial life cycles for these products may mean that the market for remanufacturing and reuse of electronic goods at the end of useful life may disappear entirely. On the other hand, targets defined by environmental legislation can act as driving forces in the opposite direction.

In Europe, the EU Directive on Waste from Electrical and Electronic Equipment (WEEE) (European Commission, 2000) is one such driver that recognizes EEE as a priority waste stream. The WEEE draft proposal directive includes the following targets:

- a minimum rate of separate collection of WEEE from private households, amounting to 4 kg per inhabitant per year by 1 January 2006;
- a total rate of reuse and recycling (of components, materials and substances) that reaches between 70 and 90% of the weight of all separately collected WEEE by 2006.

The achievement of these targets can only be expected if the costs of recovery and recycling are minimized. However, at the same time it is also important that these targets are reached at a minimum environmental impact, ensuring that on a life cycle basis reverse logistics and recycling do not result in a net increase of impacts. In some cases, this may require trading-off economic and environmental costs and finding a compromise solution. The following sections discuss how these considerations can be evaluated and assessed using the LCAA methodology. The case study of plastic panels mounted on electrical and electronic products is presented to examine the environmental and economic implications of different end-of-life options for this type of plastic product.

3.1 End-of-life options for plastic panels

The purpose of this case study is to optimize environmental and economic burdens of the end-of-life options for plastic panels used in electrical and electronic products. The particular plastic component to be investigated is the rear panel used on photocopying machines. Plastics used in the production of panels are engineering grades of Polycarbonate (PC) and Acrylonitrile-Butadiene-Styrene (ABS). The panels are mainly used for aesthetical purposes, giving the photocopier a final shape. Similar panels can be found on a number of other office equipment, such as computers, keyboards, telephones and fax machines. Although robust, plastic panels deteriorate during usage. Current volumes of reprocessed panels are high, with over 70,000 machines being recovered annually from Xerox Corporation alone (private communication with Hugh Smith, 2000). In addition to the current practice of panel reuse by refurbishment, other possible end-of-life management options for plastic panels include:

- mechanical and chemical recycling,
- incineration (with or without energy recovery), and
- disposal to landfill.

The reuse with refurbishment option involves removal of the panels from the equipment followed by the repair process where scratches and other repairable damage are filled and sanded. The panels are then re-sprayed usually using water-based paints. There are limits, however, to the extent to which panels can be remanufactured. Technological change of the equipment, high aesthetic standards, brand-specific components, logistics complexity are all reasons why a new panel may be preferred to a refurbished panel. In addition, a refurbished panel can only be refurbished once, due to problems with satisfactory re-painting of the refurbished panels.

Mechanical recycling breaks down the plastic material mechanically to yield granulate. The granulate is sometimes called "recyclate" and can be easily mixed with virgin material. Recyclate can be further reprocessed chemically through pyrolysis to obtain hydrocarbons which could be processed further and used in a closed loop to produce resin granulate, or in open loops in other processes displacing the use of virgin raw materials. Only panels with no surface treatment can currently be mechanically recycled. This means that refurbished panels cannot be recycled and implies that the panels can only be used once if the plastic is going to be reprocessed.

Of the end-of life options available, it is not immediately obvious which is preferable, as the choice depends on a number of technical, environmental and economic factors. This case study aims to analyze these options and all relevant decision-making criteria to identify the optimum solutions, and thus asks:

- is it preferable to recycle the panels and use the recyclate to make new panels?, or
- is it better to remanufacture the panels after the first use by painting (and so eliminate the possibility of recycling the panels for future use)?

3.2 The system and the life cycle activities

The supply chain and the reverse logistics for the plastic panels are illustrated in Figure 2. The figure shows the following stages in the life cycle of panels:

- the production chain producing the virgin polymer granulate,
- the manufacture of panels,
- the use phase (with photocopiers), and
- several end-of-life alternatives: reuse, mechanical and chemical recycling, incineration and landfill.

The supply chain network in Figure 2 consists of nodes, loops and direct links. The nodes signify states of the product flow. The following nodes are exhibited:

Node A: Virgin resin (a blend of PC and ABS)
Node B: Compounded polymers
Node C: New panels
Node D: Panels assembled on photocopiers ready for use
Node E: Worn panels on photocopiers after use
Node F: Photocopiers disassembled and used panels dismantled
Node G: Refurbished panels
Node H: Recycled granulate ("recyclate")
Node I: Recovered hydrocarbons
Node J: Plastic panels incineration
Node K: Landfilled panels

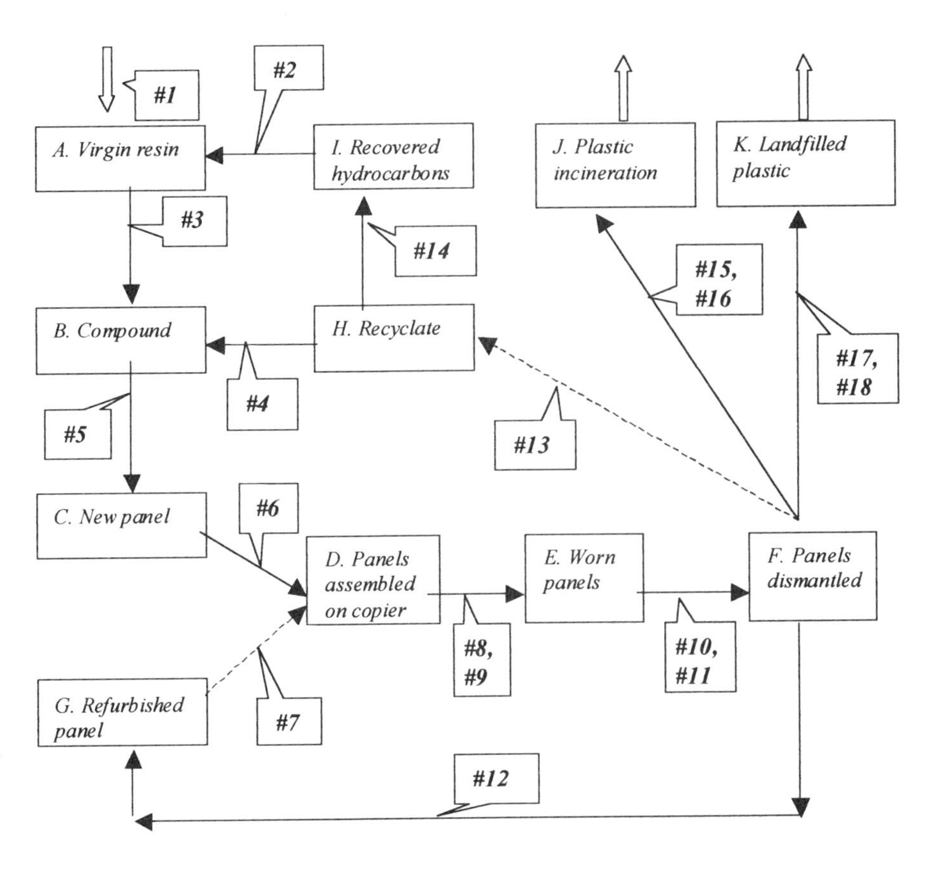

Figure 2. Flowchart illustrating the logistics of the production, distribution and recovery of photocopier plastic panels

The following loops exist: refurbishing of used panels goes from node F to node D (via node G), and the recycling of hydrocarbons and granulate goes from node F to nodes A (via I) and B (via H). These feedbacks are indicated by dotted lines in the diagram.

The following eighteen activities are considered (see Figure 2):

Activity x1 describes the production of virgin resin, which is a blend of polycarbonate (PC) and acrylonitrile-butadiene-styrene (ABS). Data representative of current industrial operations in Europe were used, available through the APME eco-profiles reports for PC and ABS (Boustead, 1997a-b).

Activity x2 describes the virtual operation of producing PC/ABS resin using liquid hydrocarbons (C4 to approx. C20), which are obtained from feedstock recycled polymers (output of activity *x14*). The environmental burdens associated with this operation are calculated using the avoided burdens approach, by subtracting the burdens of obtaining the recyclate from the burdens of the production of virgin PC/ABS.

Activity x3 represents the production of the compounded PC/ABS polymer - produced either from virgin materials (activity *x1*) or from recovered hydrocarbons (activity *x2*).

Activity x4 represents the re-compounding of PC/ABS recyclate. The output from this activity must possess the same performance specification as virgin material. This is achieved by adding flame-retardants to give the re-compound the characteristics demanded by the panel manufacturers. The inputs of this activity are recycled (output of activity *x13*) and virgin granulates (output of activities *x1* or *x2*). Currently no more than 25% of recycled granulate can be used in the production of new panels. Thus a minimum of 75% of virgin polymer has to be used. The main operations of activity *x4* include melting, blending, extruding and slicing strands into regular sized pellets. A significant amount of electricity is used for this.

Activity x5 describes the manufacture of panels. The PC/ABS polymer (0.954kg per panel) is molded into the panel shape and a small polyurethane (PU) foam gasket (0.0125 kg per panel) is attached to the panel. The production of panels takes place on a batch basis. Storage of finished panels is required prior to transportation to the photocopier assembly plant. Taking into account production losses, 0.973 kilograms of polymer are used on average per panel.

Activities x6 and x7 describe the assembly of the panel (a new panel or a refurbished one, respectively) onto the photocopier machine. This is a manual operation with minor energy inputs due to building heating and lighting.

Activities x8 and x9 represent the use phase of the photocopier, with a new panel or a refurbished one, respectively. The end-of-life options are different for each type of panel. The demand for the family of photocopiers that use this specific rear panel is currently approximately 19,000 photocopiers per year (based on 1999 data, private communication with Hugh Smith, 2000). The number of photocopiers delivered to the market is the sum of the photocopiers with new panels plus those with refurbished panels. About 90% of the used panels are refurbished and used again (see activities *x10* and *x11* below). Consequently, the number of new and refurbished panels per year is 10,000 and 9,000, respectively.

Activities x10 and x11 represent the disassembly of the panels (a new panel or a refurbished one, respectively) from the photocopier machines. The dismantling of panels is only one component step of the total dismantling of all useful parts that takes place. These are manual operations with minor energy inputs. They include visual inspection of all the panels to see if they are in a proper condition to be reused. A maximum of about 90% of all panels can be reused.

Activity x12 represents the refurbishment of used panels, which comprises cleaning, repairing, painting, and the replacement of the foam gaskets (only required by 10% of the panels). The cleaning process employs several different cleaning fluids that are sprayed onto the panel surface sequentially. The panel is then dried and repaired using a filler material, which is applied manually to the surface of the panel to cover scratches and other surface damage. The major direct environmental burdens of this activity are the emission of trace amounts of volatile organic compounds (VOCs) produced as a consequence of paint and thinner use.

Activity x13 represents the production of recycled granulate (recyclate). The input material is identified, separated, de-contaminated and cleaned. Next, the granulation of the polymer material takes place, which has an efficiency of 85-90%. The final output from this activity – the recyclate – is re-compounded according to the specific characteristics demanded by the injection molder. The overall mass loss in this activity is 27.7 %, i.e. 0.723 kilograms of recyclate are produced per kilogram of input plastic material. Recyclate can also be used in the production of other products (open loop, with possible cascade use). This would then have to be represented in Figure 2 as a separate flow in addition to those shown. This is not a part of this case study analysis.

Activity x14 describes the feedstock (chemical) recycling of plastics. The terms chemical recycling and feedstock recycling of plastics describe a family of recycling processes that convert solid plastic materials, through the use of heat, into chemical intermediates. These intermediates, usually liquids or gases, are suitable for use as feedstocks for the production of new petrochemicals and plastics.

Activities x15 and x16 describe the incineration of plastics (new panels or refurbished ones, respectively). It is assumed that no energy is recovered. Furthermore, incinerated plastic generates slag, which is disposed of in landfill.

Activities x17 and x18 represent landfilling of plastics (new panels or refurbished ones, respectively). Currently, the entire waste stream from activity *x11* (used refurbished panels) is disposed in landfills.

Optimization of the flows defined above and shown in Figure 2 requires choices to be made between a series of alternative activities. For example, both raw materials (hydrocarbons from petroleum or natural gas) and recycled feedstock (obtained from the pyrolysis of recyclate) can be used to produce virgin resin. The PC/ABS compound can both be produced by adding additives (mainly flame retardants) to virgin granulate (activity *x3*) or to a mixture of virgin material and recyclate (activity *x4*). A panel to be assembled onto a photocopier machine can be a new or a refurbished panel. Used (new) panels can be refurbished, recycled, incinerated or sent to landfill. Used refurbished panels can only be disposed of as waste in landfills or incinerated. These options and choices are analyzed on environmental and economic criteria in a number of scenarios presented below.

3.3 Scenarios and LCAA model formulation

In addition to the industrial and market characteristics, the LCAA approach permits the analyst to evaluate the effects of alternative com+binations of environmental and technology policy. Scenario analysis is used to study both current and future reuse and recycling practices. The scenarios to be solved by the model are outlined below. Scenario *A* is a base scenario, used as a reference case to which the other scenarios will be compared. Scenario *B* describes current practice and is used to validate the methodology. The other three scenarios study a mixture of current practice with future reuse and recycling practices, such as banning the disposal of panels in landfill or just considering no reuse of panels at all.

- *Scenario A* (Reference case: 100% landfilling). This scenario disregards the possibility of reusing and recycling the panels entirely, so that there are no feedback loops in the material and product flow at all. In addition, it bans incineration, so that there is only one outflow from the system and that is to a landfill. Mathematically, this scenario is obtained by setting $x_{12} = x_{13} = x_{14} = x_{15} = x_{16} = 0$. Demand for new panels is $x_8 = 19{,}000$.
- *Scenario B* (Current practice). 90% of the used (new) panels are refurbished and used again; the remaining 10% together with the used (painted) panels are disposed of in a landfill. No mechanical recycling is carried out. This scenario is similar to the reference case, but permits the refurbishment of used panels. Mathematically, $x_{13} = x_{14} = x_{15} = x_{16} = 0$. Demand for new panels is $x_8 = 10{,}000$; demand for refurbished panels is $x_9 = 9{,}000$.
- *Scenario C* (Banning plastic panels landfill; no restrictions on reuse and recycling). This scenario sets $x_{17} = x_{18} = 0$. Demand for new panels is $x_8 = 10{,}000$, demand for refurbished panels is $x_9 = 9{,}000$.

- *Scenario D* (No refurbishing of used panels; mechanical recycling of granulate; both incineration and landfill permitted). This scenario sets $x_{12} = 0$. Demand for new panels is $x_8 =$ 19,000.
- *Scenario E* (Cost minimization, all technologies are available and no restrictions on reuse and recycling). Demand for new panels is $x_8 = 10{,}000$; demand for refurbished panels is $x_9 = 9{,}000$.

As mentioned, the current waste management policies for electrical and electronic equipment do not set explicit goals (*g'*) in terms of environmental impact categories. Instead, as described in the scenarios *A* - *E*, we formulated environmental targets in terms of recovery objectives. The LCAA model for this case study is then solved in two steps. The *first step* is a conventional activity analysis model with additional constraints characterizing each scenario, as defined by:

$$\begin{aligned} \min \quad & cx + qw - py \\ \text{subject to} \quad & -A^P x + w \geq 0 \\ & (-A^I + B^I)x = 0 \\ & B^F x \geq d \\ & Hx = 0, \\ & x, w, y \geq 0 \end{aligned} \tag{8}$$

where the constraint $Hx = 0$ defines a particular scenario. For instance for Scenario *A*, the set of constraints $Hx = 0$ is defined by: $x_{12} = x_{13} = x_{14} = x_{15} = x_{16} = 0$. Thus, the model will be optimized on an economic objective (costs) while taking into account environmental constraints.

In the *second step*, the vector of environmental impacts is calculated as:

$$I(j) = F(j,i) \{(B^E - A^E)\, x^* + Dw^* - Dy^*\} \tag{9}$$

where the asterisk represents the optimal solution of (8).

The calculations presented here are intended to illustrate the application of the LCAA methodology to the alternative post-use recovery options for plastic panels. Other aspects have been simplified, including many technical and environmental considerations. The spatial dimensions of production and distribution are not accounted for, and no transportation of intermediate goods is considered. Thus, the results reported here are mainly illustrative to demonstrate the application of the LCAA methodology.

3.4 Optimum solutions

The results for the five scenarios defined above are given in Table 1, which lists the optimal levels of operation for all activities (comprising the vector x^* in (9)). The product flows are as follows:

- In scenario *A*, 18,482 kilograms of virgin resin are made into 19,000 panels. The panels are assembled, used and eventually dismantled and sent to landfill.
- In scenario *B*, 9,728 kilograms of virgin resin is made into 10,000 panels. Together with 9,000 refurbished panels, they are assembled into 19,000 photocopiers. After use, the 19,000 panels are dismantled and are routed as follows: 9,000 used new panels are refurbished, the remaining 1,000 used new panels are sent to landfill, and all 9,000 used refurbished panels are also sent to the landfill.
- In scenario *C*, 6,836 kilograms of PC/ABS virgin compound (made exclusively with virgin resin) and 2,892 kilograms of re-compound (made from $0.75 \times 2{,}892 = 2{,}169$ kg of virgin resin and $0.25 \times 2892 = 723$ kg of recyclate) are made into 10,000 panels. As mentioned earlier, a maximum of 25% of recyclate can currently be used in the production of re-compound. At the optimum, manufacturers choose to maximize the use of recyclate, which is produced using all available worn panels that can be recycled (i.e. the used non-refurbished panels). Note also that no chemical recycling is included. The reason for this is that, unless the recyclate production exceeds the needs of the re-compounding activity, extra costs will be incurred and produce a comparatively lower value product (hydrocarbons) than the re-compounded polymer. In addition, 9,000 used panels are refurbished. After use, the 19,000 panels are dismantled and are routed as follows: 9,000 new used panels are refurbished, 1,000 new used panels are processed into recyclate (yielding 723 kg of recyclate), and all 9,000 used refurbished panels are incinerated.

Table 1. Optimal levels of operation of activities, scenarios *A* - *E*. (Units: x_1, x_2, x_3, x_4, x_{13} and x_{14} in kilograms, remaining activities in number of panels)

Activity	Scenario *A*	Scenario *B*	Scenario *C*	Scenario *D*	Scenario *E*
x_1	18,483	9,728	9,005	13,862	9,005
x_2					
x_3	18,483	9,728	6,836		6,836
x_4			2,892	18,483	2,892
x_5	19,000	10,000	10,000	19,000	10,000

Activity	Scenario *A*	Scenario *B*	Scenario *C*	Scenario *D*	Scenario *E*
x_6	19,000	10,000	10,000	19,000	10,000
x_7		9,000	9,000		9,000
x_8	19,000	10,000	10,000	19,000	10,000
x_9		9,000	9,000		9,000
x_{10}	19,000	10,000	1,000	19,000	10,000
x_{11}		9,000	9,000		9,000
x_{12}		9,000	9,000		9,000
x_{13}			1,000	6,391	1,000
x_{14}					
x_{15}					
x_{16}			9,000		
x_{17}	19,000	1,000		12,609	
x_{18}		9,000			9,000

- In scenario *D*, 18,483 kilograms of the re-compound material are made into 19,000 panels. The origin of the re-compound is as follows: 75% is made from virgin resin (13,862 kg) and the remaining 25% is recyclate (4,621 kg). Again, at the optimum, the model chooses to maximize the use of recyclate. Since under this scenario no refurbishment is permitted, all 19,000 panels are freshly made and all used plastic panels can be mechanically recycled. However, after use in the photocopiers, only 6,391 panels are processed into recyclate (yielding 4,621 kg of recyclate) and the remaining 12,609 panels are sent to landfill. This quantity of recyclate corresponds to the maximum possible use of recyclate (25%) in the production of re-compound, and the remaining panels are thus sent to the least-costly end-of-life process - landfill. If landfill disposal and incineration were banned or restricted, chemical recycling would start to be operated or new markets for recyclate would be found.
- The outcome of scenario *E* turns out to be the same as that for scenario *C*, with the single modification that those panels destined for disposal (9,000 refurbished and used panels) are not incinerated but rather sent to landfill.

The corresponding optimal use of primary goods, such as material and energy from the background (the vector w^*) is shown in Table 2. A total of 15 different commodities were initially considered. To preserve confidentiality, data for some commodities have been aggregated into the following groups:

- PU foam gasket (PU foam, glue and activator),

- cleaning materials (cleaning fluids and rinse aid), and
- refurbishing materials (sand paper, filler, paint and thinner),

leading to a list of nine elements. The main resource requirements are the raw materials needed to manufacture the plastic panels: PC and ABS. Energy inputs are in the form of diesel, natural gas and electricity.

There are considerable differences in the use of resources under the various scenarios. Refurbishing and recycling generates substantial savings of PC and ABS (the use of these two polymers is down by a half) but

Table 2. Optimal use of primary goods (material and energy) from the background

Resource	Unit	Scenario *A*	Scenario *B*	Scenario *C*	Scenario *D*	Scenario *E*
PC	kg	7,393	3,891	3,602	5,545	3,602
ABS	kg	11,090	5,837	5,403	8,317	5,403
Flame ret.	kg	555	292	214	55	214
PU foam gasket	kg	276	158	158	276	158
Cleaning materials	liter		193	193		193
Refurbish. materials	kg		862	862		862
Diesel	MJ therm	1.73E+04	1.63E+04	1.52E+04	1.66E+04	1.62E+04
Nat. Gas	MJ therm	3.80E+03	3.98E+04	3.98E+04	3.80E+03	3.98E+04
Electricity	MJ electr	4.71E+05	2.97E+05	2.97E+05	4.74E+05	2.97E+05

requires inputs of cleaning fluids, filler, sandpaper, rinse aid, paint and thinner. Both refurbishing and recycling also require large inputs of natural gas.

The environmental impacts associated with different options calculated by (9) are shown in Table 3 (a selected list only). Starting with Scenario *A* (the reference case with all used panels sent to landfill), the total quantity of plastics disposed of in landfills under this alternative amounts to 20,400 kilograms.

Compared to the reference case *A*, the total weight of plastics destined for landfill in Scenario *B* has been reduced by almost a half. There are substantial reductions in air acidification and in eutrophication of water. The other impact categories also show a reduction.

The scenarios *C, D* and *E* all represent various combinations of relaxation of technical and other constraints imposed on the possible reuse and recycling and on the disposal of the end product. From the point of view of the environmental impacts, it is interesting to take a look at scenario *E* where all these constraints have been removed and all technologies (with no capacity limits) are available. The manufacturers are thus at liberty to choose

Table 3. Selected environmental impacts

Environmen -tal impact	**Unit**	**Scenario *A***	**Scenario *B***	**Scenario *C***	**Scenario *D***	**Scenario *E***
Disposal in landfill	kg	2.04E+04	1.07E+04	3.49E+02	1.46E+04	9.84E+03
Air acidi-fication	g equiv H^+	2.78E+04	1.66E+04	1.72E+04	2.40E+04	1.60E+04
Aquatic ecotoxicity	liter e^3m^3	1.56E+02	1.06E+02	9.68E+02	1.38E+02	1.03E+02
Eutrophica-tion	g equiv PO_4	6.04E+04	3.53E+04	4.02E+04	4.98E+04	3.36E+04
Greenhouse effect	g equiv CO_2	1.82E+08	1.10E+08	1.32E+08	1.59E+08	1.06E+08
Ozone layer depletion	g equiv CFC11	1.01E+01	7.07E+00	7.00E+00	1.00E+01	7.07E+00
Carcinogenic effects	DALYs *	4.74E-03	3.30E-03	3.83E-03	4.31E-03	3.23E-03

*DALYs = Disability-Adjusted Life Years

freely the system that generates the lowest cost overall. It was interesting to find out that this scenario would actually reduce the environmental impacts in every single impact category presented on Table 3 as compared to current practice *B*. As already pointed out, this is also the scenario where manufacturers would opt for maximum refurbishing and recycling.

If landfilling is prohibited and plastic panels are incinerated instead (scenario *C*), the environmental situation deteriorates: there is a sharp (more than a nine-fold) increase in aquatic eco-toxicity, and there are increases in the carcinogenic effects and in the greenhouse effect. Note that it has been assumed that no energy is recovered from the incineration of plastics. If data for an incineration plant with energy recovery (e.g. a cogeneration plant) were included in the model, the results would have been different, since the avoided burdens associated with the energy recovery would have to be subtracted from the total burdens.

Scenario *D* (no refurbishing) also exhibits a non-satisfactory environmental performance. Every single impact category exhibits a higher value, as compared to current practice. In addition, as described below, costs are higher compared to current situation (and all the other scenarios, except scenario *A*). This is due to low recovery and reuse rates with a corresponding high quantity of panels ending up at landfill.

The shadow costs (or shadow prices) of the final goods (u^F) (see section 2.3 on dual programming) are shown in Table 4 for the five scenarios. There are two final goods: the new and refurbished panels. The corresponding shadow costs account for all the costs and revenues (upstream and downstream of the use phase) associated with the panel life cycle, as described by equation (7). In the usual manner, each such shadow costs can be interpreted as the (maximal) price that the economic system would be willing to pay to obtain one more unit of the commodity in question. To protect company-level financial information, these marginal values shown in Table 4 have been normalized using the value of a new panel in scenario *A* as the normalization factor.

Table 4. Normalized shadow prices of final goods

	Scenario *A*	Scenario *B*	Scenario *C*	Scenario *D*	Scenario *E*
New panel	100.0	100.0	95.1	98.4	95.1
Refurbished panel		64.8	69.8		69.7

The cost of using a refurbished panel is 70% (scenarios *C* and *D*) or 65% (scenario B) of the cost of a new panel. Scenarios *C* and *E* present the lowest costs for new panels, approximately 95%. Scenario *B* however presents the lowest cost for a refurbished panel.

Normalized total costs (using scenario *A* as reference) for the five scenarios are presented in Table 5. Total costs are defined by the objective function in (8) and can also be calculated by multiplying the dual values of final goods by the corresponding demand values, as described by equation (7). Normalized total costs shown on Table 5 could be calculated by multiplying the normalized dual values presented on Table 4 by the corresponding number of panels, the total being divided by the total demand (19,000 panels).

Table 5. Normalized total costs

	Scenario *A*	Scenario *B*	Scenario *C*	Scenario *D*	Scenario *E*
Total costs	100.00	83.33	83.12	98.36	83.07

Scenarios *B*, *C* and *E* have similar total cost values, basically a reduction of approximately 17%, as compared to base scenario *A*. However, there is a considerable difference between the environmental impacts of these scenarios, with scenario *E* having the lowest impacts overall. Option *A* is the least preferable in both economic and environmental terms, closely followed by scenario *D*.

Thus, the value of the LCAA approach is two-fold. First of all, it analyses and optimizes economic systems to show what can be gained or lost in both environmental and economic terms and so enables the decision-makers to make trade-offs between these two types of priorities. Secondly, in cases where conventional economic analysis cannot distinguish between different options, this type of approach can help make environmentally responsible decisions that may lead to more sustainable practices and activities.

4. CONCLUDING REMARKS

The present work has demonstrated the potential of a novel tool – Life Cycle Activity Analysis (LCAA) – for integrated economic and environmental assessment of material and product supply chains. LCAA combines the advantages of the Life Cycle Assessment (LCA) methodology, that tracks the environmental consequences of a product, process or service from "cradle" (resource origin) to "grave" (final disposal), with the advantages of using mathematical programming formats of economic Activity Analysis (AA). LCAA is an extension of these methods as it recognizes the presence of several alternative technologies at each point in the supply chain. Faced with such choices, LCAA can help to select preferred technologies for the manufacture, distribution and disposal of a product by analyzing and solving "what if?" scenarios. It will search out the lowest-cost alternatives that meet the environmental targets defined. In this manner, it can be used to design and evaluate alternative packages of environmental strategy or policy, including programs of action for recycling and reuse of products, with the aim of identifying more sustainable practices for the future. Hence, LCAA is not limited to analyzing current practice but is also a powerful tool for investigating alternative hypothetical scenarios.

The case study discussed in this paper, which has considered plastic panels mounted on various electronic equipment, shows how the LCAA methodology can be used to identify more sustainable material reuse and recycling options that are both practicable and cost-efficient. Current practice within the industry does not include recycling of panel materials, nor the use of recyclate. In addition to technical problems, managers also face the difficulty that the market for recyclate is under-developed and prices are volatile. In this work, scenarios with different end-of-life options, including closed loop recycling, have been analyzed to identify the best way forward. The potential for reducing the environmental impacts have been explored together with the optimization of economic objectives. The results show that, on the one hand, a hypothetical 100% landfill scenario results in both higher environmental impacts and costs compared to current practice. On the other hand, extreme measures, such as banning the landfill of plastics panels (or no refurbishment of panels at all) although cost effective could cause a deterioration of environmental performance compared to current practice. Indeed, the total banning of panels to landfill would not be practicable – at least until the technical constraints on recycling are removed. Reductions in environmental impacts and economic costs were achieved when all technologies were assumed to be available. The LCAA method was able to select the most appropriate route, which involved a combination of reuse and recycling, and thus a reduction in classic "disposal" options, and also set the optimum level of material flow through that route – thereby optimizing the whole system.

The results indicate that the most sustainable course of action seems to be a further increase in the capacity of recycling plants and development of markets for recycled materials (currently suffering from under-development, raw material and price fluctuation), in such a way that manufactures can opt for a variety materials management technologies without suffering from current market and technical constraints. In the particular case of plastic components, an optimized set of processes with high reuse and recovery ratios may result in both environmental and financial benefits.

It is clear therefore that this type of approach to system analysis and optimization can help industry and policy makers not only to evaluate current industry practice but also to identify new strategies. LCAA is capable of determining optimal configurations and operating levels of activities, whether they be existing or entirely new, so that both economic and environmental performance is improved. A tool able to evaluate complex problems of this kind will certainly provide a significant opportunity for the development of more sustainable material and product strategies in the future.

ACKNOWLEDGMENTS

One of the authors (FF) gratefully recognizes support from the Portuguese Science and Technology Foundation (*Fundação para a Ciência e Tecnologia*), which enabled him to visit the Centre for Environmental Strategy (CES), Department of Chemical and Process Engineering and the Polymer Research Centre at the University of Surrey, UK, in 2000 and 2001. The authors would like to thank the Engineering and Physical Sciences Research Council (EPSRC) and the Department of Trade and Industry (DTI) for their financial support for the CHAMP project. Thanks are also due to Mr. Hugh Smith of Xerox and Conservus Ltd. for his help with data and information.

REFERENCES

Azapagic, A. (1996), "Environmental systems analysis: The Application of Linear Programming to Life Cycle Assessment (LCA)" Centre for Environmental Strategy, University of Surrey, United Kingdom.

Azapagic, A. and Clift, R. (1995), "Life Cycle Assessment and Linear Programming - Environmental Optimisation of Product System", *Comp. & Chem. Eng.*, Vol. 19 (Suppl.), pp. 229-234.

Azapagic, A. and Clift R.(1998), "Linear Programming as a Tool in Life Cycle Assessment", *International Journal of Life-Cycle Assessment*, Vol. 3:6, pp. 305-316.

Azapagic, A. and Clift, R. (1999a), "Life Cycle Assessment and Multiobjective Optimisation". *J. Cleaner Prod.*, Vol. 7:2, pp. 135-143.

Azapagic, A. and Clift, R. (1999b), "Life Cycle Assessment as a Tool for Improving Process Performance: A Case Study on Boron Products", *International Journal of Life-Cycle Assessment,* Vol. 4:3, pp. 133-142.

Azapagic, A., Bell, G., Faraday, D.B. and Schulz, R. (2000), "System Optimisation and Industrial Ecology: Identifying More Sustainable Options for Potable Spirits Manufacturing", *Proc. CHISA 2000*, 27-31 August, Prague.

Berg N., Hues, G., and Dutilh, C. (1996), "Environmental Life-Cycle Assessment", in *Environmental Life-Cycle Assessment,* edited by M. Curran, McGraw-Hill, 1996.

Bloemhof-Ruwaard, J., vanBeek, P., Hordijk, L., and Van Wassenhove, L.(1995), "Interactions between Operational Research and Environmental Management", *European Journal of Operational Research,* Vol. 85:4, pp. 229-243.

Boustead, I. (1999), "Eco-Profiles of Plastics and Related Intermediates: Methodology", Association of Plastics Manufacturers in Europe (APME).

Brooke, A., Kendrick, D., Meeraus, A., and Raman, R. (1998), *GAMS: A User's Guide.* GAMS Development Corporation, Washington D.C.

Charnes, A and Cooper, W.W. (1991*), Management Models and Industrial Applications of Linear Programming.* Vols I and II, Wiley, New York, N.Y.

Clift, R. and Doig, A. (1996), "The Environmental Implications of Recovering Energy from Waste", Associazone Termotecnica Italiana 3rd conference: Energy, Environment towards the Year 2000, 1996.

Clift, R., Frischknecht, R., Huppes, G., Tillman, A., and Weidema, B. (1999), "SETAC Working groups 1993-1998," *SETAC EUROPE NEWS*, Vol. 10, pp.14-20.

Clift, R., Doig, A., and Finnveden, G. (2000), "The Application of Life Cycle Assessment to Integrated Solid Waste Management: Part I - Methodology", *Transactions of the Institute of Chemicals Engineers*, Vol. 78 part B, pp.279-289.

Daniel, S., Diakoulaki, D., and Pappis, C. (1997), "Operational Research and Environmental Planning", *European Journal of Operational Research*, Vol. 102, pp.248-263.

European Commission (2000), *Proposal for a Directive of the European Parliament and of the Council on Waste Electrical and Electronic Equipment (WEEE*), (see also http://www.europa.eu.int/ September 2000)

Freire, F., Ferrão, P., Reis, C., and Thore, S. (2000), "Life Cycle Activity Analysis Applied to the Portuguese Used Tire Market", *SAE Technical Paper* 2000-01-1507, presented at the Total Life Cycle Conference, SAE, Detroit.

Freire, F., Thore, S., and Ferrão, P. (2001), "Life Cycle Activity Analysis: Logistics and Environmental Policies for Bottled Water in Portugal", *OR-Spectrum*, Special Issue: "Operations Research and Environmental Management," Vol. 23:1, pp.159-182.

Gielen, D. (1998), "Western European Materials as Sources and Sinks of CO2: A Materials Flow Analysis Perspective", *Journal of Industrial Ecology*, Vol.2:2, pp.43-62.

Gielen, D. (1999), *Materialising Dematerialisation: Integrated Energy and Materials Systems Engineering for Greenhouse Gas Emission Mitigation*, University of Delft.

Heijungs, R. (1996), "Identification of Key Issues for Further Investigation on Improving the Reliability of Life-Cycle Assessments", *Journal of Cleaner Production*, Vol.4, pp.159-166.

Heijungs, R. (1997), *Economic Drama and the Environmental Stage: Formal Derivation of Algorithmic Tools for Environmental Analysis and Decision-support from a Unified Epistemological Principle*, Research School for the Socio-economic and Natural Sciences of the Environment, University of Leiden, The Netherlands.

ISO 14040, (1997), "Environmental management - Life cycle assessment - Principles and F ramework". ISO (International Organization for Standardisation).

ISO 14042 (1998), "Environmental management - Life cycle assessment - Life cycle impact assessment," ISO (International Organization for Standardisation).

Kandelaars, P. (1998), Materials-product Chains: Economic Models and Applications, Vrije Universiteit, Amsterdam.

Koopmans, T. (1951) "Analysis of Production as an Efficient Combination of Activities", in: T. Koopmans (ed.), *Activity Analysis of Production and Allocation*, Cowles Commission Monograph N. 13, John Wiley, New York, N.Y., pp. 33-98.

Koopmans, T., (1957), *Three Essays on the State of Economic Science*, McGraw Hill, New York N.Y.

Mellor, W., Williams, E. Clift, R. Azapagic, A. and Stevens, G., "A Mathematical Model and Decision-support Framework for Material Recovery, Recycling and Cascaded use", *Chem. Eng. Sci.*, in press.

Opschoor, J. (1994), "Chain Management in Environmental Policy: Analytical and Evaluative Concepts," in Opschoor, H. and Turner, K. *Economic Incentives and Environmental Policies: Principles and Practice*, Kluwer Academic Publishers, Boston, Mass.

Thore, S. (1991), *Economic Logistics: The Optimization of Spatial and Sectoral Resource, Production, and Distribution Systems*, Quorum Books, Westport, Conn.

Thore S. and Freire F. (1999), "Activity Analysis with Environmental Variables and Recycling: An Example from the Portuguese Bottled Water Industry", printed in this volume.

Chapter 11

Ranking Commercial Products with Harmful Environmental Effects

Editorial Introduction

Abstract: A brief introduction to goal programming is given. "Goals" are soft constraints that may be violated, but at a cost. The penalty costs may be cardinal numbers or just ordinal rankings. The methods of data envelopment analysis with goal constraints are explained.

Key words: Goal programming, goal deviations, eco-taxes, Non-Archimedean numbers, goal focusing

1. ENVIRONMENTAL GOALS

Sometimes an economic policy-maker might feel concerned that purely commercial solutions to the ranking of R&D projects, such as those that we have discussed in Part I of the present volume, are misleading or skewed. In some instances they may fail to account for an excessive use of scarce and depletable resources (such as scarce minerals or ground water). In other cases, new consumer goods may release poisonous or harmful substances into the environment, during the course of their production, as they are consumed, or during subsequent disposal. A common feature of these diverse circumstances is that so-called negative external economies are felt to arise from the market solution and that there is a wish by policy-makers to reduce such environmental harm. We shall assume that the intervention can be characterized by the setting of environmental goals and that such goals have been ranked in order of their relative importance.

The technique of *goal programming* to be discussed in this chapter permits an economic modeler to deal with soft constraints, such as those that the market does not explicitly take into account. Such soft constraints can be violated, but at a cost. A goal or target level is laid down for each of a number of unknown variables (like the inputs, the outputs and the environmental consequences of the various R&D projects considered). A mathematical program is formulated, designed to search for some optimal realization of these unknowns that comes as close as possible to the goals. Penalties are levied on deviations between goals and actual performance. The penalties are cash charges assessed by some controlling agency, or may just reflect an ordinal system of priorities entertained by a policy maker. The more urgent the goal, the greater the penalty assessed for violation of the corresponding constraint. In any event, the objective of the goal program is to minimize the sum of all penalties.

In the political discussion of the need to preserve the environment, two types of methods of enforcement are proposed: (I) direct regulation of industry; and (ii) taxes levied directly on the use of scarce resources by industry. As we shall see, the direct and the dual programs in goal focusing correspond in a fashion to these two approaches. The direct program includes constraints laying down the various goals. The dual program determines the corresponding taxes that, if assessed, would induce the users of resources to modify these uses as required.

2. GOAL PROGRAMMING: A BRIEF REVIEW

In order to illustrate the basic technique of goal programming, one may look at a simple numerical example. Suppose that the management of a steel mill wants to produce 100 tons of finished steel in a given week. The production process is illustrated below.

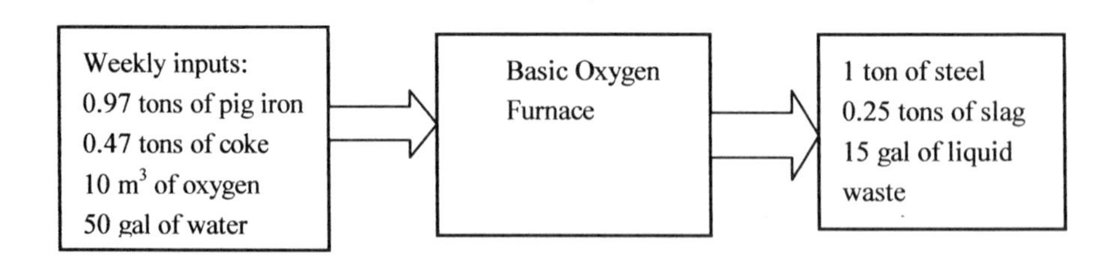

The company has ample supplies of pig iron, coke, oxygen, and water. However, the county office of pollution monitors the output of pollutants and levies charges on excess production of waste products, as listed in Table 1 below.

Table 1. Pollution targets and charges for excess pollution set by county office

Pollutant	Weekly Upper Limit	Charges for Excess
Slag	18 tons/week	4 \$/ton
Liquid waste	1200 gallons/week	15 \$/gallon
Polluted air	900 m^3	18 \$/m^3

The following notation, which will be used throughout the chapter, is helpful.

g = goal or target value of a variable
g^+ = excess performance (over-performance) relative to goal
g^- = deficit performance (under-performance) relative to goal

The actual performance of a variable is then related to the goal through the relation

$$\text{Actual performance} \quad - g^+ \ + g^- \quad = g \tag{1}$$

It must be assumed that g^+ and g^- are both nonnegative, and that $g^+ g^- = 0$, i.e. these two unknown deviations cannot both be positive at the same time. As will be seen in a moment, this latter condition will always be automatically fulfilled by the programming formulation to be written down.

Denote the environmental goals for slag, liquid waste and polluted air (listed in the table above) by g_1, g_2 and g_3, respectively. Excesses and deficits relative to the goals are denoted as explained.

Assume that the price fetched by the steel mill is \$350 per ton steel. From the gross revenues, two kinds of penalties have to be deducted: lost revenue if the quantity of steel sold falls short of the production target; and charges for excess outputs of wastes. The purpose of the linear program below is to determine a production policy that minimizes the sum of all such penalties:

$$\text{Min } 350\, g_1^- + 4\, g_2^+ + 15\, g_3^+ + 18\, g_4^+ \tag{2}$$

subject to

$$x_1 + g_1^- \geq 100$$

$$0.25\, x_1 - g_2^+ \leq 18$$

$$15\, x_1 - g_3^+ \leq 1200$$

$$10\, x_1 - g_4^+ \leq 900$$

$x_1, g_1^-, g_2^+, g_3^+, g_4^+ \quad \geq 0$

Here, x_1 is production of steel, g_1^- is the deficit in steel production, g_2^+ is the excess production of slag, g_3^+ is the excess production of liquid waste, and g_4^+ is the excess production of polluted air.

Solving program (1), one finds that the optimal steel production is $x_1 = 90$ tons. At this level of production, the steel mill falls short of total demand by $g_1^- = 10$ tons. It violates the limits on slag and liquid waste production, generating $g_2^+ = 4.5$ tons of excess slag and $g_3^+ = 150$ tons of excess liquid waste (but no pollutant air, $g_4^+ = 0$).

With these values, the optimal value of the program is $3500 + 18 + 2250 = 5768$.

2.1 Eco-taxes

To continue our discussion of the simple example of the steel mill, let us now take a look at the dual program corresponding to (2). Use the following notation:

p dual variable of the demand constraint, to be identified as the shadow price of steel;
t_1 dual variable of the environmental target on the output of slag;
t_2 dual variable of the environmental target on release of liquid waste;
t_3 dual variable of the environmental target on the release of polluted air.

With this notation, the dual program reads

$$\begin{aligned} &\text{Max } 100\,p \ -18\,t_1 - 1200\,t_2 \ -900\,t_3 \qquad (3)\\ &\text{subject to}\\ &p \ -0.25\,t_1 \ - \ 15\,t_2 \ - \ 10\,t_3 \qquad \leq 0\\ &p \qquad \leq 350\\ &t_1 \qquad \leq 4, \ \ t_2 \leq 15, \ \ t_3 \ \leq 18 \end{aligned}$$

As will now be explained, the three dual variables t_1, t_2 and t_3 can be interpreted as so-called shadow *eco-taxes* or Pigou taxes (see Pigou, 4th edition, 1952), levied on the release of one unit of slag, liquid waste and polluted air, respectively. The dual program (3) then instructs us to maximize the shadow value of all steel produced *minus all eco taxes* levied by the county office.

The first constraint of program (3) states that the steel manufacturer cannot make a profit after all eco-taxes have been paid. In fact, by complementary slackness, if production is carried out at a positive level, the shadow price will be exactly exhausted by the eco taxes.

The second constraint states that the shadow price of steel cannot exceed the market price.

The last three dual constraints state that each eco-tax cannot exceed the unit charge levied by the county office. Actually, by complementary slackness, *if the release of a harmful output violates the target set by the county office, the shadow eco-tax will be equal to the unit charge.*

Turning now to the numerical example at hand, solution gives the following dual solution: The shadow price of steel equals the market price: $p = 350$. Since the optimal releases of slag and liquid waste exceeds the targets (see the solution to the direct problem), the shadow eco-taxes on these two pollutants equal the unit penalties levied by the county office: $t_1 = 4$ and $t_2 = 15$. But the shadow eco-tax on polluted air comes out as $t_3 = 12.4$

With these values, the optimal value of the dual program equals $35000 - 72 - 18000 - 11160 = 5768$.

2.2 Non-Archimedean penalties

In the numerical example now described, cash penalties were levied on excess discharges of slag, liquid waste and polluted air. The penalties are ordinary cardinal numbers. In many applications, however, policy-makers try to induce corporations and the public to limit environmentally harmful activities without actually taking recourse to fiscal measures. Sometimes, it is helpful just to appeal to common sense and community spirits. If the management of some corporations becomes aware of the urgency of environmental factors, they may voluntarily act as if penalties were assessed for goal deviations.

One way to describe such goaling situations is to assume the presence a list of *preemptive goals* and *ordinal* penalties levied on goal deviations. In our example, one may be faced with a situation where the goals for instance are ranked by priority as follows:

- First priority: To meet the demand for steel (100 tons of steel). To reflect the high priority of this goal, we put the unit penalty for violation equal to 9,999.

- Second priority: The output of polluted air should not exceed 900 m3. Put the unit penalty for violation of this goal equal to 7,777.
- Third priority: The output of liquid waste should not exceed 1200 gallons/week. Make the unit penalty for violation of this goal equal to 5,555.
- Fourth priority: The output of slag should not exceed 22 tons/week. We set the unit penalty for violation equal to 3,333.

The unit penalties mentioned here - - the values 9,999, 7,777, 5,555 and 3,333 - - are numerical representations of so-called *non-Archimedean numbers*. They are chosen so that the differences among them are large enough to assure preemption in the goal program in the desired order. Such cardinal representations must always be verified by checking that the solution generated by them has the desired properties (i.e. that the goals are satisfied in order of their priorities, so that a goal of a higher priority always takes precedence over a goal with a lower priority, and the achievement of a higher-priority goal is never "contaminated" by the possibility of achieving a lower-priority goal).

The minimand in program (2) now reads

$$\text{Min } 9{,}999\, g_1^- + 3{,}333\, g_2^+ + 5{,}555\, g_3^+ + 7{,}777\, g_4^+ \tag{4}$$

while the constraints are the same. Solution shows that the optimal steel production is now stepped up to cover the demand: $x_1 = 100$ tons. At this level of production, however, *all* environmental limits are violated. There are discharges of $g_2^+ = 7$ tons of excess slag, of $g_3^+ = 300$ tons of excess liquid waste and of $g_4^+ = 100$ tons of polluting air.

To demonstrate the analytical power of the technique now described, let us finally switch the two first priorities. The first priority then is to conform to the limit set on the discharge of polluted air. The second priority is to meet the demand for steel. The other priorities remain as stated before. This time the minimand reads

$$\text{Min } 7{,}777\, g_1^- + 3{,}333\, g_2^+ + 5{,}555\, g_3^+ + 9{,}999\, g_4^+ \tag{5}$$

Solving again, one finds that the steel production should now be reduced to 80 tons. The two environmental goals on polluted air and on liquid waste are both satisfied. The goal with the lowest priority (on the discharge of slag) is violated, generating $g_2^+ = 2$ tons of excess slag.

For further discussion of goal programming, see the graduate textbook Thore, 1991, Chap. 7.

3. GOAL PROGRAMMING WITH ENVELOPMENT CONSTRAINTS

In order to introduce the use of goal programming in data envelopment analysis, the reader might find it helpful to review the material below, brought from Golany and Thore, 1997. Rather than seeking to determine the efficiency rating of a given observation, the aim here is the more modest one of just projecting it onto the frontier. The frontier is modified by the presence of environmental goals.

Quite generally, we are here dealing with a situation in DEA where the various decision-making units (DMUs) strive to meet target levels on some inputs or outputs and where deviations on either side are possible but may be undesired.

Each observation $j = 1,2,...n$ is characterized by a given column) vector of input variables X_j and a given (column) vector of output variables Y_j. Analyzing a given observation (X_0 , Y_0), define "best practice" input and "best practice" output in the common fashion as the linear envelopments $\Sigma X_j\lambda_j$, and $\Sigma Y_j\lambda_j$ respectively, where the λ_j are weights of all observations $j = 1,2,...n$ to be determined. Best practice inputs cannot exceed actual inputs, and best practice outputs cannot fall short of actual outputs:

$$\begin{aligned} \Sigma X_j\lambda_j &\leq X_0 \\ -\Sigma Y_j\lambda_j &\leq -Y_0 \end{aligned} \tag{6}$$

Now suppose that goals have been laid down for best practice inputs g and for best practice outputs G, in the following manner:

$$\begin{aligned} \Sigma X_j\lambda_j - g^+ + g^- &= g \\ \Sigma Y_j\lambda_j - G^+ + G^- &= G \end{aligned} \tag{7}$$

Penalities are being charged for all goal deviations. The total penalties amount to

$$M^{+} g^{+} \quad + M^{-} g^{-} \quad + N^{+} G^{+} \quad + N^{-} G^{-} \tag{8}$$

where M^{+} and M^{-} are (row) vectors of unit penalties charged for excess and deficit inputs, respectively, and N^{+} and N^{-} are the (row) vectors of unit penalties charged for excess and deficit outputs, respectively. The penalties may be cash penalties (cardinal numbers) or just ordinal rankings of these penalties (non-Archimedean numbers, see Section 2.2 above).

The goal programming DEA model now reads

$$\text{Min } M^{+} g^{+} + M^{-} g^{-} + N^{+} G^{+} + N^{-} G^{-} \tag{9}$$

subject to

$$\begin{aligned}
&\Sigma X_j \lambda_j \leq X_0 \\
&-\Sigma Y_j \lambda_j \leq - Y_0 \\
&\Sigma X_j \lambda_j - g^{+} + g^{-} = g \\
&\Sigma Y_j \lambda_j - G^{+} + G^{-} = G \\
&\lambda, g^{+}, g^{-}, G^{+}, G^{-} \geq 0
\end{aligned}$$

The model (5) is a goal programming model where the objective is dedicated to minimizing the deviation variables and where the constraints are composed of two groups. One group of constraints imposes ordinary linear constraints (read: the envelopment constraints). The other group defines the deviations. Note, however, that the envelopment constraints here only force the best practice point to have smaller than or equal inputs and larger than or equal outputs than the observation currently analyzed. They do not force the best practice point to be on the efficiency frontier. In this manner, the goal program is useful in identifying a modified best practice point for inefficient observations. Efficient observations will not be affected by the goals. But inefficient observations will be.

As an illustration, let us imagine that a company manufacturing and selling dry batteries is in the process of developing a new generation of batteries, to be used in portable radios, portable CD players etc. An entire range of new batteries is currently being tested in the R&D laboratory. The new battery type has superior characteristics compared to all competing brands in the market. Unfortunately, it also contains some highly toxic chemicals posing serious and new environmental problems.

To evaluate this situation and to rank the new battery units, we adopt the technique of goal programming with envelopment constraints. The units to be evaluated include both the new ones currently under development and a series of comparison batteries manufactured according to conventional technology. We realize right from the start that there are significant gaps between the environmental performance of the new generation of batteries currently tested and the old one. Realistically, one knows that it will be impossible to close gaps of this magnitude in the near future. The new generation seems to be locked in a severely inefficient position. There is the obvious question whether the company should go ahead with the new technology, or to shelve it entirely.

Rather than striving to achieve full efficiency, however, we now lay down some environmental goals that reflect a more moderate ambition. While these goals should still pose a challenge, they should be attainable in light of the performance of other batteries to which the units currently under investigation may reasonably be compared.

Once these more modest goals have been formulated, solution of program (5) permits the determination of a more realistic "best practice." Comparing the performance of each battery type currently under development (including its toxicity data) with its projection on the goal programming frontier, the analyst should be able to suggest possible improvements of performance.

4. GOAL FOCUSING WITH ENVELOPMENT CONSTRAINTS

The technique of *goal focusing* applies when the formulation of the goals is attached to a prior mathematical program existing in its own right (such as a conventional DEA program). It is desired to temper the objective of that program, requiring the solution values to come as close as possible to the goals. The objective function of the goal focusing program is defined as the objective of the prior (non-goaled) program adjusted by the sum of all penalties. That is, while the prior objective is still sought as long as the goals so permit one introduces the possibility of a trade-off, if not all goals can be realized exactly. The final DEA ranking may be lower, in order to avoid paying penalties.

The goal focusing version of the standard DEA program is

$$\text{Max } \theta - (M^{+} g^{+} + M^{-} g^{-} + N^{+} G^{+} + N^{-} G^{-}) \qquad (10)$$

subject to

$$\Sigma X_j\lambda_j - \theta X_0 \leq 0$$

$$-\Sigma Y_j\lambda_j \leq -Y_0$$

$$\Sigma X_j\lambda_j - g^{+} + g^{-} = g$$

$$\Sigma Y_j\lambda_j - G^{+} + G^{-} = G$$

$$\lambda, g^{+}, g^{-}, G^{+}, G^{-} \geq 0$$

where the efficiency rating θ is to be determined subject to two sets of constraints: the ordinary envelopment constraints and the definitions of the goals.

For further discussion of program (10), see Golany and Thore, *ibid.*, and the research paper immediately following.

REFERENCES

Golany, B. and Thore, S. (1997), "Restricted Best Practice Selection in DEA: An Overview with a Case Study Evaluating the Socio-Economic Performance of Nations," *Annals of Operations Research* Vol. 73, pp. 117-140.

Pigou, A.C. (1952), *The Economics of Welfare*, 4th ed., McMillan, London.

Thompson, G.L. and Thore, S. (1992), *Computational Economics: Economic Modeling with Optimization Software*, Scientific Press, South San Francisco, Calif.

Thore, S. (1991), *Economic Logistics: The Optimization of Spatial and Sectoral Resource, Production, and Distribution Systems*, Quórum Books, Westport, Conn.

Ranking the Performance of Producers in the Presence of Environmental Goals

Research paper

S. Thore and F. Freire
Instituto Superior Técnico, Lisbon

Abstract: In a study of the Portuguese bottled water industry, it was desired to rank the commercial and ecological performance of the individual bottlers of spring water. To effect the rankings, a new model type of data envelopment analysis (DEA) is proposed that includes an assessment of the performance of individual producers with respect to a list of environmental variables. The environmental concerns of society are expressed as goals, either absolute (=cardinal) goals or just preemptive priorities. Data for some 20 Portuguese table water bottlers are examined and a goal programming version of DEA is presented, ranking the performance of the bottlers with respect to recycling goals.

Key words: Environmentally harmful variables, environmental taxes, environmental benefits, step function, goal focusing, ordinal rankings of penalties, recovery targets

1. INTRODUCTION

The bottled water industry involves the production and distribution of spring water for table use. This industry presents several interesting environmental features including that of recycling. The bottles are made of glass or plastics. Recycling can take two forms: the collection of used bottles (glass or plastics) as raw material for the manufacture of new bottles, and the collection and cleaning of used bottles. Bottles that are not recycled end up in the landfills.

In the pages below, we shall discuss the mathematics of ranking the performance of bottlers and distributors of table water in the presence of environmental goals such as recycling goals. As it turns out, our study opens the door to a new *model type* within the family of DEA models. This model type distinguishes three kinds of variables: inputs, outputs and environmental variables. For each environmental variable, a goal in the sense of goal programming is formulated. That is, the goal is not a "hard" upper limit but rather a "soft" goal that may be violated, but at a cost. A piece-wise linear efficiency frontier is defined, at which the producers would make optimal use of their inputs such as spring water and packaging materials, producing and distributing the final product to the consumers, while adhering to the environmental goals as closely as possible. The producers are ranked relative to their affinity to the frontier.

How is it possible to see to it that individual producers adhere to the goals, which may not necessarily reflect their own inclinations but rather the concerns of society at large? One way of implementing the goals is for government to levy an *environmental fee or tax* (an excise tax) on any use of a harmful environmental variable that exceeds the goal.

The idea of using goal programming in environmental analysis is not new. For an early study on the subject, see Charnes, Cooper, Habbald, Karwan and Wallace, 1976 who developed a goal programming model (and a goal interval programming model) for resource allocation in a marine environmental protection program. Nor is the idea of using goal programming in DEA new, see for instance Golany and Thore, 1997 who suggested a goal programming format for ranking nations by DEA in the presence of social and educational policy constraints like target goals on the enrollment of students in secondary education. And the use of DEA in environmental analysis is certainly not new, for earlier work see e.g. Färe, Grosskopf, Lovell and Pasurka, 1989 and Färe, Grosskopf and Tyteca, 1996. But we believe that the idea of developing a goal programming version of DEA for the explicit use in environmental analysis is a novel one, first to be presented in the pages below.

Several studies of the markets for ready-to-drink beverages have been presented in the DEA literature, see e.g. A. Charnes, W.W. Cooper, B. Golany *et al.*, 1994 (carbonated beverages) and Day, Lewin,, Li and Salazar, 1994 (beer). As environmental policy has gained increased public attention, there is considerable interest in the possibilities of recycling of used glass and cans in these industries. In order to assess the performance of individual manufacturers, and of individual brands, both economic and environmental factors need to be factored into the DEA framework. The required mathematical machinery for such studies has heretofore been lacking. Hopefully our study will lay the groundwork for a new generation of studies ranking the performance of decision-makers in the presence of environmental goals.

Section 2 presents the necessary theoretical developments for the case of environmentally harmful variables. Section 3 extends the analysis to deal with environmentally beneficial variables as well. Section 4 presents a ranking of 30 Portuguese producers and distributors of mineral water and spring water. Section 5 concludes.

2. A DEA MODEL WITH GOALS ON ENVIRONMENTALLY HARMFUL VARIABLES

To begin with, let the data on $j=1,\dots,n$ decision-making units (DMUs) be organized under three headings:

- a (column) vector of input variables X_j
- a (column) vector of output variables Y_j
- a (column) vector of environmental harmful effects (or just "harms") H_j.

To simplify interpretation, we may think of the environmental harms as physical quantities of various greenhouse gases released in the atmosphere, and poisonous metals dumped into the soil. Note that the environmental harms are a kind of negative outputs - - they are undesired outputs.

The task at hand is to rate the performance of a DMU with the observations (X_0, Y_0, H_0). For this purpose, form the linear combination

$$(\Sigma X_j\lambda_j,\ \Sigma Y_j\lambda_j,\ \Sigma H_j\lambda_j). \tag{1}$$

The weights are nonnegative, $\lambda_j \geq 0,\ j=1,\dots,n$. If it so happens that

$$\begin{aligned} \Sigma Y_j\lambda_j &\geq Y_0 \\ X_0 - \Sigma X_j\lambda_j &> 0 \\ H_0 - \Sigma H_j\lambda_j &> 0 \end{aligned} \tag{2}$$

then we say that the DMU currently rated is *dominated* or *inefficient* because there exists a composite DMU that requires fewer inputs and fewer harmful effects to produce the same or greater outputs. If no such weights exist, then we say that the DMU is *un-dominated* or *efficient* and that it is located on the *efficiency frontier*.

In the common manner, it is possible to give an "input-oriented" restatement of (2), using a shrinking factor θ as follows

$$\Sigma Y_j\lambda_j \geq Y_0 \tag{3}$$
$$\theta X_0 - \Sigma X_j\lambda_j \geq 0$$
$$\theta H_0 - \Sigma H_j\lambda_j \geq 0$$
$$\lambda_j \geq 0, \text{ all } j, \text{ and } 0 \leq \theta \leq 1$$

The multiplier θ shrinks both inputs and environmental variables in an equi-proportional manner. Now we say that the DMU currently rated is inefficient if there exists a composite DMU (1) such that conditions (3) are satisfied with $\theta < 1$. If $\theta = 1$ for all such composite DMUs, the DMU at hand is rated *efficient*. (To simplify matters, we are here and in the subsequent text neglecting the possibility of non-efficient frontier points.)

The CCR model now reads (see the Appendix, program A8)

$$\text{Min } \theta \tag{4}$$
subject to
$$\Sigma Y_j\lambda_j \geq Y_0$$
$$\theta X_0 - \Sigma X_j\lambda_j \geq 0$$
$$\theta H_0 - \Sigma H_j\lambda_j \geq 0$$
$$\lambda_j \geq 0, \text{ all } j$$

Denote the dual variables that correspond to the constraints in (4) by μ, ν and ω, respectively. They are identified as virtual multipliers, or "scores". The virtual multipliers are the scores to be used to weight the individual factors:

- The (row) vector of scores μ are the weights of the output variables;
- The (row) vector of scores ν are the weights of the input variables;
- The (row) vector of scores ω are the weights of the environmental harmful variables.

The dual program to (4) then reads

$$\text{Max } \mu Y_0 \tag{5}$$
subject to
$$\mu Y_j - \nu X_j - \omega H_j \leq 0, \quad j=1,\dots,n$$
$$\nu X_0 + \omega H_0 = 1,$$
$$\mu, \nu, \omega \geq 0$$

In the common manner, program (5) may alternatively be written on the fractional programming form

$$\text{Max} \quad \mu Y_0 / (\nu X_0 + \omega H_0) \tag{6}$$

subject to

$$\mu Y_j / (\nu X_j + \omega H_j) \leq 1, \quad j=1,\ldots,n$$

$$\mu, \nu, \omega \geq 0$$

In simple words, program (6) instructs us to maximize the ratio between the virtual value of the output of a given DMU and the sum of the virtual values of its inputs and harmful environmental effects. The maximization is to be carried out subject to the condition that the same ratio, calculated using the same virtual weights, stay less than 1 for all other DMUs as well. (For earlier formulations of program (6), see e.g. Tyteca, 1996, program (29).)

Goal focusing formulation. Thus prepared, let us now impose a (column) vector of upper goals on the environmentally harmful effects

$$\Sigma H_j \lambda_j \leq H^{UP} \tag{7}$$

There is one goal for each harmful effect. The goals may be the same for all DMUs or they may be individual goals for each DMU. In any case, the goals entered in (7) are the goals that have been laid down for the DMU currently rated.

The goals are "soft" goals and they may be violated, at a cost. Now consider the goal programming DEA model (more precisely, it is a so-called "goal focusing model" first introduced by Charnes, Cooper, Schinnar and Terleckyj, 1979; for a general discussion see Thore, 1991, Chapter 7)

$$\text{Min } \theta + N s_H \tag{8}$$

subject to

$$\Sigma Y_j \lambda_j \geq Y_0$$

$$\theta X_0 - \Sigma X_j \lambda_j \geq 0$$

$$\theta H_0 - \Sigma H_j \lambda_j \geq 0$$

$$- \Sigma H_j \lambda_j + s_H \geq - H^{UP}$$

$$\lambda_j \geq 0, \quad s_H \geq 0$$

The goal formulation $- \Sigma H_j \lambda_j + s_H \geq - H^{UP}$ permits the constraint (7) to be violated, but a violation by the amount s_H entails a unit penalty cost of N. The total penalty cost is Ns_H. The vector N is a vector of cardinal numbers, such as environmental fees assessed by the government. Alternatively, the elements of N are ordinal numbers reflecting the priorities of the goals, so-called non-Archimedean transcendentals.

For precursors to the formulation (8), the reader is referred to Golany and Thore, 1997 who presented a goal programming version of DEA with goals on the input and output variables. Our present development takes this approach one step further, attaching the goals instead to a separate set of environmental variables.

Denote the dual variables that correspond to the constraints in (8) by μ, ν, ω and τ, respectively. The new (row) vector of scores τ are the weights of the goals. In the standard fashion of goal programming, they can be interpreted as virtual excise taxes levied on the harmful effects. See below.

The dual program to (8) reads

$$\text{Max} \quad \mu Y_0 \quad - \tau H^{UP}. \tag{9}$$

subject to

$$\mu Y_j \quad - \quad \nu X_j \quad - (\omega + \tau) H_j \quad \leq 0, \quad j = 1, \ldots, n$$

$$\nu X_0 \ + \omega H_0 \ = 1$$

$$0 \leq \ \tau \leq N, \quad \mu, \nu, \omega \geq 0$$

For the interpretation of the virtual taxes τ, note the following relations of complementary slackness (the asterisk denotes the value at the point of optimum):

$$s_H^* \quad \geq \sum H_j \lambda_j^* \ - H^{UP} \tag{10a}$$

$$\tau^* s_H^* = \tau^* \ (\sum H_j \lambda_j^* - H^{UP}) \tag{10b}$$

and also

$$\tau^* \leq N, \quad s_H^* (\tau^* - N) = 0 \tag{11a, 11b}$$

The virtual excise tax on any environmental variable cannot exceed the unit penalty N levied on the variable. If at the optimum, the upper limit (7) imposed on an environmental variable turns out to be violated (the slack variable s_H^* is positive), then the virtual excise tax equals the unity penalty. But a positive tax falling short of the unit penalty is also possible; in that case the environmental goal is exactly satisfied. Finally, the tax is zero if the goal is slack. (The interpretation of the dual variables of the goals in goal programming as excise taxes is due to Ryan, 1974. For a general discussion, see e.g. Thore, *loc.cit.*)

A geometric illustration may be helpful. The optimal tax rate can be viewed as a step function of the goal deviation, see Figure 1. The frontier release into the environment is measured along the horizontal axis and the optimal tax rate is measured along the vertical axis. As long as the frontier release into the environment stays below the goal, the tax rate is zero. If the frontier release reaches the goal, a positive tax rate is possible, but it cannot exceed the unit penalty N. If the frontier release exceeds the goal, the tax rate equals the unit penalty.

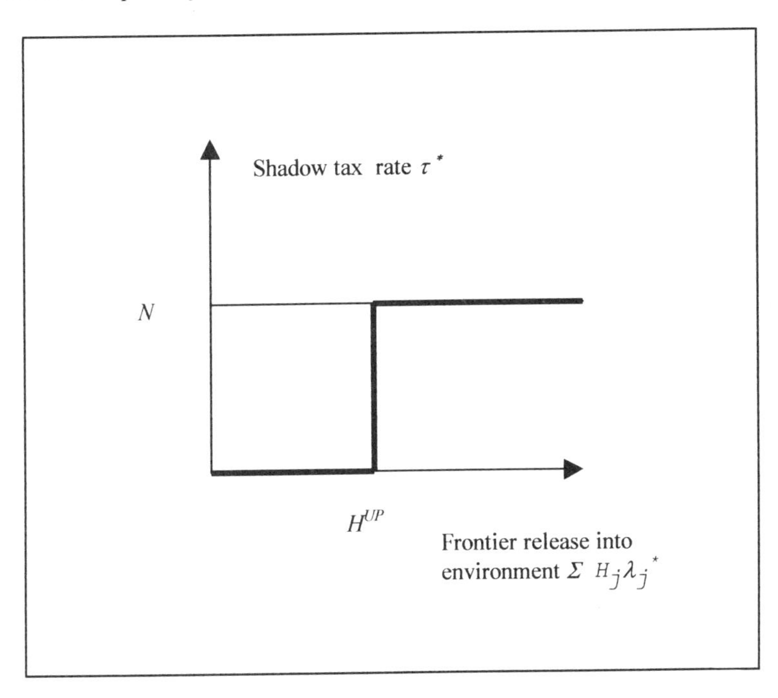

Figure 1. The shadow excise tax is a step function of the goal deviation

The magnitude of the tax rate has now been explained. Environmental harms at the frontier are only taxed if the harmful effect exceeds the goal. The amount of tax equals the appropriate tax rate times the full amount of the environmental effect.

Theorem 1 below casts further light on the nature of the tax. To derive the theorem, note that by the dual theorem of linear programming, the optimal value of the direct program (8) equals the optimal value of the dual program (9), or

$$\theta^* + Ns_H^* = \mu^* Y_0 - \tau^* H^{UP}. \tag{12}$$

Making use of (11b) and also of (10b) and collecting terms

$$\theta^* = \mu^* Y_0 - \tau^* \Sigma H_j \lambda_j^*$$

or, which is the same (the value of the denominator equals 1, see (9))

$$\theta^* = (\mu^* Y_0 - \tau^* \Sigma H_j \lambda_j^*) / (v^* X_0 + \omega^* H_0) \quad (13)$$

This result is quite attractive. In the conventional CCR model with harmful environmental effects (see program (6)), we obtained the optimal efficiency rating as given by the expression $\mu^* Y_0/(v^* X_0 + \omega^* H_0)$. In the presence of goals a similar relation now has now been established, only that the virtual value of the output this time has to be corrected by a term reflecting the virtual environmental tax levied on the DMU. This is

Theorem 1. For the DMU currently rated, the optimal efficiency rating can be written as the ratio between:

- the virtual value of all outputs, remembering to deduct the virtual excise tax levied on all environmental variables, and
- the virtual value of all inputs and all harmful environmental variables.

So, it turns out that the environmental variables blend characteristics of both inputs and negative outputs. They are to be treated as inputs in the sense that they are to be included in the denominator of the efficiency ratio, together with the regular inputs. They are to be treated as negative outputs in the sense that virtual excise taxes are levied on environmental variables and that these virtual expenses have to be deducted from the nominator of the efficiency ratio.

Theorem 2 below is a direct consequence of Theorem 1.

Theorem 2. For a DMU located at the efficiency frontier, the virtual value of all outputs equals total virtual costs, calculating these costs as the sum of the virtual value of all inputs plus the virtual value of and taxes paid on all environmentally harmful variables. But for an inefficient DMU, the virtual value of all outputs falls short of the same virtual costs.

3. ENVIRONMENTALLY BENEFICIAL EFFECTS

We now extend the analysis above to include the presence of desired environmental effects, like reuse and recycling of packaging materials (rather than their disposal in nature). Other examples include the use of bio-degradable packaging materials, non-freon propellants in aerosols, the generation of solar energy, wind and wave power etc. etc.

This time, let the data on $j=1,\ldots,n$ DMUs be organized under four headings:

- a (column) vector of input variables X_j
- a (column) vector of output variables Y_j
- a (column) vector of environmentally beneficial effects E_j
- a (column) vector of environmentally harmful effects H_j.

The task at hand is to rate the performance of a DMU with the observations (X_0, Y_0, E_0, H_0). For this purpose, form the linear combination $(\Sigma\ X_j\lambda_j,\ \Sigma\ Y_j\lambda_j,\ \Sigma\ E_j\lambda_j,\ \Sigma\ H_j\lambda_j)$. The weights are nonnegative, $\lambda_j \geq 0,\ j=1,\ldots,n$. If it so happens that

$$\begin{aligned} &\Sigma\ Y_j\lambda_j \geq Y_0 \\ &\Sigma\ E_j\lambda_j \geq E_0 \\ &X_0 - \Sigma\ X_j\lambda_j > 0 \\ &H_0 - \Sigma\ H_j\lambda_j > 0 \end{aligned} \tag{14}$$

we say that the project currently rated is *dominated* or *inefficient* because there exists a composite project that requires fewer inputs and fewer harmful effects to produce the same or greater outputs and the same or greater environmental benefits.. If no such weights exist, then we say that the project is *un-dominated* or *efficient* and that it is located on the *efficiency frontier.*

The CCR model this time reads

$$\begin{aligned} &\text{Min } \theta \\ &\text{subject to} \\ &\Sigma\ Y_j\lambda_j \geq Y_0 \\ &\Sigma\ E_j\lambda_j \geq E_0 \\ &\theta\ X_0 - \Sigma\ X_j\lambda_j \geq 0 \end{aligned} \tag{15}$$

$$\theta H_0 - \Sigma H_j \lambda_j \geq 0$$
$$\lambda_j \geq 0 \text{ all j}$$

Denote the dual variables that correspond to the constraints in (15) by μ, ρ, ν and ω, respectively. The (row) vector ρ contains the scores to be used to weight the environmental benefits. The dual program to (15) then reads

$$\text{Max } \mu Y_0 + \rho E_0 \qquad (16)$$
subject to
$$\mu Y_j + \rho E_j - \nu X_j - \omega H_j \leq 0, \quad j=1,\dots,n$$
$$\nu X_0 + \omega H_0 = 1$$
$$\mu, \nu, \omega \geq 0$$

or, on fractional programming form

$$\text{Max } (\mu Y_0 + \rho E_0) / (\nu X_0 + H_0) \qquad (17)$$
subject to
$$(\mu Y_j + \rho E_j)/(\nu X_j + \omega H_j) \leq 1, \quad j=1,\dots,n$$
$$\mu, \nu, \omega \geq 0$$

In simple words, program (17) instructs us to maximize the ratio between on the one hand the virtual values of the outputs of a given DMU and its beneficial environmental effects, and on the other, the virtual values of its inputs and harmful environmental effects. The same ratio should stay less than 1 for all other DMUs as well.

Goal focusing formulation. Retaining the upper goals (7) on the environmentally harmful effects already discussed, we now also introduce a (column) vector of *lower goals* on environmentally beneficial effects

$$\Sigma E_j \lambda_j \geq E^{LO} \qquad (18)$$

The full goal focusing model formulation is

$$\text{Min } \theta + Ms_E + Ns_H \qquad (19)$$
subject to
$$\Sigma Y_j \lambda_j \geq Y_0$$

$$
\begin{array}{ll}
\Sigma E_j\lambda_j & \geq E_0 \\
\theta X_o - \Sigma X_j\lambda_j & \geq 0 \\
\theta H_o - \Sigma H_j\lambda_j & \geq 0 \\
\Sigma E_j\lambda_j + s_E & \geq E^{LO} \\
- \Sigma H_j\lambda_j + s_H & \geq - H^{UP} \\
\lambda_j \geq 0, \text{ all j and } s_E \geq 0, & s_H \geq 0
\end{array}
$$

The goal formulation $\Sigma E_j\lambda_j + s_E \geq E^{LO}$ permits the constraint (18) to be violated, but violation by the amount s_E entails a unit penalty cost of M. The total penalty is Ms_E.

Denote the dual variables that correspond to the constraints in (19) by μ, ρ, ν, ω, σ and τ, respectively. As we shall see immediately below, the (row) vector σ can be interpreted as environmental subsidies paid by the government on benefits up to the stipulated minimum targets. The dual program to (19) then reads

$$
\text{Max } \mu Y_0 + \rho E_0 + \sigma E^{LO} - \tau H^{UP} \tag{20}
$$

subject to

$$
\begin{array}{l}
\mu Y_j + (\rho + \sigma) E_j - \nu X_j - (\omega + \tau) H_j \leq 0, \quad j=1,\ldots,n \\
\nu X_0 + \omega H_0 = 1 \\
0 \leq \sigma^* \leq M, \quad 0 \leq \tau \leq N, \\
\mu, \nu, \omega \geq 0.
\end{array}
$$

To elaborate on the interpretation of the dual variables, note the following relations of complementary slackness (the asterisk denotes the value at the point of optimum):

$$
\Sigma E_j\lambda_j^* + s_E \geq E^{LO} \tag{21a}
$$

$$
\sigma^* (\Sigma E_j\lambda_j^* + s_E^* - E^{LO}) = 0 \tag{21b}
$$

and also

$$
\sigma^* \leq M, \quad s_E^* (\sigma^* - M) = 0 \tag{22a, 22b}
$$

The subsidy cannot exceed M. If at the optimum, the minimum target (13) imposed on a beneficial environmental variable turns out to be violated (the slack variable s_E^* is positive), then the subsidy equals M. But a subsidy smaller than the unit penalty is also possible; in that case the environmental goal is exactly satisfied. Finally, the subsidy is zero if the goal is slack.

Figure 2 helps to explain the nature of the virtual subsidy. The figure plots the subsidy as a step function of the amount of frontier environmental benefits. The frontier environmental benefits are measured along the

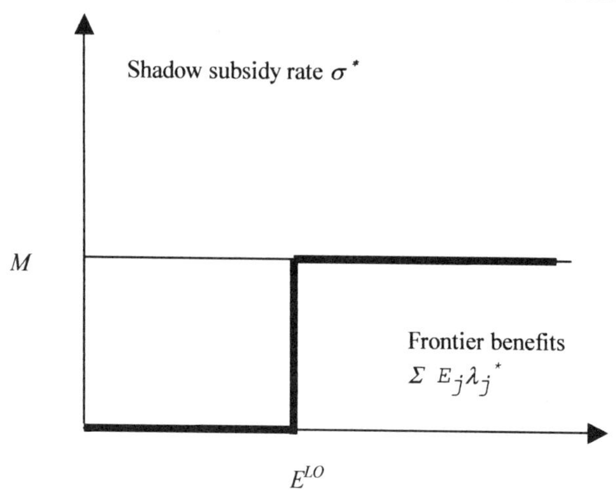

Figure 2. The shadow subsidy is a step function of the goal deviation

horizontal axis and the optimal subsidy is measured along the vertical axis. If the frontier benefits stay below the minimum goal, there is no subsidy. If the benefits reach the goal, a positive subsidy is possible, but it cannot exceed M. If the frontier benefits exceed the goal, the unit subsidy equals M.

In goal programming, "penalties" are to be paid for deviations between actual performance and the goals. As we have pointed out, the vectors of unit penalties N and M appearing in program (19) may be cash charges or just ordinal numbers represented by non-Archimedean transcendentals. A virtual excise tax obviously is a penalty. But is a subsidy a penalty? The answer is that the *absence* of a subsidy is a penalty. Consider Figure 2 again. To the left of the goal along the horizontal axis, where the benefits fall short of the stipulated minimum, the subsidy is revoked. The subsidy is zero. The purpose of the goal (focusing) mechanism in program (19) is to find a feasible solution that minimizes the total penalties paid, whether actual penalties or penalties relative to what could otherwise have been achieved.

Proceeding now as in Section 2, we derive Theorem 3 and 4 below. Again, the starting point is the dual theorem of linear programming, which in the present instance gives

$$\theta^* + Ms_E^* + Ns_H^* = \mu^* Y_0 + \rho^* E_0 + \sigma^* E^{LO} - \tau^* \Sigma H_j \lambda_j^* \quad (23)$$

which now produces

$$\theta^* = \mu^* Y_0 + \rho^* E_0 + \sigma^* \Sigma E_j \lambda_j^* - \tau^* \Sigma H_j \lambda_j^*$$

or, which is the same

$$\theta^* = (\mu^* Y_0 + \rho^* E_0 + \sigma^* \Sigma E_j \lambda_j^* - \tau^* \Sigma H_j \lambda_j^*) / (v^* X_0 + \omega^* H_0) \quad (24)$$

This proves

Theorem 3. In the case that the DMUs generate both environmental benefits and harms, the optimal efficiency rating of an DMU can be written as the ratio between:

- The virtual value of all outputs and all environmental benefits, remembering to add the subsidies paid on benefits but to deduct the virtual excise tax levied on all environmental harms;
- The virtual value of all inputs and all environmental harms.

Theorem 4. For a DMU located at the efficiency frontier, the virtual value of all revenue equals total virtual costs. The virtual revenue consists of the virtual value of the outputs, the virtual value of the environmental benefits and the subsidies paid on those benefits. The costs consist of the virtual value of all inputs and all environmental harms including the taxes paid on those harms. But for an inefficient DMU, the virtual value of the revenues falls short of the virtual costs.

4. ENVIRONMENTAL HARMS AND BENEFITS IN THE BOTTLED WATER INDUSTRY

The bottled water industry in Portugal fills, bottles, and distributes two types of table water: spring water and mineral water. Mineral water is spring water containing various mineral salts, especially the carbonates, chlorides, phosphates, silicates, sulfides, and sulfates. Various gases may also be present, e.g., carbon dioxide. Ordinary well or spring water, in contrast, contains far fewer substances, mostly dissolved sulfates.

Some brands are spring water, others mineral water. No brand covers both sections of the market. There were 16 mineral water brands in 1997, selling 389 million liters of mineral water. The largest brands were Luso,

Fastio, Vitalis and Carvalhelhos. Furthermore, there were 12 spring water brands; together they sold 210 million liters that same year. The four largest spring water brands were Caramulo, São Silvestre, Cruzeiro and Serra de Estrela. The combined production of all kinds of table water in Portugal thus comes to 600 million liters a year. With a total population of 10.5 million people, this amounts to an annual consumption of more than 50 liters of table water per capita, a quite astonishing figure. It has to be remembered, though, that large quantities of bottled water are sold to tourists in Portugal who during the summer months outnumber the domestic population.

We collected the following statistical information for each brand:

- Input X: Total production in hundreds of thousands of liters.
- Output Y: Revenue in hundreds of millions of Escudos.
- Environmental benefits $E1$: Weight of returnable glass bottles used in table water industry, in hundreds of thousands of kilos.
- Environmental benefits $E2$: Weight of non-returnable glass bottles used in table water industry and recycled back to the plants, in hundreds of thousands of kilos.
- Environmental harms H: Weight of other non-returnable packages used in table water industry (PET or PVC plastic containers, paper packs), in hundreds of thousands of kilos.

Our principal source of information was the Instituto Geológico e Mineiro (see the reference list). It lists the annual production in liters of each brand broken down by types of packaging. In order to convert these data to weights of packaging, we used the following approximate coefficients:

Weights of various packaging materials containing 1 liter of table water

Returnable glass bottles: 857 grams
Non-returnable glass bottles: 563 grams
PVC bottles: 31.9 grams
PET bottles: 39.6 grams
Cans: 60 grams.

These figures are national averages and actually vary quite considerably from one brand to another. Brands sell in many different packaging sizes, ranging from 1/3 liter bottles to 10 liter plastic containers. Hotels and restaurants sell large quantities of small bottles; the market for residential homes emphasizes large plastic containers.

In order to calculate the environmental benefits, we assumed the following national average collection factors in 1997:

Recovery rates of various packaging materials (calculated as a fraction of the packaging weight recovered)

Returnable glass bottles: 85 %
Non-returnable glass bottles: 40 %

Plastic bottles and cans: 0 %.

The returnable glass bottles are heavier than the non-returnable ones (see above) and they are typically manufactured with glass of darker tint. Upon collection, they are cleaned and refilled. Non-returnable bottles are collected in characteristic large dome-shaped green metal containers placed at roadsides all over the country. The class is crushed and used as raw material for the manufacture of new glass bottles. The collection of plastic bottles and of cans is still only on the planning stage. The weight of non-returnable glass bottles holding 1 liter of table water and eventually recycled back to the plants is then obtained as 20% × 0.1 = 0.02 kilos.

Table 1. Data for 28 Portuguese table water brands, 1997. Volume in hundred of thousands of liters, revenue in hundreds of thousands of escudos, environmental data in hundreds of thousands of kilograms of packaging

Brand	Volume	Revenue	Benefit E1	Benefit E2	Harm H
M1	144899.55	6215.26	4875.91	33.73	6110.76
M2	57229.63	3308.95	728.83	871.77	3325.48
M3	33653.64	1396.80	754.79	15.47	1445.34
M4	32056.92	1580.74	7151.16	297.86	2376.02
M5	28212.98	3649.25	12658.45	2440.21	5894.16
M6	22482.32	311.98			890.30
M7	18025.38	533.19			651.08
M8	12193.51	310.78			388.97
M9	10504.13	847.99	5705.90	601.56	1909.26
M10	8405.97	1141.63	1172.56	6.88	433.07
M11	6536.29	1159.13	2621.08	643.36	1476.36
M12	6415.77	170.86			204.66
M13	3645.10	375.28	1530.86	347.61	791.57
M14	3563.02	519.88		802.39	1203.59
M15	1173.52	103.53	226.80	176.90	308.41
M16	189.43	16.55	106.60	9.70	33.37
S1	47846.31	1823.95			1894.71
S2	37307.54	805.20			1477.38
S3	30327.64	1074.47	197.89	107.82	1346.68
S4	29713.80	930.06		56.36	1246.29
S5	23306.59	613.37			743.48
S6	15492.81	544.60	123.32		628.57
S7	13756.78	438.93			438.84
S8	10285.63	308.41			328.11
S9	1254.38	164.09	591.61	99.59	253.79
S10	922.88	19.41			36.55
S11	219.34	11.55		13.55	26.63
S12	65.27	3.32			2.08

Refer now to Table 1. It lists the given data for 1997: the input, output and environmental variables of each brand. The mineral water brands are denoted M1- M16, the spring water brands S1-S12. Note that not all brands generate environmental benefits. The mineral water brands M6, M7 and M8, for instance, sell all their water in plastic bottles. They are not recovered, and no environmental benefit ensues.

4.1 DEA with environmental benefits and harms

We first ranked the brands with respect to their commercial and environmental performance without laying down any environmental goals at all. The solution to the environmental DEA model program (15) is listed in Table 2 below.

Six brands are CCR-efficient. For these brands, the frontier environmental performance ("best practice") coincides with the actual observations. For instance, brand M5 generates 12658.45 thousand kilograms of recycled glass bottles available for cleaning and renewed use, and 2440.21 thousand kilograms of crushed glass recovered from non-returnable glass bottles, and both these figures coincide with the calculated CCR frontier values.

Table 2. DEA calculations for 1997 in the absence of goals. Environmental data in hundreds of thousands of kilograms of packaging

Brand	CCR efficiency rating θ^*	Frontier benefit E1	Frontier benefit E2	Frontier harm H
M1	0.39	6383.69	37.45	2357.72
M2	0.70	2829.52	871.77	2327.79
M3	0.37	1429.94	15.47	538.75
M4	0.96	7151.16	602.04	2270.83
M5	1.00	12658.45	2440.21	5894.16
M6	0.13	320.43	1.88	118.35
M7	0.31	547.64	3.21	202.26
M8	0.30	319.20	1.87	117.89
M9	1.00	5705.90	601.56	1909.26
M10	1.00	1172.56	6.88	433.07
M11	1.00	2621.08	643.36	1476.36
M12	0.32	175.49	1.03	64.82
M13	1.00	1530.86	347.61	791.57
M14	1.00		802.39	1203.59
M15	0.99	226.80	176.90	305.37
M16	1.00	106.60	9.70	33.37

Brand	CCR efficiency rating θ^*	Frontier benefit E1	Frontier benefit E2	Frontier harm H
S1	0.37	1873.37	10.99	691.90
S2	0.21	827.02	4.85	305.45
S3	0.40	1035.88	107.82	535.20
S4	0.33	921.36	56.36	416.72
S5	0.31	629.99	3.70	232.68
S6	0.33	559.36	3.28	206.59
S7	0.38	450.82	2.65	166.51
S8	0.36	316.77	1.86	117.00
S9	1.00	591.61	99.59	253.79
S10	0.20	19.93	0.12	7.36
S11	0.80	2.85	13.55	21.36
S12	0.61	3.41	0.02	1.26

The remaining brands are sub-efficient. One brand, M15, is very close to the frontier having the efficiency rating of 0.99 but several of the others receive surprisingly low ratings. Brand M6 scores only a meager 0.13. Low efficiency scores reflect either too low revenues per liter of production, or poor environmental performance, or both. In the case of M6, the revenue per liter of production was only 311.98 hundred of millions of escudos / 22482.32 hundred of thousands of liters = 13.88 escudos per liter, which is the lowest figure in the industry.

4.2 Goal focusing model with ordinal priorities

Thus prepared, we now turn to the goal focusing formulation. For the year 2001, we assumed the following goals:

Target recovery rates of various packaging materials (calculated as a fraction of the packaging weight recovered)

Returnable glass bottles: 100 %
Non-returnable glass bottles: 40 %
Plastic bottles and cans: 25 %.

The resulting target figures in kilograms are exhibited in Table 3. Goals are formulated only for those environmental benefits and harms that are actually generated by a given brand. For instance, brands M6-M8 fill all their water on plastic bottles. Upper limits are then placed on the amount of plastic refuse sent to the landfills (harm *H*), rather than placing lower limits on the recycling of glass bottles (benefits *E1* and *E2*). Also note that the lower limits placed on the recycling of non-returnable bottles are identical to the actual amount of such bottles recovered in 1997.

Table 3. Environmental goals

Brand	Goal benefit E1	Goal benefit E2	Goal harm H
M1	5736.37	33.73	3950.38
M2	857.45	871.77	2724.56
M3	887.98	15.47	989.91
M4	8413.13	297.86	947.23
M5	14892.30	2440.21	3660.31
M6			667.73
M7			488.31
M8			291.73
M9	6712.82	601.56	902.33
M10	1379.49	6.88	172.19
M11	3083.62	643.36	1001.63
M12			153.50
M13	1801.01	347.61	521.42
M14		802.39	1203.59
M15	266.82	176.90	267.63
M16	125.41	9.70	14.56
S1			1421.04
S2			1108.03
S3	232.81	107.82	1024.25
S4		56.36	955.85
S5			557.61
S6	145.08		455.11
S7			329.13
S8			246.08
S9	696.01	99.59	149.39
S10			27.41
S11		13.55	25.06
S12			1.56

It is instructive to compare the earlier solution figures listed in Table 2 with the goals in Table 3. Unfortunately, some of the best-run brands in the CCR model (those with the highest efficiency ratings) incur considerable violations of the goals. For instance, brand M5 processes 12 658.45 thousand kilograms of returnable glass bottles; the goal is 14892.30 thousand kilograms. The only well-run brand (having an efficiency rating equal or close to unity) that satisfies all the goals is brand M14. It is efficient and it satisfies all goals exactly. We shall have more to say about this brand in a moment.

Next, we now impose the environmental goal priorities mentioned below:
Highest priority: environmental goal *E1*,
2nd *priority:* environmental goal *E2*,
*Lowest prio*rity: goal on harm *H*.

If a brand cannot satisfy all goals, at least it should try to meet the goal placed on returnable glass bottles. The goal on recovered and crushed non-returnable bottles comes next. The goal on packaging sent to the landfills has the lowest priority.

Environmental policy is a matter of great public concern in Portugal, as in all Western countries. In the political discussion, recycling is often mentioned as a national priority. But it is difficult to translate voluminous political discussions into a simple order of priority, as we need to do here. So, our list of priorities should be seen as just an example, intended to illustrate the procedures involved in DEA goal focusing.

To implement the priorities listed, the following vectors of penalties *M* and *N* appear in the DEA goal focusing formulation, program (19):

Penalty for deviation from the environmental goals *E1*: *M1*
Penalty for deviation from the environmental goals *E2*: *M2*
Penalty for deviation from the goals on harms *H*: *N*.

The elements of these vectors are understood to be non-Archimedean transcendentals. The desired ranking of priorities is established by assuming $M1 > M2 > N$. What this means is that no positive multiple *k* of any *N* can give $kN \geq M2$, and so on (see pp. 316-317 in Charnes and Cooper, 1961). Numerically, one may provisionally use large penalties such as $M1 = 99{,}999$, $M2 = 66{,}666$ and $N = 33{,}333$, provided one checks afterward to see whether the numerical solutions that these numbers generate have the desired properties. The goals must be satisfied in order of their priorities, so that a goal of a higher priority always takes precedence over a goal with a lower priority, and the achievement of a higher-priority goal must never be "contaminated" by the possibility of achieving a lower-priority goal.

4.3 Optimal solution and discussion

The solution to the environmental DEA goal focusing model, program (19), is presented in Table 4. The first column headed "Objective function" records the optimal value of the program. For nine brands,

M4, M5, M9, M10, M11, M13, M15, M16, S9 (25)

the objective function takes on a large positive value (greater than *E+05*). These are the brands for which deviations between the goals and the actual performance cannot be brought down to zero. The result: large positive penalties. Furthermore, for those nine goal-violating brands, the efficiency rating comes out as a number greater than 1.

Ordering the brands (25) from the smallest penalty to the largest one, one obtains the order of ranking

Table 4. Optimal solution to DEA goal focusing model. All environmental figures in hundreds of thousands of kilograms of packaging

Brand	Objective function	Efficiency rating θ^*	Benefit B1	Benefit B2	Harm H	Fill deviation
M1	3.9E-01	0.39	6383.69	37.45	2357.72	
M2	7.0E-01	0.70	2829.52	871.77	2327.79	
M3	3.7E-01	0.37	1429.94	15.47	538.75	
M4	5.7E+07	1.12	8413.13	737.32	2652.37	1705.14
M5	8.8E+07	1.11	14892.30	2440.21	6288.36	2628.05
M6	1.3E-01	0.13	320.43	1.88	118.35	
M7	3.1E-01	0.31	547.64	3.21	202.26	
M8	3.0E-01	0.30	319.20	1.87	117.89	
M9	4.0E+07	1.14	6712.82	611.09	2101.25	1198.92
M10	1.1E+07	1.14	1379.49	29.06	495.63	323.44
M11	1.8E+07	1.13	3083.62	643.36	1547.37	545.74
M12	3.2E-01	0.32	175.49	1.03	64.82	
M13	1.1E+07	1.10	1801.01	347.61	839.24	317.83
M14	1.0E-00	1.00		802.39	1203.59	
M15	1.5E+06	1.01	266.82	176.90	312.44	44.81
M16	8.2E+05	1.18	125.41	11.42	39.26	24.70
S1	3.7E-01	0.37	1873.37	10.99	691.90	
S2	2.1E-01	0.21	827.02	4.85	305.45	
S3	4.0E-01	0.40	1035.88	107.82	535.20	
S4	3.3E-01	0.33	921.36	56.36	416.72	
S5	3.1E-01	0.31	629.99	3.70	232.68	
S6	3.3E-01	0.33	559.36	3.28	206.59	
S7	3.8E-01	0.38	450.82	2.65	166.51	
S8	3.6E-01	0.36	316.77	1.86	117.00	
S9	4.1E+06	1.11	696.01	99.59	272.21	122.83
S10	2.0E-01	0.20	19.93	0.12	7.36	
S11	8.0E-01	0.80	2.85	13.55	21.36	
S12	6.1E-01	0.61	3.41	0.02	1.26	

M16, M15, S9, M10, M11, M13, M9, M4, M5 (26)

The next three columns in Table 4 exhibit the solutions to the environmental variables. Again, it is helpful to look at the results for the nine goal-violating brands first. Now, we obtain more information about the nature of the violations of the goals. Which goals are violated? Looking first at the environmental variable *E1*, we see that all nine brands meet their goal listed in Table 3 exactly. Their performance in terms of the environmental variable *E2* also meets the goals, or exceeds it. (Such environmental performance above the goals occurs for brands M4, M9, M10, and M16.) In other words, the two goal variables with highest priorities are always met. But the variable *H* creates problems. This is where the goal violations occur. They all fall short of the goals, and the goal deviations are listed in the last column in Table 4.This is as it should be, since the *H* goals were postulated to rank with the lowest priority.

But for all other brands, it is indeed possible to satisfy all the environmental goals, and the objective function simply equals the optimal θ^* that is, the efficiency rating itself. The goal constraints make it possible to bring the objective function down to 1, or less than 1. The efficiency ratings then actually coincide with the ordinary CCR ratings already calculated (Table 2). This should not surprise us: when no goal constraints bind, the goal focusing formulation (19) actually boils down to (is identical to) the conventional CCR version, program (15).

Only one brand obtains the efficiency rating $\theta^* = 1$: brand M14. The remarkable performance of brand M14 is now clear. As already noted, it is the only brand obtaining a top-efficiency rating in the standard CCR model that meets its environmental goals. Its rating in the goal programming model is also unity - - the only brand to achieve this result.

Eighteen brands score efficiency ratings less than 1. They satisfy the environmental goals but they are sub-efficient, performing less well than M14. Ordering them from the highest rank to the lowest, one obtains the order

S11, M2, S12, S3, M1, S7, M3, S1, S8, S4, S6,
M12, M7, S5, M8, S2, S10, M6 (27)

So, which is the final ranking of the brands? This is a difficult question to answer because we have rated the brands according to two criteria of different dimensions: the goal-violating brands were ordered according to the magnitude of the total environmental penalties; and the goal-satisfying brands were ordered according to their conventional CCR ratings. Which one of these two dimensions is the more important one, compliance with the environmental goals or CCR efficiency? The model itself has no answer. In the last analysis, it is up to the makers of environmental policy themselves to answer this question and to determine to what extent environmental priorities should override commercial efficiency.

REFERENCES

Charnes, A. and W.W. Cooper, W.W. (1961), *Management Models and Industrial Applications of Linear Programming.*, 2 vols, Wiley, New York.

Charnes, A., Cooper, W.W., Golany, B., Learner, D.B., Phillips, F.Y. and Rousseau, J. (1994), "A Multi-period Analysis of Market Segments and Brand Efficiency in the Competitive Carbonated Beverage Industry." In Charnes, A., Cooper, W.W., Lewin, A.Y. and Seiford, L.M., editors, *Data Envelopment Analysis: Theory, Methodology, and Application*, Kluwer Academic Publishers, Boston 1994, pp. 145- 166.

Charnes, A., Cooper, W.W., Habbald, J., Karwan, K.R. and Wallace, W.A. (1976), "A Goal Interval Programming Model for Resource Allocation in a Marine Environmental Protection Program," *Journal of Environmental Economics and |Management*, Vol. 3, pp. 347 – 362.

Charnes, A., Cooper, W.W., Schinnar, A.P. and Terleckyj, N.E. (1979), "A Goal Focusing Approach to Analysis of Trade-Offs among Household Production Outputs," *American Statistical Association 1979 Proceedings of the Social Statistics Section*, pp. 194-199.

Day, D., Lewin, A.Y., Li, H. and Salazar, R. (1994), "Strategic Leaders in the US Brewing Industry: A Longitudinal Analysis of Outliers." In Charnes, A., Cooper, W.W., Lewin, A.Y. and Seiford, L.M., editors, *Data Envelopment Analysis: Theory, Methodology, and Application*, Kluwer Academic Publishers, Boston 1994, pp. 211-234.

Färe, R., Grosskopf, S., Lovell, C.A.K. and Pasurka, C. (1989), "Multilateral Productivity Comparisons when Some Outputs are Undesirable: A Non-parametric Approach," *Review of Economics and Statistics*, Vol. 71, pp. 90 – 98.

Färe, R., Grosskopf, S. and Tyteca, D. (1996), "An Activity Analysis Model of the Environmental Performance of Firms – Application to Fossil-Fuel-Fired Electric Utilities," *Ecological Economics*, Vol. 18, pp. 161-175.

Golany, B. and Thore, S. (1997), "Restricted Best Practice Selection in DEA: An Overview With a Case Study Evaluating the Socio-Economic Performance of Nations," *Annals of Operations Research*, Vol. 73, pp. 117 – 140.

Instituto Geológico e Mineiro, Lisbon, home page on the Internet: www.igm.pt

Ryan, M. J. (1974), "A Goal Programming Approach to Land Use Economics, Planning and Regulation," Ph.D. thesis, University of Texas at Austin, Texas.

Thore, S., *Economic Logistics: The Optimization of Spatial and Sectoral Resource, Production and Distribution Systems* (1991), Quorum Books, Westport, Connecticut.

Tyteca, D. (1996), "On the Measurement of the Environmental Performance of Firms - A Literature Review and a Productive Efficiency Perspective," *Journal of Environmental Management*, Vol. 46, pp.281-308.

The Mathematics of Data Envelopment Analysis

Appendix

Abstract: The central concepts of DEA are explained, including the original CCR and BCC models, the ratio model, the treatment of slacks, and economies of scale. The Appendix concludes with a listing of some simple GAMS programs for numerical calculation.

Key words: CCR model of DEA, BCC model of DEA, output-oriented models, the ratio model of DEA, returns to scale, GAMS software

1. INTRODUCTION

Economists have devoted much effort to the development of a positive theory of rational behavior for economic decision-making units, such as individuals, households, firms, banks, schools, government bureaucracies, etc. Such theories begin with the premise that, given a problem to be solved, a decision-maker first collects all available information about every possible solution, performs all the calculations needed to evaluate and compares different alternatives. He then chooses a course of action that maximizes profit, or utility, or some other objective. This technique is embodied in the assumption of the existence of a rational economic person, so-called "economic man" which is a customary assumption in economics.

Conventional economics has therefore had difficulty in explaining sub-optimal behavior by decision-makers who for one reason or another, do not arrive at the rational solution that economists prescribe. Frontier analysis is a recent development in economics, which explicitly recognizes that some decision-makers arrive at poorer solutions than other. The purpose of frontier analysis is to distinguish the optimal (efficient) decision-making units, which are said to be located at the frontier, from the sub-optimal (inefficient) ones that are located away from the frontier. Since there may be several optimal decision-makers located on the frontier, the multiple answers provided by frontier analysis indicate that an optimizing unit may exist in several forms corresponding to different ways of organizing and managing it. However, decision-makers that are not on the frontier do not make as efficient use of their inputs as some linear combination of other firms, indicating that their performance might be improved by changing some of their production or management procedures.

Data envelopment analysis (DEA) is a linear programming technique for determining how decision-makers perform in relation to the frontier. As we shall see, decision-making units on the frontier itself are assigned an "efficiency rating" of 100 percent, while units falling behind the frontier are assigned a rating of less than 100 percent. The frontier is "spanned" by the efficient units. Geometrically, the frontier is arrived at as the envelope to the set of data points represented by the inputs and outputs of each decision-making unit.

To effect the envelopment calculations, the observations of each decision-making unit have to be divided into two classes: outputs or performance indicators, and inputs or indicators of effort. DEA ranks the decision-makers in terms of their ability to convert inputs into outputs. That is, the efficiency rating is a measure of the relative performance of a unit - - relative to its use of inputs, not of its absolute output performance. It is this relative measure that we call "efficiency."

The concept of efficiency as developed and calculated in this manner rests on well-known concepts in microeconomic theory, including the notion of a feasible production set. Each feasible production point is written as a weighted average of the given observations. That is, the production possibility set and the efficiency frontier are constructed empirically from the observed inputs and outputs.

The efficiency rankings provide a ranking of all inefficient units. (There is no ranking of the efficient units because they all receive the rating of 100 percent. They are all "best.") Thus, DEA in effect is a tool for ranking the performance of units whose performance is measured by many outputs and inputs. It is easy, of course, to rank units who are characterized by a single output and a single input (just calculate the output-input ratio of each unit and use it as the ranking criterion). But the mathematical problem of ranking units that are characterized by many outputs and inputs is a difficult one. It is solved by DEA.

An efficiency score less than 100 percent signals non-optimal and non-equilibrium behavior. The performance of the decision-maker is then *non-Paretoan* in the sense that, given the outputs, it should be possible to reduce the use of each input employed in the production process. (Or, conversely, given the inputs, it should be possible to increase all outputs obtained.) DEA provides detailed information about these possibilities by calculating the projection of each observation upon the frontier. The projection point is called "best practice." Comparing the actual performance of the unit with best practice, the analyst can give detailed information about how the performance of the unit may be improved. That is, data envelopment analysis can be used as a managerial tool to monitor the performance of the units, and to provide managerial advice.

Here are some characterizations of DEA that distinguish it from other methods of data analysis.

- DEA is empirically based and involves no *a priori* theory. That is, it is a non-parametric technique that makes no assumption of a possible theoretical relationship.
- DEA fits a piecewise linear frontier. The envelope consists of "corner points" (representing the efficient observations) and the adjoining linear "facets."
- DEA is a "one-sided" estimation method in that all observations are located on or on one side of the envelope.

By contrast, a conventional data analysis method like linear regression is parametric (it postulates the existence of a linear relationship, the slope coefficients of which are parameters to be estimated), it is globally linear, and it is two-sided.

In the applications in the present volume, the "decision-making unit" is everywhere identified as an R&D project. Sometimes the projects are academic research projects; sometimes they are commercial product development projects. Sometimes they are startup companies. DEA then delivers a ranking of the priority or attractiveness of all projects currently considered.

DEA requires only weak assumptions about the nature of the underlying production structures to be estimated. There is no need to cling to the neoclassical origins of standard production or investment theory. There is no assumption that projects are ranked by net present value or by some other conventional procedure. DEA assumes neither a given and known project technology, nor that new technology is being installed in some optimal fashion. Instead, the DEA estimates reflect the behavior of real-world projects as project leaders and managers struggle, sometimes more and sometimes less successfully, with the process of developing and bringing on line new technology and new products.

2. THE CCR AND BCC MODELS

We now briefly outline the mathematics of DEA. Rather than presenting the mathematical programming models right away, we shall first spend some time explaining the conceptual background and the motivation of the programming mathematics.

Let there be $j=1,...,n$ R&D projects . For each project j , a suitable set of inputs X_{ij} , $i=1,..., m$ and outputs Y_{rj} , $r=1,...,s$ are observed. Note in particular that the concepts of inputs and outputs are not limited to tangibles such as resources used or manufactured products obtained, but extend to intangibles as well, such as measures of the quality or technological characteristics (such as the memory size of computer hardware).

In order to rate the performance of a particular project, DEA forms a weighted average of all the observations. The average represents a "composite" project. The weights are to be determined so that the composite project is located on the frontier. It will represent "best practice." The actual project at hand is then compared with its "best practice."

Denote the weights to be attached to project j by λ_j. They are to be determined so that the weighted sums

$$\Sigma_j \quad Y_{rj} \lambda_j \ , r=1,...,s, \tag{A1}$$

represent "best practice outputs" and so that

$$\Sigma_j \quad X_{ij} \lambda_j \ , \ i=1,...,m \tag{A2}$$

represent "best practice inputs." The weights are nonnegative, $\lambda_j \geq 0,\ j = 1,2,...,n$. Denote the particular project currently rated by the index "0" (it is one of the indices $j = 1,2,...,n$). If it so happens that

$$\Sigma_j \ Y_{rj} \lambda_j \quad \geq Y_{r0},\ r=1,...,s \tag{A3}$$

$$X_{i0} \ - \ \Sigma_j \ X_{ij} \lambda_j \ > 0,\ i=1,...,m \tag{A4}$$

then we say that the project currently rated is *dominated* or *inefficient* because there exists a composite project (best practice) that requires fewer inputs to produce the same or greater outputs. If no such weights exist, then we say that the project is *un-dominated* or *efficient* and that it is located on the efficiency frontier.

It is possible to give an "input-oriented" restatement of (A3-4), using a scalar "shrinking factor" θ, as follows

$$\Sigma_j \; Y_{rj} \lambda_j \qquad \geq Y_{r0}, \; r=1,...,s \tag{A5}$$

$$\theta X_{i0} - \Sigma \, X_{ij} \lambda_j \;\; \geq 0, \qquad i=1,...,m \tag{A6}$$

$$\lambda_j \geq 0, \text{ all } j, \text{ and } \; 0 \leq \theta \leq 1 \tag{A7}$$

Notice that θ is a multiplier that shrinks the inputs from X_{i0}, $i=1,...,m$ to θX_{i0}, $i=1,...,m$ in an equi-proportional manner. Now we say that the project currently rated is *inefficient* if there exists a composite project (best practice) such that conditions (A5-7) are satisfied with $\theta < 1$. If $\theta = 1$ for all such composite projects then the project at hand is rated *efficient*.

We state first the basic CCR model (see Charnes, Cooper, Rhodes 1978):

$$\text{Min } \theta \tag{A8}$$

subject to

$$\Sigma_j \; Y_{rj} \lambda_j \qquad \geq Y_{r0}, \; r=1,...,s$$

$$\theta X_{i0} - \Sigma \, X_{ij} \lambda_j \;\; \geq 0, \qquad i=1,...,m$$

$$\lambda_j \geq 0, \text{ all } j$$

Program (A8) is the input-oriented version of DEA. It looks for a maximal possible contraction of all inputs, while still delivering the same outputs. The contraction factor is θ so that the expression θX_{i0} represents the contracted inputs of the project currently rated.

In simple words, program (A8) determines the efficiency rating θ as the maximal possible rate of equi-proportional contraction of all inputs, while seeing to it that best practice outputs do not fall short of observed outputs and that best practice inputs do not exceed the contracted inputs. In other words, the efficiency rating has an immediate geometrical interpretation, as a factor shrinking the use of inputs. For instance, an efficiency rating of 0.75 means that the use of all inputs can be reduced by one quarter (some inputs may allow even further reduction) while still delivering the same outputs (or more).

The condition $\theta \leq 1$ is not included in the constraint set of (A8) because it will be fulfilled automatically. To see this, note that $\theta = 1$, $\lambda_j = 1$ for $j = 0$ and $\lambda_j = 0$ for $j \neq 0$ is always a feasible solution (i.e. it satisfies all of the constraints). Thus it is always possible to drive θ down to 1.

If the optimal solution to (A8) gives $\theta^* = 1$ then the project currently rated is efficient (the asterisk denotes the solution optimal value). If $\theta^* < 1$ then it is inefficient.

Note that the convexity constraint

$$\Sigma_j \lambda_j = 1 \tag{A9}$$

can be appended to model (A8). This will make the model correspond to the BCC formulation of DEA instead (see Banker, Charnes and Cooper 1984) rather than the CCR.

Fig. A1 illustrates the case of one single input and one single output. There are six projects, *A,B,C,D,E* and *F*. The CCR model satisfies the following “ray property”: if *(X,Y)* is a feasible project, then *(kX, kY)* is also a feasible project, where *k* is a nonnegative scalar. The ray OBM is the CCR frontier. Project *B* is CCR -efficient. All other projects are CCR inefficient. Best CCR practice for *F* is the projection *F''* on *OBM.*

For the BBC model, only convex combinations of the given projects are feasible projects. The piecewise linear frontier *ABCD* is the BCC frontier and the four projects *A,B,C*,and *D* are BCC-efficient. But a project like *F* is inefficient and best BCC practice for *F* is the projection *F'* on *AB*. *F'* can be obtained as a convex combination of the corner projects *C* and *D*.

Since the BCC program is obtained by adjoining the one additional constraint (the convexity constraint A9) to the CCR program, it follows that the optimal value of the BCC program cannot exceed that of the CCR program:

$$\theta^*_{CCR} \geq \theta^*_{BCC} \tag{A10}$$

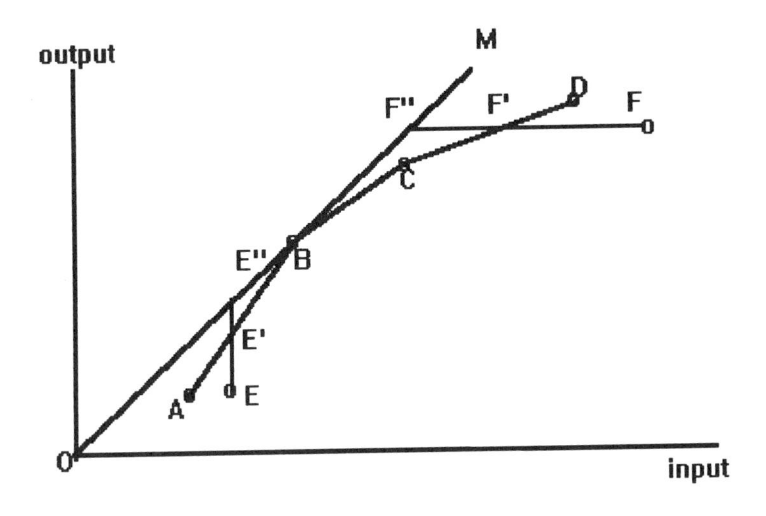

Figure A1. CCR and BCC efficiency illustrated

The two values are identical and equal to unity along the common frontier (point B in Figure 1). But for all other points along the BCC frontier, and at all points below the BCC frontier one has $\theta^*_{CCR} > \theta^*_{BCC}$.

The BCC efficiency rating is sometimes called "technical efficiency." Banker, Charnes and Cooper themselves suggested splitting the overall CCR efficiency into two factors, technical efficiency and "scale efficiency", in the following manner:

$$\theta^*_{CCR} = \theta^*_{BCC} \times (\theta^*_{CCR} / \theta^*_{BCC}) \tag{A11}$$

The scale efficiency is the ratio between θ^*_{CCR} and θ^*_{BCC}. It is unity along the common frontier of the CCR frontier and the BCC frontier, but is less than 1 everywhere else. It is a measure of the distance of a given point to the common frontier, where constant returns to scale hold.

2.1 Output-oriented models

Returning to (A3-4), efficiency and inefficiency may alternatively be stated using an "output"-oriented formulation instead. Let ϕ be a scalar expansion factor and write

$$\Sigma_j \; Y_{rj} \lambda_j \geq \phi Y_{r0}, \quad r=1,\dots,s \tag{A12}$$

$$X_{i0} - \Sigma_j \; X_{ij} \lambda_j \geq 0, \quad i=1,\dots,m \tag{A13}$$

$\lambda_j \geq 0$, all j, and $\phi \geq 1$ (A14)

This new condition makes use of a multiplier ϕ that expands the outputs from Y_{r0}, $r=1,\ldots,s$ to ϕY_{r0}, $r=1,\ldots,s$ in an equi-proportional manner. This time, we say that the project currently rated is inefficient if there exists a composite project (output-oriented best practice) such that (A12-14) are satisfied with $\phi > 1$. If $\phi = 1$ for all such composite projects then the project is efficient.

The corresponding output-oriented programming formulation of the CCR model is

Max ϕ (A15)
subject to

$$\sum_j Y_{rj} \lambda_j \geq \phi Y_{r0}, \quad r=1,\ldots,s$$

$$X_{i0} - \sum_j X_{ij} \lambda_j \geq 0, \quad i=1,\ldots,m$$

$$\lambda_j \geq 0, \text{ all } j$$

In an output orientation, the focus shifts from input resource minimization to output maximization. Returning to Figure 1, the CCR-inefficient point E is now projected onto E''.

A few results comparing an input-oriented model with an output-oriented one are listed below, without proofs:

- The envelopment surfaces (the frontier) of the two models are identical. (But the projections of a given project upon the frontier are different.)
- A project is characterized as efficient with an output orientation if and only if it is characterized as efficient with an input orientation applied to the same data.
- The optimal value of the input orientation equals the inverted value of the optimal value of the output orientation, $\theta^* = 1/\phi^*$.

The output-oriented BCC model is obtained by adjoining the convexity condition (A9) to program (A15).

The vast majority of applications of DEA reported in the literature involve the input-oriented formulation. In the ranking and prioritization of R&D projects, however, we often find it more natural to look for the maximal outputs that can be obtained from a given use of resources.

3. THE RATIO MODEL

The DEA formulations reviewed in Section 2 are all so-called "envelopment formulations." They envelop the given observations. The unknowns are the efficiency rating of the project currently evaluated, and the weights to be assigned in forming its best practice.

A different class of formulations can be obtained from the dual side of the corresponding linear programs. This brings us to the subject of the Ratio Model, the very first DEA formulation studied in the pioneering work by Charnes, Cooper and Rhodes in 1978. The ratio model has considerable intuitive appeal. Through a clever mathematical maneuver, it can be reduced to the dual of the CCR model.

The starting point is the concept of relative efficiency as used in the engineering literature and defined as the ratio of output obtained per use of inputs. This concept is straightforward enough when there is a single output and a single input. But in the multi-dimensional case one needs first to form some kind of aggregate of the outputs, and another aggregate of the inputs. Only then can the ratio between the two be calculated.

Introducing a set of "virtual multipliers" μ_r , $r = 1,\dots,s$ of the outputs, and another set of virtual multipliers of the inputs v_i , $i = 1,\dots, m$ and using them to weigh the outputs and the inputs of the project currently rated, we are thus led to form the ratio

$$\sum_{r=1}^{s} \mu_r Y_{r0} \;/\; \sum_{i=1}^{m} v_i X_{i0} \tag{A16}$$

If only the numerical values of the multipliers were known, the ratio (A16) would serve as the desired efficiency measure. Furthermore, if the ratio (A16) were equal to 1, one would say that the project was efficient. Subefficient values would be associated with ratios less than 1.

CCR found an ingenious programming approach that enables one to determine the multipliers endogenously, rather than assuming that they be known and given. The idea is to vary the multipliers so as to maximize the obtained efficiency measure (A16), while seeing to it that the efficiency measures of all projects (including the project currently to be rated) remain meaningful, i.e., that they be less than or equal to 1. Mathematically,

$$\sum_{r=1}^{s} \mu_r Y_{rj} \;/\; \sum_{i=1}^{m} v_i X_{ij} \quad \leq 1, \quad j = 1,2,\dots,n \tag{A17}$$

The resulting program is then

$$\max \left(\sum_{r=1}^{s} \mu_r Y_{r0} \Big/ \sum_{i=1}^{m} v_i X_{i0} \right) \tag{A18}$$

subject to

$$\sum_{r=1}^{s} \mu_r Y_{rj} \Big/ \sum_{i=1}^{m} v_i X_{ij} \leq 1, \quad j = 1,2,\ldots,n$$

$$\mu_r \geq 0, \quad r = 1,2,\ldots,s \text{ and } v_i \geq 0, \quad i = 1,2,\ldots,m$$

Program (A18) is an instance of fractional programming. In order to deal with it, CCR proposed to norm the virtual multipliers of the inputs so that

$$\sum_{i=1}^{m} v_i X_{i0} = 1 \tag{A19}$$

Program (A18) can then be written

$$\max \sum_{r=1}^{s} \mu_r Y_{r0} \tag{A20}$$

subject to

$$\sum_{r=1}^{s} \mu_r Y_{rj} - \sum_{i=1}^{m} v_i X_{ij} \leq 0, \quad j = 1,2,\ldots,n$$

$$\sum_{i=1}^{m} v_i X_{i0} = 1$$

$$\mu_r \geq 0, \quad r = 1,2,\ldots,s \text{ and } v_i \geq 0, \quad i = 1,2,\ldots,m$$

Inspection shows that program (A20) is the dual of the CCR program (A8). Each virtual output multiplier is identical to the dual of the output constraint (A5), and each virtual input multiplier is identical to the dual of the input constraint (A6).

By the dual theorem of linear programming, the optimal value of program (A20) is θ^*.

4. THE TREATMENT OF SLACKS

While the characterizations of DEA that we have supplied so far will be adequate for the rating of most projects, mathematical difficulties can arise that we now need to face head on. They have to do with the very definition of an efficient point. Recall that we defined an efficient point as an un-dominated point. In order to locate the un-dominated points, we constructed the CCR frontier (or the BCC frontier, as the case may be) as illustrated in Figure 1. Numerically, we calculated the frontier by the (CCR or BCC) envelopment procedure (A8).

However, a frontier point need not necessarily be un-dominated. That is the crux of the matter we now need to consider. There are cases when frontier points are dominated. It is perfectly possible that frontier points still use excessive inputs. This happens if the frontier contains a horizontal facet so that frontier points exist with different input combinations that all yield the same vector of outputs.

In order to guard against this possibility, we need to amend our search for efficient points, requiring both of the following two conditions to be satisfied:

- An efficient point must be located on the frontier, i.e. delivering an efficiency rating equal to 1.
- Efficiency also requires absence of output and input slacks, so that the conditions (A3-4) are all tight at the optimum.

In order to locate efficient points using the input-oriented CCR model, a two-stage process is then called for, searching in the first instance for the maximal reduction of inputs and determining the optimal efficiency rating. This is the CCR model as we have already encountered it, program (A8). In a second subsequent stage, the movement along the frontier onto an un-dominated point is achieved by searching for the further maximal reduction of all slacks. (A similar two-stage process is suggested for the BCC model.)

It is possible to combine these two stages of optimization into one single program, using an infinitesimally small ordinal number (a so-called non-Archimedean) ε. In the case of the input-oriented CCR model, write

$$\text{Min } \theta - \varepsilon\left(\sum_{i=1}^{m} s_i^- + \sum_{r=1}^{s} s_r^+\right) \qquad \text{(A21)}$$

subject to

$$\sum_{j=1}^{n} Y_{rj}\lambda_j - s_r^+ = Y_{r0}, \qquad r=1,\ldots,s$$

$$\theta X_{i0} - \sum_{j=1}^{n} X_{ij}\lambda_j - s_i^- = 0, \quad i=1,\ldots,m$$

$$\lambda_j,\ s_i^-,\ s_r^+ \geq 0, \text{ all } i, j \text{ and } r$$

Comparing with (A8), we see that this program features explicitly the output and input slacks s_r^+ and s_i^- respectively. All slacks are added together, the resulting sum is multiplied by the number ε, and entered with a minus sign in the minimand. What is ε, and what is the purpose of this maneuver?

The number ε is an infinitesimally small ordinal number, called a non-Archimedean transcendental. For the purpose of the numerical calculations, we may take $\varepsilon = 0.00001$ or $\varepsilon = 0.000001$.

If chosen small enough, the constant ε will be dwarfed by all other numbers occurring in the calculations. Hence, one can imagine that the calculations are effectively carried out in two stages. First, the computer looks for the maximal reduction of inputs, in effect solving (A8). This first stage preempts the determination of the slacks. Second, in the case of alternate optima to (A8), the computer searches out the combination of slacks that yields the minimal negative sum of slacks $-\sum s_i^- - \sum s_r^+$.

In the case of an un-dominated point on the frontier, no reduction of inputs is possible ($\theta^* = 1$). The sum $-\sum s_i^- - \sum s_r^+$ can only be brought down to zero, but not below zero. That is, at the optimum, all slacks vanish. But in the case of a dominated point on the frontier, this sum can be brought down to a negative number. All slacks do not vanish.

The dual corresponding to (A21) is

$$\max \sum_{r=1}^{s} \mu_r Y_{r0} \tag{A22}$$

subject to

$$\sum_{r=1}^{s} \mu_r Y_{rj} - \sum_{i=1}^{m} v_i X_{ij} \leq 0, \quad j = 1,2,\ldots,n$$

$$\sum_{i=1}^{m} v_i X_{i0} = 1$$

$$\mu_r \geq \varepsilon, \quad r = 1,2,...,s \text{ and } v_i \geq \varepsilon, \quad i = 1,2,...,m$$

which corresponds to (A20). Note that the only difference between (A20) and (A22) is that the unknowns are now effectively required to be positive rather than just non-negative.

From the dual theorem of linear programming, it finally follows that a given point is efficient if and only if the optimal value of (A21) = the optimal value of (A22) = 1.

5. RETURNS TO SCALE

DEA also provides a measure of the economies of scale of each project. In the well-known manner, constant returns to scale are said to prevail at a point on the frontier, if an increase of all inputs by 1 percent leads to an increase of all outputs by 1 percent. Decreasing returns to scale obtain if outputs increase by less than 1 percent; increasing returns to scale if they increase by more than 1 percent.

In Figure A1 above, the CCR frontier OBM exhibits constant returns to scale throughout. The BCC frontier exhibits increasing returns to scale along *A-B* (the output/input ratio is increasing; the intercept of the tangent at the origin is negative). It has constant returns to scale along *BC* (the output/input ratio is constant; the intercept of the tangent at the origin is zero). It has decreasing returns to scale along *B-C-D* (the output/input ratio is decreasing; the intercept of the tangent at the origin is positive).

But the returns to scale at the corner points A, B, C, and D are problematic because the tangential plane at these points is not uniquely defined. There is a difficulty here, and it is inherent in the use of a piecewise linear frontier. Intuitively, inspecting Figure A1, it would still make sense to say that the returns to scale at a point like C are decreasing, because even if there are infinitely many tangential planes to point C they all have positive intercepts at the origin. That is, the interval of intercepts lies entirely on the positive side. But if the interval of intercepts were to straddle both positive and negative values, no inference can be drawn.

To see how the returns to scale can be calculated by DEA, and to see how the mentioned indeterminacy can frustrate these calculations, consider now the dual formulation of the BCC program below

$$\max \sum_{r=1}^{s} \mu_r Y_{r0} + u_0 \qquad \text{(A23)}$$

subject to

$$\sum_{r=1}^{s} \mu_r Y_{rj} - \sum_{i=1}^{m} v_i X_{ij} + u_0 \leq 0, \quad j = 1,2,...,n$$

$$\sum_{i=1}^{m} v_i X_{i0} = 1$$

$$\mu_r \geq \varepsilon, \quad r = 1,2,...,s \text{ and } v_i \geq \varepsilon, \quad i = 1,2,...,m$$

This program features a new unknown u_0 which is unrestricted in sign and which can be interpreted as the intercept of the BCC model at the origin. It is precisely the intercept of the tangential plane that was discussed a moment ago. Indeed, in their original paper (1984), BCC asserted that

- if the optimal u_0 * is zero, there are constant returns to scale;
- if u_0 * is positive, there are decreasing returns to scale;
- if u_0 * is negative, there are increasing returns to scale.

This criterion is satisfactory if u_0 * is unique. But, as already pointed out, if alternate optimal solutions of u_0 * exist, things are more difficult. This situation was discussed by Banker and Thrall, 1992. Fortunately, all attendant theoretical issues have now been resolved. In particular, the reader is referred to the references Banker, Chang and Cooper 1996, Golany and Thore 1997, Golany and Yu 1998.

The calculations of economies of scale have a direct interpretation in terms of the underlying dynamic evolution. In an obvious sense, a firm with decreasing returns to scale has pushed its expansion too far, and management can be expected to consider the possibility of downsizing, laying off workers and reducing its scale of operations. Conversely, a firm with increasing returns to scale will typically be engaged in rapid economic growth. That is, these calculations tell us something about the long-term growth pattern of the firm, and the direction it may take.

6. COMPUTER CODES

Most of the computer codes used by the authors of papers in the present volume were written in GAMS (General Algebraic Modeling System). For information about GAMS, see A. Brooke, D. Kendrick, A. Meeraus and R. Raman, 1998. A demonstration version of the GAMS software can be downloaded for free from the following address on the Internet: http://www.gams.com/download/ .

To illustrate, we provide below listings of a few of the GAMS codes. The first code relates to the ranking of 14 high tech oil drillings projects pursued by the Baker and Hughes corporation described in Chapter 2. This code illustrates the computation of the input-oriented CCR model (section 2 above) combined with a non-Archimedean feature to search for un-dominated frontier points (see section 4 above). So, the software shown here does the calculations of program (A21) in the text.

With the additional requirement that the sum of the lambda weights equal unity, one obtains the corresponding BCC model. (The constraint CONVEX is included in the model "DEABCC" but not in the model "DEACCR".)

```
$OFFSYMXREF OFFUELLIST
 OPTION SOLPRINT = OFF;
 OPTION  LIMROW = 0, LIMCOL =0;
 SETS
 J directional drilling projects
    / PROJ1  short radius system
      PROJ2  re-entry motors
      PROJ3  reservoir navigation tool
      PROJ4  coiled tubing drilling
      PROJ5  expandable stabilizer
      PROJ6  thrusters
      PROJ7  air drilling motors
      PROJ8  workover motors
      PROJ9  window master
      PROJ10 near-bit stabilizer
      PROJ11 200 deg C air motor
      PROJ12 new motor design
      PROJ13 active thrusting
      PROJ14 closed loop drilling/
  R the performance criteria for each project
    / SIZE       estimated market size
      COMP       strategic compatibility with INTEQ
```

```
        DEMAND     projected market need or demand
        INTENS     competitive intensity
        PROB       probability of technical success
        POSIT      proprietary position
        COMPLX     manufacturing and maintenance complexity
        HSE        health and safety and environment/
    R1(R) attractiveness criteria with HSE excluded;
*The output and input data follow.
 TABLE Y(J,R) listing of performance data by project
            SIZE  COMP DEMAND INTENS  PROB POSIT COMPLX  HSE
  PROJ1      32   8.2    7.5    8.0    8.8   7.2    8.9  5.6
  PROJ2      50   7.6    7.2    6.4    8.6   6.2    8.6  6.0
  PROJ3      40   7.6    7.1    5.3    7.4   6.7    7.5  5.6
  PROJ4      30   7.1    7.2    5.5    6.4   6.6    6.0  6.5
  PROJ5      25   7.0    7.0    5.1    7.6   5.2    8.3  6.0
  PROJ6       8   6.0    6.1    6.9    8.1   6.8    8.4  5.7
  PROJ7       2   5.9    6.2    6.6    8.6   5.8    8.8  6.1
  PROJ8      12   5.8    5.8    5.4    8.6   4.6    8.6  5.7
  PROJ9      10   5.8    5.8    4.7    7.1   4.5    7.6  6.3
  PROJ10    0.8   5.4    5.6    6.1    7.6   4.0    8.5  5.8
  PROJ11      3   5.3    5.4    6.5    6.5   6.7    7.7  6.0
  PROJ12    300   6.8    6.1    6.4    8.8   5.4    8.9  6.1
  PROJ13     60   6.2    6.9    6.8    6.3   7.4    7.2  6.0
  PROJ14    240   6.5    6.6    7.1    7.5   7.4    7.6  6.4
  ;
 PARAMETER X(J) cost to complete each project
 / PROJ1      1.07
   PROJ2      1.06
   PROJ3      0.325
   PROJ4      1.6
   PROJ5      0.55
   PROJ6      0.2
   PROJ7      0.35
   PROJ8      0.53
   PROJ9      0.21
   PROJ10     0.16
   PROJ11     0.07
   PROJ12     1.95
   PROJ13     5.59
   PROJ14     3.1/;
PARAMETER Y0(R) performance of project currently rated;
   SCALAR X0 completion cost of project currently rated;
```

```
    Y0(R) = Y("PROJ1",R);
    X0 = X("PROJ1");
    SCALAR EPSILON infinitesimally small /0.00001/;
 VARIABLES
     OBJ objective function
     THETA
     POSITIVE VARIABLES
     EFFX    optimal costs
     EFFY(R) optimal criteria
     LAMBDA(J)
     SLACKPLUS
     SLACKMINUS(R);
  EQUATIONS
     DEFOBJ
     DEFEFFX
     DEFEFFY(R)
     INBAL
     OUTBAL(R)
     CONVEX;
  DEFOBJ..      OBJ =E= THETA - EPSILON*(SLACKPLUS
                   + SUM(R,SLACKMINUS(R)));
  DEFEFFX..     EFFX =E= SUM(J,LAMBDA(J)*X(J));
  DEFEFFY(R)..EFFY(R) =E= SUM(J,LAMBDA(J)*Y(J,R));
  INBAL..       THETA*X0 - EFFX -SLACKPLUS =E= 0;
  OUTBAL(R).. EFFY(R) - SLACKMINUS(R) =E= Y0(R);
  CONVEX..      SUM(J,LAMBDA(J)) =E= 1;
  MODEL DEABBC/DEFOBJ,DEFEFFX,DEFEFFY,INBAL,OUTBAL,CONVEX/;
  MODEL DEACCR/DEFOBJ,DEFEFFX,DEFEFFY,INBAL,OUTBAL/;
  PARAMETER BBCRSLT(J,*)
    CCRRSLT(J,*)
    BBCLAMBDAS(J,J)
    CCRLAMBDAS(J,J);
  ALIAS(J,J1);

  LOOP(J1,
  X0 = X(J1);
  Y0(R) = Y(J1,R);
  EFFX.L = X0;
  EFFY.L(R) = Y0(R);
  SOLVE DEABBC USING LP MINIMIZING OBJ;
  BBCRSLT(J1,"THETA") = THETA.L;
  BBCRSLT(J1,"OPTCOST") = EFFX.L;
```

```
    BBCRSLT(J1,"SLACKPLUS")   = SLACKPLUS.L;
    BBCRSLT(J1,"SLACKMINUS") = SUM(R,SLACKMINUS.L(R));
    BBCRSLT(J1,R) = EFFY.L(R);
    BBCLAMBDAS(J1,J) = LAMBDA.L(J);
    SOLVE DEACCR USING LP MINIMIZING OBJ;
    CCRRSLT(J1,"THETA") = THETA.L;
    CCRRSLT(J1,"OPTFUND") = EFFX.L;
    CCRRSLT(J1,"SLACKPLUS")   = SLACKPLUS.L;
    CCRRSLT(J1,"SLACKMINUS") = SUM(R,SLACKMINUS.L(R));
    CCRRSLT(J1,R) = EFFY.L(R);
    CCRLAMBDAS(J1,J) = LAMBDA.L(J);
   );

   DISPLAY "Results: BBC model", BBCRSLT, BBCLAMBDAS;
   DISPLAY "Results: CCR model", CCRRSLT, CCRLAMBDAS;
```

One of the great advantages of writing the DEA codes in GAMS (rather than using one of the several prepackaged DEA codes that are available on the market) is that it permits a seamless inclusion of all relevant mathematical steps, both before the DEA calculations proper and after. To illustrate, we show the code for the ranking of five optical electronics satellite communications projects discussed in Chapter 3.

In this application, extensive introductory calculations of costs and sales over time were necessary before the DEA computations could start. Once this had been done, the authors fitted an output-oriented BCC model to the obtained data.

```
$OFFSYMXREF OFFSYMLIST OFFUELLIST
 OPTION SOLPRINT = OFF;
 OPTION LIMROW = 0, LIMCOL =0;
 SETS
  K scenarios
     /SCEN1 intense international competition
      SCEN2 multimedia explosion
      SCEN3 social pressure/
  T time periods /1998,1999,2000,2001,2002,2003,2004,2005/
  SPAN(T) time span of product on market
                 /2000,2001,2002,2003,2004,2005/
  R outputs
    / OUTPUT1  annual sales
      OUTPUT2  annual net income
      OUTPUT3  learning achieved inside company/
```

```
 J projects
    /PROJECT1 optical memory based on spectral hole burning
     PROJECT2 optical memory based on holographic
     PROJECT3 optical processing device
     PROJECT4 broadband amplified for fiberoptics cables
     PROJECT5 satellite uplink project   /;
ALIAS(J,JA); ALIAS(T,TA); ALIAS(SPAN,SPANA); ALIAS(K,KA);
TABLE INSALES(J,K) initial sales expected in year 2000
            SCEN1    SCEN2   SCEN3
  PROJECT1   3        4       2
  PROJECT2   4        0.5     1
  PROJECT3   2        3.5     1.25
  PROJECT4  12        9       7
  PROJECT5   6        4       2.5;
TABLE GROWTH(J,K) percentage growth of sales in 1st year
            SCEN1    SCEN2   SCEN3
  PROJECT1   10        8       6
  PROJECT2   12        7       8
  PROJECT3   20        9       5
  PROJECT4    8        4       1
  PROJECT5    3        4       1;
TABLE SATLEVEL(J,K) saturation sales levels
            SCEN1    SCEN2   SCEN3
  PROJECT1  10        8       3
  PROJECT2  12        7       4
  PROJECT3   8       12       6
  PROJECT4  40       25       16.5
  PROJECT5  12        8.5     5.25;
PARAMETER
  F(J,T,K) fraction of market reached by project
  C(J,K) coefficient in diffusion equation
  ALFA(J,K) rate of exponential growth of project
  SALES(J,T,K) total sales;
F(J,"2000",K) = INSALES(J,K)/SATLEVEL(J,K);
F(J,"2001",K) = (1+0.01*GROWTH(J,K))
                     *INSALES(J,K)/SATLEVEL(J,K);
C(J,K) = (1-F(J,"2000",K))/F(J,"2000",K);
ALFA(J,K) = LOG(( F(J,"2001",K)/ (1 - F(J,"2001",K)))
                     *((1 - F(J,"2000",K))/F(J,"2000",K)));
F(J,T,K) =  1/(1+ C(J,K)*EXP(-ALFA(J,K) *(ORD(T)-3)));
SALES(J,T,K) = SATLEVEL(J,K)/(1 + C(J,K)
                     *EXP(-ALFA(J,K)* (ORD(T)-3)));
```

```
SALES(J,"1998",K) = 0; SALES(J,"1999",K) = 0;
PARAMETER
 A(T,TA) triangular unit matrix
 ACCSALES(J,T,K) accumulated sales
 MFGCOSTS(J,T,K) manufacturing costs of project ;
A(T,TA) = 0.0; A(T,TA) = 1.0$(ORD(T) GE ORD(TA));
ACCSALES(J,"1998",K) = 0; ACCSALES(J,"1999",K) = 0;
ACCSALES(J,"2000",K) = SALES(J,"2000",K);

LOOP(T,
ACCSALES(J,T+1,K) = SUM(TA, A(T+1,TA) * SALES(J,TA,K));
MFGCOSTS(J,SPAN,K) = 0.60*SALES(J,SPAN,K)*
          ((ACCSALES(J,SPAN,K)/ACCSALES(J,"2000",K))**(LOG(
          0.95)/LOG(2)))
);

PARAMETER COMCOSTS(J) project R&D costs
     /PROJECT1  14.5
      PROJECT2  12.5
      PROJECT3  20
      PROJECT4  15
      PROJECT5  12      /;
PARAMETER
      PROFIT(J,T,K) profit of project
      MKVALUE(J,T,K) market value of project;
PROFIT(J,T,K) = SALES(J,T,K) - MFGCOSTS(J,T,K);
PROFIT(J,"1998",K) = - 0.5* COMCOSTS(J);
PROFIT(J,"1999",K) = - 0.5*COMCOSTS(J);
PARAMETER
    LEARN(J) degree of learning ranked from 0 to 10
     /PROJECT1   3
      PROJECT2   3
      PROJECT3   3
      PROJECT4   3
      PROJECT5   7/
    X(J) input data arranged for DEA calculations
    Y(R,J,T,K) output data arranged for DEA calculations;
 X(J) = COMCOSTS(J);
 Y("OUTPUT1",J,T,K) = SALES(J,T,K);
 Y("OUTPUT2",J,T,K) = PROFIT(J,T,K);
 Y("OUTPUT3",J,T,K) = LEARN(J);
 SCALAR EPSILON infinitesimally small /0.00001/;
```

```
PARAMETER Y0(R)        outputs of event currently rated
          X0           input of event currently rated;
Y0(R) =Y(R,"PROJECT1","2000","SCEN1");
X0 = X("PROJECT1");
VARIABLES
     OBJ objective function
     THETA efficiency rating to be determined
POSITIVE VARIABLES
     EFFX                best practice input
     EFFY                best practice output
     LAMBDA(J,T,K)       weight attached to project
     SLACKPLUS(R)
     SLACKMINUS;
EQUATIONS
     DEFOBJ
     DEFEFFX
     DEFEFFY(R)
     INBAL
     OUTBAL(R)
     CONVEX;
DEFOBJ..  OBJ  =E= THETA + EPSILON*(SLACKMINUS +
                             SUM(R,SLACKPLUS(R)));
DEFEFFX.. EFFX =E=SUM((J,SPAN,K),LAMBDA(J,SPAN,K)*X(J));
DEFEFFY(R)..     EFFY(R) =E=
          SUM((J,SPAN,K),LAMBDA(J,SPAN,K)*Y(R,J,SPAN,K));
INBAL..          EFFX + SLACKMINUS                    =E=X0;
OUTBAL(R)..      THETA*Y0(R) - EFFY(R) + SLACKPLUS(R) =E= 0;
CONVEX..         SUM((J,SPAN,K),LAMBDA(J,SPAN,K))     =E= 1;
MODEL DEA/ALL/;
THETA.L = 0;
SOLVE DEA USING LP MAXIMIZING OBJ; DISPLAY THETA.L;
PARAMETER THETATAB(J,SPAN,K)  result table

LOOP(JA,
X0 = X(JA); Y0(R)=Y(R,JA,"2000","SCEN1");
SOLVE DEA USING LP MAXIMIZING OBJ;
THETATAB(JA,"2000","SCEN1") = THETA.L;
);
DISPLAY "Results ranking all projects", THETATAB;
```

The resulting THETATAB is Table 4 in the main text of the paper. If so desired, one may next write the concluding rank calculations in GAMS as well (the authors preferred to do them by hand).

REFERENCES

Banker, R.D., Charnes, A. and Cooper, W.W. (1984), "Some Models for Estimating Technical and Scale Inefficiencies in Data Envelopment Analysis, " *Management Science*, Vol. 30, pp. 1078-1092.

Banker, R.D. and Thrall, R.M. (1992), "Estimation of Returns to Scale Using Data Envelopment Analysis, *European Journal of Operational Research*," Vol. 62, pp. 74-84.

Banker, R.D., Chang, H. and Cooper, W.W. (1996), "Equivalence and Implementation of Alternative Methods for Determining Returns to Scale in DEA", *European Journal of Operational Research*, Vol. 89, pp.473-481.

Brooke, A., Kendrick, D., Meeraus. A. and Raman, R. (1998), *GAMS: A User's Guide*, GAMS Development Corporation, Washington D.C. This manual can downloaded for free at the GAMS web site http://www.gams.com/docs/document.htm

Charnes, A., Cooper, W.W. and Rhodes, E. (1978), "Measuring the Efficiency of Decision Making Units," *European Journal of Operational Research*, Vol. 2, pp. 429-444.

Golany, B. and Yu, G. (1997), "Estimating Returns to Scale in DEA," *European Journal of Operational Research*, Vol. 103, pp. 28-37.

Golany, B. and Thore, S. (1997), "The Economic and Social Performance of Nations: Efficiency and Returns to Scale," *Socio-Economic Planning Sciences*, Vol. 31:3, pp. 191-204.

Seiford, L. and Thrall, R.M. (1990), "Recent Developments in DEA: The Mathematical Programming Approach to Frontier Analysis," *Journal of Econometrics*, Vol. 46, pp. 7-38.

Thompson, G.L. and Thore, S. (1992*), Computational Economics: Economic Modeling with Optimization Software*, The Scientific Press, South San Francisco, Calif.

Thore, S. (1996), "Economies of Scale in the US Computer Industry: An Empirical Investigation Using Data Envelopment Analysis, " *Journal of Evolutionary Economics*, Vol. 6, pp. 199-216.

Index